IN SEARCH OF

AMERICAN

JEWISH

CULTURE

IN SEARCH OF

AMERICAN

JEWISH

CULTURE

STEPHEN J. WHITFIELD

Brandeis University Press

PUBLISHED BY UNIVERSITY PRESS OF NEW ENGLAND

HANOVER AND LONDON

Brandeis University Press

Published by University Press of New England, Hanover, NH 03755

© 1999 by Brandeis University Press

Printed in the United States of America

5 4 3 2 1

CIP data appear at the end of the book

A portion of the chapter *"Shoah"* is from *Studies in Contemporary Jewry,
Volume VIII, A New Jewry? America since the Second World War*, edited by
Peter Y. Medding. Copyright © 1992 by Oxford University Press, Inc.
Used by permission of Oxford University Press, Inc.

Brandeis Series in American Jewish History, Culture, and Life
JONATHAN D. SARNA, Editor
SYLVIA BARRACK FISHMAN, Associate Editor

Leon A. Jick, 1992
The Americanization of the Synagogue, 1820–1870

Sylvia Barrack Fishman, editor, 1992
Follow My Footprints: Changing Images of Women in American Jewish Fiction

Gerald Tulchinsky, 1993
Taking Root: The Origins of the Canadian Jewish Community

Shalom Goldman, editor, 1993
Hebrew and the Bible in America: The First Two Centuries

Marshal Sklare, 1993
Observing America's Jews

Reena Sigman Friedman, 1994
These Are Our Children: Jewish Orphanages in the United States, 1880–1925

Alan Silverstein, 1994
*Alternatives to Assimilation: The Response of Reform Judaism
to American Culture, 1840–1930*

Jack Wertheimer, editor, 1995
The American Synagogue: A Sanctuary Transformed

Sylvia Barack Fishman, 1995
A Breath of Life: Feminism in the American Jewish Community

Diane Matza, editor, 1996
Sephardic-American Voices: Two Hundred Years of a Literary Legacy

Joyce Antler, editor, 1997
Talking Back: Images of Jewish Women in American Popular Culture

Jack Wertheimer, 1997
A People Divided: Judaism in Contemporary America

Beth S. Wenger and Jeffrey Shandler, editors, 1998
*Encounters with the "Holy Land":
Place, Past and Future in American Jewish Culture*

David Kaufman, 1998
Shul with a Pool: The "Synagogue-Center" in American Jewish History

Roberta Rosenberg Farber and Chaim I. Waxman, 1999
Jews in America: A Contemporary Reader

Murray Friedman and Albert D. Chernin, 1999
A Second Exodus: The American Movement to Free Soviet Jews

Stephen J. Whitfield, 1999
In Search of American Jewish Culture

FOR MY MOTHER,

WHO LIVES FOR OTHERS

Contents

Preface

"The fact of Jewishness has been nothing but an ever-growing good to me," the poet Delmore Schwartz wrote "with gratitude," in the safety of the United States in 1944. This caprice of birth was central to his sensibility and was, indeed, "nothing but a fruitful and inexhaustible inheritance."[1] It deserves historical scrutiny; and a critical interpretation of American Jewish culture, as it has evolved over the twentieth century, is what this book is intended to provide. The questions it addresses are how a nation's culture has differed because of the presence of Jews, and how they invented a distinctive culture without the feeling of living in exile. The time is, if anything, overripe for a work that traces what their culture has meant to Jews and to other Americans. This volume purports to help meet that need, by suggesting the impact both of Jews on American culture and of America on Jewish culture.

However notable the Jews' contribution to art, thought, and expression, this minority is very small. Genesis 22:17, which is read in the prayer book at every New Year, promises that the Hebrews will be as numerous as sand. This is a pledge the deity did not keep. Though more Jews have lived in twentieth-century America than anywhere else, they rarely have risen much above 3 percent of the population. Indeed, the Jewish role in American life could easily have been ignored earlier. When the Constitution was ratified, Jewry constituted one-twentieth of 1 percent of the population, and as late as 1880 had risen to only half of 1 percent.[2] For longer than the first century of the republic, its history could be recounted without reference to Jews. Occupying a penumbra, this minority was too peripheral to matter.

Both as a percentage and in sheer numbers, American Jewry has been declining of late, a tendency that shows every sign of continuing. The twentieth century may therefore be regarded as special, a belle époque, a sublime peak in the history of Jewish involvement in a "host" society. In making themselves so smoothly and so decisively into Americans, Jews did not use tiny proportions as an alibi but have instead loomed large in the evolution of the nation's culture. They "are amazing people. They are truly amazing" was how the most admired actor of the past half century bestowed praise in 1996. "Per capita," Marlon Brando claimed in a television interview, "Jews have contributed more to American—the best of American—culture than any other single group." He asserted that "if it weren't for the

xi

Jews, we wouldn't have music. If it weren't for the Jews, we wouldn't have much theater. We wouldn't have, oddly enough, Broadway and Tin Pan Alley and all the standards that were written by Jews, all the songs that you love to sing." Piercing the mysteries of a creative patrimony that scholars have tried in vain to solve, he added: "The Jews—the secret of the Jews is their worship for the word *sachel* [good sense]. That doesn't mean that they are superior people; it just means that they are culturally advantaged in the same way that the Chinese and the Japanese are." The actor revealed that his own "kids go to a Jewish school. Because I think that the Jewish schools . . . are . . . the best."[3] This book can be read as a gloss on his remarks.

A century or so earlier, no observer of American vernacular culture could have foreseen such impact. The exemplar of Victorian seriousness, Matthew Arnold, had visited the United States in 1883–84 and, upon his return to England, put down the cultural life he had so recently observed: it was not "interesting," he sniffed.[4] That was just before Jewry was braced to play a role in making American civilization interesting. The major communal institutions that would encourage and sanction Jewish culture in the New World had already been formed. The Jewish Publication Society of America was created in 1888 to sponsor Jewish books in English, and four years later the American Jewish Historical Society was founded to explore—and celebrate—an integration so successful that the United States did not feel quite like the Diaspora. The basis for appreciating the literary antecedents of the new immigrants was established in 1899, when a Harvard instructor named Leo Wiener published his *History of Yiddish Literature in the Nineteenth Century*. In 1898 editorial planning for the *Jewish Encyclopedia* began. This monument to scholarship, realized in 1906, had then no counterpart among German and Austrian Jews, whose dazzling creativity earned them such preeminence in the Diaspora.

By the turn of the century, the impact of the newcomers from Eastern Europe could already be measured. Although the federal government had begun identifying immigrants by country of origin in 1819, the separate category of "Hebrew" was included only in 1899; and at that moment a distinctive contribution was registered. That year the *American Jewish Year Book* first appeared; in 1900 the Zionist theoretician Ahad Ha-am, based in Odessa, predicted that the United States would become "the future center of Judaism." Two years later Solomon Schechter, one of the world's most prominent Jewish savants, arrived in New York City to head the newly reorganized Jewish Theological Seminary. The JTS quickly became a key institution of scholarship and soon boasted of a major library.[5] Most of the issues entangled in the meaning of American Jewish culture were already being articulated. The attorney Louis D. Brandeis assumed the leadership of the puny Zionist movement in 1914, and the philosopher Horace M.

Kallen worked out the vision of "cultural pluralism" by 1915. The public posture of the community would be largely determined by defense agencies created in that era, such as the American Jewish Committee (founded in 1906), the Anti-Defamation League (founded in 1913) and the American Jewish Congress (founded in 1917). The cultural groove that is the subject of this book had been dug, and only the variations would be played out for the rest of the century.

Because so little rupture can be detected in the course of American Jewish culture, the story can properly begin in 1900, which is when Leo Stein, doomed to be recalled—if at all—as Gertrude's brother, observed that "the Jew is becoming more numerous and prominent, and the eyes of the community are more and more fixed upon him."[6] This new prominence was especially evident in the popular arts. In the first century or so of the history of the republic, a reader had no more reason to expect to encounter any Jews in literature than had a Gentile to meet any Jews in life. Nineteenth-century fiction had no counterparts to transatlantic figures like Sir Walter Scott's Rebecca, or Charles Dickens's Fagin, or George Eliot's Daniel Deronda. "There is not a single Jewish character who can match any of these in popular appeal, symbolic value, or influence on the popular mind," historian Louis Harap remarked, "and the Jew's place in the context of American literature before our century has been even further from the literary historian's awareness and concern."

The performing arts would mark the change before serious literature would turn to Jewish subjects. By the turn of the century, a Jewish actor named David Warfield defined the stock figure of the "Hebe," and achieved fame by playing comic Jewish businessmen. Ascending from the burlesque company of Weber and Fields (both of whom were Jewish), Warfield starred in a Broadway hit entitled *The Auctioneer* (1901), produced and directed by another Jew, David Belasco. In 1903 a Jew was for the first time represented on a movie screen. By the end of the Great War, 80 percent of the *world's* films were coming from Los Angeles.[7] There the stuff dreams are made of was produced by the Jewish immigrants who were mostly responsible for building the studios. The impact upon popular music, which Brando emphasized, was concurrent; already by the beginning of the century, Jews were dominant in the creative as well as the commercial side of Tin Pan Alley. Its songs would, for more than half a century, help unify a huge and disparate nation.

Although this book therefore spans the twentieth century, *In Search of American Jewish Culture* is not organized according to historical principles but rather to themes and genres. The subject is too fragmented and indeed too rich to allow the caprices of dates to dictate how such diversity should be treated. Take 1934, for example. What eventually became the most-admired novel in the canon of American Jewish literature was published that year: Henry Roth's *Call It Sleep*. The most important book by probably the most creative thinker in the history of American Judaism was published that year too: Mordecai M. Kaplan's *Judaism as a Civilization*. Both authors struggled to elucidate what it meant to live in an unfamiliar New World. Both were New Yorkers. But the novelist was a Communist; the author of the treatise was a professor of homiletics. Such dissimilarities thwart any attempt to situate their books in the same historical context. In the same year Milton Steinberg enhanced Judaic thought with *The Making of the Modern Jew*, as did Professor Harry A. Wolfson of Harvard with *The Philosophy of Spinoza*. Novelist Daniel Fuchs also published *Summer in Williamsburg*, and Lillian Hellman's *The Children's Hour* opened on Broadway. The American Jewish imagination defies every effort to define it in a unified way. The artifacts that could be plucked from the following year—from *Awake and Sing!* and *Porgy and Bess* to *A Night at the Opera* and *Top Hat*—are so various that I hope to be forgiven for ignoring the confinements of chronology. Instead this book sticks to certain topics and issues, and treats the century en bloc—even if Jewish culture itself eludes uniform treatment.

That culture is polymorphic, crystallizing in many forms, which is why few other historians facing such plenitude would use the same approach in defining—or addressing and analyzing—this topic. *In Search of American Jewish Culture* cannot pretend to be comprehensive. Any of the chapters and topics considered here could be expanded. Invaluable books have already shown how this minority group transplanted an Old World heritage, and sometimes invented indigenous forms, as Jews installed themselves in a culture that they enriched and altered. Readers expecting a definitive account will therefore be disappointed. For example, they may be surprised to find precious little attention given to either serious or popular literature. That is because, of all the arts, it has been by far the most studied; I thus feel no need to add anything here. Neither do I supply a separate chapter on Hollywood, because so much illuminating critical work is already available. Even the most indulgent of readers may deplore the omission of chapters on painting and sculpture, on radio and television programs, on the influence of intellectuals, on magazines, on book publishing itself—to say nothing of the Yiddish theater. Because all the conundrums associated with American Jewish culture cannot be resolved, I try only to clarify—and illustrate—them within limited space.

This volume can thus be regarded as less a book about the evolution of American Jewish culture than an example of how such a book might be conceived and extended. Although I hope that the criteria informing this book will not be dismissed as eccentric, the judgments and choices are inevitably mine alone. Ultimately there is no accounting for taste; upon meeting Ezra Pound, Mussolini praised passages of the *Cantos* as "divertente" (entertaining).[8] Nor would anyone consider it idiosyncratic to mention Gentiles in an account of the culture of the Jews. Not even the crudest ethnic chauvinist could manage to make this story hermetic, and the following pages rarely make explicit those who are *not* Jews. Anyone who infers that, say, Jefferson or Tocqueville *is* a Jew is not part of the readership that this book is intended to attract.

In injecting Jewish history into the study of American culture, I ignore the intentions of many of the most ambitious and gifted Jewish-American artists and thinkers, who did not wish to serve a manifestly ethnic or communal purpose, who did not deliberately engage themselves in the effort to preserve and revitalize a peculiarly American Jewish culture. Were this book itself conscripted for a communal purpose, in tracking the mysteries of continuity, no protest could be lodged. But my primary goal is to plug a rather large scholarly hole. The very hospitality of this Diaspora site has threatened the vitality of the community that has spawned such talent, and the final chapter in particular considers the anxieties about the sources of creativity that may have been depleted. It is hardly consoling that only with evidence that the momentum of communal particularity has been spent is the shape of such a history easier to imagine.

How an ancient but adaptable faith might somehow resist the allure of American culture is a problem that struck me in a 1995 conversation with an undergraduate enrolled in my seminar on American individualism at Brandeis University. Schuyler Abrams '97 had come to talk to me about a paper topic for the course. As he was wearing a skullcap, we chatted a bit about his own Judaic background and commitment, about his own experiences in Chicago day schools and in Israel. After I finally inquired what he might want to write about, Abrams's animated reply was unexpected: "Jerry Lee Lewis!" Why, I wondered. "He had three top hits in less than two years in the mid-'50s," he announced, "Whole Lot of Shakin' Going On," "Great Balls of Fire," and "Breathless." This Brandeis junior was enthusiastic not only about songs that had blared from jukeboxes long before he was born, but about music that was soaked in the sweaty evangelical intensity of the rural South. I would not have predicted this crossing of boundaries of religion and region. Abrams was too young for any direct knowledge of the suffering that being a Jew has historically entailed, and being an American seemed to inspire no appreciation of paradox or irony either. Cherishing the vitality of popular music and observing the strictures of Judaism seemed to come easily to him, and activated no sense of incompatibility.

How to map the boundaries of such expressiveness stems from my conviction that, if Jewish life is to prevail and prosper here, it will not be through the vicissitudes of memory alone, or the fear of others, or invocations of the Holocaust, or the emotional connection with Israel. However necessary such concerns and gestures are, in themselves they are insufficient. What will matter is not what Jews fear or remember but what they affirm, not what their ancestors died for but what they and their descendants might want to live for. That is why the study of culture is indispensable. How to define its meaning and how to assess its dynamic are my concerns here, and bring to mind the only voice other than Alex Portnoy's in his book of lamentations: "Now vee may perhaps to begin. Yes?"[9]

IN SEARCH OF

AMERICAN

JEWISH

CULTURE

DEFINITIONS

THE CULTURE OF AMERICAN JEWRY WAS BORN IN EASTERN EUROPE AND was then transplanted and refashioned in cities such as New York. In the New World the tension between the parochial and the national, the particular and the universal would be resolved in favor of satisfying mass taste. Tradition would also be invigorated, but the allure of the democratic marketplace would prevail. In retrospect, the fragility of what the immigrants brought over is easy to emphasize. But the vitality that is also demonstrable should not be obscured. If one artifact can epitomize the resources of a minority culture as well as the transforming power of the popular arts, I move the nomination of "Bei Mir Bist Du Schön" (to me you are beautiful).

The composer of the song was Sholom Secunda, who had been born in Russia in 1894 and was groomed to be a cantor. In 1906 his family immigrated to the United States, where the prodigy was billed as the "Crown Prince of *Khazonim*" (cantors). He seemed so destined for stardom that in 1915 the flamboyant impresario of the Yiddish theater, Boris Thomashefsky, introduced Secunda to another promising kid who had shown a certain flair for composition. But Secunda was shocked to learn that his potential collaborator was an ignoramus who composed by ear. A teenager with no formal classical training would be a drag. Later, George Gershwin would express his appreciation to Secunda for having made his own success possible: "If he had agreed to write with me, I, too, would now be writing music [only] for the Yiddish theater." In 1932 Jacob (Joe) Jacobs wrote the lyrics, and Secunda the melody, for "Bei Mir Bistu Shein," which immediately scored a hit in the Yiddish musical theater and at Catskills weddings and bar mitzvahs.

Even a casual perusal of the lyrics casts doubt that Jacobs was imagining a crossover triumph, as evidenced by an in-group barb like "Even if you were a Galitzyaner! / I tell you it wouldn't matter to me." (Known for their piety, Jews from Galicia were also mocked for their superstitiousness, their provincialism, their ignorance, and their naïveté.) The song was remarkably popular. But those who enriched the repertoire of the Yiddish musical theater could not count on living off the residuals. Eddie Cantor rejected a chance to introduce the song on NBC, telling the frustrated composer: "Sholom, I love your music. But I can't use it. It's too Jewish." By 1937 the team sold the rights to the song to a Yiddish music publisher, and split the $30 proceeds.

What happened next depends on who tells the story. Resort owner Jennie Grossinger claimed to have taught the song to two Negro entertainers, whose stage names were Johnny and George, in the Catskills (referred to by *Life* magazine as "the Jewish Alps"). Songwriter Sammy Cahn insisted that as early as 1935 he heard two black performers (though not Johnny and George) do the song in Yiddish at the Apollo Theatre in Harlem. Cahn, whose name had been shortened from the presumably less pronounceable Cohen, was astonished to observe the crowd rocking with delight. Perhaps no audience was more demanding than the Apollo; a number that could make it there could make it anywhere. Cahn mused privately, imagine what this song would do to an audience that understood the words. He persuaded the three Andrews Sisters to record it for Decca Records. Its president, Jack Kapp, went along—but only if Cahn and his collaborator Saul Chaplin would translate "Bei Mir Bistu Shein," which they did. English was the precondition of popular interest. Cahn, whose lyrics would help extend the career of Frank Sinatra, kept the title exotic by refusing to anglicize it, but did generate confusion by elevating it into German: "Bei Mir Bist Du Schön."

Decca released it in December 1937; and within a month a quarter of a million records were sold, along with about two hundred thousand copies of the sheet music. Soon enough records were sold to make the Andrews Sisters' single the number one hit of 1938. The song drove America wild. *Life* reported customers rushing into record stores asking for "Buy a Beer, Mr. Shane," and "My Mere Bits of Shame." But the Andrews Sisters did not have this song to themselves. Because some like it hot, Ella Fitzgerald quickly did her own version. Not until 1961, it is sad to report, did Secunda regain copyright of his hit. Upon his death thirteen years later, he left behind a huge list of Yiddish and liturgical musical works, including the score to Maurice Schwartz's Yiddish-language film, *Tevye der Milkhiker* (1939). But perhaps because Secunda's oeuvre was "too Jewish," he worked mostly in obscurity. Shortly before his death at age seventy-nine he had gone to Tokyo; in the baths there, he asked a masseuse to sing to him any American songs she might know. She complied with a Japanese version of "Bei Mir Bist Du Schön."[1] From an otherwise largely concealed minority culture, the song had circumnavigated the globe. An ephemeral community of immigrants (and then their children and grandchildren) could tap and then revise its own traditions, and somehow manage to satisfy national and even cosmopolitan tastes. Two years later, in 1976, Saul Bellow, the product of a Yiddish-speaking home in Chicago, would become the first American Jew to win the Nobel Prize for Literature—and would also be counted with Herman Wouk, grandson of Rabbi Mendel Leib Levine of Minsk, as among the most translated American authors in the People's Republic of China.[2]

Determining how this minority group has contributed to the arts, while also sustaining and altering its religion, challenges the powers of the cultural historian. But the philosophers must also be satisfied when they say: Define your terms and then defend your definition. That is the particular aim of this chapter and the next, both of which offer an interpretive overview. Each key term—American, Jewish, and culture—is problematic.

Thanks to the religious psychology of Feuerbach, the atheism of Marx, the higher biblical criticism of Renan and others, and finally the nihilism of Nietzsche, the nineteenth century destroyed the supernatural. The twentieth century destroyed the natural. No longer was the domination of Christianity inevitable. Nor did white supremacy appear to be inherent in the structure of reality, and finally patriarchy ceased to enjoy an ontological status. What has remained is "only" culture, which three methodologists of American Studies have called "perhaps the most germinal idea in twentieth-century scholarship in the social sciences and humanities."[3]

No other word occupies so privileged a place in the academic lexicon. But, as literary historian Stephen Greenblatt has complained, the term is also "repeatedly used without meaning much of anything at all." According to the historian Raymond Williams, "culture" is "one of the two or three most complicated words in the English language," primarily because of its use "in several distinct intellectual disciplines and in several distinct and incompatible systems of thought." Although by 1952 the anthropologists Alfred L. Kroeber and Clyde Kluckhohn had already managed to discriminate among 160 different definitions of "culture," Williams radically compressed that number, so that he could describe "a general process of intellectual, spiritual and aesthetic development," as well as "the works and practices of intellectual and especially artistic activity."[4] His formulations are relevant to this inquiry, especially in the form of deliberate efforts to promote and perpetuate artistic and intellectual expression. A bit easier to construe than to define, culture is now understood to be more than a pattern of meanings that is inherited. Culture is also something that is concocted. It is not only a system of behavior that is accepted, but is also a complex of beliefs that is adapted and contrived. Picked up by osmosis, culture is also consciously transmitted.

The status that the study of "society" once enjoyed in the academy has now yielded to "culture." Two trends have converged that inevitably affect how the experience of American Jewry can best be fathomed. What the pioneering social sciences achieved by relativizing what had been taken as certitudes is now done by cultural studies, whose work is similar. Cultural studies involves some sort of unmasking or demystification of the ideological aims of the institutions or groups under scrutiny. For its academic practitioners, culture is not usually "high," nor is it singular; rather, it consists of "that plurality of symbolic systems and practices that enable different groups to make various kinds of sense of their lives."

Such a definition is less indebted to Matthew Arnold than to anthropologists, one of whom has been widely influential in offering a semiotic approach to culture that is also applicable to the case of American Jewry. Clifford Geertz has referred to "structures of signification," to "an historically transmitted pattern of meanings," and to "a system of inherited conceptions . . . by means of which men communicate, perpetuate and develop their knowledge about and attitudes toward life." Such "symbolic dimensions of social action" need to be decoded, so that the ways our species make experience intelligible can be elucidated.[5] Geertz's version of anthropology as well as cultural studies are ways of taking seriously the expressive evidence by which, say, a minority group seeks to define itself, tries to give shape to its experiences, and exchanges standards and values.

Every culture, proclaimed the anthropologist Claude Lévi-Strauss, is "the result of a mishmash." Even more so is America, because its society is itself composed of minorities, "formed of all the nations of the world," according to Alexis de Tocqueville, who observed "different languages, beliefs, opinions: in a word, a society without roots, without memories, without prejudices . . . without common ideas, without a national character." He was compelled to wonder: "What serves as the link among such diverse elements? What makes all of this into one people?"[6] To this polyphony, everybody's voices could be added; and in theory they all counted —not only at the ballot box, but also in the circulation of ideas and images.

The ideal of democracy sanctioned majority rule in taste as well as suffrage. Popular sovereignty operated in culture and not only in government. The motto of the newspaper which inaugurated the penny press, the *New York Sun*, was: "It shines for ALL." The marketplace that embraced the masses became the touchstone of value. "We are the only great people of the civilized world that is a pure democracy," Henry James proclaimed in the *Nation* in 1878, "and we are the only great people that is exclusively commercial." Within two decades, when rural free delivery was established, a corporate beneficiary was Sears, Roebuck and Company, which got its mail-order catalogues classified as *educational* material.[7] In so emphatically commercial a society, its most accessible philosopher (William James) would speak of the "cash-value" of truth and the nation's wisest jurist (Oliver Wendell Holmes Jr.) would speak of the "marketplace of ideas." America's most effective dissident would speak before the Lincoln Memorial in 1963 of the "promissory note . . . of life, liberty, and the pursuit of happiness," even though the government had instead "given the Negro people a bad check."

Such metaphors come easily in a society in which aristocratic and socialist standards are weak; because American culture is broadly democratic, the popular arts aim at intelligibility. Good taste is virtually synonymous with mass taste, as Jewish immigrants quickly grasped and proclaimed. The box office, according to theatrical producer Lee Shubert, "never lies." The "mob," Irving Berlin insisted, "is always right."[8] Adolph Zukor, who founded Paramount Pictures, entitled his 1953 autobiography, *The Public Is Never Wrong*. To marketers, it is infallible.

Though studies of national character are no longer fashionable, the American has been widely believed to be something other than an ersatz European. Indeed, the first great professional historian of the United States, Frederick Jackson Turner, once characterized the American mind in terms that do not sound European: "practical, inventive, experimental." In pursuing an errand into the wilderness, the American was further driven by a "dominant individualism," with a "buoyancy and exuberance which comes from freedom." That "dominant individualism" to which Turner referred was hardly confined to the wilderness, and tended to counter collectivist aspirations. Americans were not supposed to be limited by the accidents of birth and inherited status. Truths were supposed to be self-evident, according to the Declaration of Independence; and in "Self-Reliance" (1841), Emerson insisted that "nothing is at last sacred but the integrity of your own mind." The ethos of "Americanism," Theodore Roosevelt asserted in 1899, required treating one's neighbor "on his worth as a man," and forgetting "whether he be of English, German, Irish or any other" sort of nationality, "whether he be of Catholic or Protestant faith." Even Turner, a son of the Middle Border (Portage, Wisconsin) called his fellow citizens "a mixed race, English in neither nationality nor characteristics."[9] Difference was not supposed to be a handicap. Individualism sanctioned the pursuit of personal ambition, however extravagant, for the sake of a loosely defined American Dream. The ideology of individual aspiration could therefore be compressed into a couplet for Disney's *Pinocchio* (1940): "When you wish upon a star / Makes no difference who you are."

With hierarchy impugned, authority need not relied upon; the buoyant freedom that Turner exalted promoted instincts for improvisation. Americans, a visitor noted in 1837, "live in the future and *make* their country as they go along." (Remember that during the first of Indiana Jones's adventures, he flamboyantly yells: "I'm making this up as I go along.") The arts attracted lonely pioneers, literary historian Alfred Kazin declared, each of whom "fought his way through life—and through his genius—as if no one had ever fought before. Each one, that is, began afresh—began on his own terms." American life is relatively unregulated, and its do-it-yourself "genius" is characteristically described as raw, untutored, undisciplined, uncertified, flexible, unbounded. George Herriman, the mulatto comic-strip artist, claimed that "Krazy Kat was not conceived, not born, it jes' grew"—an allusion to Harriet Beecher Stowe's Topsy; and Jes' Grew be-came, in novelist Ishmael Reed's *Mumbo Jumbo* (1972), an archetype for jazz and more broadly for mass culture. With *America as a Civilization* (1957), Max Lerner was probably the last scholar intrepid enough to write a single systematic work on that daunting topic. But in the decade it took to write the book, he conceded, so much had been transformed that much of it was "no longer valid." Even during a presumably quiescent decade, "American civilization had been changing drastically right under my fingertips as I was writing about it."[10]

It is also decentralized and diverse. A passable history can be written about "French Post-War Culture from Sartre to Bardot"—the subtitle of the 1984 book *Saint-Germain-des-Prés*, in which authors Paul Webster and Nicholas Powell focus on the cafés in only one neighborhood in one city. That sort of compression would make no sense for the United States. Its film capital was not the literary capital (if indeed there was one), and no neighborhood (not even Greenwich Village) has ever been the locus of national creativity. Even when a city like Chicago produced more than its share of important American writers, it is easy to forget how the lines of descent and influence got crossed in a multiethnic and multiracial society. The Chicago school is usually associated with "realism," and one of its pro-ponents, James T. Farrell, is considered an authoritative and authentic chronicler of the Irish-American experience. But his own development as a writer was not unmediated: Farrell was inspired by reading, and then meet-ing and talking with, Abraham Cahan. Bellow is commonly taken to be an authoritative guide to some aspects of American Jewry. But he was wary of being assigned to a "school" whose other chief representatives did not hone their skills in Chicago, and objected to the yoking of his name with Bernard Malamud and Philip Roth, as though these three novelists had become business partners, "the Hart Schaffner and Marx of our trade." Bellow squeezed off another round against such critics by adding: "People who make labels should be in the gumming business."[11]

Nevertheless, labels are often necessary to establish the proper limits of a subject. Who, for example, is a Jew? The classical definition is anyone whose mother is Jewish, even if Judaism is not practiced, so long as he or she has not converted to another faith. But a Jew is also anyone who *chooses* to be one, by undergoing (in the phrase of the Zionist journalist Hayim

Greenberg) "the process of Jewish religious *naturalization*." (Judaic law forbids any distinction to be drawn between Jews by birth and Jews by choice.) To be a Jew is tribal or it is formal, or both, which is partly why a definition gets tricky. Anyone who practices Judaism is a Jew, but far from every Jew practices Judaism. To be a Jew can be a social identity as well as a religious affiliation.

Judaism has also been defined as "whatever Jews did or do together to preserve their collective identity,"[12] even practices that may not be rituals or invested with theological meaning. Judaism in this sense may be a culture—or at least at the heart of a culture. But there can also be Jews without Jewish culture. The obverse is not true: there cannot be a cohesive Jewish culture without Jews. That is why the definition of who is Jewish is salient. Whom a burial society is allowed to inter is not synonymous with whose creative talent has been cultivated in a historically significant way. But a consideration of Jewish identity itself is a precondition for exploring Jewish culture.

Once upon a time, to be Jewish was not very problematic. Jewish identity was once so precise and rigid as to be the butt of humor, as in the psychiatrist Theodore Reik's report of a defendant who is asked by the judge: "What's your name?" "Menachem Jomtef." "What is your profession?" "I am a dealer in secondhand clothes." "Your domicile?" "Rzcezow." "Your religious creed?" The defendant can scarcely disguise his exasperation: "I am called Menachem Jomtef, I am an old-clothes man, I live in Rzcezow— I am perhaps a Hussite?"[13] So certain an identity (who is a Jew?) meant that its rationale (why be a Jew?) was unexamined. That question, the essayist Ahad Ha-Am commented, would have skirted the edges of blasphemy for previous generations—and would also have demonstrated egregious stupidity. He himself considered the question of remaining Jewish quite pointless, akin to being "asked why I remain my father's son."

Such conditions have been rarely believed to be escapable. Isaiah Berlin asserted: "A Jew is a Jew, as a table is a table. Things and persons are what they are and one accepts them naturally. I've never been either proud or ashamed of being a Jew any more than I'm proud or ashamed of possessing two arms, two legs [or] two eyes." The British philosopher added: "I take my Jewishness for granted," as something "natural." He claimed "never in my life either [to have] wished not to be a Jew, or wished to be one."[14] Citizens of the Soviet Union did not have a choice; and its system of internal passports listed Jews by "nationality," which was irrevocable. The dissident Lev Kopelev, the model for the philologist Rubin in Solzhenitsyn's *The First Circle*, could not discover "in my conscious mind anything that would link me to the nationalistic ideals or religious traditions of Jewry."[15] But Soviet law made his identity unambiguous and unalterable.

By the time the American republic had been founded, however, its residents would generally not bear the marks of origins. A nation made up of so many strangers and sojourners and newcomers does not facilitate encounters with anyone bearing names like Scipio Africanus or El Greco (to say nothing of Philo Judaeus). Because certain entertainers bore names like Ella Fitzgerald and Eddie Murphy should not mislead anyone into believing that they were Irish. Recent Cabinet officers with names like Schlesinger, Blumenthal (baptized a Presbyterian), and Weinberger were *not* Jews; others, with a name like Brown, *were*. Yet essentialism was a commonplace until rather recently. Phil Green wished to become a Jew—for eight weeks—in Laura Z. Hobson's best-selling novel and then in the Oscar-winning adaptation of *Gentleman's Agreement* (1947). But the fiancée of the journalist masquerading as a Jew to investigate the scope of antisemitism berates him for doing "an impossible thing. You were what you were, for the one life you had," Kathy Lacey tells Phil. "You couldn't help it if you were born Christian instead of Jewish." Fish gotta swim and birds gotta fly. Boys will be boys. And *a yid blaybt a yid*—even though that last piece of folk wisdom was often contested. Some Jews could wriggle out of such an identity, or try to. The financier Otto Kahn had once been a Jew, he told a companion, who responded that *he* had once been a hunchback. The conversation may be apocryphal, but the message transmitted was unambiguous: such escape routes exemplified self-delusion.[16]

Such essentialism also punctuated the Second Dialogue in Israel of the American Jewish Congress in 1963, when Max Lerner, drawing on Justice Holmes's view of truth, remarked: "Most people . . . live by 'can't helps'; most of us are what we are because we can be no other and we can do no other. We in America, I think, also have our 'can't-helps.' We can't help being part of the larger culture, but also for many of us—perhaps for most of us—we can't help being Jews." He did not "mean simply because we were born Jews or because it was thrust upon us. It might be that we would be better Jews" if we were more knowledgeable. "And yet we can't help being Jews because there is a strange, inner necessity within us which demands we be Jews in the sense of being members of the Jewish historical community and of making a contribution to that, in terms of the urgencies of time and place within America." Essentialism poses problems when its proponents disagree, however, and when proper means of adjudication and reconciliation cannot be stipulated. At the same 1963 conference, Leslie A. Fiedler showed that he shared Lerner's essentialism, even as the literary critic rejected a triumphalist notion of the Chosen People: "If you are chosen, you cannot choose! The Jews are a Chosen People because they have no choice. We are chosen; the choice is outside of us. We are Jews! Defined as Jews! Essentially Jews!"

Another product of Newark spoke at the same conference in Israel, and indicated how Jewish identity was something that was fabricated rather than inherited. Philip Roth could accept as authoritative "no body of law, no body of learning, and no language, and finally, no Lord—which seems to me significant things to be missing. But there were reminders constantly that one was a Jew and that there were *goyim* out there." What the novelist picked up from his upbringing "was a psychology, not a culture and not a history in its totality. The simple point here is . . . that what one received of culture, history, learning, law, one received in strands, in little bits and pieces. What one received whole, however, what one feels whole, is a kind of psychology." From the residue of the notion of chosenness came a psychology by which, "as one grew up in America, [one could] begin to create a moral character for oneself. That is, one had to invent a Jew. . . . There was a sense of specialness and from then on it was up to you to invent your specialness; to invent, as it were, your betterness." Roth cited two novels that he admired, written by his partners in Hart Schaffner and Marx. In Bellow's second novel, *The Victim* (1947), and in Malamud's second novel, *The Assistant* (1957), "you find the central figure having to find out what it means to be a Jew and then invent a character for himself, or invent certain moral responses, invent attitudes."[17] Making it up as she went along was also the claim of Kim Chernin, the author of a 1986 novel about an ancient sect of Jewish women (*The Flame Bearers*). The daughter of a Communist who hailed Moses as "a radical, a people's hero" and who celebrated Chanukah as a "liberation struggle against a foreign imperialist ruling class," Chernin had to become "a patchwork Jew, stitched together from every sort of scrap."[18] Identity is thus a kind of bricolage. No longer could Jews feel guided by some inner necessity or by a divine destiny. No longer did outside hostility give them little choice. Nor did they still feel fully at home only among one another, assured of their collective destiny.

The story of American Jews in the twentieth century can be told in terms of the erosion of a stable identity, so that eventually all of them would be described as Jews by choice; the momentum that had begun in Emancipation would enable its legatees to choose not to be Jews at all. Welcome to modernity. Under its auspices, according to Stuart Hall, a British exponent of cultural studies, "cultural identity" entails "becoming" more than "being." Rather than some preexisting state prior to the stimulus of historical change, identities can "undergo constant transformation. Far from being eternally fixed in some essentialized past, they are subject to the continuous 'play' of history, culture and power." Identity should be considered whatever name "we give to the different ways we are positioned by, and position ourselves within, the narratives of the past."[19] If communities are not primordial but imagined, if tradition is not ancient but invented, then identity is, according to this fashionable view, *not* something that one is born with. Identity is constructed. It is mutable, subject to collective transmission and also to individual will and agency.

But the more it becomes apparent that identities are learned rather than given, contingent rather than secure, historically positioned rather than inherent, the stronger the temptation to discern porousness even before the granting of civic equality. Even before Emancipation, Jews were not *only* Jews, exempt from the pressures that shaped their culture. Among Roman Jewry in the early modern period and with increasing momentum through the nineteenth century, Italian was heavily flavored with Judeo-Romanesco —a unique, often Hebraically based, vocabulary. There were interactions with others despite confinement to the ghetto; the cuisine varied somewhat from the local diet. Jewish subculture, according to Kenneth Stow, an authority on Italian Jewry, went beyond merely religious expression.

Or take Vladimir Medem, who cofounded the Bund in 1897, the same year as political Zionism. He had been baptized as an infant into the Russian Orthodox Church and picked up Yiddish only as an adult, without ever converting to Judaism. But such cases were somewhat freakish. Only with the revolutions of 1917 would Russian Jews achieve civil equality; and on the desk of their greatest historian, Simon Dubnow, was a picture of the liberal philosopher John Stuart Mill, whose works Dubnow called "*kitve kodesh*" (holy writings).[20] Medem and Dubnow illustrate how permeable was the eastern European Jewish society that the twin forms of totalitarianism would bury alive.

Such flexibility where the Emancipation was late to penetrate can also be found in the prototype that Hannah Arendt had applied to western European Jews: the pariah. Her four exemplars are Kafka and Bernard Lazare (neither of whom practiced Judaism); Heine, who never repudiated his youthful decision to "crawl to the cross" (but never lost his Jewish consciousness either); and Chaplin, whose ancestry was often believed to have been Jewish. Such a belief was unwarranted, as she conceded: "Even if not himself a Jew, he has epitomized in an artistic form a character born of the Jewish pariah mentality."[21]

The United States may be the site, however, that has most fully tested the category of Jew, where the definition is loose enough to embrace culture rather than religious belief or the identity of one's mother. In planning an encyclopedia on the history of American Jewish women, its two coeditors wondered about including Marilyn Monroe. She had converted immediately prior to her third marriage, after submitting to two hours of religious instruction. Was that sufficient? To solve this conundrum of identification, Paula E. Hyman of Yale asked her adolescent daughters, "who were tuned in to popular culture"; and Deborah Dash Moore of Vassar asked her "similarly situated sons." Exclusion was the unanimous verdict, which the editorial board of the encyclopedia upheld (though, in any Reform synagogue, Monroe was eligible for an *aliya*—the honor of being called to the Torah). However refreshingly democratic the procedure the encyclopedia adopted, what remains elusive is a clear set of criteria by which such a judgment is reached.[22]

Nevertheless the case for contingency and plasticity can be pushed too far. Jewish identity cannot be satisfactorily reduced to the play of capricious historical forces that make cultures into options. Even if identity is socially constructed rather than "given," who would transmit or inherit it other than a Jew? The Jewish religion can be adopted, its laws followed, its rituals practiced, its beliefs sincerely held. But how does an individual select a culture? Ordinarily only those born and raised within Jewish families, woven into the fabric of the Jewish people, could have the experiences that facilitate the use of patterns of meaning according to the heritage of that particular culture. The legacy of Jewish history becomes one's own most readily when one's ancestors were part of it.[23]

That Judaism accepts converts means only that membership in a distinctive people is not transmitted exclusively in the genes. If Jewish culture depended on choices made available to every generation, something as intricately systematic as a culture could not be perpetuated. Neither the Jewish people nor their culture can be categorized as a voluntary association, comparable to the Elks or the National Rifle Association. From birth forward, freedom of choice is never possible, even for those who belong to such organizations; the life that one lives is inevitably circumscribed. And neither Judaism nor Jewish culture could be rendered continuous if the tribal and ancestral links between the generations were severed—or defined as arbitrary. The recent scholarly emphasis on social construction obscures the determinacy that governs cultural persistence.

The modernity that Americans have found so congenial also tends to undermine the rigidity that separates Jews from others. To ensure persistence has traditionally entailed a sense of distinctiveness, and religious faith once marked as well as reinforced the singularity of membership in the Jewish people. Judaism codifies an awareness of difference and inculcates a sense of unique destiny. Judaism virtually defines itself in contrast to idolatry (which is one of the seven Noahide prohibitions), and contrasts true believers to the "nations." Indeed, "without the Other," historian David Biale has argued, "the Jew of 'Judaism' lacks definition." Judaism is not a religion famous for extolling ambiguity, but instead promotes "binarism." *Havdalah*, marking the end of the Sabbath and the beginning of the rest of the week, means "separation." Consider as well the distinctions between milk and meat, kosher and *trayf* (though there is also the third category of *pareve*), the school of Hillel and the school of Shammai, and finally Jew and Gentile. The first generation of American Jewish philosophers and literary critics, one historian surmised, showed "a mode of thinking in dichotomies," a legacy of the "intellectual structures acquired in their fathers' worlds."[24]

Because binarism is deeply encoded in historic Judaism, can it be mere coincidence that the sociologist who analyzed religion in terms of the gap between sacred and profane, Emile Durkheim, was the son of a rabbi? Nor is it surprising that the anthropologist who insisted that binary opposition (nature/culture, raw/cooked, "hot"/"cold") is locked into all social structures and mental processes is Lévi-Strauss, the grandson of a rabbi. A third French Jewish thinker, philosopher Jacques Derrida, has also argued that dichotomies are codependent. Difference is how to begin to understand culture—and indeed to grasp the making of the self, which is formed in relation to the Other.

But if the imperatives of religion cease to determine Jewish identity, which has become alterable, then the consequences are what Marjorie Garber, a cultural critic, has called a "category crisis." By that she means "a failure of definitional distinction, a borderline that becomes permeable, that permits of border crossings from one (apparently distinct) category to another: black/white, Jew/Christian, noble/bourgeois, master/servant, master/slave." This definition stems from her own investigation of cross-dressing. The category crisis of transvestism begins with a very practical question: which public restroom does one use?

Garber's analysis finds some confirmation in American life itself, which philosopher George Santayana called "a powerful solvent." The national experience is not compatible with taxonomy. Under modern conditions, Judaism itself faces a category crisis, as integration into an open society has demonstrated, according to David Biale, that "the identity boundaries between the Jew and the Other are inherently unstable." To historicize Jewish culture is to recognize that "the difference between 'Jew' and 'goy' is no longer ontological." He adds: "The relationship of Jewish culture to its surroundings was, and is, dynamic and permeable."[25] Dividing lines so clearly marked in principle were crossed in practice, and rigidities were not immune to the threat of dissolution.

After all, if gender is socially constructed, why not race and ethnicity too? None of Lenny Bruce's routines is more famous than his pair of distinctions intended to discredit traditional versions of Jewish identity: "All Drake's cakes are goyish. . . . Instant potatoes—goyish," and so are TV dinners and cat boxes and trailer parks. But though "fruit salad is Jewish," "body and fender men are goyish." Another dualistic comedian with acutely developed ethnographic interests, Jackie Mason, generalized that "you never, ever see a Jew under a car," and also noticed the absence of his co-religionists on the roster of rodeo performers. Only Gentiles would risk falling off of broncos ("I say, *shmuck*, use the other hand!"). As for jockeys, who must weigh under a hundred pounds, Mason opined, "a Jew is not going to give up coffee and Coke just to sit on a horse."[26]

It was Bruce, however, who most strikingly anticipated the academic formulation of identity as a social construction, telling his listeners to "dig [that] I'm Jewish. Count Basie's Jewish. Ray Charles is Jewish." And so is Hadassah. But neither B'nai B'rith nor Eddie Cantor were. (Here demurral must be entered. Rather than derogate the B'nai B'rith as "goyish," Bruce might have substituted, say, the American Jewish Committee; and the former Israel Iskowitz was an electric and impassioned performer deeply committed to Jewish life and to Jewish as well as other charities.) Bruce was right to assert that skin color is irrelevant. But should "soul" or spiritual authenticity or a capacity to swing or to be hip be the true signifiers of Jewish identity? That, at the risk of sounding square, is dubious. More plausible was the comedian's claim that, "if you live in New York or any other big city, you are Jewish. It doesn't matter even if you're Catholic; if you live in New York, you're Jewish. If you live in Butte, Montana, you're going to be goyish even if you're Jewish."[27]

Explaining a joke is awkward, although Bruce's routine is too extensive and elaborate to fit the label of a mere joke. In an era when the persistence of ethnicity was not a sociological commonplace, he was making such an accident of birth more decisive than class or geography or religion. That hardly establishes the soundness of his monologue, even as a loose generalization. Professor Fiedler was then living in Missoula, Montana, but was quite recognizably Jewish, having come from Newark and New York University. His eight children were from Montana, so it should be noted that most have considered themselves only "in some vestigial sense Jews." None "has at the present moment a Jewish mate; nor, for that matter, do I," Fielder acknowledged in 1989.[28] So one particular family's history indirectly confirmed Bruce's point, which, within its limits, is well taken: "kosher style" has exerted considerable impact in urban America, but has played less well in the heartland. If only for purposes of comic exaggeration, his antiessentialist riff on Jewish identity is suggestive. So democratic, so diverse, and so hospitable did the nation prove to be that a customary way of understanding the Diaspora needed revision.

Elsewhere the hegemony of Gentiles was so taken for granted that, as Sartre argued shortly before the state of Israel was proclaimed, Jews are presumably destined to represent "negativity" forever. Theirs was the permanent status of the "other." In defending them in 1946 against anti-semitism, he did not bother to read a single Jewish book and therefore could not imagine what positive contribution could be made by Diaspora Jews: "They cannot take pride in any collective work that is specifically Jewish, or in a civilization properly Jewish, or in a common mysticism." So much for the Talmud, for the Golden Age of Spain, and for the Kabbalah. Sartre was hardly alone in doubting that Jews could form a culture of their own, however permeable. The émigré sociologist Max Horkheimer also believed that his fellow Jews perpetually embodied the "negative principle," which is why by the 1970s he criticized Israeli nationalists for having become "positive themselves."

Henry Pachter, another diagnostician of Weimar culture who relocated himself in America, announced that the condition of a "rootless, cosmopolitan Jew" suited him "better than any other role."[29] Ilya Ehrenburg, who was part bohemian and part Bolshevik, defined himself as a Jew "as long as a single antisemite remains on earth." Such obduracy is undoubtedly a recipe for eternal life, if not much of an recommendation for any religious or cultural affirmation. In Ehrenburg's 1921 novel, *The Extraordinary Adventures of Julio Jurenito and His Disciples*, the protagonist asks representatives of various nations which word should be preserved from the human vocabulary: "yes" or "no." The American is not unique in picking the former; but only the Jew, the perpetual dissident, chooses "no."[30]

So familiar a condition once led Isaiah Berlin to ask: "What does every Jew have in common, whether he hails from Riga or from Aden, from Berlin or from Marrakesh or Glasgow?" Berlin answered his own question: "A sense of unease in society. Nowhere do almost all Jews feel entirely at home." His interlocutor tried to rebut by citing Sir Isaiah himself as "a counter-example. Surely you feel at ease and even amused at the most solemn state occasions, and in the company of imposing and powerful men?" Berlin answered, "You are wrong." He admitted to feeling not completely at home in the land of his adoption: "I am a devoted Anglophile, not an Englishman." Berlin added that because Jews "are a minority everywhere" except in Israel, "constantly being made to look over their shoulders to see what other people think of them," their culture developed "in an atmosphere of intermittent uneasiness."[31] Perhaps justifying his own refusal to live in Israel, Rabbi Joseph B. Soloveitchik of Boston described *Galut* (Exile) as "the essence of the Jewish people," with its triggering antecedents in the expulsion from Eden. It may not be accidental that his writings are pervaded by references to homelessness and loneliness.[32]

The depth of such estrangement should not be exaggerated. Because Christendom worshiped a Jew, the people from whom Jesus had sprung could not be ignored as ancillary to Western civilization. During the Great War, David Lloyd George told Mrs. James de Rothschild: "When Dr.

Weizmann was talking of Palestine[,] he kept bringing up place names which were more familiar to me than those on the Western Front," where British soldiers were fighting and dying. Jewish civilization and its off-shoots were not mere footnotes to the history taking place on center stage. When an Israeli archeologist guided Neil Armstrong through the Old City and showed him the Hulda Gate, where Jesus had presumably trod, the astronaut exclaimed: "I am more excited stepping on these stones than I was stepping on the moon."

The subsequent predicament of Jesus's coreligionists in the Diaspora does not stem only from exclusion but rather from feeling so integral to a Christendom that has also stigmatized them. In 1916 the radical critic Randolph Bourne identified as "the anomaly of the Jew" the feeling of being "culturally [and] racially . . . peculiar." But the Jew "has proven himself perhaps the most assimilable of all races to other and quite alien cultures."[33] A sympathetic Gentile, Bourne had already hailed the project of young Jewish intellectuals to enrich what he hoped would become a transnational America.

It was in the pages of the *Menorah Journal* that Bourne diagnosed the anomalous condition of the Jew in a cosmopolitan nation. The magazine had been founded in 1915 to articulate an American Jewish culture, to encourage something separate and continuous that Jewish immigrants and their progeny transplanted and adapted and created. In that year Horace Kallen made the most valiant effort of any Jewish thinker hitherto to legitimate ethnic difference when he coined the term "cultural pluralism." Preferring to validate the Many rather than envision the One, Kallen called for a society bound into a federation of ethnic groups. Irreversible data of birth could be converted into opportunities for self-realization; ancestry would be honored as a means of revitalizing democratic possibility. The individual could be anchored in a continuous and comforting fabric of institutions that enriched the larger community. Kallen was the pioneer theorist of resistance to the ideal of homogenization.[34]

That he also became perhaps the first intellectual to try to describe the substance of an American Jewish culture reinforces his claim to historical attention. A champion of "Hebraism" in the early issues of the *Menorah Journal*, Kallen was praised half a century later by Mordecai Kaplan for having most satisfactorily reconciled the Jewish heritage with American citizenship. Kaplan was being generous. Though Kallen had struggled to find in the ethos of "Hebraism" something peculiarly (if not uniquely) Jewish, he did not succeed in doing so. His basic text was the Book of Job, a work of resonant power, but typical neither of the Bible nor of Judaic thought. What Kallen meant by "Hebraism" remained murky: what exactly *is* "the total biography of the Jewish soul"? He had a weakness for such phraseology: by the end of his career, he forsook "Hebraism" for the very non-denominational "secularism." Such truth in labeling was admirable; but to be a secularist, you don't have to be Jewish. This had been the problem with "Hebraism" as well. Whatever it was supposed to be, it sounded suspiciously like the go-with-the-flow pragmatism, meliorism, and empiricism that had been absorbed from teachers like William James. Indeed, Kallen was so deeply indebted to non-Hebraic thought that, of the six thinkers he claimed had most influenced him (including Barrett Wendell and George Santayana), only one—Solomon Schechter—was Jewish.[35]

Kallen had failed to locate the distinguishing features of a Jewish culture that might enrich and enliven the larger American culture while also providing a striking contrast or challenge to it. The attributes of plasticity and integration make the task of specifying what American Jewish culture has been or might be fiendishly difficult. But that was the project of the children of eastern European immigrants who founded and contributed to the *Menorah Journal*. Its masthead promised devotion to "Jewish culture and ideas." The editors and contributors described such values as a response to the cruelties of bigotry, a gesture of resistance to the excesses of Americanization, a necessary adjunct to the Zionist movement, and an elaboration of Judaism itself. Less than six months after assuming the leadership of the Zionist Organization of America, even a figure as distant from Judaism as Brandeis was urging readers of the *Menorah Journal* to seize "the opportunity . . . for the further development of Jewish . . . culture."

For those who repudiated tradition and who objected to the categorization of Jewry as a religious group, the magazine offered a forum. Jewishness could be more than—and not merely—a substitute for piety. Culture was a way for a minority losing its religious moorings in the New World to sustain itself, and was assumed to be fully compatible with the exercise of critical intelligence.[36] But the question of how Jewishness and culture could be reconciled and sustained among the second generation did not resolve into any consensus or confidence. Although the debates in the *Menorah Journal* heightened the ethnic consciousness of Jewish intellectuals, the Great Depression reduced to anemia the circulation and ideological intensity of a magazine that lingered until it expired in 1962.

Could anyone specify the attributes of an American Jewish culture? In 1916 Walter Lippmann, the most brilliant American journalist of the century, dodged such an assignment, presented by editor Henry Hurwitz. Lippmann responded: "I have read Bourne with admiration and a touch of skepticism. I am considerably puzzled over the whole matter of dual allegiances, and have been for a long time." Though disclaiming any preparation "to write anything about Jewish questions," Lippmann acknowledged that "Bourne raises issues which go to the roots of political science, and it is a trifle hard for me to see just whence he derives his faith. [Felix] Frank-furter, Kallen, and I are slender reeds on which to lean . . . and just what Bourne and the rest of you mean by culture I can't make out." The co-founder of the *New Republic* then inquired: "If you get rid of the theology, and the biological mysticism, and treat the literature as secular, and refuse to regard the Jew as in any sense a chosen people, just what elements of a living culture are left of a culture that is distinct and specially worth cul-tivating?"[37]

Without specifying a category crisis, Lippmann nonetheless crystallized its problem: how could an identity without a fully formed historic ideology result in a recognizable culture? What are its attributes? Here any answer is treacherous, and generalization can be of only limited validity. But even half-truths can be valuable, and a half can still be quite a bit.

Jewish culture in the United States cannot be assessed according to the standard, is this artifact so authentic and distinctive that no Gentile could have produced it? If this distinction *were* the criterion, then no Jewish cul-ture would exist. Processes of spiritual, aesthetic, and intellectual develop-ment cannot be quarantined from the rest of America. Its culture and its Jewish segment are too firmly braided. This is the problem that faces any-one studying American Jewish culture: the larger culture seems so porous, the smaller one so fragile and indistinct. In the United States, no chasm separates the shape that Jews have given their experiences and the opera-tions of the majority culture, into which Jews fit mostly by making it up as they went along.

At the turn of the century, nobody took more starkly compelling or more enduring photographs of Lower East Side residents than Jacob Riis and Lewis Hine, neither of whom was Jewish. Nor was the legendary team of director D. W. Griffith and cameraman Billy Bitzer, who kept enlarging the possibilities of cinema in shooting *Romance of a Jewess* (1908). Anne Nichols's *Abie's Irish Rose* (1925) was such a Broadway hit that the play reached an audience of perhaps eleven million; Abie was not her coreli-gionist. Among the splendors of synagogue architecture is Beth Sholom (1954) in Elkins Park, Pennsylvania. A preacher's son named Frank Lloyd Wright is responsible. United Artists' version of *Fiddler on the Roof* (1971) may be as commonly known and appreciated as the stage play (to say noth-ing of Sholom Aleichem's tales). But Norman Jewison, a Methodist, di-rected the film. Boundaries may be blurred (or low enough to surmount), but any consideration of what Gentiles are mimicking or enhancing re-quires the assumption that there *is* an American Jewish culture. Adopting the voice of the blocked and beleaguered Henry Bech, John Updike thrice did a parody of the postwar Jewish novel that was more than passable. His own identity—literary and otherwise—is secure.

Contrast the mysterious career of Henry Harland, who has been credited with inaugurating the themes of assimilation and intermarriage that would permeate American Jewish fiction for a century thereafter. But though he wrote novels like *Mrs. Peixada* (1886) and *The Yoke of the Thorah* (1887) under the name of Sidney Luska, Harland was in fact a Protestant only pretending to be a Jew, whose phony ethnicity was exposed when one of his novels did not merely depict intermarriage but also endorsed it. He eventually expatriated himself, converted to Catholicism, and lied through his teeth to a reporter: "I never knew a Sidney Luska."[38] (Such facile shuffling of identity cards was spoofed in Woody Allen's account of a friend who kept switching back and forth on sex-change operations, because "he just couldn't find anything he liked.") Creative Jews in the United States have operated in a protean culture that makes hierarchy, authority, and rigidity an affront to democratic aspirations and the inclusive tendencies of the marketplace.

And because American Jewish subculture is neither autonomous nor impermeable, the criterion of eligibility cannot be that a Gentile could not have painted it, or drawn it, or composed it, or written it. No artifact of Jewish culture is more manifestly authentic than a *Haggadah*. But in 1512 a Franciscan monk did a Latin translation.[39] Is *it* Jewish? Not even the effort by historians of premodern Jewry to isolate an uncontaminated cultural identity can succeed. Between what is Gentile and what is Jewish in American culture, no fire wall can be constructed.

A novelist like George Eliot could imagine a Jewish protagonist, but such a projection does not make *Daniel Deronda* (1876) a specimen of Jewish culture (even though the most important Jewish literary figure in nineteenth-century America, Emma Lazarus, became sympathetic to her people's claims to Palestine only after reading Eliot's novel).[40] Leopold Bloom constitutes the radical terminus of assimilation, and imagines himself speaking to Dublin crowds in his pidgin Hebrew: "Aleph Bet Ghimel Daleth Hagadah Tephilim Kosher Yom Kippur Hanukah Roschaschana Beni Brith Bar Mitzvah Mazzoth Askenazim Meshuggah Talith." Jewish only on his father's side, the advertising canvasser is uncircumcised. He did not become bar mitzvah. He talks like an agnostic and perhaps even like an atheist. Yet no Dubliner takes Bloom to be anything other than a Jew. (In reimagining Odysseus, "only a foreigner would do," the novelist once explained. "The Jews were foreigners at that time in Dublin.")[41]

Because Bloom is barely yet unmistakably Jewish, he should intrigue the Jewish historian. But *Ulysses* is not a Jewish book, despite its decisive influence on *Call It Sleep*. The film *The Great Dictator* (1940) not only makes a Jewish barber its protagonist, but also puts Chaplin's politics on the side of the sentimental faith in surmounting bigotry that sustained so many Jews.

Perhaps that is why the comedian became a sort of honorary Jew. But his film cannot be called Jewish, any more than *Uncle Tom's Cabin* (1852) or *The Confessions of Nat Turner* (1967) can be said to illustrate black culture (even though William Styron adopted the "voice" of a slave rebel). These novels are rightly read as specimens of the souls of white folk, not black. Michelangelo's *Moses* and the spiritual "Go Down, Moses" reflect the Jewish influence on others, not the continuity of Jewish culture. Categories are not easy to establish, but they are not meaningless, nor are distinctions impossible to parse.

Should American Jewish culture be allowed to include works that do not bear directly on the beliefs and experiences of the Jews as a people? Or is *any* intellectual or artistic activity that they have initiated in the United States, whether or not such work bears traces of Jewish content, a contribution to American Jewish culture? Does Bellow's *Mr. Sammler's Planet* (1970) count, for instance, but not his *Henderson the Rain King* (1959)? Does Joseph Heller's *Good as Gold* (1979) merit consideration, but not his *Catch-22* (1961)? Or all of Malamud's novels after his first, *The Natural* (1952)? What about Ben Shahn, who illustrated Maurice Samuel's *The World of Sholom Aleichem* (1943) as well as a *Haggadah* (1966), but who is better known for, say, his artistic protest of the execution of Sacco and Vanzetti? Whether representing Jews or not, these works are expressions of the same intelligence, distilled products of the same experiences, manifestations of the same sensibility.

For the historian of Jewish culture, books and plays and paintings that depict Jews may be more revelatory and important. But to expel from consideration whatever omits Jewish subject matter unnecessarily diminishes the effort to understand the Jews who created such works, and would make the task of classification even more difficult than it already is. (How much Jewish content would count? And how overt or emphatic should Jewish themes be to merit inclusion?) Moreover, some works are not even representational. There can be no observable Jewish content in the canvases of Adolph Gottlieb, Barnett Newman, and Mark Rothko; Abstract Expressionism *has* no content. Are their paintings, or the sculpture of, say, Louise Nevelson, off-limits to the student of American Jewish culture? To define that culture too stringently risks pushing nonreferential masterpieces away, and would repudiate the interpretive possibilities inherent in Meyer Schapiro's claim that no "pure art" unaffected by experience is imaginable: "All fantasy and formal construction, even the random scribbling of the hand, are shaped by experience and by nonaesthetic concerns."[42] To insist that the artifacts of Jewish culture must exhibit overt Jewish representations, or explicit Jewish subjects, would impoverish the appreciation of that "fruitful and inexhaustible inheritance" passed on to Delmore Schwartz.

Nowhere is the word "Jew" mentioned in the fiction of Kafka, whose status among Jewish writers of the twentieth century is at least as secure as anyone else's (even if the canon itself no longer is). The word "Jew" is not mentioned in the Book of Job either, nor was its protagonist apparently a Hebrew. Indeed, it is unlikely that even Abraham, the first monotheist, was in any ethnic sense a Jew; there was no Jewish people to which he could belong. Even more obviously, Adam and Eve were not Jewish. They did their share to reinforce one rabbi's assertion that "Genesis is a very *goyishe* work. It smells of the ancient Near East with its pantheon of fatally flawed heroes and misbehaving demigods," much in need of reinterpretation "to make it conform to classical rabbinic standards."[43] But the presence of such figures in Genesis and other books does not detract from the status of the Bible as a Jewish book. (It is tempting to revise Bruce's routine, so that Genesis is goyish; Psalms, Jewish.) Written in Aramaic and Hebrew, the Book of Daniel is Jewish. Written in German, Martin Buber's *Daniel* (1913) is Jewish too. Written in English, *The Book of Daniel* (1971) should be similarly classified, and not only because E. L. Doctorow's novel is populated with Jewish characters whose multigenerational oppositional stance to bourgeois America is representative. The same author's other fiction, whether or not diagnosing Jewish life, should also be incorporated into a comprehensive interpretation of Jewish culture. So should "Visions of Daniel" (1990), by Robert Pinsky, who became poet laureate of the United States.

What then is Jewish culture? It is whatever individuals of Jewish birth (who did not sincerely convert to another faith) have contributed to art and thought. Jewish culture is not merely synonymous with Judaism. To include the philosophical and legalistic works of Maimonides, for example, but *not* his medical treatises would be to constrict the boundaries of Jewish culture. After the Enlightenment and Emancipation, which have dramatically shrunk the sphere of religion, narrowly liturgical and spiritual themes should not exhaust the meaning of cultural expression. If Jewish culture is more than Judaism, then a religious or ideological standard should not preclude an investigation of what Jews have created, adapted, and conserved. What Raymond Williams summarized as intellectual and aesthetic processes and practices suggests that an a priori determination of what is Jewish is reductive, and cannot do justice to what talented thinkers and artists have bequeathed. (By analogy, what some U.S. citizens have done in arts and letters cannot be cordoned off as un-American activities either. The American mind is too multifarious for that.)

Though "content" cannot by itself distinguish what is Jewish from what is not, a preoccupation with similar themes or ideas is not irrelevant. Clustering in certain fields demands inquiry. Disproportionate expressions of certain interests are themselves signs of the animating power of a culture. The Nazis were wrong to claim that there is a "Jewish physics." But it is not wrong to note how attracted Jews have been to physics, and to wonder why. Though not founded until 1938, the Bronx High School of Science produced more Nobel laureates in physics than all but a tiny fraction of the member states of the United Nations. Because of such statistical improbability, curiosity about the commons origins of Sheldon Glashow, Steven Weinberg, and Melvin Schwartz should be piqued. Humor comes pretty close to a universal phenomenon. But when a 1978 study calculated that four out of five professional comedians was Jewish,[44] the proportion should invite reflection on whether something like Jewish humor exists—and why, if it does, its place in Jewish culture is so secure. The Olympian Mark Spitz ranks as one of the greatest swimmers who ever lived, and the Olympian Kerri Strug among the nation's most astonishing gymnasts. But no one would claim any special Jewish disposition toward aquatic or acrobatic skills, and it would be foolish to account for such athletic gifts in other than fortuitously individual terms. But when Jews are heavily drawn to certain fields, curiosity demands to be satisfied rather than short-circuited. As with recent scholarly work on the roles of gender and sexual orientation, the challenge here is to expose something to a different light without being reductive. Attentiveness to ethnicity in the formation of the nation's culture is not intended to displace other readings, but to complement them.

The alternative of inattentiveness has consequences too. As this book was being written, two feature articles appeared in the *New York Times* on the peculiarities of foreign countries. "There is pride that Hungary has produced so many important minds" in the twentieth century, a correspondent reported from Budapest. "Hungary has produced an inordinate number of Nobel Prize winners." And from Buenos Aires came news that Argentina had more psychologists, psychiatrists, and psychotherapists per capita than any country on earth (except for Uruguay). Though the Hungarian physicists and mathematicians were reported to have fled "often . . . under the shadow of antisemitism," the *Times* failed to indicate whether any of the Hungarian geniuses were *not* Jews, at least by Nazi criteria. (In fact *none* of the great nuclear physicists were Gentiles.) Leo Szilard, Edward Teller, and Eugene Wigner, plus the mathematician John Von Neumann (who converted to Catholicism upon marrying in 1930), attended the same schools; and Wigner attributed their brilliance to the excellence of their education in Budapest and to the stimulus of expulsion and relocation.

Neither Wigner nor the *Times*, however, explained why Roman Catholics or Lutherans did not perform so spectacularly in those Budapest schools, or why non-Jewish émigrés were less successful at physics than some Jews were. Only at the end of the article filed from Argentina did the *Times* note that "a large proportion of the country's psychotherapists and patients are Jews, whose population of 250,000 is one of the largest in the world outside Israel and the United States." Readers might have wondered whether a Jewish absorption in psychology was an adequate explanation for what was called an "obsession . . . as thoroughly Argentine as the tango."[45] Such sociological imprecision is akin to asserting that the fascination that Manet, Monet, Renoir, and Cézanne showed in the play of light upon surface was distinctly "European." Such clustering may not be random after all.

There is no "Jewish economics"; consider the contrast between, say, Milton Friedman and Paul Samuelson (to say nothing of the divide between David Ricardo and Rosa Luxemburg). But there have been dispositions, susceptibilities, tendencies that Jews as a group have demonstrated and that they as well as others have not been shy about noticing. Such social observations cannot be utterly capricious and can sometimes be demonstrated. For example, a quite disproportionate flair for producing intellectuals (including theorists who have examined the strengths and weaknesses of capitalism) is among the group characteristics of modern Jewry. No minority or other collectivity has a monopoly of any of the attributes ascribed to it, and many members of the group do not exhibit such traits. But a belief in Jewish distinctiveness is familiar enough, and widespread enough, to be a datum worthy of consideration. A few examples are intended to be suggestive.

At least within the Anglo-Saxon world, Jewish culture has presented itself as more openly emotional and less restrained than the general ambience. Producer David O. Selznick aimed for electrifying feelings in his films, and urged Alfred Hitchcock not to permit Joan Fontaine to underplay the female lead role in *Rebecca* (1940). "A little more Yiddish Art Theatre [is needed] in these moments," Selznick advised the British director, "and a little less English Repertory Theatre." (On stage at least, such advice was the opposite of the standard instructions that *Ostjuden* received: "more polish, less Polish.") When Aaron Copland gushed that the "passionate lyricism" of his music made it Jewish ("it's dramatic, it's intense. . . . I can't imagine it written by a goy"),[46] he was unwittingly engaged in supplementing Lenny Bruce's ethnography by announcing: Dig—Tchaikovsky is Jewish. Bruckner is Jewish. And yes, Wagner is Jewish.

Selznick and Copland were probably on to a certain truth, but still far from the whole truth. Not even the descendants of the Psalmist have the franchise on passionate lyricism and dramatic intensity of expression. Such claims deserve skepticism not only because they look like special pleading, not only because they indulge in the unconvincing promotion of stereotypes, not only because Jewish actors and composers whose style is cooler and more cerebral are erased, and not only because Gentiles also have traits ascribed to Jews. Such claims can also be matched by their opposites: instead of passion, rumination; instead of lyricism, doubt. Though British film director Mike Leigh denied any "conscious" manifestation of a Jewish sensibility in his films, he conceded that something "inescapably Jewish" might be read into their "peculiar kind of inevitable tragicomic chemistry," plus a tendency "to pose reflective questions more than answer them."[47] Such attributes would make Chekhov Jewish too, and suggest how warily generalizations should be proposed.

Some claims are nevertheless sounder than others. Take logocentricity, for example. A religion that makes texts so integral to piety ensures that an exaltation of the word would shape Jewish culture and bestow upon it enduring power. Language "is the Jews' weapon," a British textile manufacturer once instructed his son, the future historian Simon Schama. At least in the Diaspora, "we can't really be soldiers; we must always rely on the spoken word." Or the written word. Learning was to be sweetened with honey on the alphabet, and sacred books that were too tattered to be used had to be buried (on consecrated ground) rather than thrown away. Through the remorseless ratiocination that entwined knowledge with religion, the transmission of texts, and the exegesis of legal codes, Jews have enjoyed historic advantages in what has seemed like the mass production of intellectuals, whose own religious tradition encouraged them to think of Life itself as a Book (*sefer ha-hayim*).

The meaning of Jewish culture is therefore most likely to be borne by language—which is why Philip Roth explained the significance of breaking protagonist Nathan Zuckerman's jaw in *The Anatomy Lesson* (1983): "For a Jew a broken jaw is a terrible tragedy, it was to avoid this that so many of us went into teaching rather than prizefighting." What makes such a novel so Jewish, its author insisted, is "the nervousness, the excitability, the arguing, the dramatizing, the indignation, the obsessiveness . . . above all the *talking*. The talking and the shouting. . . . It isn't what it's talking *about* that makes a book Jewish—it's that the book won't shut up."[48] It is no surprise that a Jew invented what Zuckerman undergoes (as does Alex Portnoy): "the talking cure."

Many key figures in the evolution of linguistics have been Jews; Ludwig Lazar Zamenhof believed that talking a new language would cure humanity of its post-Babel hatreds and misunderstandings. Hence he invented Esperanto. The Harvard philosopher Stanley Cavell traced his interest in language in part to his "father's unease in any language—his English accented, his Yiddish frozen," which "helped create in him, and in me, a certain passion for expressiveness. Something of this passion, so conceived, may go into various modes of Jewish discourse." Some psychometric evidence supports this interpretation. Even if Roth is wrong about Jewish verbosity, Jewish test-takers have ranked above the norm in verbal ability itself. They have also tended to earn lower scores than others when attributes such as visual ability and reasoning, as well as the conceptualization of space, are measured.[49] Jewish painters were less conspicuous than Jewish novelists and playwrights, at least until the 1940s. But even the central role of Jews in Abstract Expressionism, for example, is no more striking than their contribution to art criticism (Clement Greenberg and Harold Rosenberg) and to scholarship (Schapiro as well as refugees like Erwin Panofsky). To be sure, writing about art demands acute visual powers. But Jews may nevertheless be more important in writing about American painting and sculpture than in creating it.

An attraction to the impalpable at the expense of the tangible is a trait that the literary scholar Erich Auerbach traced to antiquity. The first chapter of *Mimesis* contrasts the Homeric poems, in which "delight in physical existence is everything to them, and their highest aim to make that delight perceptible to us," with the Hebrew Bible, in which the characters move across an undescribed landscape, and encounters take place in settings that are very difficult to visualize.[50] The characters of the Bible move, according to the British polymath Jonathan Miller, "through a purely acoustic universe, propelled by audible dictates from God. No scenery described." And when the Israelites are commanded to follow the moral law enunciated at Mount Sinai, they tell Moses, according to Exodus 24:7: *na'aseh v'nishmah* (we shall do and we shall hear). What amazes a soldier in Oscar Wilde's *Salomé* is that the Jews "only believe in things that you cannot see."

Miller, a self-described "Jewish atheist," has amplified the impression of emphatic orientation upon textuality. "Jews cluster around a book in the way that the Italians and the Irish don't. The great tradition of Jewish religious life is exegetic—argument, dispute, and exegesis. . . . Indeed, the original founding myth of Judaism is in itself exegetical and legalistic. It's a contractual relationship that we have with God," and each party may "haggle over the terms." He added: "The Jews had a head start over almost any other immigrant group in that so many of them had got, if not the fully developed yeshiva tradition, at least a familiarity with Talmudic dispute. Thus literacy and, associated with literacy, commentary, and, associated with commentary, hairsplitting dispute; out of dispute comes a comic sense, a sense of the absurd, the ridiculous, the triumphant defeat of opponents on matters of interpretation." Jews who have distinguished themselves in the performing arts tended to be drawn to "the verbal, the quick wisecracking, the arrangement of dialogue, rather than with the display of decor, for example."[51]

Other signs of greater ease with abstractions than with the natural world would not be difficult to locate. Vladimir Nabokov was not only a literary genius: as an entomologist he twitted Kafka for not realizing that a domed beetle (*Ungeziefer*) has wings, which means that the metamorphosed Gregor Samsa could have flown out of an open window when the maid was cleaning his room. "I can't write description," Joseph Heller has conceded. "In *Catch-22* there is very little physical description. There is very little in *Something Happened*." Historian Ruth Gay grew up in Queens not knowing "the names in English of common flowers, trees, or birds, or even of the spices in everyday use in our house." When she and her husband, the historian Peter Gay, bought a Vermont farm, a New England friend walking with them in a meadow elicited "amazement and dismay" by identifying the flora, making the memoirist doubt her credentials for "owning property when I could not even recognize its plant life."[52] The American Jewish novel is likely to be psychological rather than pastoral. Even Roth's *American Pastoral* (1997) is typical in calibrating the wrenching tensions within a family rather than in giving its characters the option of lighting out for open spaces.

It is also something of a truism—even if true—that American Jewish culture is urban in setting and sensibility. Few of its participants ever imagined that their problems stemmed from the denial of forty acres and a mule. The Brooklyn-born Alfred Kazin once wrote in the *Partisan Review* with such rapture about Francis Parkman's *The Oregon Trail* that an editor's eyebrow was raised: "*Our* forests, Alfred?" The family name of the Philadelphia-born Clifford Odets was shortened from "Gorodetsky," which is Russian for "urban dweller." For most of the century, Jews were less than 3 percent of the nation's population. But they were nearly *ten times* that proportion of New Yorkers. Sixty thousand Jews lived in New York City in 1880; half a century later the figure had jumped to about two million. As late as the end of the 1930s, the greatest Jewish city in the world was more than merely the nation's largest metropolis. The city's population of 7.5 million was so vast that it exceeded that of any other *state* in the Union (including the rest of the Empire State).[53] So large did New York City loom on the horizon that the most famous painter of the Diaspora delayed leaving France, even as the Nazi juggernaut was approaching. A worried Marc Chagall asked his would-be rescuer: "Are there cows in America?"[54]

Neither Oscar Hammerstein II nor Lorenz Hart—Broadway lyricists who were quintessential New Yorkers—ever learned how to drive. Before there was Woody Allen's *Manhattan*, Hart's 1924 lyrics to "Manhattan" (music by Richard Rodgers) exulted in slant rhymes: "We'll have Manhattan, the Bronx and Staten Island too," because "the city's clamor can never spoil / the dreams of a boy and goil." (Well, not *only* the borough of Manhattan.) And when cowboys profess to "know we belong to the land /

And the land we belong to is grand," such autochthonous exuberance made sense in Hammerstein's Oklahoma but not where he himself worked. He seemed largely unaware that rural life differed significantly. As a producer of *Annie Get Your Gun* (1946), he had to talk Irving Berlin into writing lyrics for rural folks, and assured him: "All you have to do is drop the 'g's" in present participles. For example, it's "thinkin'" rather than "thinking." Berlin came back quickly with the winsome "Doin' What Comes Natur'lly."[55] Anything you can do, I can do better.

And Woody Allen's films seem less appreciated in the rural Midwest, for example, than among audiences in Paris, where *Le Monde* claimed "every new [Allen] film is an event." It is also the city Allen once said he would live in, were New York ever foreclosed. "In the United States," he ruefully noted, "I do pretty well in the big cities and the college towns, but not in the rest of the country." *Alice* (1990) earned more in France than in the United States. In his *September* (1987), when an actor ad-libbed a line about a state nicknamed Big Sky, the director was vexed: "Montana? Montana? The word 'Montana' is gonna be in *my* movie?" The line was cut.[56] In Wendy Wasserstein's play *The Heidi Chronicles* (1988), a dropout lawyer named Susan Johnston is described as "brilliant" when she is introduced to the high-octane Scoop Rosenbaum. His riposte is peremptory: "Brilliance is irrelevant in Montana."[57] Perhaps just as poignant was the fate of Jews residing in Montana, whom Lenny Bruce had dismissed with a term he used pejoratively: goyish.

Of course the comedian piled a hipster's suavity on top of his urban knowingness in mocking the tedium even of towns located closer to the metropolis. Bruce's routine about Lima, Ohio, is funnier on record than in cold print. He depicted a bleakness that might have reinforced the despair of a whole caravan of Midwestern writers from Edgar Lee Masters and Sinclair Lewis and Sherwood Anderson on down (to say nothing of Gertrude Stein's famous dismissal of Oakland as the sort of place where "when you go there, there is no there there"): "When you travel to these towns there's nothing to do during the day. They're very boring. All right, the first day you go through the Five-and-Ten. That's one day shot, right?! The next day you go see the cannon, and that's it. Forget it. . . . Yeah, it doesn't make it," he sneered. "At night, [in] a city like this . . . you don't see anything but stars. Stars . . . and a Socony station."[58] Of course the heartland could be represented as different rather than just boring; and the forbidding mystery of states like Iowa and Minnesota could be mocked in the form of encounters between the likes of Alex Portnoy and Alvy Singer and the families of "The Pumpkin" and Annie Hall, respectively. But Jewish voices have rarely been village voices.

Although the style of the subculture has been urban, it has not been characteristically urbane or genteel. To be sure, a book more comprehensive than this one could not neglect the literary critic Lionel Trilling, who succeeded in the Ivy League because he was manifestly "a gentleman and a scholar."[59] Civility was an ordeal to which Jews (along with blacks and lower-class Southern whites) had some trouble submitting. Julian Rose's vaudeville routine early in the century, "Lepinsky at the Wedding," poked fun at the standards of the well-heeled. Invited to "please come in evening dress," Ikey Blatt showed up in his pajamas. An item served to guests as "tomato surprise" was no surprise to Levinsky: "I ate 'em before lots of times." When his friend Lipinsky is scolded for having "grabbed an entire roast chicken "all alone to eat," he reacts by rushing to grab some potatoes to put on the plate too.

And so forth. The title of physicist Richard Feynman's first book of memoirs came from an incident on his first afternoon as a graduate student on the Princeton campus, when the dean's wife asked whether he took cream or lemon in his tea. The future Nobel laureate answered with a gauche "both," which startled her: "Surely you're joking, Mr. Feynman." His manner of speaking was reminiscent of a Brooklyn cabbie's, and his social orientation was largely designed to puncture pretense with an impish disregard of gentility. Attuned to the subtleties of conventions he made a political point of repudiating, the radical Abbie Hoffman rejected "the notion of 'modesty' as something invented by WASPs to keep the Jews out of the banking industry"; he "always thought the idea of postponing pleasure was something WASPs dreamed up to keep Jews out of country clubs and fancier restaurants."[60]

A sweet and unself-conscious document can also be cited, if only to discredit belief in human sameness. Whoever dismisses cultural differences, or might be tempted to define Jews as distinguishable from their neighbors only in worshiping at a synagogue rather than a church, might consider a letter to the editor of *Der Tog* in 1915. The English-language play the writer had attended was deemed "passable, but the theater! It is not like our Jewish theater. First of all I found it so quiet there." This groundling reported: "There are no cries of 'Sha!' 'Shut up!' or 'Order!' and no babies cried—as if it were no theater at all!" Nor were there any "apples, candy, or soda, just like in a desert. There are some Gentile girls who go around among the audience handing out glasses of water, but this I can get at home, too." The Yiddish theater aimed to please commoners, not *feinshmeckers* (aesthetes). The demotic dimension of American Jewish culture was also shown by Allen Ginsberg, who was listed in the telephone book at least through the 1960s, when he had become probably the nation's most famous living poet. Isaac Bashevis Singer also kept his listing in the Manhattan telephone book for a while after receiving the Nobel Prize for literature. Until the demands of fame grew exponentially, he usually invited callers over for lunch, or at least for coffee.[61] Similar hospitality was not characteristic of other eminent European-born novelists; and even those, like Nabokov or like Thomas Mann, who were married to Jews are not usually recalled as *heimish*.

But notice the extent to which Jewish culture exaggerates tendencies that are already evident in American culture itself. Arriving en masse when the nation was moving from the countryside to the city, Jews were ahead of the curve. All new citizens were required to renounce aristocratic titles in a land where nobility is less cherished than mobility, and an up-from-the-bottom scrappiness has been so widely admired that Jewish indifference to politesse did not appear peculiar. In the first third of the twentieth century, American Jews were—in the hyperbolic assessment of critic Wilfrid Sheed (of British birth and Roman Catholic persuasion)—unleashing "the wildest, vulgarest explosion of talent since the Reformation." Even as congressional restrictionists were shutting the gates to further immigration, the United States was becoming home not only to the world's largest Jewish population, but also to the largest since Abraham left Ur of the Chaldees.[62] Yet Charles and Mary Beard, in their magisterial *Rise of American Civilization* (1927), make no more than a few passing references to Jews, mostly in terms of persecution and not at all in terms of their contributions to "American civilization."

From the long perspective of Jewish history, it was still possible to ignore the cultural accomplishments of the republic to which this minority would contribute so strikingly, and that were to captivate uncountable millions of earthlings. In helping to inaugurate the founding of the Hebrew University in 1925, Lord Arthur James Balfour invoked the contribution that a Jewish university might make to international culture. Among living Jews he cited Einstein, Freud, and Henri Bergson for their intellectual achievements. At that auspicious moment on Mount Scopus, Balfour saw no reason to include any American Jews.

He was hardly alone in regarding the United States as terra incognita. Historian Heinrich Graetz had defined the Jewish experience as a dialectic between prevalence over suffering and moral and intellectual creativity: he thus in 1870 noticed nothing worthy in what Jews in the United States had produced. To their community he devoted only a sentence and a half in the eleventh volume of his *Geschichte der Juden*. (To be fair, a later English edition expanded the treatment to a paragraph.) Historian Jonathan D. Sarna has come up with a different calculation, claiming that "Graetz had condescended to devote one page to America in the English edition—an improvement, but not much of one, over the single footnote to which he relegated it in the original eleven-volume German edition. But American

Jewry never fit neatly into his conception of what was important in Jewish history: It had not struggled for survival or produced a significant cultural monument." In 1890, when an Anglo-Jewish author's *Outlines of Jewish History* was slated for publication as the very first offering of the JPS, its patriotic editor noted with horror the lone paragraph that Lady Katie Magnus spent on the Western Hemisphere, squeezed in between mention of Chinese Jewry and Turkish Jews. American Judaism was dismissed as "not always in a very much better state of preservation than among the semi-savage sects of ancient civilization."[63] (One can almost see Lady Magnus's forbidding lorgnette and curled upper lip!)

In the ambitious *Seven Jewish Cultures*, which ranges from the biblical era through the modern state of Israel, four brief references are made to the United States, which is subsumed under the culture of Emancipation. According to Efraim Shmueli's criteria, in which distinctive formulations of the deity, of the Torah, and of the land are presented within a continuous wrestling with the meaning and interpretation of Scripture, nothing peculiar or divergent stemmed from the communities of the New World—a branch of European (and especially German) Jewry. Since Shmueli lived in Cleveland for thirteen years (and earlier in Chicago and Detroit), his views did not stem from ignorance of American Jewry. Nor were they unsound, given his definition of what constitutes "Jewish culture" and how its versions and variations might be assessed.[64] Some corrective is also needed to the disparagement of a hollowed-out American Jewish life that is on display at Tel Aviv's Museum of the Diaspora, where the largest Jewish community in history is vaguely situated between Canadian Jewry and Latin American Jewry and receives less attention, for example, than Babylonian Jewry.

From such a perspective, there is something insufficiently Jewish, as though threads of traditions were severely frayed, about the American instance. In the United States, Jewish culture has not been endogenous, as though outside influences could be neglected. The civil societies of the modern age make such autonomy impossible. In the Diaspora the Jew "has nothing that is peculiarly his," Ludwig Wittgenstein surmised in 1931. "It is typical for a Jewish mind to understand someone else's work better than he understands it himself." Ahad Ha-Am was also struck by the imitative adroitness of Jews, who "have not merely a tendency to imitation," he wrote in 1894, "but a genius for it." That uncanny knack went beyond assimilation: "Whatever they imitate, they imitate well." In *Zelig*, Woody Allen's 1983 cinematic exploration of the radical instability of identity, the protagonist is called "the Chameleon Man," taking on with freakish fidelity the coloration of his social setting. His polyglot counterpart may be George Steiner. Even under hypnosis he could not find a "first language."

In German, French, or English, the distinguished critic merely replied "in the language of the hypnotist."[65]

Acute receptivity to outside forces accounts for the difficulty in locating what is Jewish in American Jewish culture. But what makes that culture special is that values, symbols, and ideals have circulated in *both* directions: not merely from majority to minority, but in an interactive and reciprocal fashion. No historical moment can be discovered in which the Jewish minority was ever so insulated that its own culture could have been created apart from the play of centrifugal forces. There was no fall from grace. Because that symbolic and expressive system was so permeable, because those who worked within it could not be cordoned off from an outside world that itself proved so open to Jewish influence, categorical rigidity is impossible to sustain.

Thus the historian needs to be sensitive to three separate, sometimes intertwined spheres, in which the internal dynamic of Jewish thought and expression could never ignore either the high culture or the popular arts that evolved in the United States. "What does it mean to be a poet of an abandoned culture?" was a question that Jacob Glatstein once raised. The Yiddish poet's own definition was poignant: "I have to be aware of Auden but Auden need never have heard of me." The historian is obligated to know *both* Auden and Glatstein, to negotiate between a dominant culture and a precarious deviation from it—and to know that the dominant culture is also divided into two branches. There is an ironic twist to Glatstein's lament. In 1965 Auden himself was asked what he thought of Bob Dylan's status as a "poet," as a poll at three Ivy League institutions had revealed that the American writer whom the students most appreciated was the folksinger-turned-rocker. Auden was candid: "I am afraid I don't know his work at all."[66] This is the sort of unfamiliarity that impedes analysis of an American Jewish culture, though it is only a coincidence that Glatstein's first book of poems, published in 1921, was called *Yankev Glatshteyn*; and Dylan's first album, released four decades later, had only the singer's name as the title. *Ecce homo*, bidding for recognition through the work.

Jewish life has been strong enough to sustain itself for several generations; it has also been subject to dilution, often under the impact of the nation's popular culture. The Jewish community has hardly been invulnerable to the pressures and interventions of the larger culture. But the Jewish culture that emerged by the end of the nineteenth century has not only been mimetic, and should not be classified as merely a microcosm of the national culture. The creativity of American Jewry has also affected and altered that culture. Exchanging ideas and images with the larger culture in a network of reciprocity, Jews have borrowed freely but have also expanded the contours of that larger culture—which has itself been protean and fluid.

American Jewish culture has no essence, and has never been autonomous. But it does have a history, which social conditions have limited as well as stimulated. Because such circumstances have determined how such a culture emerged and how it might be appreciated, a historical overview is imperative.

CONDITIONS

IN THE MID-NINETEENTH CENTURY, AN AMERICAN JEWISH CULTURE WAS unimaginable. Living Jews were invisible when Emerson complained of "no genius in America . . . which [yet] knew the value of our incomparable materials" such as "Methodism and Unitarianism"; his 1842 list lamented that "our log-rolling, our stumps and their politics, our fisheries, our Negroes and Indians . . . are yet unsung."[1] Neither as a religious nor as an ethnic group were Jews detectable; that they might be made into literary subjects, that they themselves might help create a vigorous national culture was a notion foreign to the American Renaissance. The ancient Israelites had of course deeply marked the ideology of Emerson's own ancestors, and Jews occupied an honored place in the past. Henry Wadsworth Longfellow had written a eulogy for them upon visiting the Jewish cemetery at Newport, and James Russell Lowell was haunted by them. But living avatars of Jewish culture were not easily conceivable.

The poet Emma Lazarus became the first Jew Emerson ever met, in the year of the centennial. His daughter Ellen, who taught Sunday school, expressed surprise in meeting "a real unconverted Jew (who had no objections to calling herself one)." How astonishing it was "to hear how [the] Old Testament sounds to her, and find she has been brought up to keep the Law, and the Feast of the Passover, and the day of Atonement. The interior view was more interesting than I could have imagined. She says her family . . . no longer keep[s] the Law, but Christian institutions don't interest her either." (Well, one did anyway. Lazarus celebrated Christmas.) In Victorian America, a postbiblical Jew cut an exotic figure; and as her surname suggested, she seemed to have arisen from the dead, from a moribund people.[2] Her antecedents were both Sephardic and Germanic, representing the first two waves of immigration to North America; and Lazarus's visit to Concord, Massachusetts, occurred just as the cultural impact of German Jews was beginning to register.

The historian of the nineteenth century can barely overstate the prestige of *Deutschtum* as the vehicle of civilization. The German language itself enjoyed a prestige that Philo of Alexandria had assigned to Greek, relegating a person who did not speak it to the status of a barbarian. To be ignorant of Greek meant to be denied access to the discourse of philosophy and science; and the nineteenth-century linguistic equivalent was so apparent that the claims of a forthright Jewish culture among German-speakers decisively yielded to the middle-class ideal of *Bildung* (self-cultivation, self-perfection). When Theodor Herzl of Budapest (and Vienna) imagined the restored Zion of *Altneuland* (1902), his Jews make German a more important language than Hebrew. After visiting his future Jewish father-in-law in 1904, Thomas Mann wrote to his brother Heinrich: "One has no thought of Jewishness in regard to these people; one senses only culture."[3]

In the United States, Rabbi Bernhard Felsenthal went into the gumming business in announcing: "Racially, I am a Jew, for I have been born among the Jewish nation. . . . But spiritually I am a German, for my inner life has been profoundly influenced by Schiller, Goethe, Kant and other intellectual giants of Germany." The Reform rabbi added: "With a certain pride, in thought and feeling I am German." (Near the end of his life, it should be added, Felsenthal soft-pedalled such identification.) The statement was extreme but not quite abnormal: the second wave that had arrived in the nineteenth century tended to think of their culture as German(ic) rather than specifically Jewish. Indeed, in the Reform movement's 1897 *Union Hymnal*, the melody for number 95 was lifted directly from "Deutschland über Alles."[4]

Their culture was really *Kultur*. One German-American newspaper, *Der deutsche Pionier*, praised the immigrant Jews because, "without their patronage," German-language theater in the republic "would cease to exist." Socially the families of German Jewish immigrants and their Gentile counterparts sometimes operated in separate spheres, but the cultural institutions they created (such as singing clubs and reading clubs) were remarkably similar.[5] German Jews did create an early version of the Jewish Publication Society in 1845, but it is hard to discern a distinctively and conspicuously Jewish culture of German origins in the United States. Not as a collective presence but as individuals testing the openness of American democracy, Jews enlarged the possibilities of *Bildung*. Though their contribution to an explicitly Jewish civilization was negligible, their brilliance added sophistication and subtlety to the American culture that Emerson had hoped would emerge.

The roll call is awesome. Among them were scientists like the biologist Jacques Loeb as well as Albert Michelson, who became the first American Nobel laureate in physics, and later J. Robert Oppenheimer, as well as the electrical wizard Charles Steinmetz. The architect Dankmar Adler was the partner of the premier modernist Louis Sullivan, and the celebrated photographer Alfred Stieglitz was also an influential patron of advanced art. No American journalist was a more astute political thinker than Lippmann. Perhaps the first great American music critic was Paul Rosenfeld, and certainly the first great drama critic was George Jean Nathan. Though Lincoln Kirstein enjoyed many successful artistic careers, he was an indispensable demiurge of ballet. (He eventually converted to Roman Catholicism.) A leading impresario of opera was Oscar Hammerstein; a major educational reformer was Abraham Flexner. Brandeis was "the first Jew to be great both as an American, quite apart from what he did for the Jews," according to David Ben-Gurion, Israel's first prime minister, "and great as a Jew, quite apart from what he did for America." Franz Boas was a father of anthropology. Although the *Seven Arts*, which is among the most studied of highbrow magazines, was coedited by Van Wyck Brooks, his fellow editors were all products of German-Jewish families: Paul Rosenfeld, James Oppenheim, and Waldo Frank. The German background of Gertrude Stein cannot be ignored in accounting for the modernism that she helped to establish. Though born in Pennsylvania to Jewish immigrants from Germany, she lived until the age of four in Vienna, where she and her parents spoke German. Perhaps because English was her second language, she came to it as something of an outsider; her peculiar style may have stemmed from picking up something that was not quite inherited.[6] No comprehensive history of American culture and thought can omit such figures.

But their collective traces as Jews do not endure. The only significant exception was "the Mosaic persuasion" to which they subscribed. German Jews did transplant their faith, which they reformed (and then opted to reform further). Judaism at its most rational became what was Jewish about their culture; religion defined largely in terms of ethics determined what was Jewish about their identity. Reform Judaism itself was tenacious and flexible enough to persist. From the elongated perspective of Jewish cultural history, however, the legacy of the second wave of immigrants was otherwise slight. An analogy is the impact of the arrival of Leif Eriksson in Vinland.

Consider the frustrations of Mayer Sulzberger, who served as chairman of the publications committee of the Jewish Publication Society, when he tried to recruit native-born authors. He kept hitting dry holes. Discouraged by his failure to locate an American capable of writing a successful Jewish novel, he asked his friend Lucien Wolf in London to find a British author instead. Wolf suggested Israel Zangwill, whom Sulzberger met and in 1891 invited to write *Children of the Ghetto*, which became a best-seller on both sides of the Atlantic the following year.[7] Even Zangwill expressed anxiety about narrowing his "appeal exclusively to a section," and had told Sulzberger of his hope that "behind all the Jewish details, there must be a human interest which will raise it into that cosmopolitan thing, a work of art."[8] The JPS's most famous author could not have been expected to realize how false that dichotomy is; apposite, inspired arrangement of details *makes* for human interest. Nonetheless, Zangwill was willing to make literature out of Jewish subjects, even though such literature required what the Germanic branch of Jewry in the United States was reluctant to nurture: a more intense consciousness of separateness. Only then might a Jewish culture become viable.

The odds of that efflorescence would be improved if a separate Jewish vernacular were to prevail; and that prospect appeared with the arrival of the refugees from tsarism whom Lazarus's sonnet, "The New Colossus," welcomed. "Yiddish" was a term that did not itself become widespread until the end of the nineteenth century; "Jewish" was simply the language spoken by Ashkenazic Jews. Their "jargon" had the advantage of having been heard in the United States already half a century before the third wave of immigration: settlers from small towns (especially from Bavaria and Württemberg) used a Judeo-German dialect that was probably closer to Yiddish than to "standard" German. Though Isaac Mayer Wise, the Bohemian-born rabbi who championed Americanization, disdained Yiddish, he also spoke it.

The critical mass of speakers, however, came only with the third wave of immigrants. Their numbers were so great that by 1922 (when literary immortality was bestowed upon *dreck*, thanks to *Ulysses*), the capital of Yiddish-speaking culture was neither Warsaw nor Vilna nor Kiev nor Odessa. It was New York City. There Sholom Aleichem had relocated, and there he had died. There the publicist Haim Zhitlowski's collected works were published in 1917, enabling his defense of Yiddishism to become effectively disseminated back in the Old World. In that year attorney Morris Hillquit ran for the mayoralty on the Socialist ticket. The mother tongue of the Riga-born tribune was German. But to propagate socialism, he had to learn (to his chagrin) the Yiddish of New York's Jewish masses.[9]

But which Yiddish were they using? It had incorporated, as early as the 1870s, such American terms as "boss," "boy," "dinner" and "supper." Within three decades, at least a hundred English words and phrases had been inserted into ordinary immigrant speech: "never mind," "politzman," "alle right," and "that'll do." In *Yekl* (1896), written in English, Abraham Cahan has his eponymous protagonist, renaming himself Jake, rebuke the "backwardness" of his wife Gitl "in picking up American Yiddish." Although the breakup of their marriage had deeper causes, one of her errors was to have used *fentzter* instead of *veenda*. (In 1905 Boris Thomashefsky ripped off the ardently patriotic George M. Cohan's work with a show, ostensibly based on *Yekl*, called *Der Yidisher Yenki Dudl*.)

Of course Cahan, who edited the *Forverts* from 1902 until 1951, knew that Yiddish took on the coloration of wherever its speakers lived. When Mamie introduces herself, Gitl is confused: Mamie "spoke with an overdone American accent in the dialect of the Polish Jews, affectedly Germanized and profusely interspersed with English, so that Gitl, whose mother tongue was Lithuanian Yiddish, could scarcely catch the meaning of one half of her flood of garrulity."[10]

In America, Jews learned to speak freely, and the speed with which English got into Yiddish should therefore occasion little surprise. The effect of the lexicographical transformation was evident in the career of Molly Picon, who was already a veteran of the Yiddish theater in New York when she took an extended European tour beginning in 1911. The actress felt a need to improve her Yiddish, which she realized had become "completely bastardized."[11]

But English was altered as well; the language once spoken by Chaucer and Milton opened itself up in the New World. In a commencement address at Bryn Mawr in 1905, Henry James revealed his fears for the integrity of his native tongue, because the immigrants and their progeny were drawing "from the Yiddish even, strange to say," to "play, to their heart's content, with the English language, or, in other words, [to] dump their mountain of promiscuous material into the foundation of the American." In the overprotectiveness of his concern, James came across as a bit *meshuga* (another term, by the way, which Joyce dumped into *Ulysses*).

Nonetheless, James's fears were to be realized. Even as *goniff* and *kibitzer* and *chutzpah* were enshrined in the dictionary, the vernacular was studded with phrases lifted from Yiddish such as "get lost" and "he knows from nothing" and "I should worry" and "smart he isn't" and "I'm telling you." (Such phrases were mostly injected from launching sites in show business.)[12] Linguistic anthropologists have now reached a consensus that "Gimme a bagel shmeer" is how New Yorkers order breakfast, and can be translated as "I wish you a very pleasant good morning. May I please have a bagel with a bit of cream cheese?" Yinglish represented a refusal of Jews to operate within a hermetically sealed environment; to accelerate the prospects of advancement, the Lithuanian-born Alexander Harkavy published the first "English-Jewish" (that is, Judeo-German) dictionary as early as 1891. Before the outbreak of the Great War, the *Complete English-Jewish Dictionary* had already been published in eleven editions. No European immigrant group proved itself quicker than the Jews in learning English, the language in which *The Rise of David Levinsky* (1917) was written. By then a journalistic rival had accused the *Forverts* of conflating the two languages so badly that its subscribers knew neither Yiddish *nor* English. The *Tageblatt* had begun providing its readers with a full page in English as early as 1897.[13]

Such susceptibility to the American ambience secured a new home with remarkable speed, but also exposed the fragility of the Yiddish-speaking culture. It buzzed with excitement; the vibrancy that pulsed through it is recorded, for example, in Hutchins Hapgood's *The Spirit of the Ghetto* (1902). He reported that something was always brewing in the coffee-houses and tearooms of the Lower East Side: schemes for political revolution, ideas for a new play or newspaper or broadsheet, efforts to establish a Yiddish school or a teachers' institute, plans to do a translation, or just to publish something "trashy" (a *shund*) to make money.

But this world was in critical condition. Early in the century *Lider magazin*, which provided Yiddish lyrics for the sheet music of Tin Pan Alley, had already switched to transliteration, as the second generation was uncomfortable reading the Hebrew alphabet used in Yiddish. Even before the outbreak of the First World War, the magazine was transliterating a third of the lyrics that other Jews had already written in English (from "School Days" to "Wait 'til the Sun Shines, Nellie"). Or consider the two female entertainers most closely associated with juicing up English with Yiddish (whether as accent or as syntax). With a Hungarian-born mother and a French-born father, Fanny Brice denied knowing Yiddish. Nor did Gertrude Berg talk like the mother of all Jewish mothers, Molly Goldberg. The diction of the actress was "mannered and precise," utterly devoid of ethnic traces of the Bronx.[14] Neither Brice nor Berg was a native informant; they were *performers*.

An even more obvious index of the decline of the *mamaloshen* (mother tongue) was the readership of the press, which was shrinking dramatically as early as the era of the Great War, and which not even the publication of English supplements could stanch. As early as 1898 Cahan had predicted that the Yiddish press would function as "so many preparatory schools from which the reader is sooner or later promoted to the English newspaper." Immediately after the Great War, one Yiddish weekly as well as two Hebrew monthlies had to suspend publication. The use of the "jargon" probably peaked around 1930, when the census disclosed that about 1,750,000 Americans spoke Yiddish. But that figure was failing to keep pace with the growth of the Jewish population itself. The absolute number of Jews was greater in 1940 than a decade earlier, but half a million fewer of them claimed Yiddish as their mother tongue.[15] The scholarly effort to trace the contours of a self-contained world of *Yiddishkeit* is bound to be frustrated, as a democratic and commercial civilization intervened at the outset of the process of transplantation. America only accelerated the momentum of modernization that had been instigated earlier abroad.

Because all of the noteworthy Yiddish writers in the Old Country were, without exception, multilingual, receptivity to the wider stimuli of Enlightenment and Emancipation was a source of literary enrichment. But continuity was always at risk as well. In his time America's most popular Yiddish novelist was Sholem Asch, who in 1917 wrote a poignant letter to his son, then away at college. Asch admitted that he "did not know in which language to write. That is my tragedy—that I cannot write to my son in the language in which I speak to the people. I don't know English and you don't know Yiddish."

The gap was not always generational. Having come from an assimilated German family, Alma Singer, the wife of the Nobel laureate from Poland, knew no Yiddish. But the basic paradigm consisted of parents reluctant to transmit their mother tongue to their English-speaking children. The radical Adella Kean Zametkin contributed a weekly column on household management to *Der Tog* entitled "Fun a froy tsu froyen" (from one woman —or wife—to another). But neither she nor Michael Zametkin, an editor of the *Forverts*, taught Yiddish to their daughter, Laura Z. Hobson. Their aim, the author of *Gentleman's Agreement* came to realize, "was to bring up their children as total Americans, with no trace of foreign accent, no smallest inflection or gesture that was not native to this their beloved country."[16]

The options seemed limited. In "Good Night, World" (1937), Glatstein's famous poem proposes a return—at least in imaginative terms—to medieval corporatism. He vows to recover "what is deeply mine. / World, joyously I stride / Toward the quiet ghetto lights." Yet such a declaration had little practical effect, or even meaning. His children were not enrolled in any Yiddish-language school, nor did he teach them the language in which he cultivated his poetic powers. Virtually no native-born Jewish writer wrote in any language other than English; Yiddish literature could not reproduce itself in the United States. Its Yiddish culture was a mayfly that could barely survive past one or two generations.[17] Of course, brevity is not synonymous with banality. In the year "Good Night, World" was published, *Grine Felder* (Green fields) was released. As though to defy the odds, it became the biggest hit in the history of Yiddish cinema, and possibly its finest aesthetic achievement as well. The director was Edgar G. Ulmer, famed for the horror flick, *The Black Cat* (1934). Hiring talent from the Yiddish stage, raising some funding from the International Ladies Garment Workers Union, Ulmer shot the film in rural New Jersey. *Grine Felder* expressed a yearning for the reconciliation of matter and spirit, of productivity and piety, indeed a quest for wholeness and fulfillment that inexorable historical pressures would belie. Yet Ulmer could not speak Yiddish.[18]

Zhitlowsky was the chief ideologue in promoting the primary force for Jewish unity as "Yiddishism," a program he introduced in 1900 as an alternative to Orthodoxy and to Zionism. Having helped found the Socialist

Revolutionaries in exile in Zurich in 1893, he shared with Cahan the belief that Jewish workers could emancipate themselves only under socialism. Also an anti-Zionist, Zhitlowsky tirelessly advocated Yiddishism after immigrating in 1908. "We contend that our national cultural existence [in America] will be built on the foundation of the Yiddish language. Through Yiddish we will preserve all the significant treasures of universal culture as well as our own rich Hebrew heritage. We will educate our children in this language. We will establish our own educational institutions, from elementary schools to universities." He added that the "spiritual power" needed to unify Jewry "can only be the Yiddish language. Hence, our people in America will build its national future on the basis of this language. Nowhere is this being done with such drive and success as here in America." But by the end of the 1920s, even he was soft-pedalling the claim that Yiddish could serve as a secure foundation for secular identity, for the prevalence of a "culturally creative organism."[19]

An obvious linguistic alternative was Hebrew. Yet its prospects were measured with equivocation by Solomon Schechter, who could "quite understand the attachment some of us feel toward the German-jargon, or *patois*—call it what you will." He did not care to give it a name! "But let us beware lest we attach any sacredness to this dialect." In America, foreign tongues die: "No foreign language, be it ever so rich in masterpieces of literature, survives a single generation in this country." He therefore warned against dependence of Jewish expression on "this language, which is a mere accident in our history, doomed to die, and is dying before our eyes." To defend Yiddish would be foolish, Schechter contended, because it has no prospects anyway. But the option existed for Hebrew, "the great depository of all that is best in the soul-life of the Congregation of Israel. Without it we will become a mere sect, without a past, and without a literature, and without a proper Liturgy." He pointed out that "Hellenistic Judaism is the only one known to history which dared to make this experiment of dispensing with the sacred language. The result was death. It withered away and terminated in total and wholesale apostasy from Judaism." Schechter foresaw "no future in this country for a Judaism that resists either the English or the Hebrew language." Half a century later the Hebraicist William Chomsky still envisaged Hebrew as the "medium for revitalizing the Jewish community of America, for rendering it dynamic and creative"; and those who know it well would be "the backbone of a meaningful Judaism in the Diaspora."[20]

Never mind that Schechter's autopsy notes on Hellenistic Jewry would now be considered inaccurate.[21] His hope of championing Hebrew proved no more warranted than Zhitlowsky's gallant struggle to salvage Yiddish, though some Hebraists became widely admired academicians who illumined Jewish Studies, such as the literary critic Robert Alter and the historians Gerson D. Cohen and Yosef Hayim Yerushalmi.[22] Their fellow Jews generally adopted the remorseless monolingualism of their fellow citizens, who use the most influential language in all of human history. Once spoken as a mother tongue by only about seven million of Shakespeare's contemporaries, English would by the end of the twentieth century be written and spoken by about one hundred times that number and climbing.[23] English was fulfilling the prophecy in Melville's *Redburn* (1849) that upon the ruins of the tower of Babel would eventually be heard only a universal language—and one that has since become indispensable to scientists and diplomats and air traffic controllers. Not even restricted to the planet, English is the language of cyberspace and of outer space as well. The success of Zionism was to play a joke on Schechter's faith in Hebrew, which is spoken by fewer American Jews than non-Jews who can converse in it elsewhere. But they are Israeli Arabs. An irony that Schechter did not foresee is the case of Anton Shammas, an Israeli citizen who writes in Hebrew and has taught in the United States. Shammas is an adornment of Israeli culture, but does not contribute to Jewish culture; he is an Arab.

The American variant would undoubtedly have been strengthened had a vibrant separate language remained viable. But history did not work out that way; and because of the size, security, and freedom of its Jewish minority, the United States became the most important site in the twentieth century of the struggle to create and perpetuate what could be no more than a variant of the larger culture rather than a serious, cohesive competitor with it.

A knack for leading double lives especially marked the first cohort of new Americans, at least those who landed when they were young enough to figure out how to negotiate between two worlds. Historian Lawrence W. Levine, a prominent interpreter of African-American culture, has described how his own father, a grocer who arrived in 1913, felt no conflict between the two cultures and seemed to live compatibly in both. To be sure he spoke Yiddish infrequently with his children, and became not only an ardent New Deal Democrat but a New York Yankees fan. But his social life was homogeneous. His fraternal order, his friendships, his vacation sites, and finally his choice of cemetery seemed to be largely shared with other eastern European Jews or their children. It hardly needs to be added that religion was not central to his American Jewish identity—and mattered even less to the critic Robert Warshow's Russian-born father, who was decisively shaped by the *Haskalah* (enlightenment). By the age of sixteen, he had become a rationalist and a materialist; "in America he was as a matter of course a Socialist. . . . He belonged to the Socialist movement as one belongs to a certain city or a certain neighborhood," the eulogist wrote. "It gave him his friends and it embodied his culture—so fully, indeed, that he had little need for the more formal objects of culture, such as books." A businessman rather than a worker, he was nevertheless devoted enough to the cause—including declamations on street corners—to have met such Jewish radicals as Emma Goldman ("a 'crazy' and 'loose' Bohemian," the father told the son) and the brilliant but self-centered Trotsky. For the alcoholism of Eugene V. Debs, Robert Warshow's father had some disdain, stemming from "some Jewish feeling about the 'weaker' moral fiber of the *goyim*." Despite insistence on cremation rather than burial, the world he inhabited and from which he drew sustenance and comfort was almost entirely a Jewish world.[24]

Another illustration suggests the social conditions that sparked a Jewish culture. Though William and Elsie Chomsky were supporters of the New Deal, their son Noam recalled that "the next range of family, uncles and cousins and so on," was partly working-class and Communist. One uncle especially "had a lot of influence on me in the late thirties and later," and ran "a newsstand in New York which was sort of a radical center. . . . The great moments of my life in those years were when I could work at the newsstand at night and listen to all this." Noam Chomsky added that "the Jewish working-class culture in New York was very unusual. It was highly intellectual, very poor; a lot of people had no jobs at all and others lived in slums and so on. But it was a rich and lively intellectual culture: Freud, Marx, the Budapest String Quartet, literature, and so forth." What shaped Chomsky's politics was that the future linguist "grew up in an alien culture, in the Jewish-Zionist cultural tradition, in an immigrant community in a sense," that felt connected to a far wider world. The fall of Barcelona during the Spanish civil war prompted him to write his first article—an editorial in the school newspaper—shortly after he had turned ten. That peculiar culture would disappear when the Jewish working class itself would; Chomsky and many of the less famous would become tenured professors, not militant proletarians yearning to form a more perfect union or to collectivize America.[25] What is the difference between the International Ladies Garment Workers Union and the Modern Language Association? The answer to this riddle is: one generation. Allegiance to the working class proved to be about as tenuous as the observance of Judaic law.

Though embourgeoisement would doom any hope of perpetuating a milieu animated by socialist ideals, the vulnerability of a Jewish culture can be discerned even in so central a location as the editorial office of the *Forverts*. Such a culture required a particularist emphasis; weapons of resistance to unqualified Americanization needed to be fashioned. Instead, that newspaper epitomized the yearning for integration. To a historian of a viable but separate Jewish culture, Cahan's career looks dicey. As early as

1912 he was rightly identified in William Randolph Hearst's *American Magazine* as "a Jew who wields tremendous power over his people." Cahan did so with brio for half a century. But he refused to be ghettoized. In a review of *The Imported Bridegroom* (1898), William Dean Howells speculated: "It will be interesting to see whether Mr. Cahan will pass beyond his present environment into a larger American world."[26] To a considerable degree he did, and yet his broader literary fame hardly looked to his admirers like betrayal. Instead, his prestige among Jews was enhanced as his reputation grew among Gentiles like Howells, or like Lincoln Steffens, with whom Cahan worked on the *Commercial-Advertiser*. Historian Moses Rischin wrote that, from an immigrant perspective, the worthy editor "had become a real American whose advice was to be heeded" and "had achieved an English literary style of distinction."

His stature also testifies to the problematic role of religion, without which any description of an American Jewish culture is difficult. But any definition that puts religion at the center (or even that makes religion synonymous with that culture) cannot be squared with the editorial policies or the popular success of the *Forverts*. The most widely read of Yiddish dailies was secularist, more sympathetic to freethinkers than to the rabbinate. Such attitudes did not hurt circulation, which by 1925 exceeded that of every other foreign-language daily in the nation—and even of four of New York's English-language dailies.

The *Forverts* was not Judeocentric. Though sympathetic to Zionism after visiting the *yishuv* in 1925, Cahan was instinctively an assimilationist. He doubted that Yiddish could survive, and was a prophet of its death at an early age; nor did he see much point in promoting Jewish education. Jews should not try to differentiate themselves from other Americans. A proposal to add Yiddish as a foreign language in New York City's public schools died because second-generation parents failed to support it, just as Cahan had predicted. He knew his readers. He rendered Upton Sinclair's sensational novel, *The Jungle* (1906), into Yiddish,[27] and wanted to make the *Forverts* into "the workingmen's organ in their every righteous fight against their oppressors; this struggle is the body of our movement. But its soul is the liberation of mankind—justice, humanity, fraternity."[28] Such moral and political aspirations were manifestly universalist, not an assumption of responsibility to cultivate Jewish cultural interests.

Not even socialism was supposed to spike opportunities for social adjustment. "The Fundamentals of Baseball Explained to Non-Sports," as the newspaper's first article on the national pastime awkwardly phrased it, appeared in 1909. The "madness" was elucidated crisply if apologetically, and readers were helped in making the transition from the Old World to the New with a three-column diagram of the terra incognita of the Polo

Grounds. But then a year earlier Albert Von Tilzer (*né* Gumm) knew so little about this particular diamond business that when he wrote the lyrics to "Take Me Out to the Ball Game," he had never been to one.[29] Perhaps that is why his plea was so personal, given the playing of the national pastime—and his inescapable song—in stadiums to which fans have *already* been taken. The Marx Brothers use it in *A Night at the Opera* to deflate more pretentious European music, as the orchestra swoops into the baseball anthem immediately after playing *Il Trovatore*. The paleontologist Stephen Jay Gould was not alone in claiming, "My grandfather says he [got] acclimated to this country through baseball." In the 1950s the Rumanian-born, Italian-educated artist Saul Steinberg became so ardent a fan of the Milwaukee Braves that he even followed the team on its road trips; when he could not, he donned a Braves uniform and cap before sitting down in front of his television set. Countless other immigrants went through the process of acculturation and discovered their destiny not only on native grounds but also at the Polo Grounds. How quickly Jews achieved a firm grasp of the game is open to some doubt, however. An Anti-Defamation League poster depicted infielders Jackie Robinson and Hank Greenberg and outfielder Joe DiMaggio, but the caption proclaimed: "It doesn't matter what nationality he is; he can pitch."[30]

When crossover dreams could be realized so early and so quickly, the quandaries that were often posed to European Jewry seemed to dissipate. Take a 1940 Yiddish-language film entitled *Der Vilner Shtot Khazn* (The Vilna town-cantor), later released as *Overture to Glory*, in which a cantor must choose whether to join the Warsaw Opera or to remain in the Vilna Synagogue. The dilemma is serious; neither European high culture nor traditional Judaism allowed the protagonist to split the difference. Realizing too late that he has deserted his people, an emotionally spent Cantor Yoel David Strashunsky dies in the *shul* after chanting *Kol Nidre*.[31] His American counterpart is named Jack Robin, who can live out the national ideal: to have it all. The "jazz singer" can knock over the Winter Garden audience by singing "Mammy" and also honor his dying father by chanting *Kol Nidre* from a pulpit on the Lower East Side. Even as Max Nosseck was filming *Der Vilner Shtot Khazn*, the American-born cantors Jan Peerce and Richard Tucker were proving that their native land imposed no such stark vocational choices; these tenors could please audiences at the Metropolitan Opera too. They were free to slip past cultural barriers, with barely a sense that such frontiers existed.

Whether as immigrants or as their children, such figures had the advantage of birth into what might be called a "second culture." (The term was coined by the democratic dissidents who opposed Czech Communism and referred to an implicit, shadowy double, a set of "unspoken challenges"—

in journalist Paul Berman's phrase—to the official culture.)[32] For at least a couple of generations, the institutional nexus of American Jewry was thick and cohesive enough to nurture a second culture, from which the ambitious could spring into the mainstream.

Take the children of Jacob P. Adler, a luminary of the Yiddish stage. (Because *Adler* is German for "eagle," the formidable actor with the piercing eyes and the awesome stage presence had been nicknamed by his adoring public *Nesher Ha-Gadol*—Hebrew for "the Great Eagle.") A daughter from his first marriage was the actress Celia Adler, who remained rooted in the Yiddish theater, even as it was failing to hold its audience. A daughter from his second marriage was Stella Adler, who also started out on the Yiddish stage; her first role was as one of the little princes in *Richard III*. But she branched out to help form the Group Theatre, which was not exactly a clean break with her origins: two of the other founders were Harold Clurman, whom she married, and Lee Strasberg. But the Group Theatre was intended to be a progressive alternative to the crassness of the commercial stage and to the sentimentality of ethnic drama. Who can blame her for seizing the opportunity in 1935 to perform in Odets's *Awake and Sing!* and *Paradise Lost*? (She was partly the model for Bessie Berger, that most formidable of mothers.) The chance to reshape her profession was realized with the establishment of the Stella Adler Theater Studio (later called the Stella Adler Conservatory of Acting); among her alumni were Brando, Warren Beatty, and Robert De Niro.[33] However tantalizing the mainstream, that "second culture" was still proximate and accessible.

Or consider Maurice Sendak, whose writing and drawing for children have elicited exceptional acclaim. (That is, however, probably too confining a category; his books are not appreciated only by ten-somethings.) His career also had its origins in that second culture. He provided the illustrations for such books as *Good Shabbos, Everybody* (1951) and *Happy Hanukah, Everybody* (1955), both done for the United Synagogue Commission on Jewish Education, and for *Seven Little Stories on Big Subjects* (1955), done for the Anti-Defamation League. Even Sendak's apprenticeship showed, according to Selma G. Lanes, a scholar of children's literature, "an almost uncanny ability to make palpable the emotional reality of the text, the warm family atmosphere in which its characters exist and act, and the psychological sparks of life which bind them together." She already discerned "in the expressions and gestures of the grandparents and small children—as well as in the cozy, claustrophobic aura of Jewish family solidarity Sendak so clearly projects—a preview of what would become Sendak's forte: the gift for getting beneath the surface of things and revealing truths previously considered beyond the province or propriety of young children's books." He later did the uncanny illustrations for Singer's *Zlateh the Goat and Other Stories* (1966).

Admittedly such work does not measure up to the deeply personal—and more "universalistic"—achievements of *Where the Wild Things Are* (1963), which has sold eight million copies, and of *In the Night Kitchen* (1970).[34] But the speed with which Sendak established his international reputation does raise doubt whether the second culture could sustain itself long enough to give the community creative breathing space. A later generation would find a rich and credible Jewish world (one more ethnic than observant) more elusive to recall, more difficult to reinvent.

Jewish immigrants and their progeny took to America so quickly and found its culture so congenial that their fin-de-siècle impact could be already felt (which helps justify a treatment of the twentieth century as though it were a unit). The problems of adjustment were often searing and the rise of American Jewry hardly frictionless. For all of the ugly power of nativism, it ultimately failed to stanch the flow of immigration or to pervert the definition of Americanism. Probably more than elsewhere in the Diaspora, Jews found America so hospitable that status anxiety—a sense of usurpation—was stirred among those whose history and ancestry were supposed to be indigenous. The Harvard literary historian Barrett Wendell, for example, feared the declension of his own Brahmin class that had been first out of the starting gate. "Your Jewish race is less lost than we, of old America," Wendell told Kallen, his former student. "We are submerged beneath a conquest so complete that . . . I feel as I should think an Indian might feel, in the face of ourselves that were." The patriciate for whom the professor spoke doubted whether his "race—as oppressed today as yours ever was," he believed, had retained "the vitality to survive the test" of demanding multiethnic competition.[35]

How could such staid legatees of the Puritans outrun the likes of Sammy Glick? In the 1941 novel written by the son of a production chief at Paramount, the narrator muses on the East Side origins of a despicable hustler, "rocking in his cradle of hate, malnutrition, prejudice, suspicions . . . a mangy little puppy in a dog-eat-dog world." Glick's background would nourish an implacable desire to escape, cutting every corner, "proving himself the fittest, the fiercest and the fastest."[36] Faced with the rambunctious vitality, the swing-for-the-fences energy of the newcomers from the Pale of Settlement, the genteel thought of themselves as the truly disadvantaged. Though Jews in New York City never exceeded much beyond a quarter of its population, vigor and assurance made that proportion look larger. "One of the most remarkable phenomena of the time," journalist Burton J. Hendrick wrote in the muckraking *McClure's* as early as 1907, is that "New York, the headquarters of American wealth, intelligence and enterprise—the most complete physical expression . . . of the American idea —seems destined to become overwhelmingly a Jewish town." Generalizing in 1922, one fervent young intellectual could proclaim that "whatever else American civilization is, it is not Anglo-Saxon," nor was it any longer "an English Colony."[37]

From the very special angle of the expatriate Henry James, the sheer conspicuousness of the Jews was disorienting. Not that his own genealogy justified snobbery; his grandfather had been an Irish immigrant. But returning home in 1904, the novelist spoke for the native-born elite in expressing vexation with cataclysmic changes. *The American Scene* describes the Lower East Side immigrants as "a great swarming, a swarming that has begun to thicken . . . a Jewry that has burst all bounds." According to one literary scholar, "James's experience of 'terrible little Ellis Island' amounted to a fall into history, into the future of America, that left him feeling like an outsider in his homeland, perhaps even like a man without a country. Wandering the Italian and Jewish neighborhoods of the East Side, he felt assaulted by the alien sounds and smells." His olfactory nerves were as offended as his sense of hearing, in trying to absorb "a patch of alien comedy" on the Yiddish stage. The land to which he was returning injected "a new chill" in James's heart. What amazed the author of *Washington Square* was the quickness with which the "aliens" adapted to New York City: "Foreign as they might be, newly inducted as they might be, they were *at home*, really more at home, at the end of their few weeks or months or their year or two, than they had ever in their lives been before."[38]

They did so with such panache that Cahan needed to come up with a neologism for the "mushroom-millionaires" around him, and in 1906 came up with *ol-raytnikes* (*allrightniks*)—Yinglish for "parvenus." The speedy entrenchment of the immigrants meant that "American" and "Jewish" would not be exclusive terms. To the antonyms of *Deutschtum* and *Judentum*, there have been no equivalents in the United States. Already before Germany became unified, Richard Wagner had demanded emancipation *from* Jewish parvenus, whose artificiality and imitativeness were alleged to be corrupting musical life. No matter how assimilated, no matter even how sincerely baptized and converted, Jews could be regarded as a separate (or at least separable) element in German culture, as not really part of the *Volk*. But even if the judgment of the Israeli historian Gershom Scholem—that the vaunted "dialogue" was mostly a monologue—may be too unsparing,[39] what is taken for granted is the transaction of two distinct parties.

But for a Jew to make an authentic contribution to twentieth-century American culture was not widely seen as something preposterous. That is why the Jewish part of the story of creativity cannot be disentangled from the American part. Not even an embittered Truman Capote went so far as

46

to demand emancipation *from* "this god-damned Jewish Mafia" when, in a 1973 interview, he tabulated that "the entire cultural press, publishing . . . criticism . . . television . . . theater . . . film industry . . . is almost 90 percent Jewish-oriented. I mean, I can't even count on one hand, five people of any importance—of real importance—in the media who aren't Jewish. I can't." (He was probably inadvertently echoing the complaint of music critic and composer Virgil Thomson about a "Jewish Mafia that passed the jobs around among themselves.")[40]

That the interview with the novelist was conducted in *Rolling Stone*, founded and edited by a Jew, Jann Wenner, only strengthened Capote's point. Indeed, as his publisher was Random House (run by Bennett Cerf), the editor at the *New Yorker* upon whom Capote relied was William Shawn, and a major patron was CBS's William S. Paley, the novelist was not utterly deluded, however inexact his arithmetic. The "entire cultural press" covers too much terrain even for a tiny if enterprising minority to monopolize. But its conspicuousness helps explain why, according to a 1992 poll, only 10 percent of Gentiles realized that Jews numbered less than 5 percent of the population. The median estimate of their proportion was 18 percent, or about six times the correct figure.[41] So deeply implicated in American culture has "this god-damned Jewish Mafia" been that its American credentials could not disdained as ersatz. Not even Capote was willing to suggest that Jews had overstayed their welcome.

The relative openness of American society meant that the Jews who founded and ran publishing houses in New York (or who founded and ran movie studios in Los Angeles) were filling a vacuum as much as they were competing with established institutions. Capote's native South lacked publishing houses of consequence; and the career of the region's most admired novelist, William Faulkner, was inevitably entangled in the media institutions that Jews had established elsewhere. Though he tried to spend most of his life far away from metropolitan centers, Faulkner's farsighted publishers included Horace Liveright and especially Cerf (though by 1945 every novel except *Sanctuary* was out of print). Hollywood therefore became an indispensable source of income. Beginning in the 1930s, Faulkner stayed alive by writing scripts for MGM, Twentieth Century–Fox and then Warner Brothers. Such paychecks allowed Jack Warner (who had famously disdained the scenarists whom he employed as "*shmucks* with Underwoods") to boast: "I've got America's best writer for $300 a week."[42]

Such philistinism helps explain why the *American Heritage Dictionary* listed as synonyms for Hollywood (as an adjective) "tawdry," "delusive," and "meretricious." The point need not be belabored. But it is hardly obvious that Faulkner's talent would have been better served by teaching freshman English nine months a year instead of spending two or three months rewriting scripts. The movie business is of course the strongest evidence of the ease with which Jews exercised cultural power. Born mostly from within a radius of a couple of hundred miles of Warsaw, the moguls had created the fifth-largest industry in the nation by 1926, when Hollywood was making nine out of every ten films in the world. Nothing so spectacular could have been predicted at the beginning of the century; however uneasy the studio heads were with the implications of their own Jewishness, antisemitism scarcely impeded their success—or the popularity of their product. They released comedy series like "The Cohens and the Kellys" but behind the camera, as Spencer Tracy was quick to notice, "the Kellys are working for the Cohens." Such an arrangement, however, was not so unnatural as to flare into social conflict, much less to provoke political reaction.[43] Within a generation or so, outsiders were resembling insiders and were running pivotal cultural agencies with a Yankee Doodle Dandy confidence.

The speed of integration did not quite make Jews insiders, however, nor did many of them necessarily *feel* like insiders. But in a nation in which even descendants of presidents, like Henry and Brooks Adams, could tell themselves that they are losers, the distinction between outsiders and insiders may not be precise. Even by the end of the twentieth century, Jewish subjectivity did not correspond exactly with the thoroughness of assimilation; some dissonance persisted. A supplement to the Passover *Haggadah* that *Tikkun* magazine provided to its readers in 1993 included a plea to Gentiles to "understand that we too are victims, yet it's understandable why . . . [you] may think otherwise." During most of the century, the condition of American Jewry has often been so ambiguous that ambivalence made sense. Such an attitude toward American society was epitomized in the immigrant Samuel Goldwyn's insistence: "Include me out!" Less well known is the actual target of Groucho Marx's paradoxical gesture of refusal to join any club that would admit someone like him as a member. He was referring to the Hillcrest, a Los Angeles country club that was *Jewish*. The American ambience has been rife with such complications. In *Annie Hall* (1977), Alvy Singer (Woody Allen) paraphrases the remark, and then applies the line to his own "relationships with women."[44]

Especially in a nation of immigrants, Jews have been *both* outsiders and insiders. Admissible evidence can certainly be cited of their exclusion as well as their *feelings* of exclusion. "The essential nature of Jewishness," Fiedler speculated in 1963, "is, quite simply, not to belong." Much of the evocative power of *The Rise of David Levinsky* emanates from its self-exposure of homelessness, which a new American could not palliate despite the giddy sensations of prosperity and freedom. The Passover ritual, among the most widely observed of religious celebrations, encodes the extreme of marginality by asking participants to think of themselves as slaves. So deracinated were many of Cahan's fellow intellectuals that Thorstein Veblen (himself the son of Norwegian immigrants) could infer from the condition of alienation the sources of exceptional creativity among homeless Jews. Their "intellectual pre-eminence," their proclivity for dissidence were the uses they made of marginality. An extreme exemplar is the feminist theoretician Hélène Cixous. As a Jew born in French Algeria, she read in her school textbooks about "our ancestors, the Gauls." This was puzzling. Her own forebears had "lived in Spain, Morocco, Austria, Hungary, Czechoslovakia, Germany," and her neighbors were Arabs. "So where are we in history?" Cixous wondered. "Where is my place?"[45] Such dislocation typified Veblen's creative rebels. Bereft of any particular Jewish heritage, they are suspended between two worlds. Without enjoying the benefits of Judaic learning yet feeling the stigma of Jewish identity, they are merely estranged.

In the United States, however, the case for unease should not be overstated. Peoples of color have been even more marginalized. But Native Americans and Asian-Americans, for example, have not registered an equivalent cultural impact, though often they are not Christians either. Mere difference therefore cannot be all-important in engendering cultural achievement. If it were, then the contributions of the Native American and Asian-American minorities to the nation's arts and letters would be more conspicuous (or even *more* striking, as at least skin color protected Jews against the worst discrimination).

Veblen's thesis is especially dubious in accounting for the strength of American Jewish culture. Jews are not like gypsies, nor alien in a way that those afflicted with extreme physical deformities are (as Bourne himself was). Unlike blacks, Jews have been formally free, and were never really in need of any "Jew bill" to establish their rights (except briefly in Maryland in the early national period). Nor were they treated like pariahs or disruptive threats who had to be shunted off to reservations or to relocation camps or to segregated schools, as other minorities were. Jews were not utterly alien; they were not formally evicted or persecuted or deprived of rights. They have only rarely—and perhaps only for one or two generations —felt like "resident aliens." Even if Jews were made to feel like outsiders in certain circumstances, they had also become by midcentury a "model minority," achieving embourgeoisement in a society that tends to think of itself as middle-class.

To reduce Jewishness to marginality, or to the distance of "the other," is to flatten the complications of the minority condition in the United States. In 1980, a bomb exploded outside a synagogue in Paris, killing four people. That evening, in a televised statement, Prime Minister Raymond

Barre condemned "this odious attack aimed at Jews attending the syna-gogue, and which struck innocent Frenchmen who were crossing rue Co-pernic." Apart from the possible implication that Jews were *not* innocent was the easy assumption that they were not quite Frenchmen either. In the imbroglio over the recovery of Jewish assets deposited in Swiss banks during the Holocaust, Rolf Bloch, the chief spokesman for the Jewish community in Switzerland, referred to "the Swiss" as though they are a separate category from the eighteen thousand Jewish citizens living there. The chief negotiator for the recovery of the assets, Edgar Bronfman, did not refer to "the Americans" (despite his own Canadian background).[46] And across the border from Zurich, the umbrella Central Council of Jews *in* Germany does not use the preposition "of," as though to signify the sense of not quite belonging. There are books devoted to "German-Jewish relations" and "Polish-Jewish relations" and so forth. A 1994 monograph on Victorian social relations is even entitled *Englishmen and Jews*. But a phrase like "American-Jewish relations" would be nonsensical.

The ambiguities of being both outsider and insider can be framed in the genesis of an inescapable manifestation of recent popular culture: *Star Trek*. A visitor who had taken his daughter to a Jewish cemetery in Poland once told actor Leonard Nimoy of seeing a tombstone, he recalled, "that fea-tured an image of two hands sheltering a candle, their fingers splayed out in the traditional sign of blessing—with the thumb and its adjacent two fingers to one side, the other two fingers to the other, in a kind of V." The girl then asked her father: "How come the hands are saying, 'Live long and prosper'?" Nimoy laughed when he heard of the incident: "The funny thing is, the girl got it exactly right." In Boston's West End where the future "Mr. Spock" grew up, the most awesome moment in synagogue was when about a half-dozen *Kohanim* (descendants of the priestly tribe) would stand before the ark, with their large *tallit* (prayer shawls) over their heads and their extended arms. Forming a semicircle, these men would open their hands in a four-fingered *V*-configuration, which created the let-ter *shin*, signifying the name of the deity (or *Shad-dai*). "It was a very loaded moment," he recalled. "You weren't supposed to look as they be-gan chanting, for it was said that at that moment the *Shekhinah*, the holy presence of God, entered the sanctuary, and that this spirit was so power-ful, so beautiful that if you saw it you'd die." That is what happens to the Nazi raiders of the lost ark in Steven Spielberg's first Indiana Jones epic—but not to the eight-year-old Nimoy, who "peeked, and the sheer theatri-cality of the occasion indeed made a lasting impression."

When cast for *Star Trek*, he could hardly mistake what he called "the Jewish resonances of this eternally wandering exile, this alien among an otherwise homogeneous crew." Nimoy had "to fashion his whole Vulcan world as if from scratch, and one of the things I kept keying on was this notion of a distinctly hand-oriented society: the mind-meld, the neck-pinch, and so forth. And in one of the early episodes there came a moment when a salutation of some sort was called for, and it all came back to me like that—the four-fingered *V* sign from my youth. That became the gesture for 'Live long and prosper.'" Though actor William Shatner, the captain of the *Enterprise*, was also Jewish, it was fitting that the pointy-eared Vulcan was played by a Jew, who remembered that hand gesture and made it "my Vulcan *shalom*, my greeting of peace, my yearning for the blessing of peace—the age-old quest of . . . my people."[47] But of course the other point of the story is that Nimoy is *not* Spock; and as costar of a cult series beloved by "Trekkies," the actor is no outsider.

This example hints at one of the inescapable conditions of American Jewish culture: its bias toward mass entertainment. The only culture American Jews have ever known is like the only polity they have known; both are based on the ideal of popular sovereignty. Even as Emma Lazarus was visiting the Emerson household, Bert and Leon were pioneering Jewish comedy; they splattered audiences with mile-a-minute patter, pratfalls, and parodies. Take "The Widow Rosenbaum," whose "father keeps a hock shop / With three balls on the door, / Where the sheeny politicians can be found." Bert and Leon concluded by wondering "Was hast gesachta? Zu klein gemachta," and describing "the kleine kinder, looks in the winder" (not *fentzter*). In an era when group caricatures were a show-business staple, demeaning stereotypes of Jews could hardly be excluded. (Or, as Brando would later put it in his television interview, audiences were accustomed to seeing the nigger, the greaseball, the Chink, the Jap. The kike was not ignored either.) The amplification of antisemitic images bothered the *Indianapolis News* as early as 1901, however. "With the growing influence of Jews in theatrical matters," a staff writer observed, it is strange that "so little respect is paid on the stage to the Jewish character or the Jewish traditions." Despite the Jewish domination of the "theatrical business," there seemed no immediate prospect that "the frightful caricature of the Hebrew that has long served as a buffoon for the amusement of the unthinking would disappear."[48] Already at the dawn of the century, what makes some sorts of representation problematic had emerged as a topic, if not yet as a political issue.

Jews helped shape mass entertainment before participating in the elevated arts and letters that Matthew Arnold defined as "culture." The creative achievements of the National Book Award winners and the Nobel laureates in literature were "in the first years of this century being prepared not in the universities, not even in journalism," Kazin argued, "but in the vaudeville theaters, music halls, and burlesque houses where the pent-up eagerness of penniless immigrant youngsters met the raw urban scene on its own terms." An epiphany of such entertainment occurred in 1893 when Chicago hosted the World's Columbian Exposition. There, at the gaudy Midway Plaisance, the manager of all the entertainment was Solomon Bloom, and the word "ballyhoo" may have originated. There the most legendary attraction was a "hootchy-kootchy" dancer known as Little Egypt, whose navel became famous in the *danse du ventre*, staged in the so-called Persian Palace of Eros. "Simply horrid" was the reaction of seventy-four-year-old Julia Ward Howe (author of "The Battle Hymn of the Republic"), who could see "only a most deforming movement of the whole abdominal and lumbar region." Another memorable performer at the Midway Plaisance was a rabbi's son, Ehrich Weiss, who bestowed on himself a name to conjure with: Houdini.[49] No minority group was quicker to satisfy the hunger for the sensations of mass entertainment (and often for liberation from Victorian gentility) than Jewish entrepreneurs and performers, who faced far fewer impediments than serious writers and artists did. That is why Sophie Tucker had to precede the operatic tenor Richard Tucker, and Sammy Cahn the modernist architect Louis I. Kahn. Only after Louis Mayer could sponsor "more stars than there are in heaven" could Richard Meier become the architect who would win the commission to design a new Vatican church in a suburb of Rome. He wanted Pope John Paul II to inspect the model only when properly lit. "It's just my *mishegoss*, I know," Meier recalled, "but the Pope should not see the model in the dark. . . . He was very gracious."[50]

Within the commercial and democratic system of mass entertainment that was becoming so ascendant by the end of the nineteenth century, no minority group was better poised to seize both artistic and business opportunities. The movies were the purest example. What made them so distinctly Jewish, Fiedler declared, was that they were ancillary to the garment industry, "which began by blurring away class distinctions in dress and ended by blotting out class distinctions in dreams." Invited to send in the clowns, Jews also operated as minstrels and music-makers, and would "help to fit the Jew to America, and America to the Jew, with an élan that made for future creativity in literature" as well as mass entertainment, Fiedler wrote.

Kazin's description suggests how smoothly such talents could be absorbed: "The very poverty and cultural rawness of the Jewish immigrant masses, the self-assertive egalitarianism of the general temper, and the naturalness with which different peoples could identify with each other in the unique halfway house that was New York . . . gave individual performers the privilege of representing the popular mind. Never before had so numerous a mass of Jews been free citizens of the country in which they lived, and so close to the national life." This plebeian culture became "a natural habitat for the Jews," enabling the generation of serious writers who emerged in the 1930s to adopt "the language of the street" instead of "stilted moralism." As Arnold had barred even Chaucer from the pantheon because he lacked "high seriousness," one wonders how such solemn definitions of culture could have embraced wild cards like Lou Holtz and Belle Barth. Film critic Pauline Kael, whose parents had come from Warsaw, insisted that "vulgarity is not as destructive to an artist as snobbery, and in the world of movies vulgar strength has been a great redemptive force, cancelling out niggling questions of taste."[51]

She was right about the vital sources from which popular art would spring—and that includes even the aspirations a phrase like "high seriousness" once invoked. "Very possibly there may be at this moment," Howells speculated in 1915, "a Russian or Polish Jew, born or bred on our East Side, who shall burst from his parental Yiddish, and from the local hydrants, as from wells of English undefiled, slake our drouth [*sic*] of imaginative literature." This guess almost anticipated Bellow, who was born that year, though bred in the Chicago counterpart of the East Side. Such inspired speculation might also have been applicable to Malamud, born a year earlier (though in Brooklyn), or to Henry Roth (whose family had moved to the Lower East Side in 1910). However uncannily Howells had forecast how the national letters would be revitalized, other genres were responsive to the uncluttered and uncertified ambitions of talented Russian and Polish Jews. Unable to read or write music, Irving Berlin did not bother to seek remedial education: "In the time I spent taking lessons[,] I could have written a few songs." When Minnie Marx was asked why her sons went into show business, she answered with another question: "Where else can people who don't know anything make so much money?"[52] In 1905 show biz became a beat when Sime Silverman founded its newspaper of record, *Variety*. The term evoked the mishmash of the mass arts: "the racial and immigrant plurality of the American polis," one historian remarked.[53]

How fully Kazin's generalization encompasses the style and sensibility of the writers starting out in the 1930s and thereafter need not detain us here. But what matters is how closely entwined that energetic and raucous "vulgar culture" was with the achievements normally recognized as inhabiting a higher realm of art and thought. At the moment of such energetic entanglement, however, the achievement was barely noticed. What America was giving the world, and what the Jews were then giving America, was not taken seriously. The criteria of evaluation had not yet been satisfactorily formulated. The evolving culture of American Jewry scarcely resembled the *Bildung* that idolized Goethe and Schiller. The austerity associated with German high culture collided with what American Jews had created most directly in the 1930s, when some refugees were lucky enough to escape the Third Reich.

In Hollywood the contrast was most obvious. Those who had come earlier, out of choice, like directors Ernst Lubitsch and Billy Wilder, adapted smoothly. But consider the dislocation of Arnold Schoenberg, the revolutionary inventor of serialism, invited during a party at Ira Gershwin's to provide some after-dinner entertainment: "Give us a tune, Arnold." When producer Irving Thalberg once complimented him for his "lovely music," the reply was chilling: "I don't write lovely music." Schoenberg nevertheless seemed willing to score *The Good Earth*. But then he demanded a $50,000 fee, and insisted on complete control of the soundtrack, including the introduction of *Sprechstimme* instead of ordinary spoken dialogue (so that the actors' voices would be confined to the composer's own pitch and key). MGM declined. Also adrift was the novelist Hermann Broch, who was well versed in science and in psychoanalysis and had studied with the Vienna Circle of philosophers. In the United States he got the bizarre inspiration to work on a film script devoted to Einstein's theory of relativity. One can scarcely imagine the reaction of Harry Cohn (upon whom his most important director, Frank Capra, bestowed the sobriquet of "the Crude One") had Broch pitched such a script at Columbia—a name that Cohn, the president of the studio, had trouble spelling.[54]

No wonder that the fearsomely erudite Walter Benjamin was ambivalent about coming to America. Faced with the prospect of incomprehension and provinciality, he feared that "people would probably find no other use for him than to cart him up and down the country to exhibit him as the 'last European.'" No wonder that Theodor W. Adorno, who was possibly even more learned, found himself unable to dodge "the question whether the concept of culture, in which one was brought up, has not itself become obsolete" in a nation where people make up their culture as they go along.[55]

The cultural diffusion that many American Jews perpetrated, beginning early in the century and not yet run its course, came to alter the way artistic achievement itself is evaluated. The raw power of mass culture—its syncretism and its heterogeneity—helped blur the distinction that once established differences between art and entertainment. If aesthetic criteria require consideration of how the mysterious luck and self-discipline of talent can be expressed, the prestige accorded to sobriety and responsibility and subtlety means less than, say, believability and forcefulness. Mass culture has been pervasive enough to impose its own standards of judgment and appreciation. It tends to be forgotten that Van Wyck Brooks, the critic who coined the phrases "highbrow" and "lowbrow," illustrated the latter not by citing, say, the baggy-pants "Hebe comedians" or the vaudeville "coon shouters" of 1915 but the most famous American *scientist* of the eighteenth century: Benjamin Franklin. His Hon. M.A. from Harvard College and membership in the Royal Society notwithstanding, Franklin's popular writings placed him in Brooks's account in opposition to the "highbrow" Jonathan Edwards.[56] Once the machinery of mass entertainment was fine-tuned, such distinctions between "high" and "low" became less useful, as the arts became so democratized that lower versions of the "lowbrow" demanded to be appraised—and perhaps even praised. Because the conceptual apparatus of Van Wyck Brooks was not expansive enough to encompass, say, Mel Brooks, that task was first assumed, aptly, by a son of Jewish freethinkers and an astute critic: Gilbert Seldes.

Seldes became almost certainly the first serious American analyst of the popular arts. Especially in his 1924 volume *The Seven Lively Arts*, published a year before Lord Balfour's address on Mount Scopus, Seldes advanced a pioneering critical case for the value and importance of mass entertainment, while attacking the snobbery upon which the case for "high culture" often rested. By insisting upon the conscientiousness with which popular as well as "classical" art deserved to be studied, he denied a Manichaean opposition between them. What the populace enjoyed was not always to be disdained; sometimes, even often, its taste was entirely justified.

Seldes himself was no vulgarian, having served as managing editor of the *Dial* (1920–23), the avant-garde magazine that published *The Waste Land* as well as poems of e. e. cummings, Ezra Pound, and Marianne Moore. Seldes's idea of celebrating the completion of *The Seven Lively Arts*, while in Paris, was to take Picasso, Stravinsky, and James and Nora Joyce to the Ballets Russes on "Bloomsday," 16 June. In the *Nation*, Seldes had also published an early and influential appreciation of *Ulysses*. But he also believed that ragtime and comic strips and musical comedies merited the same careful analysis and evaluation as "the great arts," and wanted to jump across what he dismissed as "artificial lines . . . between the fine and the popular arts." (Seldes used the analogy of the false division "between Jews and non-Jews.")[57]

Perhaps his influence was only indirect upon Elliot E. Cohen, who served as managing editor of the *Menorah Journal* and then as the first editor of *Commentary* (1945–59). His successor was struck by "the great variety of subjects the magazine covered." This range "was not simply the mark of his limitless curiosity," Norman Podhoretz noted. Cohen refused "to define himself by his exclusions and snobberies rather than by his passions and enthusiasms." Lionel Trilling, an early contributor to the *Menorah Journal*, also recalled the eclectic scope of Cohen's nonstop "gossip— about persons, books, baseball players and football plays, manners, morals, comedians (on these he was especially good)," as well as "literary scholarship, restaurants, tailors, psychiatry." Spurning an ideal of intellectual "purity," Cohen's "mind was dominated by his sense of the subtle interrelations that exist between the seemingly disparate parts of culture, and between the commonplaces of daily life and the most highly developed works of the human mind." His legacy, both Trilling and Podhoretz stressed, was an unhierarchical view of culture. Not only did "lowbrow" expression need to be evaluated fairly; Cohen also hoped to find a way of "being both Jewish and non-parochial." Is it accidental that Walter Benjamin and Q. D. (Queenie) Leavis, two early critics across the Atlantic who measured the impact of mass culture on literature, were Jews?[58]

The revision of cultural standards is recorded early in the century in *The Rise of David Levinsky.* It flunks to be sure the exhilarating test of "the great arts." For ethnographic purposes, however, Cahan's novel is extremely useful. Dinner at the home of the Kaplans, to whose daughter Fanny the protagonist is briefly engaged, elicits this reflection: "I was ambitious to be a cultured man 'in the European way.' There was an odd confusion of ideas in my mind," however. Levinsky "had a notion that to 'become an American' was the only tangible form of becoming a man of culture (for did I not regard the most refined and learned European as a 'greenhorn'?)."[59] Note the reversal here of what is culture, which by the early twentieth century has become American (or at least modern). The result is some consternation. Are the standards to which he aspires European? Or have they become American? The ground is already shifting beneath Levinsky's feet, and in the direction of that independence that Emerson had been urging during the American Renaissance.

Cahan's novel went out of print in 1943, as though to signal the inexorable disappearance of the first generation that had fled from persecution and immiseration. Levinsky embodies the unsettling juxtaposition of success and failure, the ordeal of reconciling conflicting demands and memories. In that year a second-generation American would demonstrate his own emancipation from the burden of insecurity, self-doubt, and shame. He was a supremely indigenous instance of self-invention, in the sense that no predecessors existed upon whom Leonard Bernstein might model himself. Indeed the idea of an American-born and -trained conductor of a major orchestra was so odd that Mencken conjectured, in 1922, that "the leading American musical director, if he went to Leipzig, would be put to polishing trombones and copying drum parts."

Bernstein's own roots were of course further east. His father, Samuel Bernstein, was born in Russia, and so was his surrogate father, the conductor Serge Koussevitzky, whose own father had been a klezmer, an itinerant folk musician.[60] To advance his own career, however, the adolescent

Serge Koussevitzky had converted to Russian Orthodoxy. In so benighted a country, the yearning for material rewards and professional status so difficult to attain under tsarism should not be disparaged. The orientalist Daniel Chwolson once justified such an option in explaining that he had converted to Russian Orthodoxy out of conviction: "I was convinced it is better to be a professor in St. Petersburg than a *melamed* [Hebrew teacher] in Eyshishok."[61] (Several versions of this explanation have circulated.)

By 1943 Koussevitzky had become the conductor of the Boston Symphony Orchestra, and was able to offer his protégé some onomastic advice. Unsurpassed possibilities would be available, Bernstein recalled his idol assuring him, were it not for one impediment: "It is the name, the *nom*. He said, 'It vill be open to you all the gates from the vorld, but it vill nothing happen ven you vill not change it—the *nom*.'" Koussevitzky even had a suggestion: Leonard S. Burns. The middle initial would be a patronymic, standing for Samuelovich; that is, Samuel Bernstein, to whom the prodigy's piece for soprano and orchestra, based on the Book of Lamentations, would be dedicated. The advice could not be easily dismissed. The friendship of the conductor meant so much to Lenyushka that he would name his only son, born in 1955, Alexander Serge Bernstein; and Leonard Bernstein would make a lifetime habit of conducting while wearing the pair of cufflinks that Serge Alexandrovich Koussevitzky had given him.

But Lenyushka was irrevocably a Jew. That part of himself was unalterable, even if some names remained shames; and he knew that the United States did not require or expect conversion from Judaism. After a sleepless night, the protégé then told Koussevitzky of having "decided to make it as Leonard Bernstein, or not at all."[62] Later in 1943, when he made a sensational debut with the New York Philharmonic, the conductor whom Bernstein suddenly replaced was the Berlin-born Bruno Walter, who had lopped off his own surname of Schlesinger and had found a mentor in Gustav Mahler, who had become a Roman Catholic to take full advantage of Vienna's musical life.

Bernstein was lucky enough to do otherwise and felt free to honor both sides of the proverbial hyphen. He kept his family name, and no penalty was exacted; thus he demonstrated the plasticity of American society. He could not have imagined echoing from his own experience how Mahler had once identified himself: "I am a thrice homeless man: as a Bohemian among Austrians, as an Austrian among Germans and as a Jew among the people of the whole world." The first conductor to record the full Mahler cycle, Bernstein would begin his formal relationship with the Vienna Philharmonic in 1966—even before resigning from the New York Philharmonic. In leading the orchestra of Mahler's own city, Bernstein achieved a personal triumph as well as an ethnic vindication.[63] Even while helping to legitimate Jewish difference at home, he did not shun the ambition to reach out to a wider constituency that also typifies the democratic thrust of his native land. In that interplay can be found the dynamic of American Jewish culture.

MUSICAL THEATER

No epicenter of American Jewish culture exists. There is no capital that is akin, say, to the vicinity of St.-Germain-des-Prés where postwar French culture could be situated. But if there were such a locale, it would be Broadway. The New York stage was the thrilling showcase for the talents of Fanny Brice, Al Jolson, Eddie Cantor, Bert Lahr, and (briefly) Barbra Streisand. For more than half a century, such performers could electrify audiences. Broadway also spawned some of Hollywood's stars and rivaled it in glamour, and incubated the Tin Pan Alley tunes that a nation would sing in unison. The pulse of a common culture could be taken on Broadway, validating the etymology of *entertain*: to hold together.

But the emergence of both rock and roll and television in the 1950s had the effect of weakening the American musical. The center could not hold; it shifted to the small screen (which also made the Broadway genre in retrospect look classier and more estimable). Its babies deserved to be appreciated for having found a European-derived operetta and created an indigenous art form that one historian elevated into "New York opera." It flourished, John Dizikes has claimed, between 1940, when *Pal Joey* opened, and 1960, when *Camelot* opened and Oscar Hammerstein II died. "New York opera" showed its vitality before and after those dates as well. The city inflected the musical as completely as Vienna marked the waltz and Paris the cancan, and yet also managed to project a *national* style. This "distinctive form of American popular opera" was easily recognized wherever it was staged, "in its propulsive energy, its brashness and naïveté and unshakable optimism." The Broadway musical was incontestably native, as though honoring Emerson's plea that the truly "American scholar" should cease listening to the courtly muses of Europe.

Unlike opera, Broadway preferred actors who could sing to singers who could act, so that "spoken dialogue moved the stories forward." But that is why Dizikes's label is misleading. Opera stars are expected to sing, as Rex Harrison, for example, could not. Yet he was designated—indeed destined —to be Henry Higgins before the songs in *My Fair Lady* (1956) were finished. They were accordingly shaped for him. Nor did Richard Burton quite sing in *Camelot*. In the rehearsals for *Guys and Dolls* (1950), the role of Nathan Detroit seemed so perfectly cast that nobody took seriously Sam Levene's disclaimers about his vocal range. In fact he was so bad that he was blocked from leading the title song in act 1 and was even *ordered* not to sing along.[1] They do it differently at La Scala.

Broadway represented showmanship at its most flamboyant because the goal was to sell tickets. This demotic spectacle was driven by commercialism, not a bid for artistic immortality. Or as lyricist E. Y. (Yip) Harburg wrote: "Mozart died a pauper, / Heine lived in dread, / Foster died in Bellevue, / Homer begged for bread. / Genius pays off handsomely— / After you are dead."[2] A cantor's son from Dessau, Kurt Weill ached for success on Broadway, in contrast to Schoenberg, who "said he is writing for a time fifty years after his death." But Weill insisted in an interview with the *New York Sun* that he was writing "for today" and claimed not to "give a damn about writing for posterity."[3] The nation from which Henry James had expatriated himself was animated by a democratic commitment to popularity, unalloyed by vestiges of royal or aristocratic patronage; and Broadway typified the yearning to transform citizens into customers. At its best this art form nevertheless proved to be enchanting and indelible.

It also has a history, a cohesive and continuous legacy that is inextricably associated with the gifted Jews who invented and extended it. Deborah Dash Moore, a leading social historian of American Jewry, has described its condition during the interwar years as *At Home in America* (1981). But what she really meant (as her subtitle indicated) was at home in New York City—where so many Jews were packed that the seating capacity of Temple Emanu-El exceeded that of Saint Patrick's Cathedral.[4] Virtually all of those composers and lyricists who heard America singing their Broadway songs were Jewish New Yorkers, without whom it is hard to imagine the history of musical comedy in the United States. There certainly would have been theater, and music, and comedy. But the combination was virtually a franchise enjoyed by one minority group, whose achievements in this genre are considered here.

Broadway was attractive to Jews because "New York opera" was *not* opera. Their "portable talents," Jonathan Miller suspected, could operate in fields "which are not respectable, therefore not heavily guarded at the entrance by white Anglo-Saxon Protestant custodians." Such openness also accounted for Hollywood, whose studios were built by the same sorts of men who operated theater chains and produced plays and musicals. In the first half of the century, nobody could avoid reckoning with the Shuberts. Levi, Shmuel, and Jacob Szemanski were three sons of a Lithuanian peddler (who also had three daughters). As Lee, Sam, and J. J. Shubert, they exerted supreme booking power through their ownership of theaters in virtually every major city (including six in New York and three in Chicago).[5] No one else operating at the business end of show business would be so dominant—except perhaps for David Merrick, who produced more musicals than anyone in the history of Broadway. So brazenly did he operate that by the 1960s his name (originally Margulois) was no less familiar than the names of the performers and directors who did his bidding. Showmanship should not be confused with sainthood, since Merrick's personality was so excruciatingly unpleasant that one star vowed: "I'll never work for him again until he offers me another great show." By the mid-1970s, such gifts were no longer possible; and the Broadway he knew had ceased to flourish.[6]

But two features of the history of Broadway justify its claim (rather than Hollywood's) to be considered the epicenter of American Jewish culture. One is the audience. In 1968 the scenarist and novelist William Goldman offered "a conservative guess" that Jews filled half the seats in Broadway theaters, which benefitted financially from the theater parties that stemmed from a tradition in the Yiddish theater. David Levinsky, who recalls his own "considerable passion for the Jewish theater," participates in this sort of fund-raising activity, in which blocks of seats (and sometimes even entire houses) are sold by charitable or fraternal groups.[7] The cinema was obviously far more of a mass art than Broadway ever aspired to be, and therefore also seduced a far wider range of talent than "New York opera" needed. More so than behind the screen, the talent behind the stage was for more than half a century virtually the monopoly of one ethnic group. That is the second feature that locates Broadway at the center of Jewish culture.

When Hammerstein was working with Jerome Kern on adapting Donn Byrne's biography of Marco Polo, the lyricist inquired: "Here is a story laid in China about an Italian and told by an Irishman. What kind of music are you going to write?" Kern's answer was jocular: "It'll be good Jewish music."[8] That was the lullaby of Broadway, so that even those who did not satisfy *halachic* (Jewish legal) standards adapted to the prevailing ethnic sensibility.

That was true of Hammerstein himself, whose mother, a Presbyterian, had him baptized as an even more upscale Episcopalian. He grew into adulthood practicing no religion (except perhaps the faith that his next show had to be a hit). But his social and professional circle was so inescapably Jewish that, if any American could be said to have shaped Jewish culture without actually being Jewish, Hammerstein would be a prime candidate. His first marriage was to Myra Finn, a cousin of his second famous collaborator, Richard Rodgers. (Hammerstein was divorced in 1928, and married Dorothy Blanchard—a Protestant—the following year.) His career was not unique in demonstrating that talents were not only portable but intertwined. Ira Gershwin was a high school classmate of Harburg's, and would soon introduce him to Burton Lane (*Finian's Rainbow*), who wrote his first show at the age of fifteen and served as a rehearsal pianist for Ira's younger brother George. Rodgers had served as Kern's rehearsal pianist, and was sixteen when he met the twenty-three-year-old Lorenz (Larry) Hart, who played songs for him that afternoon on his Victrola.

Hart attended the same Catskills summer camp for the German Jewish upper crust as had Rodgers; another camper was Herbert Sondheim, whose son Stephen would meet Oscar Hammerstein II during the launching of *Oklahoma!* (1943). Sondheim would repay his debts to Hammerstein for private tutorials and gentle friendship by dedicating the score for *A Funny Thing Happened on the Way to the Forum* (1962) to him, and would also amplify and enhance (and upend) the whole musical tradition that Hammerstein and Kern invented with *Show Boat* (1927). Indeed, Hammerstein's death forced Rodgers to work with other lyricists—including Sondheim—so that the intricate mesh of collaborations and personal relationships (and rivalries) stretches from the Americanization of the operetta all the way down to the lingering postmodern death of the Broadway musical.[9]

Because lines of apprenticeship and collegiality were so taut, outsiders had to learn what the natives seemed to be doing naturally. The most celebrated mimic was a Yale-educated Episcopalian from Indiana. Cole Porter's postwar hits included *Kiss Me, Kate* (1948), with a libretto by Samuel and Bella Spewack, and *Can-Can* (1953), with its book based on an original story by Abe Burrows. Success had come slowly for Porter, an expatriate socialite in the 1920s who yearned to outgrow the private parties his songs enlivened. So what catapulted his career? One account has him asking George Gershwin for the secret of Broadway success and being advised to "write Jewish," instructions that Porter interpreted as "write Middle Eastern." The result was "Just One of Those Things" and "I've Got You Under My Skin," which were noteworthy for their tropical rhythms, their extended melody lines, their moody and exotic aura of romance. The conversation with Gershwin may be apocryphal. But Rodgers distinctly recalled Porter telling him that Broadway required a talent for writing "Jewish tunes," a claim that Rodgers decoded as the use of strongly chromatic, sensuous "minor-key melodies" that would sound "unmistakably eastern Mediterranean." Rodgers saw what Porter meant with "Night and Day," "Begin the Beguine," and "My Heart Belongs to Daddy." What Porter thereafter called his "magic formula" was evidenced in "I Love Paris" (1953), which, according to music historian Alec Wilder, should have been entitled "I Love Russia"—though most Jews who had emigrated from

Russia *hated* it. (Indeed, a pogrom was the earliest childhood memory of Porter's good friend Irving Berlin.)[10]

But perhaps the meaning of Porter's "magic formula" is not liturgical but sociological: the injection of the somewhat exotic and therefore alluring. He was irrevocably a *goy*. Porter was gay too, and thus an outsider in another way, adept at "passing," and no doubt achingly familiar with lamentations. In any event, he overcame his pedigree enough to impress an MGM executive producer named Sam Katz, who gushed, when Porter played "Good-bye, Little Dream, Good-bye" (1936) for him: "You know, Cole, that song is beautiful, it's—why, it's Jewish."[11] For those whose tuning forks were pitched toward the marketplace, no praise was higher.

Perhaps some "Jewish tunes" could be traced, in a vague way, to the synagogue. Berlin's father had been a part-time cantor, a job at which composer Harold Arlen's father had worked full-time. One musicologist detected "an uncanny resemblance" between the folk tune "Havenu Shalom Aleichem" and the spiritual "It Take a Long Pull to Get There" from *Porgy and Bess*, a "folk opera" that Gershwin undertook after getting stymied in adapting S. Ansky's *The Dybbuk*. But the direct musical influences upon the plangent notes projected from the orchestra pit were unlikely to be liturgical; the Jewish accent on Broadway was not obvious. Nor is there much direct evidence of the impact of the Yiddish theater, though Harburg regularly attended it with his father after synagogue on Saturdays. The lyricist claimed to recall "everything" about the plays that had "set me afire. . . . The Yiddish theater was my first break into the entertainment world." He considered Jews to be "born dramatists, and I think born humorists too."[12] Such essentialism now looks rather quaint; nonetheless, although Harburg's explicit indebtedness to the Yiddish theater was rather exceptional, others did not completely obliterate evidence of their own ethnicity.

Because their shows were often set in New York, its lingo could sometimes be injected. Contrast the cinematic *West Side Story* (1961), in which the leader of the Jets informs "Dear kindly social worker, / They tell me: get a job, / Like be a soda jerker, / Which means like be a slob." But expected to work at a soda fountain as a way to "earn a buck," Riff sneers in a less sanitized version, "which means like be a *shmuck*." (The sociolinguistics may not be entirely plausible for a 1950s hood.) Or take *Guys and Dolls*. Its songs were by Frank Loesser, its book by Abe Burrows, and its initial staging by George S. Kaufman; its pugs and thugs included the aforementioned Nathan Detroit, who declares his love to Adelaide in a daisy chain of internal rhymes: "All right already, I'm just a no-goodnik. / All right already, it's true. So *nu*? / So sue me, sue me, what can you do me? / I love you." Such idiomatic lyrics propelled the momentum of musical comedy far from the ambience of *The Merry Widow*, and even further from the libretti of Lorenzo Da Ponte, *né* Emilio Conigliano (1749–1838), the Venetian Jew who was baptized in adolescence and joined Mozart for *Le Nozze di Figaro, Don Giovanni*, and *Così fan tutte*. Da Ponte's migration to New York, where he taught Italian at Columbia, proved that the city was not quite ready for opera. Identifying himself as "the inspiration of Salieri . . . and of Mozart" (in that order), Da Ponte nevertheless feared a humiliating oblivion in which "my remains might become food for the dogs." [13]

What American audiences eventually craved was something else, and from the Viennese operetta came something new and wondrous. Here too there were bloodlines: the father of composer Frederick Loewe, for instance, had sung the role of Count Danilo in the original Berlin production of *The Merry Widow*. In the 1920s her frippery was exchanged for less fancy ready-to-wear clothing. Her lyrics were injected with slang; and so sassy and brassy did the rhythms of her songs become that, for the next half-century or so, musicals were integral to American culture. [14]

So much so that, before the 1920 season, the owner of the Boston Red Sox did something preposterous. So eager was he to finance a Broadway hit that he sold Babe Ruth to the New York Yankees. Even though Giacomo Puccini and later Kurt Weill wanted to make operas out of *Liliom* (1909), Ferenc Molnár supposedly rebuffed them. But the Hungarian playwright was willing to sell the rights to Rodgers and Hammerstein so that the dream team could make *Carousel* (1945), which in 1958 became one of the two musicals chosen to represent American culture at the World's Fair in Brussels. (The other was *Wonderful Town* [1953].) Broadway supplied studios like MGM and Paramount with talent and themes for cinematic musicals, and generated material for jazz artists as well. (Miles Davis, for example, did his own version of *Porgy and Bess* in 1958; and John Coltrane recorded "My Favorite Things.") So sensational was the soundtrack to United Artists' *West Side Story* that for fifty-four weeks it was the nation's most popular album. [15]

And Broadway had its own bridge to politics. Shortly after 22 November 1963, a grieving Jacqueline Kennedy told ace reporter Theodore White of how she and her husband had played the soundtrack of *Camelot* in the evenings. Thus was the spirit of John F. Kennedy's thousand days in the White House to be invoked—especially the lyric about a "brief shining moment." At Choate, Alan Jay Lerner had coedited the yearbook with the future President. In 1942 a Spanish immigrant named his newborn son for Jerome Kern, which is how the guitarist for The Grateful Dead came to be Jerry Garcia; yet, when the President of the United States played saxophone at the Reduta jazz club in Prague in 1994, in the presence of Václav Havel, the musical heritage that Bill Clinton shared with his Czech accompanists was not rock and roll but "Summertime" and Rodgers and Hart's "My Funny Valentine." Probably no other American music was at once more familiar and more fabulous.[16]

Though it was popular, its matrix was not populist. Hart had attended Columbia, as had Rodgers and Hammerstein. The latter had also earned a law degree from Columbia; the former was the son of a highly successful physician who took his family to operas as well as musicals. Kern studied at the University of Heidelberg. Lerner's father had founded Lerner Shops and sent his son to Harvard; he graduated the same year as Leonard Bernstein. Sondheim studied music at Princeton after graduating from Williams College. Of course not everyone who succeeded on Broadway had been nurtured among the *allrightniks.* Berlin quit school at the age of fourteen; George Gershwin dropped out when he was two years older. Conscious of gaps in his musical knowledge, he wanted to study with Maurice Ravel, whose music he admired. But Ravel refused, possibly for fear of restricting an untutored genius like Gershwin, whose brother Ira got as far as a few semesters in college. Though Loesser's father was a piano teacher and his mother a translator and a lecturer on modern literature, the future song-writer somehow managed to get expelled from both high school and college.[17]

That several of Broadway's leading figures were nevertheless born into comfort may have reinforced a national and generic addiction (to quote from *South Pacific*) to "happy talk." The most glowing dream of the Great White Way was to see your name in lights (even if that name had been an-glicized), and thus success was both celebrated and certified. Unlike Euro-pean operas, musicals encouraged the pursuit of happiness and promised it. Broadway reinforced the national faith in fortune, in the buoyant conse-quences of pluck and luck; such an ethos could not flourish in the gloom. Thus the operative word is electricity. The dazzling technology of neon lighting reached Broadway in 1924—the very year that the Gershwins did. Though the brothers usually wrote for Gentile performers, like Ethel Mer-man ("I Got Rhythm"), or the cast of *Porgy and Bess*, or Fred Astaire, who became a star thanks to *Lady, Be Good!* (1924), the dancer aptly remarked of George Gershwin: "He wrote for feet." The raucous exuberance of such musicals, with their jaunty lyrics and their rousing scores, reflected an in-souciant spirit. Though L. Frank Baum's 1900 fable, *The Wonderful Wiz-ard of Oz*, makes no mention of a rainbow, Harburg installed it in the MGM film. The lyricist explained to the son of the great clown Bert Lahr: "Man's imagination is what takes him out of his misery."[18]

Broadway itself was a symbol of hope, promising liberation from the shadows of the past, from the pall of Old World *Kulturpessimismus.* In 1931 Walter Benjamin characterized himself as "one who keeps afloat on a shipwreck by climbing to the top of a mast that is already crumbling";[19] and the *Trauerspiel*, about which he wrote at the University of Frankfurt, has no American equivalent. No "sorrow play" could be expected to click on Broadway, which aspired not to the tragic but instead to make magic. When Curly first strutted onto a stage to exult in "what a beautiful mornin'" he was enjoying in Oklahoma, and to predict that "ever'thin's goin' my way," the disjunction could not have been greater. The Nazi death camps were operating around the clock; the battle of Stalingrad had ended only a month earlier; and the following month, at Mila 18, the suicidal revolt of the Warsaw ghetto fighters would erupt. Only in America could Curly's optimism have seemed remotely credible.

Musicals committed all sorts of crimes against complexity, and it is easy to condescend to the reductiveness of the genre. But the cockeyed, optimistic innocence of the national sensibility could not be blamed on Broadway alone, and tacked-on happy endings were also endemic to the West Coast branch of show business. In exculpation it might be noted that schmaltz is not the only serving the customer on Broadway might expect. Jud Fry is a genuine villain in *Oklahoma!* Lieutenant Joseph Cable dies in *South Pacific* (1949), as does the Siamese monarch Mongkut in *The King and I* (1951). Julie Jordan loves a man who brings her much unhappiness in *Carousel* and ends up a widow. Bess is a drug addict and prostitute. In *Show Boat* Julie LaVerne is an alcoholic who almost certainly dies prematurely (offstage), and no one who hears Joe sing about being tired of livin' and scared of dyin' can believe that existential despair is a European monopoly. Critics of cloying sentimentality might consider the first stanza of Ira Gershwin's last hit, "The Man That Got Away" (1954), with Arlen's music: "The night is bitter, / The stars have lost their glitter; / The winds grow colder, / And suddenly you're older." The loss is heartbreaking, "and all because of the man that got away."[20]

Perhaps the best example of a serious musical is Marc Blitzstein's *The Cradle Will Rock* (1937), a response to Bertolt Brecht's question to him: "Why don't you write a piece about all kinds of prostitution—the press, the church, the courts, the arts, the whole system?"[21] Even a title like *The Most Happy Fella* (1956) was at least not *self*-deceptive: Loesser once remarked, "I usually look for the worst in people. And I'm never surprised."[22] With Hammerstein, Rodgers worked in a more upbeat fashion than with Hart, whose lyrics the composer praised because they were not addressed to "boy and girl idiots of fourteen." Indeed, Hart knew that romance was dangerous and sex unsafe, as he noted in *Babes in Arms* (1937): "The furtive sigh, / The blackened eye, / The words 'I'll love you till the day I die,' / The self-deception that believes the lie— / I wish I were in love again." Rodgers and Hart both considered *Pal Joey* their best musical, though its themes, as summarized by musicologist Geoffrey Block, included "adultery, sexual exploitation, blackmail, the somewhat unwholesome moral character of the principals, and a realistic and unflattering depiction of the seamy side of Chicago night life." The *New York Times* reviewer Brooks Atkinson acknowledged that *Pal Joey* was "expertly done," but then plaintively asked: "Can you draw sweet water from a foul well?"[23] (The un-American answer was yes.)

Because these lyricists and composers were not writing for an audience largely composed of adolescents, what was often prized was rue taking flight as irony and sophistication. Whatever the genealogical validity, Hart's claim of lateral descent from Heine had the exactitude of identifying bloodlines of cleverness. Perhaps Hart's absorption in the quiddity of words stemmed from his capacity to see English from the outside: he grew up in a German-speaking home and remained fluent in the language. Broadway lyricists reached heights of literacy that were unequaled before or after, making it permissible to speculate about a Jewish absorption in the mystique of language itself. Who still puts so polished a spin on it, as Hart did in "Bewitched, Bothered and Bewildered": "I'm wild again, beguiled again, a simpering, whimpering child again"? Who writes that way anymore? The answer is: only Sondheim, who claims to have learned that Broadway is about mind as well as heart while studying mathematics at Williams, where a music professor "took all the romance away from art. Instead of the muse coming at midnight and humming 'Some Enchanted Evening' into your ear, music was *constructed*."[24]

To impose the bliss of order upon inchoate feelings required painstaking creative effort: to do so with flair entailed genius. The pointless agony of false starts and the desolation of utter failure afflicted even the most gifted. Rodgers and Hammerstein had tried for more than a year to solve the problems of adapting *Pygmalion*, and gave up. Refusing to heed Hammerstein's warning ("It can't be done"), Lerner thereupon did it. Indeed *My Fair Lady* proved so triumphant that T. S. Eliot told Rex Harrison: "Bernard Shaw is greatly improved by music."[25] (Such was the estimate of one Nobel laureate in literature for the high-carat dramatic gem of another.) Lerner himself was a profile in *tsuris*, however: a chain-smoker who became dependent on amphetamines, and a compulsive nail-biter who had to wear gloves to save his cuticles. The anguish of doing a Broadway show had not been envisioned in Dante's *Inferno*, but that work is nevertheless suggestive. *My Fair Lady* fitted Lerner's book and lyrics so seamlessly to Loewe's score that it was hard to imagine such sublime results as *constructed*. Shortly before dying, in and out of consciousness, Lerner revealed to a night-shift nurse that he had written that musical. No wonder she thought her patient was delirious.[26]

The success of these shows required the exercise of craft, which at its best was pitched to literate adults. As the lyricist for *West Side Story*, Sondheim disclaimed knowledge of either poverty or Puerto Ricans; he was hired for artifice rather than authenticity. "It's alarming how charming I feel," he later admitted, would more likely be uttered by a guest in a Noel Coward drawing room than an adolescent shopgirl from San Juan. Nor would she use internal rhyme schemes in claiming to feel "so pretty / A committee should be organized to honor me."[27] Broadway is not expected to convey verisimilitude: not even lovers nor actors offstage normally burst into song to express their feelings. The aim instead is to provide aesthetic delight *and* to make some order amid chaos, despite the insistence of Alexander Herzen, Tsarist Russia's great public intellectual, that history provides "no libretto."[28]

Broadway offered lyricists a chance to become poets, to show off their virtuosity and wit and even on occasion to suggest a wider world of literacy and learning. The formal constraints were excruciating. "A lyricist generally has 75 to 100 words in which to tell the main story," musicologist Jesse Green has explained. "At least 8 of those words (and as many as 20) rhyme; they must sit properly on the music and move when it does; provide big, open vowel sounds for high notes and avoid unsingable consonant clusters; and of course make sense for the character and the dramatic situation of the libretto." Even to achieve simplicity, arduous work was entailed—at least for Hammerstein, who sometimes needed a few weeks to lock his lyrics in place. The work habits of Rodgers, by contrast, gave the impression of inspiration rather than perspiration; he could match melodies to Hammerstein's words while the dinner guests were still sipping their coffee. Preparing for *South Pacific*, Hammerstein gave his collaborator the typed lyric for "Bali Ha'i." Rodgers briefly examined the page before turning it over, went into another room, and five minutes later returned with the finished melody, surely among the most haunting of the thousand songs that he composed in his lifetime.[29]

Writing lyrics was usually more demanding than writing music, as Ira Gershwin once noted in listing the necessary credentials: "Given a fondness for music, a feeling for rhyme, a sense of whimsy and humor, an eye for the balanced sentence, an ear for the current phrase, and the ability to imagine oneself a performer trying to put over the number in progress—given all this, I still would say it takes four or five years collaborating with knowledgeable composers to become a well-rounded lyricist." Still, he mastered his craft quickly enough to write with his brother almost a thousand songs in only thirteen years, and then to collaborate with Kern, Arlen, Weill, and Copland in attempting to embellish the vernacular, "to capture the ways people spoke to each other—their slang, their clichés, their catch-phrases," and thus to reach ordinary people in an inclusively democratic art.[30]

These musicals defied snobbery, in the name of gusto, brio, force, robustness. To stir the crowd those responsible for such shows needed dynamism, and even something demonic and lunatic, a wild excess of energy, an anarchic superhuman force. The best performers had to project a vividness of personality that could hurtle across the footlights and up into the balcony. The stars of these shows did not so much sing as roar, and were not satisfied with wooing the audience; they wanted to knock it out. Loesser was famous for instructing his singers: "Loud is good." Out of such base metals, the golden age of an art form was forged; and a certain vulgarity proved to be the correct aesthetic choice. The Pulitzer Prize committees formed to honor American drama didn't quite know what to do with Broadway. In 1931, when *Of Thee I Sing* became the first musical comedy awarded the prize, the winners were librettists George S. Kaufman and Morrie Ryskind and lyricist Ira Gershwin (whose brother's score was ignored).[31] Not until 1949, with *South Pacific*, did a Broadway musical team win the Pulitzer Prize for drama.

Let George Gershwin's career serve to illustrate the opportunities that could be conferred, as well as the insecurities that were associated with a form so uneasily related to "high culture." Broadway gave Gershwin a forum (yet imposed a limitation), offered a chance to reach the masses (yet induced a need to outgrow the constraints of such shows). After spending three weeks writing *Rhapsody in Blue* (1924), the twenty-six-year-old was unable to orchestrate it. He started with hit tunes, graduated to showstoppers and then moved on to concert pieces like the *Concerto in F for Piano* (1925), which is on the short list of the most often performed piano concertos of the twentieth century. Then he tried his hand at opera, but without violating the democratic impulses that Broadway had fostered. "I hoped to have developed something in American music that would appeal to the many rather than to the cultured few," Gershwin said in 1935, when *Porgy and Bess* was done. The following year the composer also reassured a Hollywood studio executive with a telegram: "Rumors about highbrow music ridiculous. Stop. Am out to write hits."[32]

Which Gershwin continued to produce, as he imagined his ideal listeners to be "young girls sitting on fire escapes on hot summer nights in New York and dreaming of love." Such yearnings were music to his ears. Opera had not spoiled him; songs as simple and as enchanting as "Love Walked In" and "Love is Here to Stay" were done shortly before a brain tumor killed him at the age of thirty-eight. "Where might he have gone from there?" critic Martin Gottfried wondered. Gershwin contemplated "a musical about the making of a musical. Almost forty years later, such a musical was produced." *A Chorus Line* (1975) was Marvin Hamlisch's first score for Broadway, for which he won the Pulitzer Prize denied to his predecessor. "It's not that George Gershwin was ahead of his time. It's that all the possibilities of the musical theater seemed to flow from him."[33]

His funeral at Temple Emanu-El was an occasion of national sadness; heading the pallbearers was Mayor Fiorello LaGuardia, followed by former Mayor Jimmy Walker, a lineup that suggested what the composer meant to New York. His tunes would constitute the score for the 1979 film that Woody Allen simply entitled *Manhattan*. Less widely known is that the three musicals Gershwin composed before *Porgy and Bess* were all political satires: *Strike Up the Band* (1930), *Of Thee I Sing*, and *Let 'Em Eat Cake* (1933). The last one warned of an American fascism that might result from the demagoguery that takes advantage of misery, poverty, and unemployment (Kaufman and Ryskind wrote the book). Though the composer himself considered the disturbing dissonance and aggressiveness of *Let 'Em Eat Cake* the best score he had done till then, the show was a flop—even if it prefigured the seriousness of *Lady in the Dark* (1941), which Weill and Ira Gershwin wrote, and later of *West Side Story*.[34]

In the liberalism of his politics, George Gershwin was hardly unique. The emphatically Jewish audiences in New York tilted Broadway leftward in a way inconceivable to movie producers, who could not afford to offend white Southern distributors and moviegoers in particular. The Great White Way was more hospitable to blacks than were the studios, which firmly drew the color line even while blacks were doing mainstream revues and other shows in the 1920s. Broadway could usually ignore the volatile racism of the solid South, where even so tame a lyric as "You've Got To Be Carefully Taught" could draw fire from Georgia state legislators. In 1953, when the road company of *South Pacific* reached Atlanta, a law was introduced—but not passed—to ban entertainment that advocated "an underlying philosophy inspired by Moscow," as Hammerstein was providing "justification of interracial marriage."[35]

Broadway could occasionally glance at serious issues, such as civil rights, in which Jews had more than a passing interest. In Berlin's "Supper Time" (1933), Ethel Waters conveyed how a Southern black woman might tell her children that their father will not be coming home. He has been lynched. *As Thousands Cheer* constituted an early recognition of the racial tragedy, and came four years after the black lyricist Andy Razaf's "Black and Blue" (1929). But Razaf wrote it only under duress, after the major investor in *Hot Chocolates* demanded that Razaf insert a "colored girl's" lament in the revue, slammed the lyricist against a wall, shoved a gun in his face, and told Razaf that either he would write such a song or he would never write anything else. The finicky investor was Arthur Flegenheimer, a brutal, hot-tempered Jewish gangster better known as Dutch Schultz. *Finian's Rainbow* (1947) boasted of a score by Burton Lane and lyrics by Harburg (who also coauthored the book), and of a chorus of which half consisted of blacks who played sharecroppers. A Southern Senator is "punished" when a bolt of lightning paints him black. His name is Billboard Rawkins, in an era when Theodore Bilbo and John Rankin were the blatant racists whom Mississippi Democrats were sending to Washington. Contrast *Finian's Rainbow* with *Song of the South*, a film Disney had released a year earlier. It became so embarrassing in its nostalgia for the Old South that a video-cassette is yet to be released in the United States.[36]

Harburg was Broadway's most engagé lyricist. It was apt that his career began in 1929, the year of the crash, as he was responsible for the anthem of the Great Depression. "Brother, Can You Spare a Dime?" The song was written, he recalled, while he "couldn't stop crying. . . . I write with what they call in Yiddish *gederim*—it means the very vitals of your being."[37] Though best known for his collaboration with Arlen on *The Wizard of Oz* (1939), Harburg was also credited with an early antiwar musical entitled *Hooray for What?* (1937); with the first musical devoted to feminism, *Bloomer Girl* (1944); and with a song for the incipient civil rights movement called "The Eagle and Me" (1944). During the Vietnam War, he advised Berlin to rename "God Bless America" "God Help America." Though "too foivent" for Bert Lahr's tastes, Harburg was not all that much of an "insoijent." He was simply capable of seeing under the rainbow too.[38]

Because the subjugation of blacks appeared so intractable a dilemma, concern for the victims of bigotry could be more safely deflected to Asians. They were the subject of three of Rodgers and Hammerstein's musicals: *South Pacific, The King and I,* and *Flower Drum Song* (1958). When *The King and I* opened three years before *Brown v. Board of Education*, any hint of miscegenation was startling, critic Margo Jefferson observed about half a century later. She observed even then how "the audience happily held its breath when the handsome brown-skinned Asian king placed his hand on the waist of the fair-skinned, hoop-skirted English lady." They in particular are engaged in several "racially, sexually and culturally charged encounters that are perfectly pitched between full-hearted expression and tasteful, titillating repression." Jefferson added that "the ballad of forbidden longing that Lun Tha sings to Tuptim has gone on to become an emblem for every kind of love that dared not speak its name once upon a time." The Gay Men's Chorus has crooned "We Kiss in a Shadow" in an especially evocative way, making even more poignant the suppression of the Twentieth Century–Fox version of *The King and I* (1956). It cannot be legally shown in Thailand, where the movie is deemed antiroyalist, even though the grandson of Rama V, Bhumibol Adulyadej (Rama IX), who ascended the throne in 1946, played the saxophone and contributed a song ("Blue Night") to a 1950 Broadway revue.[39]

The injection of race as an impediment to romance suggests an enduring theme on stage: the yearning to overcome social barriers for the sake of love. This topic is of special concern to Jews; and here the pivotal text is nonmusical: *The Melting Pot* (1908). Luckily for Arthur Miller, Israel Zangwill decided to reject the initial title he gave to his four-act melodrama: *The Crucible*. His protagonist, David Quixano, is an immigrant violinist and composer who finds happiness with Vera Revendal, even though his family had been murdered in the Kishinev pogrom for which her father, a tsarist cavalry officer, was personally responsible. Quixano loves visiting Ellis Island and hopes to write his American Symphony. He represents the faith that Jews would give something wondrous and fresh to their new society, that their creative talents will express their gratitude to a blessed land. His most appreciative audience consists of "the orphans of the Settlement House," which gives his American Symphony its premiere. At the end of the play, "the softened sound of [their] voices and instruments [are heard] joining in 'My Country 'Tis of Thee.' The curtain falls slowly."

The thrust of Zangwill's electrifying work was toward the extinction of ancient loyalties, which is why the president of the United States yelled out from his box at the Washington premiere: "That's a great play, Mr. Zangwill!" Indeed *The Melting-Pot* was dedicated in its later published form to Theodore Roosevelt (an ardent foe of hyphenated Americans) and is animated by the faith that exogamy might erase the antagonisms that had long cursed the Jewish people. Intermarriage was proof that the egalitarian ideal could become actualized, that the particularist bonds of the past could be slipped. Mr. Zangwill's great play was, among other things, an important opening salvo in the battle to transform intermarriage from a stigma into an ideal, from a disgrace into a cause. No wonder that Rabbi Judah L. Magnes of New York's Temple Emanu-El denounced *The Melting-Pot* for "preaching suicide to us." For if "all men will give up the particular traditions of their own history and be formed into a new people of freedom," Magnes inferred, then "Americanization means just what Mr. Zangwill has the courage to say it means: dejudaization."

The assimilationist message of *The Melting-Pot* can be overstated, however. The Irish domestic Kathleen is after all sufficiently impressed by the *Yiddishkeit* of Quixano's observant aunt to be keeping kosher herself by act 4, which suggests that Judaism may survive the flames of the crucible. Such a faith may be fireproof. Nor are the injustices that have permeated Jewish history to be forgotten. The father of Quixano's beloved Vera, Baron Revendal, becomes so guilt-stricken over the Kishinev pogrom he orchestrated that this presumably stone-cold Jew-hater gives his pistol to

David and asks to be killed, which the young musician cannot do. In a 1914 afterword, Zangwill seemed to draw back from its logic by making a racialist case for the durability of Jewry: "the toughest of all the white elements that have been poured into the American crucible, the race having, by its unique experience of several thousand years of exposure to alien majorities, developed a salamandrine power of survival."[40]

This is a message that theatergoers might well have missed, as *The Melting-Pot* so strongly predicts that the bigotry that elsewhere marked the Diaspora would dissipate in the irenic atmosphere of the New World.

The dream of romance across such chasms was reactivated in Leonard Spigelgass's *Majority of One* (1959), for which Gertrude Berg won a Tony, playing a Brooklynite who falls for a Japanese widower. To be sure, a conflict that lovers long to surmount is a dramatic device at least as old as the Shakespearean play that inspired *West Side Story*. But the hope that ancient rivalries and prejudices might be spurned for the sake of love has intrigued Jewish dramatists and librettists, who gave it a kick that consciousness of their own status might well have heightened.[41] Nothing else raised more clearly the possibility of the Jews' absorption into the larger society, or testified more convincingly to the belief that the confinement imposed on their ancestors might be superseded.

No such sensitivity to ethnic or racial conflict can be discerned in the work of Cole Porter. But the ineluctability of this theme can be found in the love between Lieutenant Cable and Liat in *South Pacific*, in *Flower Drum Song* and in Rodgers's *No Strings* (1962). The sources of this artistic concern were not the dictates of Judaism but the condition of membership in a minority group. After his bar mitzvah, Rodgers ceased subscribing to Reform Judaism, and defined himself as Jewish for "socioethnic reasons rather than because of any deep religious conviction."[42] The same was true for Berlin, whose Annie Oakley upholds the exogamous ideal in imagining that "I'm an Indian Too": "With my chief in his tepee, / we'll raise an Indian family . . . with two papooses on my back." And speaking of Indians, the Disney musical *Pocahontas* (1995) has its eponymous heroine and a white colonialist fall in love, even as she rebukes Virginians for their Eurocentrism. The lyrics are by Stephen Schwartz: "You think the only people who are people / Are the people who look and think like you. / But if you walk in the footsteps of a stranger, / You'll learn things you never knew you never knew."

The richness of the Broadway tradition and the subtlety of its Jewish ambience can be illustrated by four landmark musicals.

1927 was a year that tested the laws of improbability. Lindy landed in Paris. The Bambino broke sixty. Jolson talked and sang. Films had no monopoly on excitement—at least not in New York, where the weekly attendance for Yiddish plays that year soared in the range of 120,000. Second Avenue audiences had never been larger, and would never be so great again. On Broadway, when 264 shows opened in seventy theaters, the 1927–28 season set a record; and among the musicals were fifteen smash hits out of thirty-eight productions. Such figures are a bit inflated thanks to the prodigious Gershwins, who had three musicals running simultaneously.[43] Among the biggest risks was *Show Boat*, which Florenz Ziegfeld Jr., had feared "hasn't got a chance except with the critics, and I'm not producing for critics and empty houses." Frivolous was good.[44]

Such worries proved unjustified when the *Cotton Blossom* first docked on 27 December; and *Show Boat*'s unsuspecting ticketholders were bombarded, after the overture, with three astonishing ballads in quick succession: "Make Believe," "Ol' Man River," and "Can't Help Lovin' Dat Man." And that was only act 1. "You Are Love" begged to be compared to a Puccini aria; and even the bluesy "Can't Help Lovin' Dat Man," sung by the mulatto Julie LaVerne, did not exhaust the sequence of knockouts ("Why Do I Love You?" and "Bill"). No previous musical had ever been gilded with six show-stopping songs. But that night was different from every other night. The songs made sense in the context of the show, enhancing plot and characterization in a seamless fashion. *Show Boat* raised doubts about the practice of interpolation, by which what is deleted one year might be injected in a very different show a couple of years later.[45]

Such integration of songs within a story meant that they had to advance the plot, reveal character, and somehow be enchanting on their own terms. The cohesiveness of *Show Boat* could be contrasted with a hit musical of only two years earlier. While working on *The Cocoanuts*, Irving Berlin was so indifferent to the dialogue that he walked out when lines were spoken. His music so annoyed George S. Kaufman that the playwright walked out during the singing. On stage the Marx Brothers inserted so many ad-libs in *both* the lyrics and libretto that Kaufman muttered during a run-through: "You know, I think I just heard one of my own lines."[46] *Show Boat* helped shatter the habits of mishmash, and Cap'n Andy Hawks therefore kept the promise he made after the overture: "You've never seen a show like this before." Its settings and scenes appeared to flow as naturally as the Mississippi itself, from the music. Those 574 performances marked a pivotal moment. Two eras split the history of the musical theater: before and after *Show Boat*.[47]

But what exactly was it? "An operetta," answered Leonard Bernstein in 1956, because the America portrayed on stage "is far from the experience of the very Broadway public for whom it was created." In picking a theme from the Deep South, the creators of *Show Boat* risked presenting material that might "seem foreign to the New York public," which is why he classified the show as an operetta. But the categorization is wrong. No music was more American or immediate than what had seemed to waft up from the South, which inspired Tin Pan Alley songwriters throughout the 1920s to devote themselves to the charms of the region. Much of act 2, after all, takes place in Chicago, the capital of the "urban jazz" that Bernstein argued was "the essence of American popular music," and that he would soon deploy in *West Side Story*. In refusing to stitch a made-in-the-U.S.A. label onto *Show Boat* because urban jazz is not integral to its score, he was reductively imposing an "essence" that his country's music is too variegated to display. *Show Boat* encapsulated the history of entertainment, from the cabaret to the stage to the radio, and embedded black music in the story, from spirituals and ragtime to jazz and the Charleston.[48]

Beginning in 1887 and stopping four decades later, *Show Boat* exuded an aura of *la longue durée* and implied as its theme the epic grandeur of the nation itself. A river runs through it, indeed, the world's longest. The Mississippi on which the *Cotton Blossom* floats had notoriously flooded in the year that *Show Boat* opened, destroying the homes of more than half a million destitute people. The story acknowledged the scale of the dreams of those who live on the river, and also pointed out the persistence of the sins. Love is idealized but those who are afflicted—like abandoned women—are luckless. (In Edna Ferber's novel, Gaylord Ravenal drowns; on Broadway his life is spared.) When Harold Prince revived the musical in 1994, one precocious ten-year-old in the audience was dazzled, announcing to me that this musical was "Broadway with brains": it confronted without froth the problem of loving the "wrong" person. Even in 1927 *Show Boat* was capacious enough to boast of interracial casting. In both senses this was an "integrated" musical—though, as the critic John Lahr observed, "the lives of the white folks have taken wild turns of fortune, but the black stories remain fundamentally static."[49]

As the first musical to be entrenched in the Broadway repertory, *Show Boat* broke loose from the category of operetta, only to become the first Broadway show to enter the *operatic* repertory when the New York City Opera staged it in 1954. Such shifting definitions were only fitting. The composer and lyricist of *Show Boat* had themselves been suspended between high culture and popular culture, between Europe and America—an ambivalence that historian Ronald Sanders claims "characterizes American-Jewish culture in particular." Kern came from a solidly bourgeois German-Jewish milieu. His mother had wanted to help him launch a career as a concert pianist, but only while studying in Heidelberg did he realize that classical music was uncongenial. Back in New York City he brought Ferber's 1926 novel to the attention of Hammerstein, who had been named for his grandfather, a producer of grand opera who owned and operated the Manhattan Opera House. (The father of Oscar Hammerstein II was a theatrical manager.) Having collaborated on operettas like *Rose Marie* (1925) and *The Desert Song* (1926), the lyricist and librettist was eager to tackle material that hinted at the depths of tragedy. But Ferber still needed to be convinced that her novel was stageworthy. So Kern showed up at her apartment, sat down at her piano and played a number he had just composed. It was called "Ol' Man River," and its immediate effect she recorded in her autobiography: "My hair stood on end, the tears came to my eyes, I breathed like a heroine in a melodrama." Such music "would outlast Jerome Kern's day and mine."[50]

Show Boat was nevertheless a product of the Tribal Twenties, and made its case for racial enlightenment in that context. In London in 1928 and on Broadway in 1932, Paul Robeson created a sensation as Joe by singing "Ol' Man River," which helped advance the singer's career as an ardent champion of civil rights. A liberal, Hammerstein referred to "Ol' Man River" as "a song of resignation with a protest implied." Philip Furia, a careful student of Broadway poetics, has drawn attention to Hammerstein's "manipulation of verbs (a part of speech seldom used for rhyming) to reflect the thematic tension in the song between the singer's physical power and social powerlessness, a tension contrasted, in turn, to the river's power in repose." Furia has shown the contrast between two simple verbs: "the blacks 'work' while the 'white folks play,'" with the labor described next in participles ("Pullin' dose boats . . . gittin' no rest") and then in imperatives ("Don' look up an' don' look down, / you don' dast make de white boss frown; / Bend your knees an' bow your head, / an' pull dat rope until you dead"). Even if there is human vanity in struggling against the natural force of the river, the systematic exploitation of blacks is apparent.[51]

In the original Broadway production, the first word that audiences heard was a word that appears in *Uncle Tom's Cabin*, frequently in *The Adventures of Huckleberry Finn*, and in later works like William Styron's *The Confessions of Nat Turner*. In part because white farmworkers use the term in *Of Mice and Men*, John Steinbeck's novel became one of the most censored books in public schools in the 1990s. The word constituted the title of black comedian Dick Gregory's 1964 autobiography, and a decade later was used in the title of black comedian Richard Pryor's album (*That Nigger's Crazy*). Hauling bales of cotton on a Natchez dock after Reconstruction, a chorus of black stevedores sing: "Niggers all work on the Mississippi / Niggers all work while de white folks play." The first verse of Joe's "Ol' Man River" opens the same way.

The vagaries of racial politics then affected vocabulary and made *Show Boat* a part of the history of civil rights. The London production in 1928 had "coloured people" working on the river; and when Ziegfeld brought

Robeson to Broadway in 1932, "colored folks" were working in "Ol' Man River." Though other euphemisms were later substituted, from "darkies" (Hammerstein's 1936 screenplay) to the historically untrue "Here we all work on the Mississippi," the lyricist repeated Robeson's version for MGM's *Till the Clouds Roll By* (1946), a biopic of Kern, who had died a year earlier: "colored folks" were expected to "work while de white folks play." Two decades later, a revival at Lincoln Center played it safe by removing the chorus of black stevedores, whose absence gave audiences the impression that *nobody* worked on the mighty river. Another revival had "brothers all work[ing] on the Mississippi."[52]

The continuing power of *Show Boat* to sting and to provoke (and thus to distance itself from the frivolity of operetta) was demonstrated when producer Garth H. Drabinsky revived the show in Toronto in 1993. An organization called Coalition to Stop *Show Boat* said that "the entire play, its plot and characterizations demean black life and culture." One protest leader, a school trustee named Stephanie Payne, publicly denounced *Show Boat* as an instance of "hate literature" directed at blacks, and claimed that Jews bore responsibility for most of the works that degraded blacks (Ziegfeld was, incidentally, a Catholic). Arnold A. Auguste, the publisher of Toronto's black newspaper *Share*, also cited the ethnic origins of those who had created and who were reviving *Show Boat*. Of all people, Jews should "know what it is like to be reviled, denigrated and to suffer abuse," he lamented. "I feel my people's pain just as surely as you feel yours." Angela Lee, the general manager of Canadian Artists' Network: Black Artists in Action, added: "The portrayal of blacks as shuffling, mumbling, dancing, singing caricatures enhances the picture of a people who are not only happy in their condition but obviously better off with somebody looking after them." According to her, "slavery, Reconstruction and the post-Reconstruction period in the Americas was [*sic*] not about singing, dancing and joyful celebration."[53] Never mind that the musical (like Ferber's novel) takes place *after* the period of slavery and Reconstruction, and that to depict bigotry is not to endorse it. *Show Boat* was racially sensitive in the 1920s, and its artistry is so affecting as to suggest that it is timeless. Perhaps that is why the picketers' entreaty to "Stop This Racist Play" failed to abort the rebirth of a classic.

Kern nevertheless failed to see *Show Boat* as a binding precedent that should govern how musicals are constructed, and spurned four years later Hammerstein's proposal to adapt Lynn Riggs's play, *Green Grow the Lilacs* (1931). When Rodgers envisioned its musical possibilities as well, Hart declined to collaborate with him and considered the corniness of the theme and setting uncongenial. The lyricist's own worsening alcoholism and depression forced Rodgers to turn to Hammerstein as a collaborator, even as the riding accident that crippled Porter and the early death of George Gershwin all marked the decline of urban sophistication as the touchstone of the Broadway musical. An orientation to regional and rural themes coincided with the popularity of Thomas Hart Benton's paintings and murals, with the "Scarlett fever" that afflicted readers of Margaret Mitchell's novel and then David O. Selznick's adaptation of *Gone With the Wind*, with the celebration of Midwestern virtues in *The Grapes of Wrath*, and with the realization in MGM's *The Wizard of Oz* that there is no place like home in Kansas. Copland, whose father had been born in Lithuania and became president of a Brooklyn *shul*, was affected too, and composed the exuberant *Rodeo* (1942) and *Appalachian Spring* (1944).[54] When the forty-seven-year-old Hammerstein joined the forty-year-old Rodgers to adapt the Riggs play, they brought the integrated musical to its maturity and thus proved showman Mike Todd wrong. The Minneapolis rabbi's son had attended the New Haven tryout but saw no future in the *Gesamtkunstwerk*: "no girls, no gags, no chance."[55]

The revolution that *Oklahoma!* wrought offered no forewarning; on opening night, 31 March 1943, the St. James Theater even had empty seats. The dilemma to be addressed—whether the square-jawed Curly McLain or the squalid Jud Fry will escort the pert Laurey Williams to the box social —hardly seemed momentous amid a world at war. Nor did the musical open with a robust production number; the first notes of the slow "Oh, What a Beautiful Mornin'" are even heard offstage. But then the momentum built, from the dawn of the century in which *Oklahoma!* is set to what publisher Henry Luce proclaimed in 1941 as the American Century. For the next two decades or so, until the Vietnam disaster punctured the victory culture, just about ev'rythin' seemed to be goin' the way the United States wanted it to go. In proclaiming that "you're doin' fine, Oklahoma! / Oklahoma, O.K.!", Curly was implicitly approving the course of empire. Set in the Indian territory to which Huck Finn would flee, this musical throbbed with the ebullience that would endure as the national mood until a President was assassinated seventy miles south of the Oklahoma border.[56]

The postwar prestige that would attach to the American Way of Life was mirrored in the success of the show itself, which set a new Broadway record of 2,212 performances. In 1938 the first original cast album had been *The Cradle Will Rock*, but its sales were easily surpassed when *Oklahoma!* quickly sold 1.3 million copies. (The Decca executive who produced the cast album was Jack Kapp, who had made "Bei Mir Bist Du Schön" a crossover hit.) Then there were the ubiquitous touring companies, one of which reached beleaguered West Berlin by 1951. Classified as a "folk operetta" by the *Times'* critic, Lewis Nichols, this musical provoked little opposition. A badly outnumbered dissenter was James Agee, who condemned the "white disease" of *Oklahoma!* that "the great corrupted audience" had taken to its sentimental heart. While conceding that some of the tunes "have a pseudo-folksy charm," he did not have a compelling case; certain that the show "would be bad," Agee was candid enough to admit that he had not actually bothered to *attend* it.[57]

But let us now praise famous men: Rodgers and Hammerstein were tracing how a community makes the rules that allow it to become civilized, how farmers and cowboys might make themselves eligible for statehood. In their chipper way, Rodgers and Hammerstein were showing how a society regulates itself after the frontier has passed. The tension between egalitarianism and individualism that is unsolvable on the plane of democratic theory is concretized when Aunt Eller sings: "I don't say I'm no better than anybody else, / But I'll be damned if I ain't just as good!" Friction can be acknowledged, if kept within limits; order can be upheld, even though the waywardness of love must be accepted as well; hopefulness was propulsive, even though the shadows could not finally be dispelled. But if the origins of the state were a microcosm of the creation of the republic itself, *Oklahoma!* exposed the difficulties that musicals face in accommodating social themes. The price that community exacted was unmentioned. This jaunty Broadway riposte to the "Okies" of Steinbeck (and even of John Ford) did not acknowledge the conquests of the Sooners, their complicity in carnage. Grampa Joad "took up the land," the tenant farmers admit, "and he had to kill Indians and drive them away."[58] Only whites exist in *Oklahoma!* even though blacks also lived in Oklahoma—including the families of novelist Ralph W. Ellison (born seven years after statehood was achieved) and historian John Hope Franklin (born in 1915).

In terms of historical complication, *Oklahoma!* was a regression after *Show Boat*, as Rodgers and Hammerstein formed a bubble of faith in a beneficent nation that was bound someday to burst. Their sole original movie musical, *State Fair* (1945), could be interpreted as a rebuttal to the nativist lament of the eminent sociologist, Edward A. Ross: examining garment workers in Union Square at the turn of the century, he claimed only 38 of 368 exhibited "the type of face one would find at a county fair in the West or South." In *Oklahoma!* Rodgers and Hammerstein spoke for the inclusion of whites, without considering how widely a net of community needed to be cast. Nevertheless the narrowness of imagination that it is now easier to see should not obscure what Rodgers and Hammerstein managed to achieve: to consolidate the sense of sharing a transcontinental culture, to make nothing seem more appealing or more normal than blueberry pie (or more corny than Kansas in August). And despite (or because of) the souring of the national mood after the shocks of the Sixties, their legacy lingers:

about 2,700 productions of their shows are still mounted in the United States *annually*.[59]

In 1957 Hammerstein went to Washington, D.C., to attend the opening night of a new musical, and afterwards approached its composer (Bernstein), its lyricist (Sondheim), its librettist (Arthur Laurents), and its choreographer-director (Jerome Robbins). "Congratulations to all of you," Hammerstein announced. "This is an incredible milestone in the theater."[60] Although *The Music Man* would win the Tony that year for Best Musical, he was prophetic. *West Side Story* was a milestone—and was lucky to have reached Broadway at all. Here was a musical, Bernstein recalled, "where there are two bodies lying on the stage at the end of the first act and everybody eventually dies . . . a show that's so filled with hatefulness and ugliness."[61] Here was a tragedy that emphatically communicated its plot through dance, that showed teenagers energized by violence, that reminded audiences of the gritty unpleasantness of life outside the theater, that looked at "America" from the sardonic perspective of stigmatized outsiders. No wonder critics were initially puzzled; while Brooks Atkinson admired the craftsmanship, he was too flustered to comment on the lyrics or even mention who wrote them. *West Side Story* did not exactly fail at the box office. But only after the movie adaptation, which won eleven Oscars (including Best Picture), was the greatness of this show appreciated.[62]

No previous musical had ever been conceived, choreographed, and directed by one person. In pushing the ideal of integration beyond Rodgers and Hammerstein, Jerome Robbins required dance to advance dramatic action and expected the same performers to sing, dance, and act. He too was giddily suspended between the two realms of high culture and the popular arts. The first Broadway show he ever choreographed was *On the Town*, based on the ballet "Fancy Free" (1944), in collaboration with Bernstein. But in that era dancing was separated from singing and acting, as was the set piece that enhanced his fame: "The Small House of Uncle Thomas" for *The King and I*. Robbins would go on to direct *Gypsy* (1959), *Bells Are Ringing* (1956), and fittingly *Fiddler on the Roof* (1964), as he and Sholom Aleichem originally had the same surname: Rabinowitz. At the peak of his acclaim, however, after supervising *Funny Girl*, Robbins quit Broadway to rejoin the New York City Ballet. There he quickly conceived "Dances at a Gathering," among his most admired pieces. A year after *West Side Story* opened, he founded "Ballets: USA," and as a choreographer enjoyed a lengthy connection with the New York City Ballet, for which he created more than three dozen works (including "The Age of Anxiety," from Bernstein's Symphony no. 2, and *The Dybbuk*).[63]

The genesis of *West Side Story*, the first musical Robbins directed, occurred about 1948, when a friend was preparing to play Romeo. Having trouble getting into the role, the actor asked the choreographer for help. "I tried to imagine Shakespeare's story in terms of today," Robbins recalled, "and that clicked in." He thought of "Romeo's passions" as "so extreme, so intense, so adolescent. It's all new and fresh. The love you're feeling is the greatest in the world. Death is nothing. . . . I became fascinated by the subject." He telephoned Bernstein, whose diary early in 1949 noted:

> Jerry R. called today with a noble idea: a modern version of *Romeo and Juliet* set in slums at the coincidence of Easter-Passover celebrations. Feelings run high between Jews and Catholics. Former: Capulets, latter: Montagues. Juliet is Jewish. Friar Lawrence is the neighborhood druggist. Street brawls, double death—it all fits. But it's all much less important than the bigger idea of making a musical that tells a tragic story in musical comedy terms, never falling into the "operatic" trap.

Such a work would tap the tradition of urban jazz. Could such a work succeed? Bernstein wondered. "It hasn't yet in our country. I'm excited. If it can work, it's a first."[64]

From conception to opening night took another eight years. Two were spent locating a producer for so peculiar a musical, Robbins recalled. Even with his descriptions of his dances, even with Bernstein playing piano and eventually with Sondheim singing his lyrics, backers could not easily be found for what would become a full-scale dance musical. Questions hovered. Because the score was so operatic, where were the hit tunes? How could the arias be hummed? Why were there no stars? And did the ending have to be such a bummer? The ethnography seemed off-key too, and not only because Anton, a "Polack," happens to be a Russian name, not Polish. (Actor Larry Kert, who played the original Tony, was Jewish.) Gangs composed of Jews and Catholics somehow reminded the Flatbush-born Laurents too much of *Abie's Irish Rose* (to which the musical bore no resemblance). So the Sharks were switched from Jews to Puerto Ricans,[65] who are swarthy and speak with accents and are exotic strangers, in contrast to their lighter adversaries.

In fact the odd notion that victimized minorities were interchangeable was a commonplace in that era. When Laurents's 1945 play *Home of the Brave* was transposed to a film four years later, the target of bigotry is altered from a Jewish soldier in an otherwise all-Gentile unit to a black soldier in an integrated unit, as though bigots have interchangeable targets (and as though desegregation of the military had already occurred). When RKO adapted a 1945 novel, *The Brick Foxhole*, into an assault on anti-semitism entitled *Crossfire* (1947), the producer explained in a memo that

Richard Brooks's fictional killer "murders a fairy. He could have murdered a negro, a foreigner or a jew. It would have been the same thing."[66] But the "PRs" in *West Side Story* should not be taken for surrogate Jews, whose history reveals a tendency to leave neighborhoods when trouble comes. The Sharks are different; with no suburbs to escape to, they fight (back) and are more overtly resentful, suspicious, and devout as well.

The menacing turf warfare (alien to Jewish behavior) pervaded the rehearsals. According to Carol Lawrence, who played Maria, "we were never allowed to even communicate with the opposition. It was a battleground. The right side of the stage was earmarked for the Sharks and the left side for the Jets, and you didn't cross that line." A relentless perfectionist, Robbins "never called us anything but our character names when we were rehearsing. . . . He would purposely incite people to antagonistic behavior."

Yet what disoriented major reviewers, who used terms like "savage" and "horrifying" to describe the occurrences on stage, would later be dismissed as tame and even sentimental. Jonathan Miller later complained: "As always with New York–Jewish-Showbiz, and I speak as a Jew who can recognize it a mile off, there is a kind of sentimental, saccharine tosh that runs through everything." That feature of *West Side Story* he found "quite insufferable." Take "Somewhere," for instance. "You find yourself wanting to say: 'No, Lenny, there isn't such a place.'" Miller was unfair, since Bernstein neither wrote the lyrics nor bore primary responsibility for conceiving *West Side Story*, which is noteworthy for its fatalism, its tragic ending, the novelty of taking lethal ethnic antagonism as a subject.

Nor did Miller consider the need for dramatic counterpoint. To be sure, Shakespeare's Juliet dies; and Robbins's Maria lives, after Tony is shot, the victim of what would later be classified as a hate crime. She too was supposed to die at the end of the musical. But Rodgers suggested how to solve a problem like Maria, who "is dead already" when Chino murders Tony: "Her life is over. You don't need to kill her. It's sadder if she has to live on alone." Because the act I curtain already descends on two corpses, a repeat with the final curtain would have been too much.[67]

Does *West Side Story* wriggle out of "the operatic trap" that Bernstein feared had been prepared for it? Certainly heroic measures were taken. Carol Lawrence was nineteen when she was cast as Maria, and her untrained voice was exactly what was sought, she recalled. "They were *not* looking for an operatic sound." The rehearsal pianist for her and for Larry Kert noted that "Gershwin was a songwriter who grew into a serious composer. I am a serious composer trying to be a songwriter," Bernstein observed. "Gershwin's was by far the more normal way: starting with small forms and blossoming out from there. My way is more confused: I wrote a symphony before I ever wrote a popular song." Nonetheless, the two composers did share eventual operatic vindication. Two decades after *Porgy and Bess* had initially flopped, it was mounted at La Scala. In 1985, Deutsche Grammophon cast operatic singers in *West Side Story*, and sold more albums than any recording in the history of the company.[68]

A Hasidic belief that Kafka appreciated holds that God created humanity in order to tell stories.[69] Perhaps the divinity willed that narrative drives musicals forward too. But what if they were organized around "concepts" instead? The career of Stephen Joshua Sondheim has been an effort to answer that question, and his inventiveness has given the genre a postmodernist momentum that has ensured a singular status as the epigone of the Broadway creators of the past.

Able to pick out tunes on the piano by the age of four (as could Richard Rodgers), Sondheim was early enchanted by Broadway and particularly by Oscar Hammerstein II, who became so cherished a friend that the protégé recalled: "I have no doubt that if he'd been a geologist, I would have been a geologist." But because Hammerstein wrote libretti and lyrics, he was called on to provide a critique for a musical that the fifteen-year-old had written. "It's the worst thing I have ever read," Hammerstein recalled telling him, "but I didn't say it was untalented." With such authoritative encouragement, Sondheim grew into a composer and lyricist who, more than anyone, would dismantle the sunny-side-up sensibility that Rodgers and Hammerstein exemplified—often with the active collaboration of director-producer Harold Prince, whom Sondheim had met at the original production of *South Pacific*. Indeed, he was among the first to grasp the artistic difficulty of continuing to do musicals like those of Rodgers and Hammerstein. Though *Follies* (1971) pays wry homage to the tradition from which Sondheim sprang, he has presided over its last rites. No *kaddish* for his artistic antecedents could be more definitive than, say, *Sweeney Todd* (1979), which upends faith in a benign universe. (*Tod* is the German word for "death.") As though reversing the roles of Yul Brynner and Gertrude Lawrence, *Pacific Overtures* (1976) makes the Westerners into the barbarians rather than the rightful tutors of Asia; and *Into the Woods* (1987) poses the most explicit ideological challenge of all, by discrediting any expectation of happy endings.[70]

Sondheim was forty when *Company* premiered in 1970, and it constituted his first collaboration with Prince. Set in New York City, the musical had no chorus and no stars, although the actors and actresses had to dance and sing. Everything blended. Boris Aronson, the son of a Kiev rabbi, designed a chromium and glass structure, with skeleton elevators, so that the action tended to move vertically, giving audiences a sense of how human traffic moves in a city of skyscrapers. Based on one-act plays by George Furth, *Company* is devoted to the subject of marriage, which protagonist

Robert resists. Played by Larry Kert (Tony in *West Side Story*), he is a bachelor whose surprise thirty-fifth birthday party serves as the opening and closing scenes of *Company*. Fearful and resigned, "Bobby Bubbie" is torn between the need to overcome loneliness and the desire to protect his own autonomy. In an age of anxiety, Robert knows that the glow of romance is not credible, and presumably speaks for Sondheim: the pieties of the past have been invalidated. But even as the protagonist appreciates the dangers of surrender,[71] he knows that the chill of aloofness is terrifying too.

Here was a musical that was supremely adult in its exposition of the vulnerability that emotional commitment risks, in its calculation of the loss of independence that is the price of intimacy. The ending is open (or ambiguous), and the mood is hardly upbeat. *Company* skirted the abyss when Robert's final song was supposed to be "Happily Ever After." It was such "a scream of pain," the composer-lyricist recalled, that "Being Alive" was substituted, in which the protagonist concludes that "alone is alone, not alive." So astringent and caustic an exposition of contemporary alienation represented the maturation of Broadway—or perhaps its mordant culmination. By presenting the tricky fragility of relationships without the plot devices of earlier libretti but instead through musical interludes that constituted variations on a theme, *Company* became a landmark of roughly the same order as *Show Boat, Oklahoma!* and *West Side Story*, and won not only the New York Drama Critics' Award but six Tonys (including Best Musical, Best Music, and Best Lyrics).

Variety nevertheless demurred, warning its readers that *Company* was "for ladies' matinees, homos and misogynists"—constituencies that must have been numerous enough to keep the musical going for 690 performances.[72] In finding himself "sorry-grateful," Walter Kerr of the *Times* expressed an ambivalence that mirrored Bobby's sensibility. Sondheim himself said that disappointment in *Company* stemmed from the bleakness of a message that "relationships are *impossible.*" That was a misreading. *Company* was intended to say that "relationships are *difficult.*" Broadway was once accused of peddling sentimentality and schmaltz, but Sondheim was accused (falsely, he claimed) of the opposite: nihilism. He also discerned critical frustration when there was no "strong story line" to follow.[73] What "was shocking about the show was that it had no plot," he remarked. "I don't know of any other commercial musical, except for revues like the Irving Berlin Music Box musicals or the New Faces shows, that had no plot." The popular success of *A Chorus Line* and other musicals in revue form accustomed audiences to spending a couple of hours with a group of characters who do not weave in and out of a single story. That apparent formlessness is what *Company* pioneered.[74]

Though Sondheim would loom large in any comprehensive account of the Jewish influence in the popular arts, the Jewish component in the most personal of his works is extremely small. *Company* includes an interfaith marriage; and since Paul is Amy's "first Jew," the sociology circa 1970 is about right. They are wed in a church, with the frightened bride worrying that "perhaps / I'll collapse / In the apse." The heavy-drinking Joanne alludes to Jewish creativity across the Atlantic when she sneers (again in triple rhyme) at the ladies who lunch. They typically spend "another long, exhausting day, / Another thousand dollars. A matinee, / A Pinter play, / Perhaps a piece of Mahler's." It is fair also to conjecture about something implicitly Jewish in the remorseless psychologizing and brooding self-consciousness that hovers over Sondheim's work, though the uncertainties and equivocations are supremely modern and urban even without an intensely ethnic reinforcement.[75]

An unabashed proclivity for intellectualizing can also be advanced as a sign that a Jew is more likely than others to exhibit—for example, a musical that explores the genesis of pointillism. That work, *Sunday in the Park with George* (1984), earned Sondheim the Pulitzer Prize that eluded Gershwin. No one in the history of the musical has been more honored than Sondheim, who had won already by 1987 five Tonys (including a stretch of three years in a row) and six awards for best musical from the New York Drama Critics Circle. As both a lyricist and composer, he is rivaled only by Berlin and Porter.

But those predecessors also wrote smash hits; and in achieving the full integration of songs into shows, Sondheim left himself open to the accusation that his songs lacked a life of their own. The accusation is unfair. "His lyrics are, in their wit and dexterity, satisfyingly autonomous," critic Brad Leithauser claimed, and proof can be found by noting their inclusion in poetry anthologies (a freeze-dried fate, incidentally, that Hart strenuously sought to avoid). Though Sondheim is a theater composer, which means that his songs must serve the requirements of character and dramatic situation, his songs *can* stand on their own; eight of them did not seem to detract from the huge success of Streisand's *The Broadway Album* (1985). (When she asked him to change lyrics in the seemingly perfect "Send In the Clowns," that request—which he honored—sent lexicographers scrambling to update the definition of *chutzpah*.)[76]

His great predecessors operated when Shubert Alley was adjacent to Tin Pan Alley, which could extract popular hits from Broadway shows because there were few other options. But the exponential growth of the youth market, to which records, cassettes, compact disks, radio and television programs, and movies were increasingly attuned, made adult ambivalences neither popular nor profitable. Sondheim was too cerebral for the tastes of teenagers ignorant of Heine and Schopenhauer and Seurat. In *Merrily We*

Roll Along (1981), he poked fun at himself (or his detractors) when the producer tells a songwriting team that its "songs are too highbrow": "There's not a tune you can hum. / Why don't you throw them a crumb?"[77]

If Sondheim has refused to do so, if he has come across as uncompromising in his standards, the explanation lies in the diminishing interest in a once-"popular" form. Sondheim was the last private pupil of the serialist Milton Babbitt but did not share his austere ambitions. Despite the intricacy of Sondheim's work, he still aims to please, though the spin he puts on it would have baffled Irving Berlin: "I won't be happy until everyone likes my shows. If they ever do, I'll worry they're not liking them for the right reasons." In no other form, in no other genre is the creativity of one figure so pivotal, which Martin Gottfried summed up in lapidary fashion: "Stephen Sondheim sits at his piano with the door open beyond him—the door not only to his future but to the future of the Broadway musical. He seems incapable of the safe or conventional."[78] Thus Sondheim entwines his own vocation with the fate of the genre itself. He took its legacy so far beyond its own origins that comparisons of the Broadway musical to Viennese operetta no longer matter. It is not his fault that American musical culture has fragmented so utterly that Broadway no longer exercises the hegemony it once did.

Perhaps Broadway is less dead than diverted; perhaps it is only playing possum. The tradition has a way of rejuvenating itself, of encouraging younger Jews to enhance and perpetuate it. Consider the career of Alan Menken, who grew up listening with enchantment to his father, a New Rochelle dentist, playing on the piano the music of Kern, Gershwin, and Rodgers and Hammerstein. Menken's first collaborator was his mother, with whom he worked on a synagogue adaptation of the *Bintel Brief* section of the *Forverts*. His next collaborator was Howard Ashman, who died of AIDS in 1991; later lyricists included Stephen Schwartz and David Zippel. In composing the music for such Disney films as *The Little Mermaid* (1989), *Beauty and the Beast* (1991), *Aladdin* (1992), *The Lion King* (1994), and *Pocahontas*, Menken won eight Oscars and twelve Grammys. In reaching an audience of children (or at least of the young-in-heart), he has been operating in an optimistic tradition, in which happy endings are guaranteed, that harks back to Rodgers and Hammerstein. But their songs were not put across by animated characters, and the cassettes of their movies are not relegated to the children's bins in video stores. That "drives me crazy," Menken has complained. "These are musicals. They're written as musicals."[79]

Such is the wistfully uncertain status of the show music that Jews had invented in the early decades of the twentieth century. Broadway became resplendent not long after blacks gave birth to jazz; by the end of the century, the competition was over. The music that black Americans created has triumphed over the music that Jewish Americans cultivated; the United States has become a rhythm nation, pulsating to rock, rhythm-and-blues, or rap.[80] Indeed, if there is any rival in popularity, it is country and western music—another sign of the twilight of Jewish impact. Broadway nevertheless remains a heritage that is accessible, recoverable, and blissful. It can also be historicized and, in retrospect, fully appreciated as music that made America a little less disparate.

What endures of the legacy from *Show Boat* to Sondheim is good music. But is it, as Kern assured Hammerstein, good Jewish music? Any answer must be hesitant, any claims tentative. As a datum of the Diaspora, where the forces of acculturation and secularism have corroded the claims of piety and peoplehood, Broadway merits the same seriousness of study that has been devoted to other forms and genres bereft of traditional Judaic themes. If the fiction of Kafka can be designated Jewish, if psychoanalysis can be better appreciated by fathoming rather than ignoring its Jewish origins, if the civic profile of this minority can be praised or denounced for its proclivity for liberalism and its passions for social justice, if the sciences (or law or medicine) can be considered in the light of Jewish attraction to such fields, why not the musical theater? To neglect it would leave unrecognized and unstudied too many works that have reverberated like Caliban's New World isle, "full of noises, / Sounds and sweet airs, that give delight and hurt not" (*The Tempest*, III, ii). Kern's guarantee to Hammerstein not only promised such pleasure to their audience, but enlarged the boundaries of an American Jewish culture as well.

MUSIC

WHAT IS JEWISH MUSIC? AT THE FIRST INTERNATIONAL CONGRESS OF Jewish Music in Paris in 1957, musicologist Curt Sachs offered the following answer: "that music which is made by Jews, for Jews, as Jews."[1] This definition sounds simple and incontestable. But its ambit is dubious. Under the conditions of the Diaspora after the Enlightenment, anyone can join the audience, or at least overhear the music. The conditions of mass culture also mitigate against restricting the size of the audience. Why should only Jews be reached? When popularity is a key to financial security, when aristocratic or royal patronage has evaporated, music composed and performed only *for* Jews guarantees poverty. (Not that the prospect of destitution should affect the definition.)

Nor is it clear what it means to compose music *as* a Jew. In 1933 the rise of Nazism stirred Arnold Schoenberg to convert *back* to Judaism, from the Lutheranism into which he had been baptized in 1898. After a ceremony in Paris (where one of the two witnesses was Chagall), Schoenberg committed himself to writing specifically Jewish music: not only his unfinished opera *Moses and Aaron* (1932) but also, near the end of his life, choral compositions. He wrote explicitly *as* a Jew.[2] But such was his renown and his importance to modernity that he was not merely writing *for* Jews. The "no trespassing" signs could not be posted.

A definition that requires music to be *by* Jews risks distorting the role of performers, whose ethnic loyalties may be more emphatic and even of greater symbolic value than the programmatic efforts of composers. A case in point is the most popular classical pianist of the century. At his death in 1982 at the age of ninety-five, Arthur Rubinstein's two hundred records had sold ten million copies. He was a prodigy whose bar mitzvah ceremony had been perfunctory. Neither did he practice Judaism thereafter. But from his father he derived a strong Zionism, and upbringing in a working-class family in Łódz hardly spared him from witnessing the antisemitism of his neighbors. Because he had ascribed guilt for military aggression to Kaiser Wilhelm after the First World War, he refused ever to play in Germany after 1914. After the Second World War, Rubinstein pleaded with American concert agencies to block the rehabilitation of such conductors as Herbert von Karajan and Wilhelm Furtwängler, who had advanced professionally under the Third Reich. In 1975 he joined Bernstein, Isaac Stern, and others in protesting publicly against the UNESCO decision to cut off funds to Israel, where he instituted a quadrennial, international piano competition in Tel Aviv. Rubinstein was also generous in supporting Israeli cultural causes. The fervor of his Zionism gave him a certain posthumous authority in Jerusalem, whose mayor, Teddy Kollek, convinced the rabbinate to make an exception to the rule that prohibits cremation, so that the virtuoso's ashes could be buried in a municipal park, in a pine forest named after him. The pride he had taken in his own Jewish roots was neither erratic not superficial, even if not decisive to his professional accomplishments.[3] The firmness of those feelings leaves no doubt as to his Jewishness; the historian of *American* Jewish culture must also consider Rubinstein's nationality. The peerless interpreter of Chopin got an American passport in 1946, long after Rubinstein was famous, and long after uprooting from his native Poland. Thus the career of so cosmopolitan a figure also makes problematic the weight to be attached to citizenship in placing Jewish culture within political frontiers.

Sachs's 1957 definition looks even less applicable to Eastern and Central Europe after the Holocaust *and* after the cold war. Communism was systematic in stifling Jewish culture. In murdering some of its leading creators and custodians in the Soviet Union, Stalin came dangerously close to finishing off what the Third Reich had begun. After Germany itself was reunified in 1990, only about 50,000 Jews were living among a populace of roughly 80 million; among 12 million Czechs, there were 3,500 Jews; and among 38 million Poles remained perhaps as many as 15,000 Jews. But the music of this remnant flourished in Berlin, Kraków, Vienna, and other cities, where Yiddish songs and klezmer music attracted enthusiastic crowds. Few Jews were left to explain that *kle zemer* (instruments or vessels of music) is a Yiddish contraction of the Hebrew, and also refers to the performers of such music. A klezmer band in Austria calls itself, quite accurately, the *Gojim* (the Gentiles); and a rival group, in Bremen, is named the *Klez-goyim*. Some of the best collections of klezmer music may have been produced by German record companies, which provide thorough liner notes as well and add to the havoc wreaked on Sachs's definition.

Narrow conceptions are placed at further risk during Kraków's Festivals of Jewish Culture, which have been held periodically since 1988. Neither of the organizers—Janusz Makuch and Krzysztof Gierat—is Jewish, nor are the overwhelming majority of the attendees at this "Jewish Woodstock," which ends with a final concert in the main square, as young Poles and others dance in the early morning hours to klezmer bands. Among them has been a Polish band named *Kroke*, whose skill impressed Steven Spielberg enough to subsidize its tour of Israel. Mini-Jewish Woodstocks have been hosted by other Polish cities and towns. Sometimes the ghosts that are summoned need not be klezmer musicians. In 1992 the most successful Czech rock band was named *Shalom*, which that year sold well over a hundred thousand cassettes, records, and compact discs, even as the group was filling concert halls with fans who wore *kippot* and stars of David to demonstrate their loyalty to a band that sprinkled Jewish motifs in its lyrics.[4] At least in pockets of Eastern and Central Europe, something remarkable has happened: at least in fragments, *Jewish culture can exist without Jews.*

Such a prospect was unanticipated at the beginning of this century, and punctures Sachs's definition in particular. Jewish music played by Gentiles for Gentiles is the recent fate of klezmer. But even a century before Kraków hosted a Jewish Woodstock, the men performing such music for Jews were not always circumcised themselves. A historian of the genre has noted that its repertoire included and reinterpreted the music of Gentiles: "Klezmorim performed this broad repertoire for both Jews and non-Jews, and their ensembles sometimes included non-Jewish musicians."[5]

Such music was secular, and benefited from the belief that to play a musical instrument was a lesser transgression against the Commandment against "graven images" and "likenesses" than the visual arts. To *paint* David trying to soothe the soul of King Saul by playing an instrument was worse than to play that instrument. The postbiblical taboo on pictorial and plastic representation was, or could be invoked as, biblical; the prohibition against instrumental music was only postbiblical. Exceptions were granted. On the High Holidays worshipers could hear the blowing of the *shofar*, which has usually been a ram's horn, or "sort of like a Jewish saxophone," as Rabbi Joshua Plaut explained when President and Mrs. Clinton attended Rosh Hashonah services at the Martha's Vineyard Hebrew Center in 1994. The other exception was granted to klezmorim who, though Ashkenazic, had their Sephardic and Oriental Jewish counterparts. In prayer, vocal music was an inextricable part of the liturgy; observant Jews did not so much speak to God as sing or chant to the deity. In traditional communities singing was ubiquitous, in daily prayer and outside the *minyan* as well.[6]

No wonder then that, when George Eliot invented a Jewish character whose lofty devotion to artistic truth exposes the superficial dilettantism of the British upper crust, the novelist did not pick a writer like herself, or a painter, but a professional musician. Professor Klesmer in *Daniel Deronda* may have been modeled on Anton Rubinstein, the pianist who fifteen years earlier had established the first music conservatory in Saint Petersburg, even as his brother Nicolas was directing the Moscow conservatory. Their parents had them converted to Russian Orthodoxy, as baptism was the price usually exacted upon the ambitious and the talented. To paint or to sculpt for a living was restrictive (and a sharp break with the Second Commandment); to write was financially—and sometimes politically—hazardous. But in European civil society, music offered options for conducting and performing as well as composing, and appealed to Jews early enough for Professor Klesmer to be sociologically plausible. Unlike Heine, for example, who spent his exile in Paris writing in the German of his oppressors, composers were admired for working within a universal language, accessible to all but the deaf. Such accessibility had special meaning for a minority forced to scale barriers of prejudice and bigotry, for a people who hoped that the power of individual talent would count more than the misfortunes of birth and the caprices of snobbery. A ticket to a concert hall might be a badge of acceptance that would admit the bearer to the grandeur of Western civilization itself.

The composers entered it one by one. They formed no school, and bequeathed nothing distinctive or separable from the legacy of others. Biblical subjects inspired Jacques Halévy to write his opera, *La Juive* (1834). Felix Mendelssohn wrote not only the oratorio *Elijah* (1846) but also set psalms to music. But Gentiles hardly ignored what they called the Old Testament (which is indeed what Mendelssohn himself deemed it, as his Lutheran piety seems to have been quite sincere). Not even the best-known version of *Kol Nidre*—for cello and orchestra, composed by Max Bruch in 1880—is, strictly speaking, Jewish, as he was not. Nor was there any unanimity in taste. Jews favored and resisted Romanticism. Not even so scurrilous an antisemite as Wagner stirred uniform opposition; one ardent Wagnerite was a rabbi's son, the obsequious Hermann Levi, whom Peter Gay called "the most accomplished conductor in the German Empire." Jews were hardly the only "good Europeans" either. The careers of Giacomo Meyerbeer, Jacques Offenbach, and Anton Rubinstein did transcend national borders. Yet Handel and Haydn also managed to speak the international language that music was purported to be.[7]

Should "From Jewish Folk Poetry" be embraced as Jewish music? Dimitri Shostakovich did not display a merely haphazard or half-hearted curiosity about Jewish music, which had influenced his Second Piano Trio (1944) and his First Violin Concerto (1948). In 1962 he would famously set Yevgeny Yevtushenko's poetic outcry against antisemitism, "Babi Yar," into the Thirteenth Symphony. But paradox haunts the story of "From Jewish Folk Poetry." In the 1940s, because Soviet composers were expected to find inspiration in folk sources, it was not far-fetched for Shostakovich to turn to the Jews. But it was rotten timing that "From Jewish Folk Poetry" was finished just as Stalin's campaign against one particular Soviet "nationality" and against "rootless cosmopolitanism" was reaching fever pitch. Thus Shostakovich's song cycle was put in the drawer, not to be performed in public until 1955, two years after the dictator's death. As a Gentile, Shostakovich doesn't count in Sachs's definition. But then Mahler doesn't make the cut either. He found his inspiration not in the "folk" sources that would influence Shostakovich but in German folk songs: for example, settings drawn from poems for *Des Knaben Wunderhorn*. Neither composer wrote directly for Jews. But it was Shostakovich who was more inspired by Jewish culture, and it was Mahler who disproved Wagner's claim that composers whose background included synagogue cantillations were disabled from championing the serious music rooted in "folk" (or *völkisch*) song and dance.[8]

The political burden imposed on Shostakovich's song cycle should also be a reminder that "Jewishness" is also affected by national variations and historical accident. Personal choices and lucky breaks enabled the music of those born in Russia, or those whose parents had been born there, to flourish in the United States, where the barriers were easier to surmount. Jews there were poised to seize such opportunities. In a novel by Henry Harland, a.k.a. Sidney Luska, *As It Was Written: A Jewish Musician's Story* (1885), set in New York City, a Gentile poet named Daniel Merivale predicts that "the Jewish element . . . will leaven the whole lump" of American culture by enhancing and enlivening the arts and by injecting "passions, enthusiasms" into the populace.[9] In 1907, after attending a show on the Lower East Side, Hamlin Garland wrote of the performers: "They have a facility in music which the Anglo-Saxon does not possess." The Midwestern storyteller was "certain" that such Jews "will change the character of New York musical life," and added that "these young violinists, these actors, these literary folk are to be the leaders in their lines."

Inspiration did not require direct experience with Garland's own heartland. Though Aaron Copland composed a piano trio entitled *Vitebsk* (1928) and a piece for piano and voice entitled "Zion's Walls" (1952), he is best known for finding in native American sources that which drew Mahler so ineluctably to German folk songs. It was all too transparent a strategy of acculturation for a Brooklyn-born composer to find in the Western landscape the creative sources for ballet scores like *Billy the Kid* (1938) and *Rodeo*. Though of Orthodox, not Shaker, antecedents, Copland won a Pulitzer Prize for *Appalachian Spring*. The title is drawn from the poet Hart Crane, who referred to water rather than a season; and when Copland finally got around to visiting West Virginia in 1972, he learned that he had been mispronouncing Appalachia. (The third syllable should have a flat *a*).[10]

His oeuvre does not fit Sachs's definition. But to exclude Copland would omit not only one of the most admired and performed of the century's composers, but would leave out virtually all other Jews whose background lent to their citizenship a special urgency in seeking inclusion and legitimation. Virtually nothing in Copland's music, Bernstein argued as early as 1939, could be traced to Jewish or Hebrew sources. Where Copland was born was decisive; his ancestry was only a "tempering force." Even the music of Ernst Bloch, whose aims were "programmatically and deliberately Jewish," was better appreciated as a "post-Romantic" composer. Only by reading the program booklet, Bernstein asserted, would the listener realize that "Hebraism" was supposed to be shaping the melodies, apart from a few exceptions like Bloch's *Schelomo* (1915; subtitled "Hebrew Rhapsody for Cello and Orchestra").

Such programmatic claims were not without consequences. In 1984, when the New York Philharmonic wanted to play *Schelomo* in Malaysia, Muslim influence caused the piece to be banned; and the tour was cancelled.[11] But how such music could reinforce "Zionism" is much harder to detect in America, where favorable conditions encouraged so much Jewish talent to be so variously expressed that too precise a categorization risks reductiveness.

Because Jews were present at the creation of the national marketing of popular music, they erased whatever fine lines might be drawn between what is Jewish and what is American. Techniques of mass production had made pianos less costly in the 1880s, generating an enormous demand for sheet music. To satisfy a swelling market, a group of first- and second-generation Jewish immigrants turned music publishing into a business. The most successful were Maurice Shapiro and Louis Bernstein, Leo Feist, Edward Marks, Joseph Stern, and the Witmark brothers. They did not consider the creative process as mystifyingly ethereal, or exalt composition as an act of inspiration that only the muse could summon. As one music publisher announced, songs were "Made to Order"; they were commodities that could be hawked. Such a conception came naturally to businessmen who had earlier sold neckties (Stern), or notions and buttons (Marks), or corsets (Feist). How different could be it to market a charming blend of melody and lyric?[12] These entrepreneurs were the counterparts to the Shubert brothers, who shamelessly defined the theater as "a machine that makes dollars."[13]

If America was itself an experiment that encouraged improvisation, if democracy was based on the faith that no one was better than anyone else, then Charles K. Harris was a supremely representative figure. As the Jew who wrote "After the Ball" (1892), he showed how easy it was to for the untutored to make it up as he went along. Harris could neither read nor write music. He would hum or whistle a melody that came to him, and then have a trained musician transcribe the melody for piano. "After the Ball" was the biggest hit of the 1890s, indeed, of the nineteenth century, and sold an astonishing five million copies of sheet music. Harris was less successful but no less poignant in the mood which he struck with "The Rabbi's Daughter" (1898). She sings: "I love a man with all my heart, without him I can't live." But when "the Rabbi looked down at his child, 'One question answer me, / Is he of Jewish faith or not?'—her head sank on his knee." Her father makes clear how heartbroken he would be if she marries her beloved, and Harris shows the consequences of a commitment to endogamy: "The Rabbi found his only child had died for love that night."

A more joyous song was one of Harris's first, entitled "Bake That Matza Pie." Such works drifted from city to country, where "folk" singers sometimes adapted the lyrics and melodies. "There were hillbillies out there singing his songs—all in different forms from how he had written them," according to musicologist Bill Malone. Songwriters like Harris became absorbed so seamlessly into the common culture, and found so much in the New World to celebrate, that among the ethnic hits of 1915 was the patriotic "Lebn Zol Columbus" (long live Columbus).[14]

Such was the clatter coming from open windows on West Twenty-eighth Street, between Broadway and Sixth Avenue, that journalist Monroe Rosenfeld was reminded of pots and pans being hit, and the name he bestowed in 1909 on the songwriting district stuck: Tin Pan Alley. In less than two decades, the music publishing firms became centralized and coordinated, even as their practice rooms and tryout rooms moved north to the neighborhood of Times Square. There were the biggest booking agencies, the radio networks, the recording studios and labels, and the theaters and emporia that showcased the performers. In 1914 the American Society of Composers, Authors, and Publishers (ASCAP) was founded; this conglomerate handled the nation's leading musicians, songwriters, and singers.[15] The hegemony of great Protestant and patriotic hymns such as "The Battle Hymn of the Republic" and "America the Beautiful" would henceforth face competition from Times Square, which effectively promoted countervailing values that could be summarized as hedonism.

"Ain't We Got Fun" (1921) set the mood that is indelibly associated with the Roaring Twenties. That decade, in the words of Gus Kahn, promised pleasure "Every morning / every evening" and even "in the meantime / in between time." When a mysterious bootlegger wants to celebrate his reunion with Mrs. Tom Buchanan, Jay Gatsby makes the apt request that a guest play "Ain't We Got Fun."[16] Rivaling it in popularity during that decade, however, was "Tea for Two" (1924), in which lyricist Irving Caesar proposed: "Picture you / upon my knee; / just tea for two / and two for tea." The song points to the intensification of desire, as the lyric ignores "tea for two," which is mentioned only once.[17] In a decade that seemed to champion sexual liberation, such songwriters described the thrills of "makin' whoopee" (the phrase itself was coined by Walter Winchell, *né* Weinschel). In Ziegfeld's *Whoopee* (1928), Kahn traced the descent of a marriage into adultery: "She feels neglected / and he's suspected / of makin' whoopee." The lyricist continued: "He says he's 'busy' / but she says 'Is he?' / He's makin' whoopee." So nonjudgmental a song no doubt reinforced the ire of Henry Ford, whose *Dearborn Independent* blasted the "rotten" "lasciviousness" of Hollywood, the "filthy tide" emanating from Broadway, and the "song factories" of Tin Pan Alley that had abrogated the "clean" ditties of the late nineteenth century. Belonging to the party of Eros, Jews were charged with conspiring to corrupt the morals of a God-fearing nation.[18]

Even as mass culture was reducing the isolation of rural and village America as effectively as the Model T, a Jewish subculture managed to operate simultaneously with Tin Pan Alley. At the turn of the century, one Lower East Side bookstore specialized in sheet music for popular songs, with Yiddish lyrics substituted. The translations, before effective copyright protection could be instituted, were often free. Sometimes the transpositions were easily accomplished (a telephone song like "Hello, Central, Give Me Heaven" was entitled "Hello Central, *gib mir gan eden*"). Sometimes there were topical references, such as a nod to the bombastic twenty-sixth President: "Teddy *mitn shtekn*" (stick). Nonetheless, however distant from the anglophone originals, such songs stimulated adjustment. For newcomers hearing a strange language, historian Fred Somkin wrote, "the rhythms and lyrics of American popular music supplied an inexhaustible and ever-changing cornucopia of ordinary and idiomatic expressions, of sayings, slogans, and faddish wisecracks from vernacular life." He concluded: "When these were rhymed in Yiddish and sung out to the galleries, the theater became an enlarged schoolhouse where, whatever the technical deficiencies of pronunciation, audiences participated in a ritual of acclimatization to the 'Yankee' world, and where they could become attuned to its fashions and feel themselves at home in America."[19]

No one broke out more spectacularly from the Lower East Side and into the wider world of popular song than Irving Berlin, who became famous even before taking out citizenship papers. The former Israel Baline exemplified the Americanization of Jewish music, although another greenhorn deserves an assist for having introduced "Alexander's Ragtime Band" (1911). As a New York–based "coon shouter," Jolson first belted out the song and helped it quickly sell two million copies of sheet music in the United States and in Britain. Within six years the protagonist of Cahan's rags-to-riches novel would confess to a desire to change places with the

"Russian Jew who holds the foremost place among American songwriters and whose soulful compositions are sung in almost every English-speaking house in the world."[20]

Nor was Cahan's cloak manufacturer alone in his insight. As Jerome Kern wrote in a 1924 letter to Alexander Woollcott: "Irving Berlin has *no* place in American music, HE IS AMERICAN MUSIC."[21] *The New Grove Dictionary* later called Berlin perhaps the century's "most versatile and successful American popular songwriter" (even though the scarcely two columns he was allotted were less than the space granted, for example, to one Jan Levoslav Bella). Alec Wilder's authoritative history of popular music called Berlin "the best all-around, over-all song writer America has ever had." Virgil Thomson failed to find "five American 'art composers' who can be compared, as song writers, for either technical skill or artistic responsibility, with Irving Berlin." Stravinsky was willing to designate him a "genius."[22]

Although Berlin's reputation has been damaged by corniness and jingoism, his work cannot be narrowly confined. The roughly fifteen hundred songs he published displayed an amazing variety: "ethnic novelty" songs and "coon songs," torch songs and parodies, revue hits and patriotic stanzas, and the tenderest of ballads (like "All Alone" and "Remember"). His music was ubiquitous. In Brooklyn, when an immigrant family that renamed itself Gershwin purchased the status symbol of a piano, the beneficiary was intended to be older son Ira, an excellent pupil. But his kid brother, to the surprise of everyone in the family, sat down at the instrument, and the first song he played was an Irving Berlin hit, "You've Got Your Mother's Big Blue Eyes." (Berlin was born a decade before George Gershwin, but outlived him by more than half a century.) When Marion Davies sang "The Girl on the Magazine Cover" in a revue called *Stop! Look! Listen!* (1915), William Randolph Hearst fell for her unreservedly, until death did them part. When the Marx Brothers inflated the meaning of ain't-we-got-fun, in *The Cocoanuts*, Berlin wrote the songs; and in 1926, when an otherwise forgotten show called *Betsy* introduced "Blue Skies," the singer was called back for twenty-four encores. The next year, when Jolson broke the sound barrier, the first song he did was "Blue Skies." Radio crooners in need of hits were especially indebted to Berlin, who gave "Say It Isn't So" to Rudy Vallee and "How Deep Is the Ocean" to Bing Crosby. For *Ziegfeld's Follies* in 1919, Berlin provided the theme song, "A Pretty Girl is Like a Melody," and nearly three decades later proved that he could also write an integrated musical, avoiding interpolated songs in *Annie Get Your Gun.*[23] No wonder that a classic list song like Porter's "You're the Top" (1934) flaunts such superlatives as the Louvre, Botticelli, Keats, and "a Berlin ballad."

Though this modest tunesmith liked to tell interviewers that the simplicity of his lyrics stemmed from his limited education, he also contrived works so elegant (like "Puttin' on the Ritz" in 1929) that a satirist named Lew Brown marveled three years later at "Park Avenue librettos [penned] by children of the ghettos." Surely some of Astaire's reputation for stylish elegance is due to songs like "Cheek to Cheek," "Let's Face the Music and Dance," and "Top Hat, White Tie, and Tails." Such sophistication "frankly astounded" Alec Wilder. Even though the disarming "Cheek to Cheek" was begun and finished in a day, its sixty-four bars make it the longest of Berlin's hit tunes, double the normal length. "It seems to keep turning in on itself and then escaping, and turning in on itself once again," biographer Laurence Bergreen noted.[24]

Indeed, no song was more redolent of the glamour of romance. In *The Purple Rose of Cairo* (1985), the Depression-era waitress Cecilia (Mia Farrow) is pursued by an actor who abandons her, leaving her to find solace by watching *Top Hat*. Cecilia's problems remain unsolved, but she can at least manage a smile by watching Astaire and Rogers dance to "Cheek to Cheek." That song is played in two later films set in World War II in Europe: Claude Lelouch's *Les Misérables* (1995) and Anthony Minghella's *The English Patient* (1996). "Cheek to Cheek" is restorative, a sign of the struggle for normality. Such versatility and power were not the results of a meek autodidact's fortuitous skill; Berlin was a relentless perfectionist, a scrupulous craftsman. During the swing era, clarinetist Benny Goodman once took such liberties with a Berlin song that the composer exclaimed: "That was the most incredible playing I've ever heard. Never do that again!"[25]

The fast tempo of urban and modern life had its analogue in Berlin's modus operandi. During a Manhattan cab ride, when rehearsals for *Annie Get Your Gun* were stalled, he wrote "Anything You Can Do." Needing a Christmas number for the movie *Holiday Inn* (1942), the cantor's son in one weekend came up with a song. A song? "Not only . . . the best song I ever wrote," he gushed to his transcriber on Monday morning, "it's the best song *anybody* ever wrote." If popularity is the criterion, Berlin did not exaggerate. Bing Crosby's version of "White Christmas" is the most famous. But it competes with more than three hundred recorded versions, including Streisand's and Elvis Presley's; in a sly act of jujitsu, Mandy Patinkin's Yiddish rendition appeared in 1998. More than forty million records of the song have been sold. "White Christmas" has even sold more *sheet* music than any other American song, and was—along with "Alexander's Ragtime Band"—among the scores that the Office of War Information circulated most successfully in the Soviet motherland (then an American ally). Probably no American song is more cherished.

No exception should be made for "The Star-Spangled Banner," which was not designated the National Anthem until 1931, just in time to beat out "God Bless America." When Berlin's song was introduced on Memorial Day in 1939, the spectators at Ebbets Field rose and removed their hats, as though hearing what Francis Scott Key should have written. Whatever difficulties the song might have posed for the Establishment Clause of the First Amendment, "God Bless America" is nonpartisan enough to have been sung, already in 1940, at *both* the Republican and Democratic conventions. It is also the bittersweet finale to Michael Cimino's *The Deer Hunter* (1978), an ironic index of the desolation of the national spirit during and after the Vietnam war. Berlin came to define American music so completely that, in Sidney Lumet's *A Stranger Among Us* (1992), the failure of a Hasid to recognize Astaire and Rogers dancing to "Changing Partners" on the television screen exposes the insularity of the ultra-Orthodox sect.

Of course longevity helps explain Berlin's influence. When he began composing, Teddy *mitn shtekn* was in the White House; in 1986, when Ronald Reagan occupied it, Berlin was still writing lyrics. In fact, Reagan had been *born* in the year "Alexander's Ragtime Band" became a hit. Berlin's last Broadway show was called *Mr. President* (1962), and was considered a failure, though it ran eight months. Mortality lasted long enough for him to enjoy The Beatles and to hear Willie Nelson sing "Blue Skies." By then the copyrights on Berlin's earliest songs were already expiring; "Alexander's Ragtime Band" had become public property while its composer was still alive.[26] He lived to 101.

Was such a national treasure of song outside the parameters of Jewish music? Though Berlin had attended *cheder* to prepare for his bar mitzvah, studying was an ordeal—unlike the joy of joining his father in a synagogue on the High Holy Days. "It was singing in *shul* that gave me my musical background," Berlin once speculated. "It was in my blood." It got thinner thanks to Americanization. But Jewishness did not utterly disappear. "Sadie Salome, Go Home" (1909) recounted the saga of a young Jewish woman who acts like a Gentile, and who even has a "*shaygetz*" (Gentile) boyfriend. But "Sadie Salome," which helped make Brice a star in the Ziegfeld *Follies*, was just another item in the immense Berlin inventory, and can barely be distinguished from the "coon songs" that were the prewar fashion. Another hit that Brice sang for Ziegfeld's annual *Follies* was the Yiddish-inflected "Good-bye, Becky Cohen" (1910). Berlin's "Yiddle on Your Fiddle, Play Some Ragtime" also helped fan the flames of that craze. Jewish themes subsequently interested him no further until after the Second World War. Then, for *Miss Liberty* (1949), he set Lazarus's "The New Colossus" to music in "Give Me Your Tired, Your Poor." A decade after the birth of Israel, he wrote an anthem by that name. But this attempt to provide a Zionist counterpart to "God Bless America" failed, perhaps inevitably. Berlin was too much an assimilationist for that. Outside of the aesthetic and commercial norms of Tin Pan Alley, patriotism was perhaps the most genuine emotion he felt. Grateful to America, he didn't see the point of remaining Jewish, as that condition provoked unwarranted persecution.[27]

As though "Irving Berlin" could be too much to bear, he would sometimes sign letters to the old bunch as "Izzy," which childhood friends from the Lower East Side continued to call him. So did biographer Alexander Woollcott, perhaps to help jog Berlin's most authentic memories. Izzy Baline was manifestly a product of the Lower East Side, with an accent that betrayed his Cherry Street origins. But Irving Berlin was a chameleon who could write in a variety of ethnic modes, "whatever suited his whim and whatever he decided the market demanded," as Laurence Bergreen, a later biographer, wrote. And beginning with ragtime, black music was especially enthralling. However, in order not to write as a Jew, Berlin insisted that he wrote as a Caucasian (which entitled him to write in any dialect and on any theme).[28] "Our popular songwriters . . . are not Negroes" but "of pure white blood," he reassured one interviewer;[29] and the disclaimer was both mean-spirited and false, a denial of the heterogeneity of American musical culture. To generalize that so many other top songwriters were of "Russian . . . ancestry" was misleading, a fudging (at least for public consumption) of ethnic particularity. Such "Russians" did not consciously write music as Jews, and Berlin married a Christian. But one effect of his music was to diminish the power of the majority faith.

Indeed, as a deutero–Philip Roth exults, "God gave Moses the Ten Commandments and then he gave to Irving Berlin 'Easter Parade' and 'White Christmas.' The two holidays that celebrate the divinity of Christ . . . and what does Irving Berlin brilliantly do?" The lapidary reply is that "he de-Christs them both! Easter he turns into a fashion show and Christmas into a holiday about snow."

Of course, "Izzy" did not accelerate desacralization all by himself. Rodgers and Hammerstein did their part to suggest that nothing is sacred with "You'll Never Walk Alone." This stirring glee-club staple manages to omit mention of any deity, despite the contrivance of Billy Bigelow's ascent to heaven. By expressing faith in faith itself, this song from *Carousel* should be classified as a secular hymn (if that is not an oxymoron). *The Sound of Music* (1959) does something similar: "Climb Ev'ry Mountain" is another paean to the beneficence of no particular God at all, even though sung by a mother superior in thoroughly Catholic Austria. It is unsurprising that the 1965 film version about an ex-nun won an Oscar for Best Picture. The effectiveness of de-Christing the story was unnoticed by either Protestants or Catholics: *both* the National Council of Churches and the National Catholic Office selected *The Sound of Music* as the year's Best Film. Mormons loved it too. In the first nineteen months of its release, more than half a million tickets were sold for *The Sound of Music* in Salt Lake City, despite a census count for the city of 190,000 souls.[30]

In so latitudinarian and unstable a society, with its kaleidoscopic permutations of ancestry and its geographical restlessness, to produce America's varied carols did not require rootedness or pedigree. To feel attached to the musical culture of the nation, it was sufficient to celebrate one region above all. The idea of the South inspired a pool of melody in which anyone —black or white, Jew or Gentile—could dip. In idolizing Stephen Foster, Berlin did not want to share his predecessor's impoverishment (the thirty-eight cents found in his pocket at his death) but to absorb a tradition in which Southern atmospherics pervaded popular taste, in which the aroma of honeysuckle and magnolias could be inhaled. The region was so easy to romanticize that Jolson begged audiences to "let me sing of Dixie's charms, of cotton fields and mammy's arms," in Berlin's 1930 Warner Brothers musical, *Mammy*. "Alexander's Ragtime Band" mentions that "Swanee River" could be played in ragtime, too, and other Jews cheerfully trod the postbellum road to reunion that reduced sectional friction by paving over the hopes of blacks to win equal rights.

Some songwriters were so eager to succeed—to write hits—that research would have been superfluous. In the first line of "Waiting for the Robert E. Lee" (1911), the Odessa-born L. Wolfe Gilbert depicted "the levee, in old Alabammy"—though that state is about 150 miles east of any such levees; nor had he ever been on a paddle-wheel steamer. Gershwin's most popular hit song was "Swanee" (1919). Its lyricist was Irving Caesar; and they visited the river only *after* "Swanee," thanks to Jolson's rendition, had taken the nation by storm. The muddy creek was so unimpressive that the lyricist recalled: "I was shocked."[31] Rustic bliss was never more lovingly evoked than in the campfire favorite, "Shine On, Harvest Moon" (1908), introduced by colyricist Nora Bayes (real name Dora Goldberg) in Ziegfeld's *Follies*; its composer, Harry Von Tilzer (*né* Gumm), was no husbandman either.

Immigrant tunesmiths converted themselves into facsimile Southerners with ease. The Hungarian-born Jean Schwartz, along with Sam Lewis and Joe Young (also Jews), hit the jackpot in 1918 with "Rock-A-Bye Your Baby with a Dixie Melody." The ubiquitous Jolson made it famous; then in 1956 Jerry Lewis put it back on the Top 40 for fifteen weeks, when his single sold 1.4 million copies. Though Kahn was born in Koblenz and grew up in Chicago, he provided the lyrics for "Carolina in the Morning." The South inspired so much music that Caesar wondered, "Is It True What They Say About Dixie?" sharing credit on that one with Sammy Lerner and Gerald Marks. The singer who made it a hit was—again—Jolson,[32] who was kidded in a Warner Brothers film, *The Singing Fool* (1928), for having "rhymed 'Mammy' with 'Alabammy' 1981 times. . . . [He] did more for Dixie than Robert E. Lee."[33]

Of course it could be argued that Tin Pan Alley was designed to catch the fluctuations of mass taste, not to provide accurate geography lessons. Shakespeare's reputation is secure, even though Lucentio believes Padua is in Lombardy rather than Venetia in *The Taming of the Shrew*, (I:1), and even though a coast is added to Bohemia (which lacks one) in *The Winter's Tale* (III:3). In making "Saskatchewan" an official anthem of the province, its government did not upbraid Irving Caesar for celebrating skiing and mountains in a part of Canada where the terrain is flat. Of course no one personified the untutored commercialism of Tin Pan Alley better than Berlin, who could neither conduct an orchestra nor play a musical instrument except for the piano—and even that only in the key of F sharp. He needed a special piano that would mechanically transpose keys by shifting a lever. As he could neither read music nor notate it, a trained musician had to sit next to him to write down what Berlin was playing by ear.[34]

And yet his "A Russian Lullaby" was the first song that Leonard Bernstein remembered hearing. In a very different way, Bernstein too enjoyed the sort of musical career of which no one else could have dreamed. Because he was a second-generation American, it is tempting to see some divergences from Berlin in such terms. Already acculturated, Bernstein was certainly less desperate to assimilate. Nor did he know poverty. His family belonged to Boston's Congregation Mishkan Tefila, where Lenny went to Hebrew School and became bar mitzvah. Hebrew and Aramaic texts are encrusted in his symphonic works, and a ballet score is entitled *The Dybbuk*. Immoderate in many ways, he felt no need to be demonstrative in his patriotism. He loved America without having to make a big deal of it— at least not so effusively as to invoke God's blessings. Contrast Berlin's straightforward, simplistic nationalism with the satiric piquancy and dissonance of "America" in *West Side Story*. Without the insecurity of a naturalized citizen, Bernstein championed enough causes to activate FBI scrutiny, which began in 1943 (the year of his sudden fame) and eventually resulted in a staggering 666-page dossier.[35] Above all he acutely sensed the symbolic resonance of his own Jewishness, which could be reconciled with citizenship without the friction that an earlier generation might have expected.

That awareness was evident when his family was in New York City for a performance of his song cycle in 1943. Unexpectedly he told his parents to cancel their plans to return to Boston. Because Bruno Walter was stricken with flu and Artur Rodzinski could not come down from Stockbridge quickly enough, Lenny would be at the podium that afternoon, though without an opportunity to rehearse the New York Philharmonic for its national broadcast on CBS radio. His parents were told to pick up their tickets at Carnegie Hall, and their immediate reaction was time-honored: "*Oy, gevalt!*" In the hall, when it was announced that Maestro Walter would be replaced by a conductor who happened to be American-born and American-trained, some patrons walked out. He had been picked only three months earlier as an assistant to Rodzinski, who felt so insecure about the hiring decision that special advice was needed. "I asked God whom I should take," the music director of the Philharmonic recalled, "and God said, 'Take Bernstein.'"[36]

The deity was wonderfully prescient. Kid brother Burton Bernstein later remembered little about the music he heard, "except that it sounded all right to me and that Lenny seemed to know what he was doing." When the concert was over, "the house roared like one giant animal in a zoo. It was certainly the loudest human sound I had ever heard—thrilling and eerie. . . . Again and again, Lenny came out to bow, looking skinnier each time." The debut was front-page news in the *Times* and the *Herald Tribune*. The *Daily News* had to resort to an analogy that its readers might appreciate: the sudden substitution for Walter was like "a shoestring catch in center field." This was how Toscanini's career was launched in Rio de Janiero in 1886, and Rodzinski's four decades later. But they were Europeans. What Bernstein had done was so singular that beauty-salon owners in New England insisted on placing orders directly with Samuel Bernstein rather than through his salesmen, to be able to claim to have spoken with the father of a famous conductor who had a special significance for Jews. As his mother Jenny wrote her twenty-five-year-old son before his second Philharmonic concert: "We will be thrilled to hear you on the radio. . . . I'm sure most of the Jews in the country will be listening to you, so do your best, dear."[37]

Four years later, in 1947, Bernstein paid his first visit to the Near East, and conducted the Palestine Symphony Orchestra, which had been formed a decade earlier. Zionism had formed an orchestra before a state, and what became the Israel Philharmonic Orchestra forged a special bond with Bernstein. He conducted it during the War of Independence in Beer-Sheba, for example, only a day after the Hagganah had taken the city from Egyptian forces. No concert hall existed, and so the orchestra played in the desert, on a battlefield that was still mined. "We performed for five thousand young soldiers," Bernstein recalled. "They had heard about the concert on the radio, and they came on camels and horses, in jeeps and trucks. We played Mozart and Gershwin for those troops, and I will never forget looking about us and seeing the ground filled with shoes which the Egyptians had taken off in order to run faster." They would play for the rest of 1948 under fire and during air raids. "But there was never an empty seat, and we never missed a concert."

But probably no concert was more drenched in emotion than on Mount Scopus, on 9 July 1967, in the wake of the victory in the Six-Day War that reunited Jerusalem. The program featured Mendelssohn and Mahler—one baptized as a Lutheran, the other baptized as a Roman Catholic, both emblematic of the anguish of Emancipation. When the ensemble played in West Berlin in 1978, not far from where the logistics of the Final Solution had been devised and implemented, Bernstein included his own *Kaddish* in the program. One member of the orchestra considered the concert "like a revenge for us, on Germany. They had tried to exterminate us; and here was a Jewish orchestra, with a Jewish conductor and composer, playing in this place, and playing compositions based on Jewish tradition." His *Mass* in memory of John F. Kennedy includes the line "*Baruch ha'ba b'shem Adonai*" (blessed is he who comes in the name of the Lord), in a language that was foreign to, say, Mendelssohn and Mahler. Whatever Bernstein's private beliefs were, he refused to conduct on Yom Kippur; in the aftermath of his determination to pursue a career under his own unchanged name or not at all, both Tel Aviv and Jerusalem named squares "Kikar Leonard Bernstein."[38]

So pronounced a Jewish identity he traced to his father, whose avocation was reading the Talmud; and *shul* provided Lenny with a glimpse of his own vocation. "We didn't have a piano until I was ten," the maestro reminisced, "so my first exposure to music was in the synagogue we attended regularly. The music director at the temple in Boston, Solomon Breslavsky, was an extraordinary musician, and I owe my first musical thrills to him. After I began going to Hebrew school at eight, I really understood the words being sung in the synagogue, so that words and music became inextricably bound up."

But Samuel Bernstein harbored doubts about Lenny's career—and indeed, why not? It did not seem imaginable until he actually did it. When he had finished conducting a Town Hall concert in 1943, the owner of the Samuel Bernstein Hair Company was heard to whisper: "That's all very good, but where's the money?" A year after the Philharmonic debut, Samuel Bernstein asked composer David Diamond: "Do you think he's ever going to make any money?" Not that his father had any objection to music, which would be fine as a hobby. "You can play the piano all you want," he advised his son. "It's a wonderful thing to come home at night and relax at the piano after a hard day. But if you're going to be a *mensh* and support a family, you can't be a klezmer."[39]

The blazing promise that his son exhibited did not elude others, and his versatility in crossing the boundaries of musical culture made the 1943–44 season special. Compositions included not only the ballet "Fancy Free," but also the score for *On the Town*; and *Jeremiah*, a symphony that premiered in 1944. Jews had conducted major American orchestras before Bernstein: George Szell, Bruno Walter, Otto Klemperer, Pierre Monteux, Erich Leinsdorf, William Steinberg, Eugene Ormandy, Fritz Reiner, and George Solti. But all of them were immigrants. (Indeed the last three were from Budapest.) Before 1943–44 no conductor who was American-born and -trained had exercised such responsibility as had Bernstein, whom Koussevitzky visited backstage after *On the Town* opened and warned: "If you do this any more, I'm not going to give you the Boston Symphony." That stopped Bernstein, who seemed willing to confine himself to classical music. But after Koussevitzky died and the baton of the BSO was passed to Charles Munch instead, Bernstein was free to compose the scores to *Wonderful Town* and to *Candide* (1956).

He seemed to have it all. But when the board of the New York Philharmonic invited him to serve as its music director, a condition was imposed: Broadway was off-limits. He agreed, and assumed the post—as the first American-born conductor of a major American orchestra—just in time. In that very month, *West Side Story* opened. With "Keep Out" signs posted along Broadway, Bernstein served the Philharmonic for eleven years, during which millions of its recordings were sold and an unparalleled eminence was attained.[40] Few if any conductors have ever known greater adulation. But he craved what Samuel Gompers of the American Federation of Labor claimed workers wanted: "more."[41]

Bernstein's curse was precisely that he *was* American: he believed that all possibilities are open, that irrevocable choices need not be made, that composing and conducting and serious music and Broadway were always available to him. But not even Bernstein could escape the antinomies. His derivativeness as a composer of serious music appears to be a unanimous (posthumous) judgment. Copland was among the most obvious influences on him, and in 1949 offered what must have been a hurtful assessment: though Bernstein's music had "irresistible elan," "immediacy of emotional appeal," and often provided "a terrific dramatic punch," the work "at its worst" gave listeners nothing but "conductors' music—eclectic in style and facile in inspiration." Bernstein "was promiscuously overendowed as a musical talent," Jonathan Miller declared. "He could do anything he wanted to do. Except write really serious, original music. Which, of course, is what he *most* wanted to do." John Rockwell, a music critic for the *New York Times*, recognized that Bernstein's virtues as a composer of "serious" music were, in effect, what made his work so enchanting for Broadway: "He has a moving melodic gift, something especially rare in our time. . . . His vernacularly inspired rhythmic dash and syncopated swagger, and the theatrical directness and accessibility of even his most ostensibly 'serious' scores, make him a composer of undeniable gifts and popular appeal."[42] When asked if his music was "American," Bernstein issued a denial, then asserted that "none of it could have been written by a composer who was not an American." Then he added that "one would have had to be an American Jew to have written these pieces."[43]

What he meant is gnomic. But here is one interpretation: what he injected into classical music was the flamboyance and brio of Broadway, the showmanship that is integral to democratic appeal, what Ahad Ha-Am had considered very American: "big noise and publicity."[44] Certainly what Bernstein did on the podium was noted with distaste almost from the beginning. "He shagged, he shimmied and, believe it or not, he bumped," Virgil Thomson complained, and added in 1946: "With every season his personal performance becomes more ostentatious, his musical one less convincing." Critic Harold Schonberg told *Times* readers after one 1961 concert that "Mr. Bernstein did a pretty good job upstaging Mr. [Sviatoslav] Richter," and "made almost as much noise on the podium as his colleague did on the piano. Such foot stompings have not been heard since the 55th Division was on parade. . . . Towards the end of the Lizst Concerto, he rose vertically in the air," like Nijinsky. "His footwork was magnificent last night." Schonberg nevertheless "wish[ed] that there had been more music and less exhilaration."[45] The title of Bernstein's opera, *A Quiet Place* (1983), did not apply to the podium when he was on it, and in the last phase of his career, accusations of uninhibited vulgarity stuck with greater force than ever, as the showman seemed to overwhelm the artist. In Berlin in 1989, he celebrated the crumbling of the Wall by trying to upstage Schiller (if not Beethoven), changing *Freude* to *Freiheit* in the Ninth Symphony. Giving performances that were often mannered and always dramatic, Bernstein seemed to follow Cunégonde's motto in *Candide*: "Glitter and Be Gay."[46]

America made the compulsions to mix high and low difficult to resist, and encouraged the faith that popular appeal and artistic fidelity could be reconciled. On Tin Pan Alley Bernstein had worked briefly as an arranger; his alias was "Lenny Amber" ("amber" in German is *Bernstein*). But within a decade he became the first native-born American to conduct at La Scala, and later would know the elation of having the Vienna Philharmonic under his baton. No serious composer and conductor registered more sensitively the pressures of a commercial and democratic civilization. The consequences, he believed, were eclecticism; nothing else could do justice to the myriad vernacular influences that shaped—and above all jazzed up—his country's culture.

Mahler, the composer-conductor whom Bernstein most wanted to join on the pantheon, had also been charged with incongruity of styles and tones and the exaggeration of emotion.[47] But Mahler was not an American, nor—at first—was Weill. But when their names are added to others who juxtaposed classical forms with popular idioms, like Gershwin's and Marc Blitzstein's, then Bernstein's own suspicion that only an American Jew could have written his music may be exposed to light. Where popular taste has pressed so directly on the arts, where hierarchies of status and sensibility are harder to defend, talented and aspiring Jews are likely to cherish the breadth of opportunity offered.

A comprehensive analysis would have to consider as well the Jews who composed for the movies, the art form that most fully satisfied Henry James's emphasis on the democratic and commercial features of American civilization. His own *Washington Square* was transferred to the screen as *The Heiress* (1949); for its score Copland picked up an Oscar. The most versatile and ingenious of Hollywood composers, however, was Bernard Herrmann. The first film he scored was *Citizen Kane* (1941), which required him to create "Salaambô," a pastiche grand opera. That score did not, however, win an Academy Award, which was given instead to *The Devil and Daniel Webster*—music by Bernard Herrmann, who would evoke dread in the nine films he did for Hitchcock and would cap his career with *Taxi Driver* (1976).

Herrmann was a revolutionary film composer, who did not devise flowing melodies to illustrate what was shown on the screen but instead suggested moody and even disturbing metaphors. Brilliant as his scores were, he preferred to have established himself as a "serious" composer and conductor, at which he was far less successful. When the Los Angeles Philharmonic recorded Herrmann pieces on the Sony Classic label in 1996, the film scores rather than classical compositions were selected—just as Mstislav Rostropovich especially enjoyed conducting the suite from Bernstein's score for *On the Waterfront* (1954) rather than his formal symphonies.[48]

Bernstein's career was certainly taken as exemplifying how to prosper in the mélange of high and low culture. One musician who learned from this model was André Previn, the son of Jewish immigrants from Nazi Germany. He was still a teenager when MGM hired him to orchestrate and then compose movie scores; among his fifty-plus works for the movies, four won Academy Awards. Beginning in the 1950s Previn transformed himself into a conductor of classical music, and in the following decades served as the jet-setting music director of the London Symphony, the Pittsburgh Symphony, and the Los Angeles Philharmonic. Although his legacy has come to include more than two hundred recordings of classical music, he never abandoned another career as a jazz pianist and a composer who has been described as "a stylistic chameleon whose language is conservative and eclectic." For much of his life, *Sir* André (as of 1995) has recalled being asked: " 'Why don't you just . . .?' and you can fill in the blank. 'Why don't you just compose?' 'Why don't you just play the piano?' 'Why don't you just conduct?' But I like to do a lot of things, and as long as people allow me to do them, I will." In cultivating such virtuosity, Previn acknowledged Bernstein as a model.[49]

The affiliation was even closer for Michael Tilson Thomas, who won the Koussevitzky Prize at Tanglewood at the age of twenty-four, and then became a last-minute substitute for an ailing William Steinberg in the middle of a BSO concert in 1969. Tilson Thomas proved up to the task, which reminded everyone (including Bernstein) of what had happened in 1943. A friendship was forged, beginning with their discovery in their first meeting of a shared favorite among musical moments: a plangent oboe solo from Mahler's "Das Lied von der Erde." They also professed to have in common an eccentric capacity to sing excerpts from *Porgy and Bess* in Yiddish. Though groomed as a possible successor to Bernstein at the New York Philharmonic, Tilson Thomas lost that option after an airport arrest for drug possession: "People found out I was not the model of a nice Jewish boy." Instead he became the conductor of the San Francisco Symphony, where emphases on certain composers (Mahler, Ives, Stravinsky, and Copland) have suggested the lingering influence of Bernstein, whose portraits hang on the walls of Tilson Thomas's office.[50]

One interviewer has depicted him as "a nonstop entertainer" in his conversational style, "quoting Whitman one moment, mimicking the sinister conducting style of Fritz Reiner the next, switching accents and languages with ease, and savoring his own shtick. When it's time to be serious, he often steers the conversation toward two figures: Bernstein and Boris Thomashefsky," the Yiddish theater impresario once famous enough for his name to be rhymed with "Dostoyevsky" in the Gershwins' *Let 'Em Eat Cake.* Theodor Herzl Thomashefsky needed to emancipate himself from the burden of a celebrated father by becoming Ted Thomas, a writer for movies and television in Los Angeles. In the late 1980s the British press bestowed on *his* son a double name, like Vaughan Williams.[51]

Though Tilson Thomas's grandfather died seven years before the future conductor was born, familial background has lent authority to the claim that the Yiddish theater constituted an invaluable precedent for an American musical culture that does not separate "high" and "low" ingredients. The "*shund* plays—melodramas on contemporary issues, discrimination, sweatshops, assimilation," Tilson Thomas once remarked, alternated with "classics—*King Lear, Hamlet.* My grandfather even performed a version of *Parsifal* with Wagner's music! Many of the historians of Yiddish theater emphasize the classics," he added; "but I think if we looked today, we would be more impressed with the [impact of the] 'low' plays."[52]

How the shadow of show business falls even on the most exalted of musical forms could be briefly shown in the career of Beverly Sills. Born in Brooklyn as Belle Miriam Silverman, she sang on the radio (on *Uncle Bob's Rainbow Hour*) by the age of four and then, from the age of nine until twelve, as a Sunday regular on another radio program, *Major Bowes' Amateur Hour*. She toured in a Gilbert and Sullivan repertory company at the age of sixteen for one of the ubiquitous Shuberts (J. J. in this case). Playing Nanki-Poo to her Yum-Yum in *The Mikado* was Buddy Israel, later the father of actress Amy Irving. In the summer of 1952, when Sills sang at the Catskills' Concord Hotel, the backup orchestra was Sholom Secunda's. Joining the New York City Opera three years later, the soprano became its prima donna before finally getting roles at the Met beginning in 1975. Even afterward she could not confine herself to high culture, whether doing a television special with comedienne Carol Burnett the following year, or chatting with Johnny Carson on NBC. While serving as director of the New York City Opera, Sills introduced English supertitles to make lyrics and plot intelligible; she also programmed Broadway classics like *South Pacific*, *Sweeney Todd*, and Lerner and Loewe's *Brigadoon*.[53] In bridging the gap between her art and the masses, no one did more to vindicate faith in democratic enlightenment.

In a 1914 revue entitled *Watch Your Step*, Irving Berlin had "ragged" Verdi, who is depicted as protesting at first but then as graciously welcoming such syncopation. For the 1941 Broadway musical *Lady in the Dark*, Ira Gershwin injected "Tschaikovsky," a list song that named fifty-one Russian composers. An era of popular culture that reckoned with the prestige of serious music ended when Chuck Berry urged Beethoven to roll over and to inform Tschaikovsky of the new hegemony of rock 'n' roll. Americans would thus be "deliver[ed] . . . from the days of old."

Or consider the periodization of popular music in another way. Nineteen twenty-four marked the first collaboration of the Gershwins, *Lady, Be Good!*. The era closed with "Johnny B. Goode" in 1958, when Chuck Berry hailed the rise of a Louisiana rocker. The sartorial metaphor for the urbanity to which New Yorkers aspired was Berlin's "Top Hat, White Tie, and Tails" (1935); the wardrobe that doomed the Jewish dominance of popular music was "Blue Suede Shoes" (1956), which was first categorized as country and western but did as well on the pop and the rhythm and blues charts, too. When Berlin had gone from ragtime to riches, he moved his mother from a packed Cherry Street apartment on the Lower East Side in 1913 to the Bronx, which they deemed "the country." Carl Perkins, who wrote and first recorded "Blue Suede Shoes," *was* country, the son of a sharecropper in Tennessee, where on one plantation every impoverished family except his own was black. The very "hand" who taught Perkins to pick cotton also got him a guitar, but the first real instrument he owned was purchased only with a promise that it would be paid for when the crops came in. "Blue Suede Shoes," made famous in Presley's version, was written on a potato sack while Perkins and his wife were living in government-owned housing.[54]

Such a biography could not be replicated on Tin Pan Alley; nor could artistic ideals of cleverness and wit survive the challenge of hard-scrabble soulfulness and grit redolent of a South that could not be romanticized. No longer would New Yorkers or Chicagoans, whose birthplaces had sometimes been tsarist Russia, be able to talk Southern. When rock and roll swept across the nation, authenticity became the key criterion, defined as roots in the blues, in gospel, and in country and western music.

Jews were not absentees from the annals of rock and roll. The term itself was popularized, though not coined, by Alan Freed, a Cleveland disc jockey; and Max C. Freedman and James Myers helped write the pioneering hit "Rock Around the Clock" (1955). But compared to what Jewish influence on Tin Pan Alley and Broadway and Hollywood (to say nothing of classical music) had been, the decline was precipitous. Without Jewish innovativeness, the histories of popular song, or of the musical, or of movies, would not merely have been different; they would have been close to inconceivable. After inspecting *The Rolling Stone Illustrated History of Rock and Roll*, however, which identifies the most important groups and individuals, historian Anthony Rotundo discovered that only two of them—Bob Dylan and producer Phil Spector—are Jews. Italian-Americans were considered more pivotal, and were given a separate chapter. After checking *The Illustrated Encyclopedia of Rock*, which lists 215 Americans, Rotundo calculated that thirty-nine (or 18 percent) are Jews. "Yet even these numbers are misleading," he warned. "The Jewish contingent is heavily weighted with some of the most non-rock figures in the book," which is encyclopedic enough to cite Burt Bacharach, Neil Diamond, Melissa Manchester, Barry Manilow, and Bette Midler.

What accounts for this ethnic erasure? Because rock came late, Rotundo explained, it was not needed for rapid social ascent. Rock is "libidinal," and the directness and aggressiveness of the feelings it expresses contradict both *shtetl* and middle-class norms of moderation. To yield to such music was to take a walk on the wild side, to accept the intuitive and the spontaneous, to cast off some of the shackles of civilization. Indeed, the emotional immediacy of such music made it readily available for export; in projecting the urgency of unobstructed wants, rock around the bloc in Eastern Europe exercised some effect in discrediting Communism (especially in the country from which the families of Irving Berlin and Leonard Bernstein and Boris Thomashefsky had fled). Like jazz earlier, rock music exerted power because it came across as emancipatory, as free of constraint. Grounded in the sometimes frenzied oral culture of poor Southern blacks and whites, such music was therefore foreign to Jews, whose culture exalted textuality and literacy. Many rock and roll performers were shaped as children by gospel music, which has never reminded observers of the cantillations heard in *shul*.[55]

The plausibility of such explanations makes more surprising the success of the Jewish songwriters who churned out early hits for such labels as Atlantic, Columbia, and RCA. At 1619 Broadway, young New Yorkers like Barry Mann and Cynthia Weill wrote "You've Lost That Lovin' Feelin'" and "Uptown"; Jeff Barry and Ellie Greenwich wrote "Chapel of Love" and "Leader of the Pack." From cubicles in the Brill Building, Carole King and Gerry Goffin wrote "Will You Love Me Tomorrow" and "The Loco-Motion." There Doc Pomus and Mort Shuman wrote "Teenager in Love," "Save the Last Dance for Me," "This Magic Moment," "Young Blood," "Sweets for My Sweet," and other hits. Also from the Brill Building came the hits of Neil Sedaka and Howie Greenfield, like "Calendar Girl" and "Happy Birthday, Sweet Sixteen." Sedaka was something of an exception among these white teenagers, as he put over his own material. That authenticity was to come to define rock and roll by 1965: after the examples of The Beatles and Bob Dylan, performers were *expected* to interpret their own material. And after 1965, Jews were hardly slackers. Besides Diamond and Manilow and Carole King, the list of singer-songwriters included Paul Simon, Carly Simon, Randy Newman, and Laura Nyro. In all cases, however, their affiliation with rock and roll was remote or at least contestable. Nor were Jews absent from the blues to which rock and roll was so indebted. But Mike Bloomfield, Paul Butterfield, and Al Kooper were slotted in *urban* blues.[56] Their work was distinctive, but not seminal to the genre.

That is what makes the career of Bob Dylan so singular. He was not a Southerner nor had he or his family tilled the soil; his father, Abraham Zimmerman, operated a hardware and appliance store in the Minnesota mining region. But Dylan was not a New Yorker either, and therefore suggested something autochthonous. Perhaps, to hear America singing, it helped to spring from the Midwest (if not Middle America). He was not what Stalinist postwar propaganda considered the Jewish fiend: a "rootless cosmopolitan." Nor was he some primitive "folk" artist either. Barely a decade after Ginsberg's "Howl" (1956), barely half a decade after walking out of the Sigma Alpha Mu fraternity house, Dylan would inject dense and obscure imagery as well as introspective ambiguities into what became mainstream music. He developed "a rich, figurative language, grafted literary and philosophical subtleties onto the protest song, revitalized folk vision by rejecting proletarian and ethnic sentimentality, then all but destroyed pure folk as a contemporary form by merging it with pop," critic Ellen Willis asserted near the end of the decade of Dylan's stunning ascent. The revolution he wrought was mostly in the words he used.[57] Very few songwriters either on Tin Pan Alley or on Broadway had been more creative and fertile; none had been more esoteric. Indeed, the influences of modern poetry often resulted in lyrics so cryptic as to defy Wittgenstein's claim that a private language is impossible.

After Dylan, rock albums included lyric sheets; and in 1974 his song lyrics were published, as *Writings and Drawings*, by the eminent firm of Alfred A. Knopf. When asked to give an opinion of his author, its eponymous chairman emeritus not only answered a question with a question, but inadvertently echoed Auden: "Now you get me to a point where I have to say, 'Who's Bob Dylan?'"[58] Perhaps Knopf's problem was generational; Tin Pan Alley had not distinguished between young and old, and typified the aim of mass culture to find one size that fits all. But the young Dylan expected elders to step aside, warning them in 1964: "Your sons and your daughters are beyond your command." Parents in that decade were further instructed: "Don't criticize what you can't understand" (not what they *didn't* understand). One senior citizen who did not heed such advice was Yip Harburg, whose *Darling of the Day* (1968) opened on Broadway a year after the "summer of love." The show lasted for only thirty-one performances, after which he quit the business. About a decade later, Bert Lahr's son visited the lyricist for *The Wizard of Oz* and noticed Dylan's *Writings and Drawings* on the coffeetable. Harburg had studied—and even tried to imitate—such lyrics, but was repulsed: "They communicate only emotional intensity. They're crude. It upsets me. You're living in a savage world; and when you listen to the shrieks and savage cries in the songs, you know it."[59] The urbanity that Broadway took to be a sign of civilization was suspect in rock music.

Yet some of the cognoscenti admired Dylan's work more than that of any other American rock musician. The Pulitzer Prize–winning poet Stanley Kunitz, whose immigrant mother had reported to the *Forverts* on her visit to Palestine, reported "listen[ing] with pleasure to Bob Dylan. . . . The interest taken in him is a healthy sign, for there is no reason why popular art and a more selective, esoteric art can't cheerfully coexist."[60] Though none of Dylan's singles landed at the very top of the charts, his influence on the best educated among the young in particular was enormous, if not easy to specify. Even a sort of populist like Jimmy Carter had to show his sophistication, and not only his common touch; when he began his run for the presidency in 1974, he professed to be "a lover of Bob Dylan's songs and Dylan Thomas's poetry."[61] In 1970 the dropout from the University of Minnesota became Dr. Bob Dylan when Princeton awarded him an honorary doctorate, along with Walter Lippmann. (Those seeking to discover unities in Jewish creativity should be required to juxtapose those two names.) Dylan's influence within his own métier was also unmatched. Just as D. W. Griffith worked out the essential grammar of the cinema soon after its birth, so too Dylan brought rock and roll to its maturity scarcely a decade after its emergence. Since then, none of his American successors advanced the genre much further.

Just as Griffith extended the one-reeler into a full-length spectacle, so Dylan broke the barrier of three-minute air play. "A Hard Rain's A-Gonna Fall" (1962) was written during the Cuban missile crisis, "when I didn't figure I'd have enough time left in life, didn't know how many other songs I could write. . . . I wanted to get the most down that I knew about into one song."[62] Perhaps of even greater importance was "Like a Rolling Stone" (1965). At six minutes and nine seconds, it was double the length that a single was expected to be; and in using a band rather than only a guitar, Dylan broke out of the confinements of folk music *and* of mainstream ballads. "Like a Rolling Stone" "wasn't about dancing or driving or teenage love lost and found. This was an electric epic, simple in its music but remarkably complex and ambitious in its scope," rock chronicler Fred Goodman noted. " 'Like a Rolling Stone' erased every rule of pop music." What Dylan was saying was mysterious and undecidable; but the fifteen-year-old Bruce Springsteen was stunned listening to "a guy like I've never heard before or since." Childish in its resentment and yet grown-up in its cry of pain, the song touched something more complicated than Jerry Lee Lewis's "Whole Lot of Shakin' Going On" (which John Lennon once asserted that neither The Beatles nor anyone else had improved on, as the aesthetic ideal of the rock lyric was supposed to be simplicity).[63] Dylan obviously disagreed. In confronting disillusionment—or the threat of nuclear war, or the urgency of civil rights—without contaminating the poetry with self-righteousness, he reclassified the job of pop musician as audaciously as Lenny Bruce was redefining the role of a comedian.

In some quarters both of these figures were being taken (that is, *mistaken*) for mystagogues, for modern initiators into the mysteries of creation. The pop musician seemed to assume the mantle of visionary; as his Columbia label's ad campaign insisted, nobody sings Dylan like Dylan. Berlin wrote for others: so thin and reedy was his voice that, after doing his own "Oh! How I Hate to Get Up in the Morning" for Warner Brothers' *This Is the Army* (1942), a grip remarked: "If the fellow who wrote this song could hear this guy sing, he'd roll over in his grave."[64] But Dylan's nasal whine, his lack of vocal or verbal polish, indeed the melodic thinness, certified his sincerity. With a voice that seemed to come straight from the adenoids, how could he *not* be communicating a bitingly personal *Weltan-*

schauung? How could he *not* be reaching toward a truth that made the elegance and charm of the Broadway song look superficial and even phony? Performer and prophet were one.

But if authenticity rather than artifice was to be the aesthetic of rock (which was to flaunt its roots instead of exuding razzle-dazzle), then Dylan was oddly vulnerable. "I don't believe in Dylan," Lennon objected. "Zimmerman is his name."[65] The new surname was picked for unclear reasons, perhaps to strike pop-western associations (Marshall Dillon), perhaps to honor the prolix Dylan Thomas. To bestow a new patronymic is to test the possibilities of self-invention. Reaching maturity just before the cusp of ethnic assertiveness, Dylan behaved no differently than Carole King (*née* Klein), whose *Tapestry* (1971) exceeded sales of any of Dylan's own albums. But her Queens College classmate, Paul Simon, did not bother to change his name, even though a team called Simon and Garfunkel would sound like a department store. After the mid-1960s an adopted name risked looking too laden with show-biz ambition, too obviously an effort to "pass." But installing himself at first in the folk tradition, Robert Zimmerman may well have understood that he had to make it as Dylan or not at all.

The onomastic switch made a point: he affirmed his own right to be anyone from anywhere, emerging from a hazy and partly fabricated past to wriggle out of any fixed identity. A fierce refusal to sustain a consistent style has been the most consistent feature of his music. Nothing so aptly captured the protean quality of national possibility as his 1965 line: "He not busy being [re-]born is busy dying" (from "It's All Right, Ma, I'm Only Bleeding"). In shuffling cards of identity so often, Dylan developed the most unstable persona in rock history. Transforming himself first from Zimmerman, he became "visionary and crank, innovator and conservator, irritant and stimulant, skeptic and proselytizer, rebel and sellout, pathfinder and lost patrol," as one music critic summarized so unpredictable a career.[66] Dylan's identity has been more elusive than anything the Federal Witness Protection Program has yet devised.

He inevitably flummoxed the essentialism long entwined in Jewish identity. Showing up at the Western Wall in 1971, celebrating his son Jesse's bar mitzvah in Jerusalem twelve years later, vaguely affiliating for a while with the Lubavitcher Hasidim, Dylan has professed religious beliefs: "I've always thought there's a superior power, that this is not the real world and that there's a world to come." His 1983 *Infidels* album offered something unexpected: "Neighborhood Bully" is a remarkable capsule history of the Jewish people itself. Spitting out the song rapidly, in a tone of ironic bitterness, he blended a millennial history of unjust persecution with an unnuanced defense of a beleaguered Israel. The case he made is one that Likud could have easily endorsed. Yet Dylan denied that "Neighborhood Bully" "is a political song," and once more refused to be pinned to the mat: "I'm not a political songwriter."

Whether he is a Jewish songwriter is a question that is probably unresolvable, despite the inclusion of "Blowin' in the Wind" in the songbook of the Reform movement's National Federation of Temple Youth. Dylan also studied at a Christian Bible school in California, and by the late 1970s seems to have accepted some version of Christianity. Songs on the 1979 album *Slow Train Coming* could easily be added to Protestant hymnals, although Dylan assured an interviewer five years later of having been born only once. Calling the Old and New Testament equally valid, however, amounted to a renunciation of Judaism.[67] His case is special. Formally satisfying rabbinic rules of inclusion, Dylan has operated only barely (if at all) within Jewish culture. While remaining a Jew in the *halachic* sense, he has been ecumenical, sometimes expressing in lyrics and interviews attitudes that cannot be considered Jewish, sometimes offering tantalizing affirmations of that very identity. He shattered the difference between the Jew and the Other as though the historic boundary had never existed.

Perhaps no one considered "Cheek to Cheek" and "One Hand, One Heart" and "Blowin' in the Wind" to be Jewish songs when they were first heard. They satisfy no liturgical criteria; they were composed neither to enhance the sublimity of worship nor to complement the concerns of believers. They were not written *for* Jews, *as* Jews. Such works are evidence (as if any further proof were needed) of the desacralization that permeates the modern condition. But perhaps novelties of experience encourage definitions to be expanded. Such songs may be Jewish because Berlin and Bernstein and Dylan wrote them, which means that a conception of what constitutes "Jewish" music has become wider but thinner. The Psalmist once lamented, while sitting "by the rivers of Babylon," the loss of a homeland and the anguish of exile, but then asked: "How shall we sing the Lord's song in a foreign land?" (Psalm 137). A century of creativity in another Promised Land has bequeathed a few unexpected ways to think about that question.

THEATER

Tocqueville had been struck not only by the equality that seemed the axial principle upon which American society turned, but also by the "energetic passions" with which its citizens pursued private gain. Such impulses seemed barely frustrated by communal impediments; no Western nation was less encumbered by the residues of feudalistic guilds. Jews too were animated by this fervor for commerce, and had special reason to appreciate the fluidity of the economic system that liberalism sanctioned. Having generally been denied the right to own land elsewhere in the Diaspora, Jews had become a mercantile people—so much so that the sociologist Werner Sombart advanced the dubious thesis that Jews were primarily responsible for the formation of capitalism in early modern Europe.[1] American Jews were historically enmeshed in an economic system that collective ideals did not cushion. No wonder then that serious Jewish playwrights have highlighted the social problems that capitalism has exacerbated.

This chapter highlights the special sensitivity of such dramatists to the corrosive effects of business and to the resulting enfeeblement of the family and the ravaged ties of community. Such writers have made the high cost of capitalism pivotal to the moral critique of America itself. What was wrong with "free enterprise" was the frustration of ordinary decency, the damage inflicted on the hopes for contentment, and the persistence of misery. But then in the second half of the century, success was achieved, and the disenchantment that set in stemmed from affluence (at least for the upper-middle class where many Jews were located). Then Jewish identity came into critical condition, and the diagnosis was grim. After so much fragmentation, after so much centrifugal force had fractured the Jewish family, the continuities of peoplehood were imperiled. Drama offers a searing entrée into the consequences of integration into so bountiful a society; the myth of individual upward mobility exacted a high spiritual price upon what the immigrants called *menshlichkeit* (uprightness).

Such tensions surface early in the work of Clifford Odets. Born into an immigrant family that had moved from Philadelphia to the Bronx, he managed to escape the sorts of economic pressure that afflicted families like the Bergers in his first major full-length play, *Awake and Sing!*, written when he was 28. His early success was spectacular. When the one-act agit-prop *Waiting for Lefty* opened at the Group Theatre that year, the twenty-eight curtain calls that the production garnered stunned its author, who soon had four other plays running simultaneously in New York. (Another was *Till the Day I Die*, a 1935 drama about the Nazi persecution of German Communists—not Jews.) Odets himself is notorious for having succumbed to the commercial passions, for becoming addicted to Hollywood luxury. He exemplified the sellout whose idealism is corrupted, whose talent is squandered by self-inflicted blows. The last of the films that he scripted and lived long enough to see completed was a 1961 musical entitled *Wild in the Country*, starring Elvis Presley.[2]

This parabola of artistic self-destruction should not detract from the salience of Odets's early plays, which expose the desperation and misery of the Great Depression, when the system itself seemed to turn Jewish immigrant dreams rancid. Trying so hard to get by, his characters stare into the abyss of poverty, and brace themselves for the shock of utter failure.[3] Inspired by his idealistic but ineffectual grandfather Jacob, the patriarch of this family of Jews without money, Ralph Berger proclaims in *Awake and Sing!*: "We don't want life printed on dollar bills."

But legal tender is what such families need. His struggling mother Bessie knows the truth: "Here without a dollar you don't look the world in the eye. Talk from now to next year—this is life in America." The manipulative matriarch of this Bronx family knows the price of self-respect, and tells her brother, a clothing manufacturer proud of his fur gloves, that "Ralph should only be a success like you, Morty. I should only live to see the day when he drives up to the door in a big car with a chauffeur and a radio. I could die happy, believe me." This vision does not acknowledge the unattractiveness of this role model: Uncle Morty is a man who has resisted the temptations of tenderness because it might enfeeble him in business, which "don't stop for personal life." He vows to knock striking workers "in the kishkas."

Romance—Ralph's girlfriend—threatens Bessie Berger's vision of future security; and a typical passage conveys generational conflict, plus the social anxiety, the self-pity, and the bitter sarcasm with which family members communicate with one another. "A girl like that he wants to marry," Bessie complains. "A skinny consumptive-looking . . . six months already she's not working—taking charity from an aunt. . . . Miss Nobody should step in the picture and I'll stand by with my mouth shut." Ralph replies: "Miss Nobody! Who am I? Al Jolson?" Bessie changes the subject: "Fix your tie!" Eager to flee this combat zone of a household, with its barest thread of dignity, the son insists: "I'll take care of my own life." To which his mother is scornful: "You'll take care? Excuse my expression, you can't even wipe your nose yet! He'll take care!" Such gritty cadences and pungent rhythms compelled one critic to claim in 1946 that Odets was not just a dramatist; he had "by a considerable margin [made] the most important achievement in the literature of the American Jews."[4]

Not the least of his legacies was the introduction of an idiom electrifying in its Yiddish-driven intensity. He made memorable and searing what he called the "struggle for life amidst petty conditions." After Odets, English would have a whiplash sting. The two-bit hoodlum Moe Axelrod gives Hennie, who is about to embark on a marriage of convenience, some staccato advice: "Cut your throat, sweetheart. Save time." "To my own worst enemy I don't wish such a life," a humiliated Sam Feinschreiber says. In the original version of the play, called *I Got the Blues*, the characters use some Yiddish. In *Awake and Sing!*, however, even *mitzvah* becomes "blessing"; and the family speaks almost entirely in English. Observing no religious rituals on stage, the Bergers seem to have little ethnic consciousness either, and do not place themselves in any overt way in the nexus of Jewish history. Perhaps that is why Cahan hailed the play as a defining moment in the *American* theater.[5]

Odets's title is lifted from Isaiah 26:19, and a certain biblical righteousness hovers over another play from that era. *The Little Foxes* reveals not only the extent of acculturation but also the corrosive effects of cunning and greed. The unscrupulous Hubbards resembled so closely the family of Lillian Hellman's mother, the Newhouses, that some of the playwright's relatives threatened to sue her for libel when *The Little Foxes* opened in 1939. No wonder, since her great-uncle Jake is described in her memoirs as "a man of great force, given to breaking the spirit of people for the pleasure of the exercise." In *The Little Foxes* the Hubbards are so rapacious that Horace Giddens tells his wife Regina how "sick" he is "of your brothers and their dirty tricks to make a dime. . . . You wreck the town, you and your brothers, *you* wreck the town and live on it." The Hubbards are so wicked that their black maid, Addie, alludes to "people who eat the earth and eat all the people on it like in the Bible with the locusts. And other people who stand around and watch them eat it. (*Softly.*) Sometimes I think it ain't right to stand and watch them do it"—as indeed Regina Giddens watches her vaguely resistant but sickly husband die rather than come to his aid with a bottle of medicine. In Hellman's rigidly moralistic melodrama, the avarice of the already very comfortable middle class cannot be squared with human decency.[6]

Such plays were written from a pretty-in-pink angle, and it was from a niche sympathetic to dialectical materialism that bourgeois materialism was criticized. (Hellman's intractable "progressivism" did not deter the U.S. Geological Survey from later naming a crater on Venus for her.) Neither she nor Odets knew or cared enough about Judaism to imagine *its* value system as a measure of responsibility. Especially in the fervent decade of the Popular Front, both writers were close as handcuffs to Communism.

That same accusation was *unfairly* lobbed at the most important of the playwrights of Jewish origin, and one who underlined the costs of capitalism in his brief against American society. Indeed, the work of Arthur Miller has shown continuous interest in what befalls those who accept too credulously the promise of abundance. Having seen *Waiting for Lefty* in 1935, he was inspired to write "plays that shook you up," works powered by the immediacy of direct address.[7]

Death of a Salesman (1949) is the most haunting and trenchant of his dramas, and has elicited the greatest scholarly interest as well as general impact. Literary scholar Harold Bloom alone has edited *Arthur Miller's* Death of a Salesman (1988) and *Willy Loman* (1991), as well as *Arthur Miller* (1987) and *Modern Critical Views: Arthur Miller* (1987). This happened to be Abbie Hoffman's favorite American play, in part because his own father, who sold pharmaceutical supplies on the road, had felt the anxiety of surviving with a shoeshine and a smile. David Mamet has also praised *Death of a Salesman* as "the greatest American play, arguably." His maternal grandfather had been a traveling salesman in the Midwest, who came home only one day a week and whom the playwright remembered as "a great storyteller."[8] Mamet's father was a Chicago labor lawyer well acquainted with the underside of competitive capitalism. Like *Awake and Sing!* the plot of *Death of a Salesman* hinges on a life insurance policy and ends with a suicide. Also, Broadway's first Willy Loman, Lee J. Cobb, was, like Odets, a product of the Group Theatre and its artistic repudiation of a deforming business civilization. (Cobb had been cast in *Waiting for Lefty*.)

In the 1949 London production, the most illustrious veteran of the Yiddish theater, Paul Muni, died the death of a salesman. But a truly Jewish tang did not bubble to the surface of anglophone versions until the 1984 Broadway revival, when Dustin Hoffman, who had portrayed Bernard in a 1965 recorded version (with Cobb), got old enough to replace him. Hoffman's own father had been a traveling salesman, and Miller's play was the future actor's stunning introduction to dramatic literature. Because the most famous interpreters of Willy Loman—Cobb, Muni, Hoffman—were all Jews, the choice of Fredric March, in Columbia Pictures' disastrous film version, constituted nontraditional casting. The Bergers are certainly Jewish, the assimilated Hubbards just barely. But who exactly are the Lomans? Willy could be experiencing the anguished failure of any father, indeed the plight of a salesman so ineffective that a map of misreading could result. "I always said that New England territory was no damned good," Miller once heard someone in the audience mutter.[9]

Critic Mary McCarthy, whose brother Kevin played Biff in the 1951 movie, was disturbed that Willy was presented as "a capitalized Human Being without being anyone." He "seemed to be Jewish, to judge by his speech-cadences, but there was no mention of this on stage. He could not be Jewish because he had to be 'America,' which is not so much a setting as a big, amorphous idea." Because Loman was supposed to represent a national or even a universal type, "the puzzle for the audience . . . is to guess where these living-rooms roughly are, and who is living in them, which might make it possible to measure the plausibility of the action." Living somewhere south of Yonkers, this family sports a background as mysterious as what fills those sample cases. The "crypto-Jewish characters" of *Death of a Salesman* represented an abstraction invoking the human family. Critic Diana Trilling complained about this midcentury trope: "Under our very eyes, we see the Wandering Jew become the wandering man, the alien Jew generalizing into the alienated human being."[10] Literary scholar Sidra D. Ezrahi wondered whether Loman "is a Jew at all—neither his name nor his attire, neither his language nor his behavior betrays his ethnic origin," which is why Ellen Schiff excludes him from consideration in her standard scholarly account of stage Jews, *From Stereotype to Metaphor* (1982).[11] "He never knew who he was," Biff remarks in the Requiem, but no hints are offered that Jewishness or Judaism had unjustly been lost along the way. Willy could barely remember his father, an itinerant seller of flutes who went west and abandoned the family; Willy's mother "died a long time ago"; and his entrepreneurial older brother Ben fled to Alaska while still young. Virtually from the beginning, Willy was on his own. There is no reason to believe, however, that the family this self-made man never really had was Jewish (nor is anything revealed in the play about the origins of Linda Loman).

Such vagueness led even an admirer of the play to complain of betrayal. Willy's "story is never avowed as a Jewish story, and so a great contribution to Jewish and to Jewish American history is lost," David Mamet lamented. "It's lost to the culture as a whole and, more importantly, it's lost to the Jews, its rightful owners." "Well, *he* got it," Miller shot back, "so it couldn't have been lost." Mamet's proprietary claim inspired a newspaper columnist to wonder: "Are Jews the rightful owners of *Death of a Salesman?* . . . Would *Death of a Salesman* be a better play if the Lomans were portrayed as Jewish? How? Why?" The "tragedy of assimilation" was hardly the preoccupation of leftist writers of the 1930s and 1940s, and did not become Miller's own concern until *Broken Glass* in 1994.[12] To ask an earlier generation to address later problems is anachronistic and unfair. The way Miller chose to tell Willy's story was expressionist, and what critics were in effect demanding was the greater specificity that is the agenda of naturalism. But its superiority as a dramaturgical method is not obvious. Would the presentation of particular cultural clues have improved *Antigone*?

Mamet's concern that the patrimony of one ethnic group could not afford to be lost was not misplaced. Apart, however, from the legal technicalities of licensing and copyright, the rules of cultural life cannot be rewritten to designate certain minorities as the rightful heirs of works of art. Who, incidentally, owns *Porgy and Bess*? Or, for that matter, *American Buffalo* (1975) or *Oleanna* (1992), plays in which Mamet overtly portrays no Jews at all? Does *Hamlet* properly belong to the Danes, or to the British? Or can anyone else join in? The story of American Jewish culture can be told as an incessant struggle to retrieve what might otherwise be hidden, to reinterpret what might not have been initially recognized as relevant, and to spurn the temptation to erect impenetrable boundaries between what belongs to Jews and what belongs to other Americans. The first noteworthy American Jewish leader, Mordecai Manuel Noah, also happened to be a playwright; nonetheless his melodramas were not overtly placed in the service of Jewish interests, and were barren of Jewish characters.

Another Jewish playwright, Donald Margulies, reworked the family dynamics in Miller's play in *The Loman Family Picnic*, staged at the Manhattan Theatre Club in 1993. Pivoting on the bar mitzvah ceremony of the elder son in Brooklyn in 1965, Margulies' bitter comedy places the desperate wife (Doris) rather than her husband (Herbie) at the center. Though the family does musical routines at the edge of the abyss, Herbie's plight is ethnically coded and expressed but largely unchanged, with "nobody buying. / Shmoozing and losing / never stopped trying." He's "sweating and shlepping / . . . But knowing I'm dying."[13] Here was one resolution of the controversy over the proprietary rights to *Death of a Salesman*.

The "universalism" to which Miller was committed once seemed to be artistically problematic, a homogenizing "progressive" bias. So puzzling was the playwright's genealogy to one unsophisticated theatergoer that he was heard to wonder after *Death of a Salesman*: "If his mother is Jewish and his father is Jewish, how come *he* ain't Jewish?" The rhetorical question demands a brief rebuttal (and defense). A Jewish family was the subject of Miller's first play, *Honors at Dawn* (1936), which the Hillel Foundation produced at the University of Michigan; his 1945 novel *Focus* had diagnosed domestic antisemitism. On stage, with *Incident at Vichy* (1965), and on television, with *Playing for Time* (1980), Miller tackled the *Shoah*. He also cared enough (at least for the sake of his parents' sensibilities) to encourage his second wife, Marilyn Monroe, to convert to Judaism in 1956. Miller's ancestral allegiances were not pronounced; yet, in retrospect, the

artistic instincts and ideological limitations that he showed in his masterpiece have been vindicated. A more accessible—and moving—play is not
easy to imagine; *Death of a Salesman* was a hit in Falangist Spain as well as
in post-Maoist Communist China. In 1956, when Luchino Visconti directed a production in Rome, the unknown who played Biff was Marcello
Mastroianni.[14] So pervasive has been the appeal of this play that any obligation of Jewish artists to eschew an abstract cosmopolitanism has been
decisively invalidated.

This worldwide acceptance does not mean that the ethnic provenance
of Miller's play is automatically negated. A 1951 production of *Toyt fun a
Salesman* in Brooklyn caused a reviewer for *Commentary* to suspect that
"this Yiddish play is really the original." The celebrated Broadway premiere "was merely—Arthur Miller's translation into English." Linda Loman had said that "attention must be paid," a phrase the reviewer found
less forthright than "gib achtung." The Broadway version had situated Loman nowhere. In Brooklyn the play was transformed into the conflict of a
Jewish family, whose Yiddish lexicon included no word for "salesman."[15]
In that borough and others, it might be added, leftism came with the territory. *Death of a Salesman* more than hints that something has gone wrong
with business, as the son of Willy's former boss is clearly more engrossed
in the virtues of mechanical equipment (like a tape recorder) than in the
pathos of his New England salesman disintegrating in his office. (In *The
Adding Machine* [1923], Elmer Rice [*né* Reizenstein] had traced the displacement of a discharged employee by an enormous adding machine.)

But in inculcating no higher ambition than to be "*well*-liked," in impugning the work ethic, Willy is no paragon of a parent. Partly because
Miller was subpoenaed by the House Committee on Un-American Activities in 1956 (four years after Odets and Hellman testified), the hostility
of *Death of a Salesman* to capitalism can be exaggerated. Miller noted
that "the most decent man" in the play is "a capitalist," Willy's neighbor
Charley, whose son exacts the revenge of the nerds by becoming a hotshot
lawyer arguing before the Supreme Court, playing tennis on a friend's private court, "making it."[16] Bernard's success does not seem unmerited, just
as the failure of Biff and Happy to mature into productive, independent
citizens is not shown as palpably unjust.

Even as the Loman brothers were becoming marginalized, as Americans
after the Second World War became a "people of plenty," such prosperity
did not obliterate a willingness to expose the flaws of the corporate culture.
Even during the "golden age" of early television, Jewish dramatists engaged in such scrutiny. Among those who were not subjected to any blacklist, the most famous was Rod Serling, who condemned the indignities of
the marketplace in such dramas as *Patterns* (1955) and *Requiem for a Heavy-*

weight (1956). He was rewarded for such criticism with six Emmys, the first of which was bestowed for a script for *Kraft Television Theatre*.

The protagonist of *Patterns* is Fred Staples, a name that somewhat mirrors the writer's. Staples (Richard Kiley) is a promising young executive at Ramsey and Company who shares offices and a secretary with Andy Sloane (Ed Begley), an industrial relations expert; they become friends. In a much-cited night scene, Staples encounters Sloane, who is on his way down after suffering too much humiliation from Ramsey (Everett Sloane). Staples urges his friend to quit before Ramsey, a megalomaniac with a mean streak, has utterly deprived Sloane of his self-respect. But Staples, who is sensitive and ambitious, has mixed motives; Ramsey has hired him, in effect, to replace Sloane anyway. After the boss's bullying has brought on Sloane's fatal heart attack in front of other company executives, vice president Staples is determined to quit the company. Then, in the climax to *Patterns*, an unapologetic, manipulative Ramsey persuades him to stay, and Staples accepts the challenge of maintaining his conscience *within* the hierarchy of the high-rise building. It is a position Staples's wife has wanted for him anyway. This rather remorseless if brief peek inside executive suites was assailed in the *Wall Street Journal* the following day as "Marxist." But *Patterns* won Serling the first of three straight Emmys for Outstanding Dramatic Writing—as well as a reputation for injecting moral outrage into his teleplays.

That sensibility had been cultivated at the Binghamton Jewish Community Center. Serling was especially indebted to its director, Isidore Friedlander, who was himself a playwright as well as a translator from the Yiddish and Hebrew. Serling saw himself as something of a maverick, and his sense of vocation was explicitly dissident. The writer, he asserted in 1968, should "menace the public's conscience" and should "see the arts as a vehicle of social criticism." Nor could Serling's own Jewish origins have been irrelevant to his assertion, a year earlier, that "the singular evil of our time is prejudice. It is from this evil that all other evils grow and multiply."

Yet he was quickly defanged; Tocqueville proved prophetic in observing the enormous power of business values within American democracy. A career that had begun so strikingly with *Patterns* ended with television commercials. Serling became so conspicuous a shill for floor waxes, toothpaste, beers, sprays for rust-proofing and other products that his obituary in *Variety* identified him not only as a "writer" but also as a "commercial spokesman."[17] Such sobriquets anticipated the curriculum vitae of Mikhail Gorbachev, who capped his service as the last prime minister of the Soviet Union not only by publishing his memoirs but also by appearing in 1997 in a Russian commercial for Pizza Hut. History has no libretto.

At the same time that Dustin Hoffman was asking for attention to be paid on Broadway, a new pitch-black comedy marked the tailspin of Willy Loman's American dream. It so happens that both plays won Pulitzer Prizes; other resemblances were coincidental. Whatever Willy's other faults, at least he had made an honest living (though Joe Keller had not, in Miller's 1947 exposure of the ethics of the fathers in *All My Sons*). David Mamet's businessmen inhabit a different moral universe in *Glengarry Glen Ross* (1984), which reduces the plenitude of life to an injunction: "Always be closing." In a real estate office (perhaps like the one near O'Hare Airport where Mamet had worked for a year),[18] savagery has replaced the wish to be well liked. Because salvation depends on the leads, the credo that "the public be conned" replaces "the public be pleased." These cynics, who are not hawking real estate pro bono, subscribe to a code that prohibits suckers (once known as "customers") from keeping their money. They are kinsmen of Mamet's Teach, the deadbeat in *American Buffalo* who is evidently a close reader of Tocqueville in defining free enterprise as "the freedom . . . of the *Individual* . . . to Embark on Any Fucking Course that he sees fit. . . . The country's *founded* on this."[19] Like the pack of cynical Chicagoans operating out of the press room in *The Front Page* (1928; coauthored by Ben Hecht), indeed like the Hollywood predators in Mamet's *Speed-the-Plow* (1988), the denizens in the shark-infested waters of the real estate office make "business ethics" an oxymoron.

Nor could the hucksters of *Glengarry Glen Ross* dream of the self-respect with which Willy tries to comfort—and define—himself. His new boss may be insensitive and indifferent, and is rightly concerned about the drop in Willy's productivity. But Mamet's salesmen are subjected to a grueling competition, with the biggest closer that month winning a Cadillac; the number two man will only get a set of steak knives; third place and below receive pink slips. Willy's suicide is inextricably connected to his failure as a husband and father; but Shelly (the Machine) Levene, whose daughter is hospitalized, seems the only salesman pitching real estate for whom family matters. Mamet's women are derogatorily associated with weakness and timidity (in contrast to Linda Loman, who is bucking for sainthood). That did not stop Miller from praising the "real bite" of *Glengarry Glen Ross*, a "very electric" work he compared to the "heightened, constructed language" of Odets.[20]

Mamet's slimeballs are endowed with Jewish names like Levene, George Aaronow, and presumably Dave Moss—a sign of some confidence in Gentile tolerance, so that negative stereotyping need no longer be feared. Thus, in *Other People's Money* (1989), Jerry Sterner named his protagonist Larry (the Liquidator) Garfinkle, because the playwright professed acquaintanceship with such corporate marauders. Though Larry the Liquidator may not be a full-scale *goniff*, his operating style suggests classification among the ethically challenged. The popularity of Sterner's play did not oblige the staff of the Anti-Defamation League to put in overtime, even as the decade's notorious Wall Street inside traders, like Michael Milken, Martin Siegel, Ivan Boesky, and Dennis Levine, were being fingerprinted and booked. For the 1991 adaptation, Warner Communications rather gingerly cast Danny DeVito in the lead and altered the character's name to Garfield.

Perhaps the name change did not matter much in the heartland, where, Sterner conjectured, his protagonist was not recognized as a Jew but was merely stereotyped as a New Yorker. Half a century ago, it did matter to Warner Brothers, which decided to give a falso to Jules Garfinkle, the young actor who had appeared in the Group Theatre premiere of *Awake and Sing!* As for that new surname, "what kind of name is Garfield, anyway?" Jack Warner wondered. "It doesn't sound American." When the actor mentioned a president of the United States, another studio executive was proposing a switch to "James Garfield." "But that was the President's name!" the actor replied. "You wouldn't name a goddamn actor Abraham Lincoln, would you?" "No, kid, we wouldn't, because Abe is a name most people would say is Jewish and we don't want people to get the wrong idea." Finally Garfinkle resigned himself to becoming the movie star known as John Garfield.[21]

Half a century later, it was no longer necessary to change the names to protect the guilty, or to use such subterfuges to uphold the honor of the Jewish people. Identification was easier, but identity itself was imperiled. By the 1980s the levels of assimilation had become too high to be ignored, even by playwrights working in a tradition that minimized such problems. Among those playwrights to realize that valuables have been left unattended were Herb Gardner, in *Conversations with My Father* (1992); Donald Margulies, in *Sight Unseen* (1992); and most important, Mamet himself.

His start in the theater in Chicago had been promoted by his uncle, the director of broadcasting for the Chicago Board of Rabbis, which hired Mamet as an actor on televised religious programs. For the 1991 documentary *The Yiddish Cinema*, he also delivered the narration. The meaning of Jewish identity he tentatively explored in *The Duck Variations* (1975) and in *Goldberg Street* (1985), which uses speech cadences inflected with Yiddish patterns. The stalled effort to recapture, or at least understand, the past is also the theme of the three segments that comprise *The Old Neighborhood* (1997). The protagonist is Bobby Gould, a former Chicagoan who comes home to confront a past in which family, community, and ethnicity are intertwined. Divorced and troubled, detached from normative Jewish life, he cannot succeed in resuscitating what was left behind or connecting it to the present.[22]

In *The Old Neighborhood*, shmoozing does not quite lead to the resolution that might come from unsparing communication, and talking is no cure. But the characters fulfill what Mamet has wanted his dialogue to achieve: "No one really says what they mean, but they always mean what they mean." *Homicide* (1991), a film he wrote and directed, has Bobby Gold—this time a cop—confront the ambiguous resurfacing of Jewish affiliation. His situation the playwright compared to his own upbringing. "I found the Reform Judaism of my childhood nothing other than a desire to 'pass,' to slip unnoticed into the non-Jewish community," he recalled. The chief benefit of the religion he picked up at Chicago's Temple Sinai "was that it would not embarrass us."[23] Mamet felt "very deracinated," too marginal to be fully assured as an American yet too disaffiliated from tradition to feel very Jewish.

Homicide depicts an urban battleground pockmarked by ethnic resentment and fear, quite unlike New York City Mayor David N. Dinkins's "gorgeous mosaic" or the benign melting pot that Zangwill had envisioned. The name given to the film's Jewish policeman is virtually the same as that of the movie producer in *Speed-the-Plow*. Bobby Gould has something of a conscience in considering which films to authorize, enough for underling Charlie Fox to remind him that this is Hollywood (the morally and culturally repellent terrain that Odets had explored in 1949 in *The Big Knife*), where no one considers the Baal Shem Tov much of a role model. Indeed, nowhere is the collision of *menshlichkeit* with business more directly stated than at the end of *Speed-the-Plow*. Gould has momentarily forgotten (after Karen has seduced him) that moviemaking is not an eleemosynary activity. Instead his job is to "*make the thing everyone made last year*"; coming to his senses, he refuses to "green-light" her proposal to adapt an apocalyptic novel warning of environmental danger. "I know what you wanted, Bob," his underling—the latest of the little Foxes—tells him. "You wanted to do good." Gould agrees: "I wanted to do Good. . . . But I became foolish." Fox concludes: "Well, so we learn a lesson. But we aren't here to 'pine,' we aren't put here to *mope*. What are we here to do [*pause*], Bob?" Gould answers: "We're here to make a movie"—which will be a pointless, violent but maybe profitable prison spectacle.[24]

The way in which such Jews satisfy their commercial passions in *Speed-the-Plow* is repugnant; in other plays, it is merely tacky, worthy of ridicule instead of resentment. In Neil Simon's first play, *Come Blow Your Horn* (1961), the Baker family business is waxed fruit. In Wendy Wasserstein's first play, *Uncommon Women and Others* (1977), Holly Kaplan's father makes velveteen, among the fabrics actually patented by Morris Wasserstein, a successful textile manufacturer (and the playwright's father). In Wasserstein's *Isn't It Romantic* (1983), Janie Blumberg dates the heir to a restaurant chain specializing in popovers. In Miller's *The Price* (1968), the ancient Gregory Solomon applies his canny wisdom and all his worldly experience to the appraisal of junk. Miller disclaimed any "interest in the selling profession," which marks an historic contrast with Jerry Sterner, who came to dramaturgy not to escape from poverty but as a sideline to be pursued while syndicating partnerships as the president of a real estate firm.

Instead of playing up the conflict between private enterprise and *menshlichkeit*, Sterner's *Other People's Money* is neutral on the subject. Larry the Liquidator is so energetic, purposeful, and clever that New England Wire and Cable (the old-style family manufacturing company he yearns to acquire) looks stagnant and doomed. *Other People's Money* is a novelty item. Sterner invented a recognizable, life-sized Jewish character who uses terms like *bubkes* and *putz*. In addition, the ambitious, greedy, "pushy," and rather unappealing Garfinkle personifies the spirit of innovation that the economist Joseph Schumpeter claimed capitalism requires for its organizational reinvigoration.[25]

In the half-century after Schumpeter advanced such an argument, the faith of many Jews in the opportunities that American "free enterprise" could bestow was validated. Within a couple of generations at most, a gravity-defying ascent to material comfort and security was experienced. The trajectory can be traced from Odets's lower-class Bergers to Miller's lower-middle-class Lomans to Wasserstein's Rosensweig sisters, who range from a banker based in London to an international travel writer to the leader of the Temple Beth-El Sisterhood of Newton, Massachusetts. The problem for the character portrayed by the Group Theatre's Garfinkle in the 1930s was how to make money; the problem for Broadway's Garfinkle in the 1980s was how to make his money make money. Increasingly Jewish characters represented the beneficiaries rather than the victims of capitalism, which had triumphed so decisively by the fall of 1992 that Russian president Boris Yeltsin publicly favored a GOP victory because Bill Clinton might prove to be too much of a "socialist."[26] The international Communist movement that had once elicited the sympathy of Odets and Hellman was also so fully discredited that one of the few remaining American comrades refused to discuss the rampant factionalism in the Party: "We don't want to air our dirty Lenin in public."[27]

But the triumph of American capitalism did not mean that its blessings were fairly distributed. Serious concerns remained about the growing proportion of children born into poverty (roughly one in four), and about the long-term stagnation or decline in real wages for blue-collar workers and in productivity in skill-intensive manufacturing. In a populace with more patent attorneys than inventors, *homo economicus* was typified less by the makers of products than by the makers of deals, the specialists in leveraged buyouts with other people's money. In 1988 the $25 billion RJR-Nabisco deal capped the buccaneering, let's-make-a-deal capitalism of the Reagan years, and included $1 billion in "fees" for these bankers, lawyers, and underwriters. The preeminence of such "paper-entrepreneurs" led Robert B. Reich, later Clinton's secretary of labor, to conclude: "Rarely have so few earned so much for doing so little." Among the chief architects of that deal was Bruce Wasserstein, who happens to be Wendy's brother. (An older sister became a high executive at Citicorp.)[28] A certain familiarity with that world may explain why the playwright's characters, who take for granted the comforts of young urban professionals, come out ahead of the progeny of the Bergers and the Lomans.

Capitalism itself had never been more immune to challenge. But it was less impressive in enforcing the ideal of community than in promoting rampant individualism. Here certain historic Jewish values might have offered a perch from which to observe the stages of capitalism. Hillel's injunction not to be separate from the community could be contrasted with the right of self-determination that has resonated through American history. Miller believed that "the Jew in me shied from private salvation as something close to sin. One's truth must add its push to the evolution of public justice and mercy." That may collide with the drive toward self-fulfillment that Tocqueville discerned as the badge of the democratic citizen. Such impulses were not supposed to be frustrated; and for at least a generation, the children of the middle class generally appear to have lived apart from the pressure of material needs, largely unfettered by interdictory creeds. But social change did not overcome isolation: the feminist heroine of Wasserstein's *The Heidi Chronicles* feels "stranded, and I thought the point was that we wouldn't feel stranded. I thought we were all in this together."[29] Hers is rueful knowledge of solitary confinement.

To be sure, none of these playwrights' voices is explicitly Jewish in expressing disenchantment with a society that has left so many feeling stranded. None writes from an overtly Judaic perspective; none sees his or her work as a form of community service. Yet they seem to be revealing the failure of a meaningful collectivity to cohere. If their exposure of a dehumanizing capitalism is not grounded in Judaism, perhaps that is because neither the dramatists nor their characters have sufficient learning in religious tradition to make such criticisms stick; the absence of an intense Judaic faith nourishing characters who at least have ethnic names testifies to the effects of Americanization. Much of Jewish dramaturgy takes an adversarial stance against the national ethos, and when speaking of it, we really mean business, as Mamet once noted. Without "alternative systems of support . . . [such as] an extended family, of a tradition, a religion," he claimed, money enables "everyone . . . to fix himself on the great chain of being. . . .

It comes out of a very human urge to find out where you stand in relation to your fellows."[30]

Such linguistic neglect of the second sex suggests a further fragmentation of allegiances, beginning especially in the 1960s, as the felicitous ideal of equality extended itself to new forms of inclusion. When the *Times Book Review* identified contributor Wendy Wasserstein as "the author of several plays about women," a protest letter was published that inquired if we "will be seeing any reviews by David Mamet, the author of several plays about men." Though both playwrights have something in common other than talent, such as an interest in the enigma of Jewish identity and a sense of loss at its disintegration, the divisions of gender have required a hospitality to fresh thinking and a sensitivity to the discrimination and diminution that persist. Writers who might once have been confined to ethnic or religious or regional categories sometimes insisted on being better understood as men or women, just as AIDS made the perennial dilemmas of living together and dying alone all the more wrenching.

Running out of impediments to the chances of boy meeting girl and loving girl, the theme of boy-meets-boy has been noteworthy in the works of Jewish playwrights, especially in the shadow of the plague. (The dealmakers' fees for the 1988 RJR-Nabisco buyout was double the amount spent that year in the United States trying to find a cure for AIDS.)[31] Beginning with Harvey Fierstein's *Torch Song Trilogy* (1982), which was staged two years after Patient Zero, suffering from Kaposi's sarcoma, was diagnosed, a short list would include: Larry Kramer's *The Normal Heart* (1985) and *The Destiny of Me* (1992), written by the cofounder of the Gay Men's Health Crisis and the more militant ACT UP, and centered on a dying middle-class Jew named Ned Weeks; Paul Rudnick's comedy *Jeffrey* (1994); William Finn's musical, *Falsettoland* (1992), which entwines AIDS and a bar mitzvah; and above all Tony Kushner's *Angels in America*, which the Eureka Theatre in San Francisco first commissioned in 1987. His epic drama underwent several versions before reaching Broadway in 1993, where it won the Tony for Best Play in two successive years (for *Millennium* and then for *Part 2: Perestroika*). Kushner's central villain is Roy Cohn, who voices the typical postmodern version of identity by refusing to define homosexuals as "men who sleep with other men." Instead they "are men who in fifteen years of trying cannot get a pissant anti-discrimination bill through City Council. Homosexuals are men who know nobody and nobody knows. Who have zero clout." Identity is socially—or politically—constructed.[32]

Unlike the historical Roy Cohn, Rudnick claimed to have been "amazingly lucky" in dealing with his own homosexuality, which "has never been a problem for me. Now being Jewish—that's been a nightmare! My parents took me to doctors who had no idea why it happened." What was culturally, if not genetically, transmitted, he told an interviewer, was an irrepressible comic perspective, plus the confidence that stemmed from the "*bubbela* syndrome," defined as "whatever our baby wants is great." Had he wanted to become a serial killer, Rudnick claimed, his parents would have approved the choice—"as long as you're good at it," or "as long as you get an A."

Final mention should be made of Marilyn Cantor Baker, whose original story, "Sidney Shorr," was transformed into an NBC movie and then the television series *Love, Sidney*. The childless Shorr was played by Tony Randall (himself Jewish), who thus became the first television star to play a gay character. Shorr is portrayed as talented and successful and not, as the writer remarked, "for cutesy laughs as a hairdresser, interior decorator or blind date."[33] Such playwrights have not assigned themselves the responsibility of speaking for the Jewish people (or even necessarily *to* it). And yet a sensitivity to the pain of exclusion, an empathy for others who feel stranded, is the very least that can be conjectured to explain the disproportionate number of Jewish writers who have addressed gay themes.

The historical significance of such works needs to be highlighted in another way. Odets, Hellman, and Miller were like war correspondents in reporting on the life-or-death conflicts that rippled through the nuclear family. Of course, that subject was also put onstage by Eugene O'Neill and Tennessee Williams and William Inge. Such plays have certainly not disappeared. But as the grandfather shrieks in *Awake and Sing!* "Marx said it: abolish such families!";[34] and Jewish dramatists have mostly followed such advice. Even Neil Simon's bittersweet elegies, *Brighton Beach Memoirs* (1983) and *Broadway Bound* (1986), are confined to the childhood that inspired the most successful playwright in American history. The nuclear family has largely disappeared in the dramas of the younger generation of Jewish playwrights, and is absent in the stagecraft of the two most admired and salient among them: Mamet and Wasserstein.

Wasserstein became the laureate of upper-middle-class urban Jews, of those who pursue happiness and prize cleverness, who make wisecracks out of their anxiety and vulnerability and loneliness, and who find purposiveness elusive but cannot make sense of Judaism any more. In the explicitness and plenitude with which she has examined their lives onstage, Wasserstein is by far the most important legatee of the tradition Odets inaugurated.

Unlike the desperate Bergers, however, struggling in the pit of the Great Depression, Wasserstein's Jews do not worry where the next meal is coming from. They try instead to reconcile the ideal of female independence with a yearning for intimacy and maternity. Wasserstein has written far more directly as a woman than as a Jew. Having turned thirteen when

Betty Friedan's *The Feminine Mystique* (1963) specified "the problem with no name," the playwright once admitted: "I can't understand not being a feminist." That, more than Judaism, is the perspective offered in her plays, in which feminism is espoused even by the faux furrier Mervyn Kant. He punctures the cliché that Jews Do Not Drink, that they are shmoozers but not boozers: "I think it's a myth made up by our mothers to persuade innocent women that Jewish men make superior husbands. In other words, it's worth it to put up with my crankiness, my hypochondria, my opinions on world problems, because I don't drink."[35]

Though the social problem that *Isn't It Romantic* addresses is defined with a New York Jewish accent, the twenty-eight-year-old Janie Blumberg is deft at playing back the mixed messages that her mother has communicated to her. Having already achieved emancipation to become both bourgeois and "bohemian," Tasha Blumberg is asked: "Did you teach me to marry a nice Jewish doctor and make chicken for him? You order up breakfast from a Greek coffee shop every morning. Did you teach me to go to law school and wear gray suits at a job that I sort of like every day from nine to eight? You run out of here in leg warmers and tank tops to dancing school." Then Janie adds: "Did you teach me to compromise and lie to the man I live with and say I love you when I wasn't sure? You live with your partner; you walk Dad to work every morning."[36] It is hard to miss the envy for an earlier generation that, at its luckiest, managed to combine intimacy with security, and to blend expanded vocational and "lifestyle" possibilities with a panoply of middle-class comforts.

The special burden of expectation for women to marry is a recurrent theme in Wasserstein's work, and an even heavier burden is placed upon Jewish women to marry within the faith. World Jewry is not even a blip on the demographic screen, and continuity requires philoprogenitiveness and endogamy. These values are not inseparable either from the ideology of feminism or from the pleasures of romantic love. The pressure comes from parents who do not want their own child to be *aharon ha-aharonim* (the last of the last), a terminal Jew, and that anxiety is erratically conveyed, with mixed and uncertain results. Thus Holly Kaplan phones (or pretends to phone) a young Jewish physician in Minneapolis, but fears to establish such a connection even as she seeks it. Thus Janie Blumberg is comically fixed up with a Russian cabdriver. And isn't it romantic that Heidi Holland, who is neither more nor less "Jewish" than Willy Loman, cannot escape from the clutches of Scoop Rosenbaum, even at the raucous Jewish wedding that ratifies his compromising decision to marry someone else. In the climax to *The Heidi Chronicles*, the protagonist has adopted a daughter; she becomes a single mother. Thus Gorgeous Teitelbaum wishes that her sister's loneliness might be cured, and tells Tess Goode, her niece: "I always said to mother, if only Sara would meet a furrier or a dentist." The fifty-four-year-old Sara is permitted to wonder whether her one-night-stand gentleman caller merits a longer commitment. "You're just like all the other men I went to high school with," she tells Merv Kant in *The Sisters Rosensweig* (1992). "You're smart, you're a good provider, you read the *Times* every day, you started running at fifty to recapture your youth, you worry a little too much about your health, you thought about having affairs, but you never actually did it, and now that she's departed, your late wife Roslyn is a saint."[37] Guys like him and Scoop Rosenbaum and perhaps even the unseen and unheard Silverstein have the right vocational credentials to embody success and security. But they also threaten the autonomy and egalitarianism that a feminist vision encourages and that an expanding economy sanctions.

The ideology of the women's movement can collide with the dictates of patriarchal Judaism, though Wasserstein's writing betrays no awareness of such tension. Religious faith and ritual have become a diminished thing in the observably Jewish but unobservant families her satire dissects. Their goal is to be classified among the "good ga davened," whom Holly Kaplan, the lone Jew among the *femmes savantes* at Mount Holyoke, defines as "those who davened or prayed right. Girls who good ga davened did well. They marry doctors and go to Bermuda for Memorial Day weekends. These girls are also doctors but they only work part-time because of their three musically inclined children, and weekly brownstone restorations." It is akin to "a 'did well' list published annually, in New York, Winnetka, and Beverly Hills, and distributed on High Holy Days." Upward mobility and a securely middle-class status have become so central to the ethos of American Jewry that even a far less savvy undergraduate than Holly cannot fail to notice. Six years after graduating, she is unmarried, her life in limbo. To find the right (Jewish) man has become dicey. Jet planes had already made Miami no harder to visit than the Catskills, narrowing the distinctive sites for dating and mating, as Kutsher's came to be considered a last resort.[38]

Reluctant to compromise, Holly may have to remain single. Refusing to compromise, her creator forfeited a chance to bring *Uncommon Women and Others* to Broadway. One producer considered the play "too wistful" and proposed an upbeat ending: "When everyone asks Holly, 'What's new with you?' she should pull out a diamond ring and say, 'Guess what? I'm going to marry Dr. Mark Silverstein.'" The playwright herself thought: "Well, she'd have to have a lobotomy, and I'd have to have a lobotomy too."[39]

The focus of *Isn't It Romantic* is the third of the inalienable rights that Jefferson had enumerated: the pursuit of happiness. Its possible incompatibility with Jewish continuity spins off the major theme of the only one of Wasserstein's first four major plays to feature parents. Janie Blumberg knows she can please them by making them grandparents. But she can't tell them, "Here are your *naches*" (joys). At least not yet. How Simon Blumberg and especially his wife scheme to *kvell* (burst with pride) and seek to ensure bliss for (and through) the children gives their relationship the tone of an adversary proceeding. Tasha Blumberg serenades Janie with a prenuptial "Sunrise, Sunset" (from *Fiddler on the Roof*). Antisemitism has not been entirely eliminated from their world. When the uncommon women play conjugal games with one another, Samantha Stewart realizes that she can't "marry" Holly because back home "there would be a problem at the club."

But secularism has narrowed the gap between Jew and Gentile, who occupy the common ground of cultural pluralism and status-seeking. Contemporary mores even encourage a certain philo-Semitism, as when Janie's friend Harriet (Hattie) Cornwall studies the *Oxford Companion to Jewish Life* and her mother Lillian tells Tasha that both of them "deserve a little nachos [*sic*]." Intermarriage has ceased to be a fear and has become a fact. (Guess who's coming to the *seder*.) The Blumbergs' son Ben has married a Nebraskan named Chris (whom the parents call "Christ"), and Cynthia Peterson, who is only a voice (Meryl Streep's in the Broadway production) on Janie's answering machine, wonders—intertextually—whether she "should have married Mark Silverstein in college." Religion is no barrier to friendship or romance.

One of Janie's options is Dr. (again!) Marty Sterling, *né* Murray Schlimovitz, a kidney specialist with a love of Jewish cuisine. His restaurateur father has prospered, but risks losing his status as "Toastmaster General for the United Jewish Appeal" because his television commercials promote free shrimp at the salad bar. Though such lapses make the Jewish community a tempting target for satire, the playwright does not mock the comfort that Marty himself derives from *ahavat yisrael*, from solidarity with the Jewish people. "I worked on a kibbutz the second time I dropped out of medical school," he tells Janie. "Israel's very important to me. In fact, I have to decide next month if I want to open my practice here in New York or in Tel Aviv." He worries about assimilation (of which the most striking indices are "intermarriage, Ivy League colleges, the *New York Review of Books*"). Stability and continuity are the watchwords of his faith.

But does Janie want what Marty offers? Does she *love* him? He is nice enough to be appealing. But his very attractiveness also seems to foreclose the future, to block her freedom of choice. As with some of the uncommon graduating seniors, Janie sees tracking as a threat to be avoided, a conventionally bourgeois life as something to be dreaded. "He's decided to open his practice here next month," she tells Hattie, "and he's invited me to his parents' house for Chanukah." He upholds traditional ways, preferring to live in the parts of Brooklyn "where people have real values." The attenuation of *l'dor vador* (from generation to generation) seems to be reversed: "My father thought my brother was crazy when he named his son Shlomo." Janie still resists facing a destiny that is signed, sealed, and delivered, that entails too many expectations to fulfill; using a joke to escape a yoke, she phones her mother: "This morning I got married, lost twenty pounds, and became a lawyer."

Yet Wasserstein plays fair by allowing Marty the dignity of decent ambitions. He too wants "a home, a family, something my father had so easily and I can't seem to get started on." He has also "wanted something special [as well]. Just a little. Maybe not as special as you turned out to be, but just a little. Janie, I don't want to marry anyone like my sister-in-law." Though Janie can imagine a wedding at the Plaza Hotel, where "baby Shlomo could carry the ring in one of my father's gold-seal envelopes," it wouldn't be right. As for her own "settling down," she raises no principled objections, "but it just isn't mine right now."[40]

A sympathetic and sprightly romantic comedy about young people just starting out in Manhattan, mixed up with the daughter's mother very much on the scene and a possibly amorous foreigner, sounds a little like *Barefoot in the Park* (1963). *Isn't It Romantic* is indeed indebted to Neil Simon, whose protagonist attorney announces that he had won his first case, though the court awarded his client only six cents. Paul Bratter adds that his law firm would henceforth give him "all the cases that come in for a dime or under"—a punchline akin to Janie's pride in getting to write the letter *B* on *Sesame Street*: "If they like this, they'll hire me full-time. In charge of consonants." In such plays rising dramatic tension tends to get deflated into the dénouement of self-deprecating humor, as a local anesthetic, as Wasserstein is the first to acknowledge: "The real reason for comedy is to hide the pain. It is a way to cope with it." The perky wit, if not chastened wisdom, of her typical protagonist "gives her the ability to distance herself from situations,"[41] which are the vortices that the tragic hero cannot avoid (nor, for that matter, can broken and dispiriting figures like the Bergers, the Hubbards, and the Lomans).

The Heidi Chronicles does mark a more serious turn, though Wasserstein's flair for snap-crackle-and-pop dialogue and satiric observation were still very much on display. The quarter of a century that the play spans ends in desolation, with the loss of friends, the stretching of bonds to the breaking point, and the plague of AIDS raging outside. Above all the play is a chronicle of abandonment. Sisterhood is powerful—but not enough to resist infection by the culture of narcissism. Heidi Holland is at least vaguely aware that no meaningful substitute has been found for the cohesiveness of earlier generations of families. Until she adopts the infant Judy, her isolation may reflect the almost one-quarter of the nation's households that by the last decade of the century consisted of one person (up from only 8 percent in 1940).[42] Though nuclear families remained standard and got reconstituted, they frequently divided too, and other loyalties were articulated. The first edition of Friedan's classic was dedicated to her husband "and to our children—Daniel, Jonathan, and Emily." After a divorce, a new 1974 edition of *The Feminine Mystique* was instead dedicated to "all the new women, and the new men."

Even if men could change sufficiently (and by 1986 even Superman was becoming "more vulnerable" and "more open about his feelings," according to a vice president of DC Comics), a gendered community like the company of women envisioned in Charlotte Perkins Gilman's 1915 *Herland* is an unrealized utopia as well. Nor does Heidi have the option of re-creating the "loveless intimacy" of the Brownsville neighborhood that, in 1951, Alfred Kazin could at least summon from his memory: "We had always to be together: believers and non-believers, we were a people; I was of that people. . . . We had all of us lived together so long that we would not have known how to separate even if we had wanted to. The most terrible word was *aleyn*, alone."[43] He could still recall the ethics of the fathers, still savor the cooking of the mothers. But "Brunzvil" had its obvious limitations, and only one of them was a diminution of women.

The challenges and mysteries of Jewishness are central to *The Sisters Rosensweig*. An identity crisis can be tiring: "You really don't understand what it is to have absolutely no idea who you are!" the bisexual Geoffrey Duncan tells Pfeni Rosensweig.[44] But as a theme in American Jewish drama, identity was not yet tiresome. Indeed, it had almost never been faced, from Mordecai Manuel Noah through Elmer Rice and Sidney Kingsley and well into the 1980s. But Wasserstein makes the faulty transmission of *Yiddishkeit* central, while hugging the shore of gender that she found most congenial. The five uncommon women have been reduced to three and have become middle-aged as well. Two of them are single, but all are Jewish.

By making them sisters, the playwright has injected Chekhov into the Jewish family constellation. Perhaps as directly from him as from any other source, Wasserstein learned to combine detachment with sympathy, objectification with wry feeling. The distinction between the cosmic and the comic is, after all, a matter of spacing (and, at least onstage, of pacing). In *The Sisters Rosensweig* the author's nimble humor is intact; her particular version of Moscow does not believe in tears.

One would even be tempted to announce that in this play Chekhov meets Neil Simon, except that they had already been formally introduced: Simon had already paid homage on Broadway to the Russian master in *The Good Doctor* (1973), and Chekhov was no slouch in extracting mellow laughter from the stupendous folly of human behavior. (If his plays are laden with a reputation of unsparing gloom, the performances and the translations may be accountable.) The three American Jewish sisters may not pine away nor suffer so unbearably from ennui. Indeed, from Newton to Nepal, their lives vibrate with excitement. But the sisters are not exactly fulfilled either, and feelings of disappointment and frustration are among the promises that the structure of human existence never fails to keep. Disenchantment and misplaced dreams are also familiar to the sisters Rosensweig.

They are, in the playwright's categorization, "a practicing Jew, a wandering Jew, and a self-loathing Jew." They are also a gloss on the poet Randall Jarrell's line: "The ways we miss our lives are life." In the closing scene of the play, Tess Goode, who is seventeen, asks Sara: "Mother, if I've never really been Jewish, and I'm not actually American anymore, and I'm not English or European, then who am I?" It is a question that goes beyond the special status of the expatriate adolescent, that taps into the peculiar history of the Jew: the extraterritorial, "the wandering Jew" (as Pfeni calls herself). American identity can be protean.

But Jewish identity itself is too impalpable and too demanding to be easily transmitted; and the institutions that have been built to foster and sustain it *The Sisters Rosensweig* treats ambivalently, as objects of respect as well as of satire. On behalf of the American Jewish Congress, for example, Merv Kant has been monitoring Eastern European antisemitism; and his commitments are taken seriously, or at least not undercut by any of the other characters. But what to make of Gorgeous Teitelbaum? Endowed with the silliest given name, she matches a stereotype so completely that even Merv falls for it: "So you're the sister who did everything right. You married the attorney, you had the children, you moved to the suburbs."[45] Yet she is not to be scorned: members of synagogues like Beth El—and their Sisterhoods—have kept Judaism alive for yet another generation.

That responsibility is hardly shared by thoroughly modern Sara, who wonders: Why light Sabbath candles after electricity has been harnessed? Disdaining the Fourth Commandment ("Remember the Sabbath Day to keep it holy"), she orders Pfeni to "blow out the god-damned candles" that Gorgeous has lit and sanctified with the Hebrew blessing. Yet Sara offers no substitute, no alternative signal to convey to her own daughter the sublimity of Judaism. The international banker whose birthday has drawn the sisters from America and from Asia is deracinated. In London she herself may have rubbed against some genteel bigotry, embodied in Nicholas Pym. Jews in Britain, as the South African writer Dan Jacobson once put it, felt as though a room in the house had been given to them, but they were treated like boarders rather than members of the family. Sara is even more adrift and alienated. Despite two appearances on the cover of *Fortune*, "I'm a cold, bitter woman who's turned her back on her family, her religion, and her country! And I held so much in. . . . Isn't that the way the old assimilated story goes?"[46] The play offers no clues, however, to account for the psychic sources of such utter self-denial. Her sensibility is hardly exceptional. Yet for well over a generation, American society was being pulled in other directions, whether in exalting ethnic diversity and the rediscovery of "roots," or in continuing to harbor the most pious Christians in the industrialized world.

Sara has propelled herself furiously away from the parochialism of the Jews and the rituals of their faith. Twice divorced and homeless, she cannot return home. Her ties to her people are very tenuous. But they are not completely forfeited. Significantly, they reach only backward into the past, as when Sara and Merv discover common ground: the spa resort named Ciechocinek, "the Palm Beach of Poland." There she had gone to provide financial expertise; there his own grandparents had vacationed. And now, "fifty years after the lucky few had escaped with false passports, Esther Malchah's granddaughter Sara was deciding how to put bread on the tables of those who had so blithely driven them all away." (To such a resort town come the doomed, assimilated Middle European Jews in Aharon Appelfeld's 1980 allegory, *Badenheim 1939.*) Sandra Meyer, to whom the play is dedicated, told an interviewer: "That Polish resort town in *The Sisters Rosensweig* is really where my grandparents had their villa, with tennis courts and their own pastry chef." Lola Wasserstein's father—and Wendy's grandfather—had escaped from Poland; while living in Paterson, New Jersey, Simon Schleifer wrote some Yiddish plays. But it would be idle to speculate that the sisters Rosensweig represent the playwright herself in triplicate, or that she has created a surrogate in Pfeni, the youngest of the three sisters, and the only writer among them. The peripatetic Pfeni is an invention.[47]

With her charming Gentile companion, she is also unaffiliated with institutions that might keep her (or indeed her generation) from being terminal Jews. When Geoffrey, flushed with excitement, imagines their future kids as so dynamic "they'll be running Metro-Goldwyn-Mayer before age seven," Pfeni asks: "But will they be Jewish children?" Geoffrey rebuts with an eccentric case for remaining within the fold: "They'll have to be if they're going to run MGM." Forty-year-old Pfeni's biological clock is ticking away, but the British theater director is probably not going to succeed as a "closet heterosexual." Pfeni is an advocacy journalist, endowed with a passion for social justice, a champion of the rights of women in Tajikistan. Yet she realizes that such concerns may preempt other forms of self-expression: "Somewhere I need the hardship of the Afghan women and the Kurdish suffering to fill up my life for me." Pfeni has a capacity to empathize with other groups (but not with her fellow Jews).

Compared to Sara and Pfeni, the defense can therefore make out a pretty good case for Gorgeous. Not an airtight case: she is flaky, garrulous, materialistic. Nor are her ambitions noble: *The Dr. Gorgeous Show* might expand from a radio call-in into a cable TV talk show ("talking has always come easily to me"). Challenged to reveal the provenance of that professional prefix of "Dr.," she replies with another question: "You've heard of Dr. Pepper?" Gorgeous does invite ridicule, but she gets briefly beneath her shallowness when she—rather implausibly—voices the Chekhovian hope "that each of us can say at some point that we had a moment of pure, unadulterated happiness! Do you think that's possible, Sara?" More than an ethnic caricature, less than a full-scale figure of pathos, Gorgeous also gets to deliver one of the play's few searing lines: "How did our nice Jewish mother do such a lousy job on us?"[48] No one has an answer or a comeback, yet it is not obvious that their mother *did* muck up their lives. The charge rings false. And to whom, in any case, should Rita Rosensweig be compared? To Tennessee Williams's Amanda Wingfield, or to Eugene O'Neill's Mary Tyrone, or for that matter to Mother Courage? And why should Maury Rosensweig, described as a manufacturer of "Kiddie Togs," get off the hook?

Stumbling through their disillusionment, Wasserstein's women try to make do nearly a century after Zangwill had envisioned an "America where God wipes away all tears." The integrationist ideal he promoted was subjected to more withering criticism at the end of the century than nativists had mustered earlier. They had tried to block the process of amalgamation. Though the English playwright had foreseen the new American as the product of multicultural fusion (a "superman" would be forged in the intense heat of the melting-pot), the nativists doubted that any crucible could produce temperatures high enough to be effective against their bogus concept of race. In professing to speak for Nordic Americans after World War I, the Imperial Wizard of the Ku Klux Klan asserted that "the melting pot was a ghastly failure." Hiram W. Evans added that "the very name was coined by a member of one of the races—the Jews—which most determinedly refuses to melt."

Seven decades later, doubts about the faith that had animated *The Melting-Pot* tended to come from *anti*racists and *anti*nativists, who made the cultivation of diversity integral to egalitarianism. Champions of multiculturalism thus breathed new life into the issues that the British playwright had raised. In 1996, playwright Ari Roth even revised and restaged this "wildly melodramatic" work at the University of Michigan. "How might the characters of Zangwill's turn-of-the-century scenario fare in our more stridently tribal times?" he asked Ann Arbor students. How could *The Melting-Pot* be revived "by recontextualizing the debate within a contemporary frame"?[49]

An indirect answer came from the versatile Elizabeth Swados, whose play *The Hating Pot* (1997) cast mostly adolescents who explored their diverse ethnic and racial differences through musical encounters. (The video version was subsidized by Spielberg's Righteous Persons Foundation and by the Covenant Foundation.) At the end of *The Hating Pot*, the cast of Jews and Gentiles—including blacks, Hispanics, and Germans—sing that "everyone's the same."

Such a cliché is misleading at best, false at worst. It leaves conflict unexplained and, if taken literally, would not even distinguish between bigots and their targets. Nor does such a claim take the ethos of multiculturalism seriously. "Everyone's the same" ignores the genuine divergences that emerge from the wide range of cultural practices, from the integrity of religious and national traditions, and from the psychic divisions due to gender. And to *want* everyone to be the same is to honor the ideal of equality without respecting the right to be different. Striking the proper balance is not easy to achieve; hence the rather appealing ambivalence of Zangwill himself. As a Zionist he was uncertain about how badly he wanted his own people to melt; as a racialist he doubted how much the Jews *could* melt. His melodrama was staged when they were only one among the many uprooted peoples arriving from Europe. *The Hating Pot* was conceived when Swados's fellow Jews were continuing to experience a singular condition: remaining conscious of being a minority, they were separated by class and cultural values from many of the "peoples of color" whose roots could be traced to Latin America, to Asia, to Africa. Still differentiated from the majority of Americans, Jews in the United States lacked a history of searing injustice comparable to the suffering of blacks or Indians in particular; thus they escaped the notice of multiculturalism.[50]

In Europe no minority was more conspicuous or had been treated more unjustly than the Jews. In the United States their counterparts were blacks, whose systematic exclusion from the enjoyment of basic rights and opportunities affected American Jews more deeply than any other group. The presence of blacks in the New World—but not the Old World—also made American Jewish culture distinctive, and merits a separate chapter.

RACE

IN RECALLING THE ORIGINS OF *Les Nègres* (1958), JEAN GENET MENtioned that "one evening an actor asked me to write a play for an all-black cast. But what exactly is a black? First of all, what's his color?"[1] The playwright was not just being perverse, as was his wont. Those trick questions suggest that so seemingly observable a trace as race is not a biological fixity. Race can be pliable. Its power in America can be ascribed as much to Uncle Sam as to Mother Nature.

Such a shift in the meaning of race struck me in 1966, when teaching on a New Orleans campus. I was among the first whites permitted to teach in an institution that before 1965 had been all black. The undergraduates I was teaching had all grown up under Jim Crow; one morning, while I was crossing the parking lot, one of them yelled out at me: "Hey, man, you go to Saint Aug?" At first I was taken aback; Saint Augustine was the city's Roman Catholic parochial school for Negroes. Seeing my green eyes and brown hair and pale skin, were my interlocutor and his friends just having some fun at Whitey's expense? Only later did it occur to me that, despite the evidence of the senses, I *had* to be black: at Southern University in New Orleans, who *wasn't*?

My hunch was confirmed later that year when undergraduates staged Lorraine Hansberry's drama, *A Raisin in the Sun* (1959), which has only one white character, a devious realtor who blocks the Youngers' search for a home in a new neighborhood. To recruit me for the cast was necessary, given a thin applicant pool. While we were rehearsing, the chairman of the chemistry department came over and, dropping the impeccable English he had previously used when chatting with me, exclaimed: "Hey, Whitfield, I didn't know you was blood!" Sheepishly I replied that I was not. A lesson was nevertheless learned that would mark the understanding of race: it is *only* "race," however decisive in affecting lives, however necessary in modifying generalizations about Americans. In an indirect fashion, such incidents may have spurred a book which addresses a question analogous to Genet's: What exactly is a Jew? First of all, what's his or her religion?

Though racial anxieties have long run deep in America, the cultural impact of blacks cannot be measured by the terrible social barriers erected against them. Those whose ancestors had been brought in chains from Africa would make American civilization different. According to the Swiss psychiatrist Carl Gustav Jung, who visited America before the First World War, whites seemed to be walking, talking, and laughing like Negroes. He believed the blacks—despite their subjugation—to be "really in control," and was inspired to define the American as "a European with Negro manners" (and an Indian soul). By then "the vanishing American" was inconspicuous. But six decades later black modes of expression had become so ascendant that, "so far as their culture is concerned," historian C. Vann Woodward remarked, "all Americans are part Negro."[2]

Such powers of resilience were amazing, especially since the acknowledgment of what a degraded, segregated minority had done was begrudged and unappreciated for so long. The enthusiasm of the versatile James Weldon Johnson is therefore pardonable when he declared in 1917 that the "only things artistic in America that have sprung from American soil, permeated American life" that could be recognized "as distinctively American," were "the creations of the American Negro." Alluding to folklore, dance, and sacred and secular music, he later made an exception of the skyscraper, and added that the blacks' "lighter music" was becoming even more important than the sublimity of the spirituals, which the philosopher Alain Locke identified in 1925 as "America's folk song."[3]

In 1939 came scholarly amplification with the submission of a Harvard bachelor's thesis on "The Absorption of Race Elements into American Music." Its argument could not have been more forceful: "The jazz influence is common to *all* Americans," so that, because of "the incredible popularity of this art, Negro music has finally shown itself to be the really universal basis of American composition." The author made sure that no reader could mistake his drift. However discernible the influences of Latin America, of French New Orleans, and of hymns originating among white Protestants in Tennessee, "the greatest single influence upon American music as a whole has been that of the Negroes." The Harvard senior's claim was not contested, and honors were awarded, despite the qualms of musicologist Hugo Leichtentritt, who "thoroughly disapprove[d] of Mr. Bernstein's arrogant attitude and of the air of superiority assumed by him" (which may also account for the C he received in one music course).[4]

In generalizing that "Negro music" had become "the most powerful . . . influence upon American music," Bernstein confirmed the injunction that Anton Dvořák had issued at the end of the nineteenth century: Negro melodies constituted "the folk songs of America" to which its composers "must turn." So fully was that advice followed that in 1914 Zangwill marveled at the "spiritual miscegenation" by which "the ex-African has given 'rag-time' and the sex-dances that go with it, first to white America and thence to the whole white world." Had the protagonist of *The Melting-Pot*, yearning to compose his own "American Symphony," followed Dvořák's advice, David Quixano would have resembled his own coreligionists, who were trying to create and sing music like Negroes. In the Old World the violin was almost as Jewish an instrument as the *shofar*. In the New World a "Yiddle on Your Fiddle" was expected to "play some ragtime," as Irving Berlin wrote in his 1909 song about a Jewish wedding, in which the violinist uses syncopation and is addressed by one guest, Sadie, as "mine choc'late baby."[5]

The black presence made the culture of the Jews different from anywhere else in Exile. Because Jews so sensitively registered such influence, however, they energized American culture and helped make it mulatto. Music offers the strongest and most convincing evidence, though that art alone need not be cited. The importance of what Jews made of black cultural resourcefulness is what this chapter is intended to demonstrate.

A poet and a Tin Pan Alley songwriter, James Weldon Johnson was himself a key figure in accentuating black influences upon the nation's arts. But he was no racial chauvinist. He conceded that "this lighter music has been fused and then developed, chiefly by Jewish musicians, until it has become our national medium for expressing ourselves musically in popular form; and it bids fair to become a basic element in the future great American music" (which was getting widely accepted overseas as well).[6] Johnson appreciated what some students of Diaspora Jewry were more broadly claiming: that its mimetic powers were the attributes of a modal personality. Arthur Ruppin, a pioneering sociologist of the Jews, agreed that theirs was a special gift for empathy, for intersubjective adeptness. In hailing Dada as "the chameleon of rapid and interested change," the Rumanian poet Tristan Tzara spoke from experience. He himself was a chameleon, having been born Sami Rosenstock. Woody Allen's Jazz Age character known as "The Chameleon Man" turns himself black as he sings with the Negro staff in the servants' quarters. Leonard Zelig thus personifies the "mongrel Manhattan" that historian Ann Douglas has made the capital of the 1920s.

Snugly adapting to the host society has a long history. The Hebrew poets of medieval Spain used Arabic syllabic meters; and the celebrated Yehuda haLevi, historian Raphael Patai has claimed, "could easily duplicate the structure, rhythm, and rhyme scheme of any of the Arabic song hits of the day." (The day was the early twelfth century.) In Renaissance Italy poets like Immanuel of Rome, Moses Rieti, and Abraham Yaghel Gallici used Dante as their model.[7] In America Jewish entertainers imitated blacks.

The adaptive as well as creative powers of Jews would fuse black music in particular into something distinctively American by the turn of the century. What drew the newcomers and their progeny, paradoxically and mysteriously, into the vortex of American culture was association and identification with a minority that was far more marginalized—but also more manifestly familiar with American life and also more numerous. (In 1940 there were three blacks for every Jew, in 1970 more than four for every Jew.) To give black song and humor a Jewish inflection was often a gesture of Americanization.

This is of course a story of cultural transmission from which evidence of condescension and exploitation cannot be excised, and from which other whites cannot be excluded either. Consider a very short list. Neither the composer Stephen Foster nor the minstrel star Dan Emmett, who put nineteenth-century black musical styles in circulation, were qualified to be counted in a *minyan*. The most famous of all abolitionist novels featured a gallery of memorable black characters; and though one New York stage version of *Uncle Tom's Cabin* was mounted in Yiddish,[8] its literary source was written by a Calvinist. (Stowe maintained that her novel had actually been written by God—with Whom, incidentally, royalties were not shared.) After the Great War neither plays like O'Neill's *The Emperor Jones* (1920), nor novels like DuBose Heyward's *Porgy* (1925) and Sherwood Anderson's *Dark Laughter* (1925) emerged from the Jewish community. Even as the Iowa-born Carl Van Vechten was making himself the leading white sponsor of the Harlem Renaissance, Paul Whiteman had become the "King of Jazz" (though his coronation, it can be safely surmised, was not held in Harlem). Freeman Gosden and Charles Correll were the leads on *Amos 'n' Andy*, which ran on the radio for nearly four decades. The most controversial of neo-abolitionist novels was *The Confessions of Nat Turner*, which Styron told in the first person. A Jack Kerouac narrator admits to "wishing I were a Negro, feeling that the best the white world had offered was not enough ecstasy for me, not enough life, joy, kicks, darkness, music, not enough night." Though Keourac's own Italian-American alter ego found himself "wishing I could exchange worlds with the happy, true-hearted, ecstatic Negroes of America,"[9] the author's own parents were French-Canadian immigrants. This inventory is hardly exhaustive.

Jews have nevertheless felt most intensely the magnetic pull of black culture. They have been more likely than other whites to shiver with the sentiment Langston Hughes conveyed of "night coming tenderly / Black like me."[10] If identity is indeed constructed and contingent, then the Jewish artist and intellectual could, more easily than anyone else, empathize with the Other who is black. Because culture cannot be reduced to race (which, after all, is only "race"), then those who repeat annually at their *seder*, "this year we are slaves, next year we shall be free," readily assigned themselves the task of arranging the "part-Negro" components of the national style. No other phenotypically Caucasian minority was so willing to construct out of its own historic rejection and humiliation a bridge to the African-American experience.

With his aptitude for the odd half-truth, Lenny Bruce once put it differently. Rather than observing that feelings of stigmatization predisposed Jews to become fractionally black, he averred instead that "Negroes are all Jews." He did not acknowledge that the terms are not mutually exclusive. *Some* Negroes *are* Jews, like the most famous Jew-by-choice, Sammy Davis Jr., or like the writer Julius Lester, whose *Lovesong* (1988) is among the great American Jewish autobiographies, an unusual invitation to accompany its author through the labyrinth of genuine and mysterious faith. Though the Antigua-born novelist Jamaica Kincaid has served as the president of her synagogue in Bennington, Vermont, her work remains to be included in the canon of American Jewish literary studies. Some Negroes have also *married* Jews; such intimate links are as ancient as Solomon, the king who was most legendary for his wisdom, and who was wed to the queen of Sheba. Among black writers and artists married to Jews were Richard Wright (twice), Lorraine Hansberry, Alice Walker, John Edgar Wideman, Harry Belafonte, and Diana Ross. The first wife of the writer LeRoi Jones, who became a black nationalist named Imamu Amiri Baraka, was Hettie Cohen, whose 1990 autobiography records the allure of black life, beginning with the aura of jazz and terminating in the belief that the white suburbs blinded its residents to reality.[11] But the claims of cultural proximity are even stronger, so that the obverse of Bruce's remark can also be noted and modified. Not all Jews are white (or married to whites). Some Jews are Negroes.

Milton (Mezz) Mezzrow, a clarinetist and saxophonist, at least thought of himself as a Negro, and thus reversed the journey that James Weldon Johnson's anonymous narrator takes in *The Autobiography of an Ex-Coloured Man* (1912). After moving from Chicago to New York in 1929, Mezzrow married a black woman and, when sentenced to Riker's Island for selling marijuana, asked to be assigned with the black prisoners. "I became a Negro," he reported in his 1946 autobiography. After all, he added, inner-city folk were "my kind of people." Even his draft card identified "Mezz" as Negro. "He felt he had scrubbed himself clean, inside and out, of every last trace of his origins in the Jewish slums of Chicago," his collaborator, Bernard Wolfe, surmised. Mezzrow "pulped himself back to raw human material, deposited that nameless jelly in the pure Negro mold, and pressed himself into the opposite of his birthright, a pure black."[12] No one personified more relentlessly the notion of race as social construction.

Mezzrow did not consider himself to be merely a "white Negro." That phrase Norman Mailer gave currency in describing—and advocating—a less complete but still audacious brand of empathy. Mailer's bar mitzvah speech had recorded a desire to emulate "great Jews like Moses Maimonides and Karl Marx." The novelist's career didn't quite work out that way, and he generally advertised himself to his readers as a non-Jewish Jew. But he also fit into a certain groove to which his own ethnic group was prone, plunging himself imaginatively into a demi-monde that challenged the conventions of genteel society. In his 1957 essay in the social-democratic *Dissent*, Mailer internalized the role of the "hipster," whose riskiness and aggressiveness could be endorsed as a morally admirable stance in a world haunted by the memory and the threat of mass extinction. The ghetto black "could rarely afford the sophisticated inhibitions of civilization, and so he kept for his survival the art of the primitive."

In romanticizing the irrationality of violence as a manifestation of genuine and unmediated feeling, as an acceptable response to the prospect of a bureaucratized and administered death, Mailer legitimated the sociopathic extremities of black experience. This justification for black criminality distanced its author so fiercely from the historic Diasporic yearning for civil restraint and legal regularity that the coeditor of *Dissent*, Irving Howe, regretted the decision to publish intact an essay that considered the ethics of "beat[ing] in the brains" of a storekeeper. (Howe's own father had been a Bronx grocer.) One sign of how far Mailer had crossed the racial boundary in identifying with the outlaws was revealed from Folsom Prison in California, where a rapist named Eldridge Cleaver wrote in praise of "The White Negro" as a "prophetic and penetrating" essay, "one of the few gravely important expressions of our time."[13]

A phrase like "white Negro" was a way of blurring the lines that were once legally (and often violently) enforced, a way of undermining the rigidity once believed to be a genetic justification. Racism dictated an either/or. Yet the relationship of two novelists in the 1920s constituted a tantalizing challenge to the dichotomy prescribed by law, ideology, and custom. Waldo Frank and Jean Toomer were *Doppelgänger* who cast shadows on the antinomies of dark and light, especially in 1922, when they visited the South to soak up for modernist purposes the local atmosphere of black life. The Jewish novelist was saturnine enough for blacks to accept him as one of their own, as a "professor from the North." They asked about his vocation and his church, but "never: Are you a Negro?" Toomer later passed for white; in becoming an ex-coloured man, he invited the question of what *is* a black (and what's his color). Their sojourn, mostly in Spartanburg, South Carolina, helped inspire novels that the two friends initially hoped would be published on the same day in 1923.

Holiday was Frank's vivid protest against the stereotypes of "primitivism" and against the mob violence from which blacks suffered in the region. *Cane* became an enduring literary monument of the Harlem Renaissance, even though Toomer had never lived in Harlem and as early as 1925 refused to allow his part-black ancestry to determine his identity. "I do not expect to be told what I should consider myself to be," he told their mutual publisher, an imaginative and reckless Jew named Horace Liveright, whose firm pioneered in the promotion of the Harlem Renaissance. Frank wrote the foreword to Toomer's *Cane*; Toomer reviewed Frank's *Holiday*. Can the *Survey* reviewer be blamed for suspecting that both were written by the same novelist? In the following year Frank's wife left him for Toomer, shattering a bond that had seemed to erase the color line.[14]

"Melanctha" (1909) was a pioneering act of crypto-blackness that is justly admired. Gertrude Stein had put herself inside a black woman's skin; and Richard Wright was so taken with this section of *Three Lives* that he applied a simple democratic test, reading passages aloud to uneducated black stockyard workers in Chicago. Their animated responses—howling, stomping, laughing—suggested how smoothly literary art could cross the color line. Wright called Stein's first-person narrative "the first long serious literary treatment of Negro life in the United States," and recorded its effect upon him: "As I read it my ears were opened for the first time to the magic of the spoken word. I began to hear the speech of my grandmother, who spoke a deep, pure Negro dialect." The "struggling words" that Melanctha utters "made the speech of the people around me vivid." Johnson also praised "Melanctha" as "marvelous," because it treated blacks as "normal members of the human family."[15]

Perhaps Stein showed such a gift for ventriloquism precisely because her Jewish consciousness was very limited or absent. Perhaps the triumph of "Melanctha" was sui generis; Stein was, after all, a genius. Indeed, along with Whitehead and Picasso, she was one of the only three geniuses whom Alice B. Toklas ever met, according to her *Autobiography*, written of course by Stein, the chameleon woman. Her interest in black life was not fleeting. She wrote the libretto for the opera *Four Saints in Three Acts* (1934), which used an all-black cast of singers, and was capable, like Lenny Bruce, of inspired half-truths, as when she "concluded that negroes were not suffering from persecution, they were suffering from nothingness." Three decades later, Martin Luther King Jr., told a group of white clergymen from his jail cell that their pleas for patience were unwarranted "when you are forever fighting a degenerating sense of 'nobodiness.'"[16]

The suspension between being and nothingness is a constant in the work of Kafka. He never visited America, but managed to suggest that it has differed from the Old World because of "the shadow of the Ethiopian" (the phrase is the Southern writer George Washington Cable's). Characteristically unfinished, Kafka's *Amerika* is a fantasy of living alone and unafraid in an incomplete country, where Karl Rossman renews himself so completely that "the first days in America might be likened to a rebirth." To land a job at the (Nature) Theater of Oklahoma, the sixteen-year-old protagonist has to surrender his name and provide another. Without reflection, Rossman calls himself by an earlier nickname, "Negro."

Other Jewish novelists meditated more fully on the meaning of that identity. A tale of a white man who turns black, *The Very Dark Trees*, was accepted by a publisher in San Francisco. How good was this first novel, by an author in his mid-twenties? No one will ever know, as Saul Bellow destroyed the manuscript. Perhaps his protagonist could be described in two senses as The Man Who Disappeared—which was Kafka's provisional title for *Amerika*.[17]

Let two events, occurring in New York City in 1932, suggest the powers of artistic empathy that talented Jews could demonstrate. When Annie Nathan Meyer's play, *Black Souls*, was produced, the ubiquitous Johnson hailed her work as "one of the most powerful and penetrating plays yet written on the race question." Her onetime protégée, Zora Neale Hurston, went further in praising the sensitivity of Emma Lazarus's first cousin. "No one in America has a better grasp" of interracial issues than Meyer, Hurston stated, and added: "Never before have I read anything by a white person dealing with 'inside' colored life that did not have a sprinkling of false notes."[18] That year Gilbert Seldes attended a party enlivened by Paul Robeson's singing. Asked about "Ol' Man River," Robeson reportedly told Seldes: "Musically it is a complete miracle, the creation of a tone of the Negro spiritual by an alien to the Negro's traditions." Robeson could prove such a claim by "sing[ing] it between two spirituals, and it is not a false note. There is no change in the emotional response of the audience."[19]

He himself enjoyed a special status among Jews, as his prodigious and multifarious gifts vindicated the faith that accidents of birth bore no relation to the aristocracy of talent. That he was Red as well as black did not hurt his popularity among so leftward an ethnic group either. No wonder then that, in 1930, the social-democratic *Forverts* paid special tribute to Robeson, who personified "the cry of an oppressed people . . . the cry of an insulted and driven race. The cry of pain of a race through the mouth of an artist, through the musical lines of a performer. The cry was directed to the world, the appeal was made to all of mankind, but the first country that must listen should be—America."[20]

Robeson repaid this gesture of solidarity nearly two decades later, but in Moscow, in the very country where the tsarist Black Hundreds had assaulted Jews so violently that "lynch law" was introduced into the Russian language (*zakon lyncha*). Visiting the Soviet Union after the Second World War, he could not help sensing the noose tightening around Yiddish culture: the actor-director Solomon Mikhoels was murdered in 1948, and in Robeson's hotel room the writer Itzik Feffer drew a finger across his throat to signify his own imminent fate as well. When the singer performed his final concert, in early June 1949, he stayed in character by mentioning nothing about how Stalinism (which had made him a pariah at home) was extinguishing Yiddish culture. In such an atmosphere, however, he knew the political implications of Jewish music; his single encore, he explained, was an expression of faith in the cultural relations between American and Soviet Jewry. After referring to his own friendship with Mikhoels and Feffer, Robeson translated into Russian the lyrics of the Jewish partisans' "Zog Nit Kaynmal," which he then sang in Yiddish:

> Never say that you have reached the very end,
> When leaden skies a bitter future may portend,
> For sure the hour for which we yearn will yet arrive,
> And our marching steps will thunder: we survive!

The effect was electrifying, as Muscovites broke down, sobbed, and rushed the stage to touch and to hail "Pavel Vasilyevich."[21]

No art was more congenial than music in conveying the hunger for the justice that eluded too many Jews and blacks, and such yearning proved especially suitable for the blues. A New York songwriter named Lewis Allan, for example, was so wrenched by a photograph of a Southern lynching that he wrote a poem, which he then set to music. A friend named Barney Josephson owned a nightclub and persuaded one of his performers, Billie Holiday, to introduce the song at his Café Society. As "Strange Fruit," it became one of her standards, though its theme was so painful that singing it made her sick. So central was "Strange Fruit" to her repertoire that her ghosted autobiography brags that she helped write the song as well.

That boast was false. Allan did, however, get a kick out of the occasional assumption that the composer-lyricist of "Strange Fruit" had to have been black. His real name was Abel Meeropol, and his parents were Russian-Jewish immigrants. After teaching English in the New York City public schools, he became a full-time writer in 1945; his credits included the lyrics to "The House I Live In." He was also a Communist, and in 1953 served as a pallbearer at the funeral of the Rosenbergs, whom he had never met. Meeropol and his wife Anne adopted and raised the orphans of Julius and Ethel Rosenberg. The history of "Strange Fruit" proved, their sons later noted, that "you don't have to be black to hate lynching or to compose bluesy music."[22]

True enough, though perhaps it helped to be Jewish. Even in a canonical text of modern Zionism, *Altneuland* (1902), a leading character in Theodor Herzl's utopian novel discerns "one problem of racial misfortune unsolved . . . [that] only a Jew can fathom. I mean the Negro problem." The scientist named Professor Steineck was "not ashamed to say, though I be thought ridiculous, now that I have lived to see the restoration of the Jews, I should like to pave the way for the restoration of the Negroes." Or take *Babouk* (1934), which is narrated by the eponymous Mandingo storyteller. He describes an insurrection in Santo Domingo, and seeks to join with other captive Africans to challenge their white masters. Its author was Guy Endore, the nom de plume of the New Yorker Samuel Goldstein, a Communist, a Hollywood scenarist, and a blacklist victim in the 1950s.[23]

Arnold Perl also ran afoul of the blacklist in the movie industry, and turned to the stage. *The World of Sholom Aleichem* (1953) consisted of dramatizations, and *Tevya and His Daughters* (1957) became the basis for Joseph Stein's book for *Fiddler on the Roof.* But Perl was fluent enough in crossing racial and cultural divides to cowrite the scenario (with Ossie Davis) for the cinematic adaptation of Chester Himes's novel, *Cotton Comes to Harlem* (1970).[24] Perl also cowrote the script for *Malcolm X* (1992), even though his collaborator, Spike Lee, insisted that such a biopic required a director like himself, "an African-American who knows what it feels to be . . . a second-class citizen. You needed someone who know what it feels like to have a white woman cross the street or clutch her purse when she sees you coming." (Would a movie centering on *her*, however, need a white female director?)

Verisimilitude marked *Nothing But a Man* (1964), which portrayed the struggles of Southern blacks with the frustrations of romance and of family pressures as well as the ever-present threat of racism. *Nothing But a Man* was directed and cowritten by the German-born Michael Roemer, who claimed to have "immediately connected with the black experience. . . . The whole issue of not being allowed to be a man, a human being, touches something very personal in me." Jews were "cousins," co-star Ivan Dixon noted of those behind the camera. "I for one had never been led to believe that Jews were white people." For *Malcolm X*, Spike Lee may have felt that Arnold Perl's Red Scare reduction to second-class citizenship qualified him to help write the scenario about a black nationalist with freckles and reddish hair, an autodidact who once "deconstructed" race by praising Spinoza because "he was black. A black Spanish Jew."[25]

That is the sort of error that would not have been made by the scholarly W. E. B. Du Bois, who was several times assumed to be Jewish while traveling in central Europe. Seeking lodgings in a Slovenian village, he was asked: "*Unter die Juden?*"[26] But the fluidity with which the identities of blacks and Jews might be switched, and especially the ease with which Jews adapted to American culture and deliberately did their part to paint it black, did not escape notice by the 1920s. Immigrants and their children were invoking the right to expose, exploit, and draw inspiration from a culture that was supposed to be impenetrable. They were daring enough to claim to be lifting the veil that has obscured it, to know the trouble that the singer of the spiritual had seen, to bridge the chasm another lyric announces: "Got one mind for white folks to see, / 'Nother for what I know is me; / He don't know, he don't know my mind."[27] It was obvious by the 1920s that Jews in the performing arts had nominated themselves as surrogates for blacks. In an era when racial segregation and discrimination pervaded every aspect of American society, Jews in show business stepped forward to tap—and to appropriate—the power of blackness.

What came to be regarded as the most notorious medium of impersonation was blackface. The East Side exercised no monopoly on this show-business staple, which George M. Cohan used at the outset of his own career, and which can be seen as late as *Babes in Arms* (1939), with Judy Garland, and *Holiday Inn* (1942), with Bing Crosby. Already by the mid-nineteenth century, minstrelsy was blackening white faces; and in the dramatizations of *Uncle Tom's Cabin*, the white actors who played Tom, Eliza, and Topsy wore blackface.[28]

Only a few Jewish entertainers practiced this version of minstrelsy. But they were among the most famous, and a paradox worth considering is that *The Jazz Singer* (1927) is not only the primordial cinematic exploration of American Jewry but also remains the most famous of all blackface musicals. When it was released and changed the movies forever, the reviewer in the *Forverts* discerned "so many points of resemblance between Jews and Negroes." Indeed, could it be accidental that "at least three of the most popular makers of music on the American stage should be Jewish boys, two of whom blacken their faces and sing Negro 'mammy' songs while the third has written many songs in Negro dialect"? The reviewer wondered why "the most famous black face singer in the world, Al Jolson, would be the son of a cantor? How is it that the second most popular black face artist should be an East Side boy, Eddie Cantor, and that Irving Berlin, author of so many Negro songs, should be an East Side scion of a line of *Chazonim*?"[29]

No direct answer was given, nor is a satisfactory one obvious even now. An ethnic impulse seemed to be at work, to elude the ordeal of civility that gentility required, to emit the galvanic and mysterious glow of alterity, to go into overdrive in order to inhabit on stage the peculiar and unsettling space where Wright claimed "America likes to see the Negro live: between laughter and tears." Perhaps, as musicologist Mark Slobin argued, blackface offered performers born in poverty and obscurity "the ritual mask of the powerless," bestowing "sacred strength in this strange and dangerous New World." Perhaps blackface was a way of conveying emotions too deep to be expressed directly, too melancholy to be confronted in a promised land. Perhaps only when hidden behind a veil could the sadness that is endemic to life be weighed, which may be why Seldes once observed that Jolson, despite his compulsive buoyancy, "created image after image of longing."[30] By cavorting in blackface, he and Cantor and Brice and George Burns and George Jessel were perhaps taking out their citizenship papers. By laying claim to the most popular and enduring manifestation of nineteenth-century vernacular culture, perhaps these performers were invoking their right to be Americans.

Or something more sinister could have been operating. According to historian Michael Rogin, the Jews who inherited the conventions of minstrelsy blocked the entrances through which blacks might somehow have come and been given a chance to speak for themselves. Their absence gave Jews a chance to ascend, by masquerading in the guise of a more despised and excluded minority. "Blacking up and then wiping off burnt cork," he has argued, could "be a rite of passage from immigrant to American."[31] Blackface thus signified a strategy of assimilation, achieved through a consciousness of whiteness. That was the price of national inclusion, through the avenue of upward mobility that show business provided. Blackface was a way of reinforcing the humiliation of blacks: the mimicry in which white performers engaged on stage and screen injected a painful reminder of the enforced silence and civic inferiority of blacks. That other racial and ethnic groups were also cruelly stereotyped in popular culture offered little consolation, as no other group was so consistently victimized. That others besides Jews used blackface should no more draw scholarly attention away from the appeal of burnt cork than the obvious indifference to it of most Jewish entertainers.

It does seem counterintuitive, however, that blacking up was the vehicle for becoming white, that the way to secure a place at the top of the racial hierarchy was to pretend to be at the bottom. It seems dubious that such performers would call attention to their own whiteness by showing how easily they could slip across the color line. But the allure of blackface was that through its artifice such entertainers could separate themselves from the Old World. What was at stake was not their race but their nationality. By walking and talking like Negroes, Jewish performers could transform themselves, and the masses whom they represented, from outcasts into Americans.

Whether that process would be successful was not yet evident in the first third of the century (before blackface went into eclipse). Despite the phe-

The fate of no song better reflected both the power and the vulnerability of the internal "second culture" of American Jewry than Sholom Secunda's. The composer is shown at left.

The crowds gather at Warner's Theatre in New York, where *The Jazz Singer* opens in 1927. The sound barrier is broken.

Something wonderful happened when composer Richard Rodgers, seated, teamed up with lyricist Oscar Hammerstein II, shown here in 1953. UPI/ Corbis-Bettmann.

"He wrote for feet," Fred Astaire said of George Gershwin (center), here shown with his lyricist brother Ira (at right). The results included *Lady, Be Good!* and *Shall We Dance*. Photofest.

Rehearsing for a milestone, cast members of *West Side Story* join composer Leonard Bernstein, standing, and lyricist Stephen Sondheim. © Museum of the City of New York.

Making American culture mulatto are lyricist Jerry Leiber, seated at left, and composer Mike Stoller, at piano. Immediately to the left of The Coasters is Atlantic Records' Jerry Wexler. Photo courtesy of Showtime Archives (Toronto).

Bob Dylan visits the Western Wall in 1971, scarcely a decade after his songs had begun to circumnavigate the globe and to reshape indigenous American music. United Press International.

Never was the Jewish family more painfully exposed than when the Group Theatre staged *Awake and Sing!* in 1935. From left are John Garfield, Morris Carnovsky, and Stella Adler. Culver Pictures.

Broadway's first Willy Loman, Lee J. Cobb, prepares to record *Death of a Salesman* in 1965 with a new Bernard, Dustin Hoffman, who would play Willy on Broadway in 1984. Magnum Photos, Inc. © 1965 Inge Morath.

At Fifth Avenue and 43rd Street, Temple Emanu-El is dedicated in 1868. A seating capacity of 2,300 also measured pride, wealth, and confidence. Library of Congress.

Dit is een foto, zoals ik me zou wensen, altijd zo te zijn. Dan had ik nog wel een kans om naar Holywood te komen. Maar tegenwoordig zie ik er jammer genoeg meestal anders uit.

Annefrank.

18 Oct. 1942
Zondag.

'This is a photo of me as I wish I always looked. Then I might still have a chance to come to Hollywood . . ." Anne Frank, 1942. © AFF/AFS Amsterdam the Netherlands.

Architect James Ingo Freed designed a space for contemplation—the Hall of Remembrance, at the U.S. Holocaust Memorial Museum, opened in 1993. © Timothy Hursley.

One man's family: Mordecai Kaplan is shown with his father Israel Kaplan, daughter Judith (center), wife Lena Rubin Kaplan, and daughter Hadassah in 1914. Judith would become the first bat mitzvah in history. Reprinted from *Judaism Faces the Twentieth Century: A Biography of Mordecai M. Kaplan*, by Mel Scult.

The Skirball Cultural Center opened in Los Angeles in 1996, and was intended to evoke the synthesis of Jewish creativity and American citizenship. © Timothy Hursley.

nomenal popularity of *The Promised Land* (1912), despite its heartfelt account of an immigrant's faith, Harvard's Barrett Wendell sniffed at Mary Antin's "irritating habit of describing herself and her people as Americans" —a term he wished to reserve for those like his wife, whose ancestors had landed three centuries earlier. However coldly Wendell also refused to permit himself social intercourse with blacks, he would not have impugned their status to be considered Americans. On the Jews, however, not all the precincts had yet reported. To abandon the Old World, as Jung observed at that moment, was to take on, however unconsciously, the mannerisms of the Negro.

And on stage the imitation was conscious, a projection of a certain idea of blackness that was so fully a caricature that these gestures of racial impersonation could be kidded, as Jolson himself did by using Yiddish inflections. By then blackface was something of a cruel joke: even Bert Williams, the West Indian star of Ziegfeld's *Follies*, performed in blackface.[32]

He also wrote "coon songs," as did other black musicians. The most popular of these works was "All Coons Look Alike to Me" (1896), which was written by a black vaudevillian named Ernest Hogan. Another composer, Irving Jones, hinted that not every ethnic group could be expected to be sympathetic to his fellow blacks, by writing "St. Patrick's Day is a Bad Day for Coons." To have substituted holidays like Chanukah or Purim would have made no sense, as Jews were not commonly accused of bigotry. But they picked up the musical fashion quickly enough. Though Leo Friedmann was best known for writing "Let Me Call Me You Sweetheart" (1910), a decade earlier he had written "Coon, Coon, Coon—I Wish My Color Would Fade." Gustave Edward Simon immigrated from Germany, changed his name to Gus Edwards, and became famous for composing such hits as "In My Merry Oldsmobile" (1905), "School Days" (1907), and "By the Light of the Silvery Moon" (1909). (He would occupy a niche in the history of popular culture for having created *School Days*, the variety show that discovered Cantor, Jessel, Walter Winchell, and the Marx Brothers.) But it was a coon song that launched Edwards's career: "All I Want is My Black Baby Back" (1898).

The opposite sentiment had been expressed the previous year by Monroe Rosenfeld: "I Don't Care If You Never Come Back." It was written for Bert Williams (for whom Irving Berlin would write his first successful ballad, "Woodman, Woodman, Spare That Tree"). Though Will Vodery served as Ziegfeld's musical director, Williams managed to remain for a decade Broadway's only black man in an otherwise all-white show,[33] and joined Cantor in a father-son blackface act in the *Follies*. They addressed each other as "Pappy" and "Sonny" offstage as well. Having never gotten past grade school, the scrappy Cantor was especially impressed with the impeccable "English with a light West Indies accent" that Williams employed. He was, Cantor recalled, "a true gentleman."

The line dividing black from blackface could not considered distinct when Brice got twelve encores—and a contract with the *Follies*—thanks to a coon song called "Lovie Joe" (1910). Its composer, Joe Jordan, was black. No female performer seemed to extract such comic possibilities (or to have sprung with greater immediacy) from the Jewish immigrant masses than Fanny Brice. Yet her career also suggested the stageworthy importance of imitating the souls of black folk.[34]

The entanglement of race and ethnicity also marked the shtick of Sophie Tucker, whose early specialties included ragtime, Yiddish ballads, and "red-hot momma" songs. But when she switched from the Yiddish stage to burlesque houses, Tucker became so smoothly Americanized that she was billed as a "Manipulator of Coon Melodies." Indeed, for about four years, she was the nation's best-known practitioner of the genre, and was so adept at black imitations that, according to historian June Sochen, "audiences shrieked with surprise" when Tucker took off her gloves to show her white wrists and hands. The first song ever written by Eubie Blake and Noble Sissle, "It's All Your Fault" (1915), she turned into a hit; and expressly for her, the black songwriter Shelton Brooks composed the lyrics and music to "Some of These Days" (1911).

That bluesy combination of coon song and romantic ballad became indelibly linked with a performer who had taken singing lessons from Ethel Waters, which is further proof of how difficult it is to detach Jewish and black musical styles from one another. Sartre should therefore not be scoffed at for having his protagonist in *Nausea* (1938) mistake Tucker for a black singer. Antoine Roquentin sinks into the pit of nihilism while listening to a recording of "Some of These Days." Little scholarly support can be found, however, for the puckish view of A. J. (Joe) Liebling, who traced existentialism to "the last of the red hot mommas."[35] Putting on blackface had not, incidentally, been Sophie's choice; and the persona she had adopted trapped and pained her. But coon-shouting was popular, and in mass entertainment the customer is always right. Then, at least according to apocrypha, her makeup and costumes got misplaced, and she was forced to step on stage as her unadorned Caucasian self. When the audience did not rush to the exits, Tucker announced: "I'm through with blackface." Jewishness could not be so casually or so irrevocably abandoned, however; "My Yiddishe Mama" not only released the most intense of sentiments but affirmed the tribal bonds of family and ethnicity. Tucker thus demonstrated the compatibility of *Yiddishkeit* with the mask of blackness.[36]

Watching and listening to Jolson when *The Jazz Singer* opened, the film reviewer for the *Forverts* saw no "incongruity in this Jewish boy with his face painted like a Southern Negro singing in the Negro dialect." On the contrary, what was obvious was "the minor key of Jewish music, the wail of the *chazan*, the cry of anguish of a people who had suffered. The son of a line of rabbis well knows how to sing the songs of the most cruelly wronged people in the world's history." A spectacular career apparently began when Jolson played an extra in a mob scene in the stage version of Zangwill's *Children of the Ghetto* (1899). Though fluent in Yiddish, he did not manage to achieve Tucker's synthesis, and earned stardom as "the un-crowned king of minstrelsy." For his Broadway debut in 1910, he applied burnt cork to belt out "Paris is a Paradise for Coons." The composer of this "coon song," oddly enough, was Jerome Kern, whose "Smoke Gets in Your Eyes" (1933) would be revived by The Platters, five black doo-wop singers who made it a hit a quarter of a century later, during the classical age of rock and roll.

Indeed, Jolson made blackface an advertisement for himself. Upon first seeing him in action, Cantor got so rattled that his own act was hurt. He was Jolson's closest rival. But Cantor was candid enough to admit: "I can't compete with Jolson." The inventor of the one-man Broadway show sang "You Made Me Love You" (1913) for Woodrow Wilson in the White House. Al Capone was such a fan of "April Showers" (1921) that Jolson was once obliged to give a private command performance by singing the song in Chicago. (Technically the invitation was not a kidnapping; none-theless, the gentlemen relaying Scarface's request had conspicuous bulges under their armpits.) Jolson's billing as "The World's Greatest Entertainer" didn't seem at the time to be too much of a hype.[37]

That he was sensational did not mean that he was entirely original. "Folks, you ain't heard nothin' yet" was filched from black vaudevillian Joe Britton; and by flouting the grammatical "have" and dropping the final *g* in the noun, Jolson's signature phrase flaunted what Ann Douglas called "the most easily recognized characteristics of the Negro dialect." So much for the 1915 effort of the American National Council of Teachers of English to devote the month of November to "Ain't-less Weeks" and "Final-G Weeks." Not until 1929 would Thomas (Fats) Waller's lyricist, Andy Razaf, step forward to reassure schoolteachers: "Ain't Misbehavin'." Jolson's taste was as peccable as his pronunciation. He wanted to mount *Porgy and Bess* as a blackface musical but lost the literary rights to Gershwin; and "My Mammy" (1921; not to be confused with "My Yiddishe Mama") was a highlight of *The Jolson Story*, a biopic released in 1946.

That date revealed how little moral or artistic discomfort Jolson had felt in the acts of racial impersonation that so largely defined his career.[38] Per-haps that is because he appreciated the galvanic effect that could result from the allure and the appropriation of blackness. Jolson was an assimilationist, but he was not assimilated. There was something demonic about him, something that could not be contained within the thin membranes of Victorian order. His performances emitted something so raw that he seemed possessed. "John the Baptist was the last man to possess such a power," critic Robert Benchley told readers of *Vanity Fair.* "It is as if an electric current had been run along under the seats."[39] The emotional voltage Jolson could unleash was so high that Seldes saw corybantic equivalents only in religious exaltation, only in mob hysteria, only at the stock exchange. The critic was speaking for his fellow whites (and not for his fellow Jews) in recognizing the inspirational source of such furious energy. "In words and music," he wrote in 1923, "the negro side expresses something which underlies a great deal of America—our independence, our carelessness, our frankness, and gaiety. In each of these the negro is more intense than we are."[40]

No other minority group was more exempt from the staid moralistic interdictions of the early twentieth century. But such prohibitions buttressed the system of white supremacy that excluded and silenced that minority. With one form of repression reinforcing another, members of another minority group could seize the opportunity to step on stage and transmit something of Negro ardor. Jolson, Brice, and Cantor were "racially out of the dominant caste," Seldes conjectured. "Possibly this accounts for their fine carelessness about our superstitions of politeness and gentility." Such performers "go with more contempt for artificial notions of propriety, than anyone else."[41] In doing so, the first superstar conveyed the excitement of emancipation—and in the first sound film is fully identified with the "sounds and sweet airs, that give delight and hurt not" in the New World.

Jazz is what the cantor's son is supposed to be singing in the paradigmatic film about the rise of an American-born, American-bred entertainer. Jazz is the music that insinuated itself so fully into the national consciousness that F. Scott Fitzgerald bestowed the name on an entire age. Jazz was also the sole cultural achievement attributed to blacks in Charles and Mary Beard's grand historical survey, published in the year that ended the silent film era. Yet the racial minority which created that music is nowhere seen or heard in that Warner Brothers' movie. "Jazz had rushed into the mainstream," Baraka acidly observed, "without so much as one black face." Only blackface. The omission was understandable and indeed deliberate.[42] In no way does *The Jazz Singer* purport to be about the genesis of such music. Filmed in part on the Lower East Side, the movie is not set in New Orleans or elsewhere along the Mississippi River, which was the African-American provenance of jazz.

Far less defensible, however, was Samson Raphaelson's peculiar definition of jazz as the *absence* of blacks. Inspired by a Jolson performance, he published a short story entitled "Day of Atonement" in 1922, which he expanded three years later into a Broadway play before it became a film. In the preface to the published version of what was his first play, Raphaelson explained: "I have used a Jewish youth as my protagonist because the Jews are determining the nature and scope of jazz more than any other race— more than the negroes, from whom they have stolen jazz and given it a new color and meaning." Performers who exemplified "the rhythm of frenzy," like Jolson and Tucker, had "their roots in the synagogue. And these are expressing in evangelical terms the nature of our chaos today." Raphaelson was thus promoting the transvaluation of values: "Jazz is prayer. It is too passionate to be anything else." Indeed, the fervor it aroused in the nightclubs and dance halls, he argued, could be compared only to the emotions that might be felt in evangelical churches, or on the Day of Atonement.[43]

The music had become ubiquitous. *The Waste-Land* (1922) already digs "that Shakespeherian rag" (section 2, line 128). Almost instantaneously, jazz had become so universal a musical language that it belonged to no one in particular, not even its inventors. Jazz was so tantalizing and so irresistible that the step taken to obscure the creative primacy of blacks was a short one. That is why the *Dearborn Independent* headlined its report on the craze as follows: "Jewish Jazz Becomes Our National Music." That Henry Ford's weekly did not intend to bestow praise on this trend can be inferred by the newspaper's definition of jazz as "Yiddish moron music." A New England music critic in the ragtime era had also denounced such "rude noise which emerged from the hinterlands of brothels and dives, presented in a negroid manner by Jews most often," who were endowed with "oriental extravagance and sensuous brilliance."[44] Jazz was what blacks had invented and extended. But Jews also did something to it and with it. Jazz was not only Jews, but jazz was *also* Jews.

Though the standard definition of a genius is an ordinary child born to Jewish parents, Morris and Rose Gershwine (formerly Gershovitz) could make out a strong case for their younger son. The first time George tried his hand at a major instrumental work, the result was a veritable evocation of the jaunty go-get-'em aura of the Jazz Age: *Rhapsody in Blue*. No serious musical work of the century is more familiar; probably none has been more often performed (by, among others, Bernstein, Tilson Thomas, Oscar Levant, James Levine and the Chicago Symphony—and Duke Ellington). Gershwin's own indebtedness to black music was deep, and perhaps no other white composer showed a more intuitive appreciation of the blues. His early idols were jazz pianists James P. Johnson and particularly Luckey Roberts; his good friend was Fats Waller. The ebullient composer of "I Got Rhythm" did not seem out of place in Harlem's nightclubs and parties; nor did he have any trouble substituting himself for the lead "shouter" in a black church in South Carolina, while preparing for *Porgy and Bess*. For *George White's Scandals* of 1922, Gershwin inserted a Harlem operetta saturated with spirituals, ragtime, and the newly fashionable blues. Harburg once cited Gershwin's "My One and Only" from *Funny Face* (1927) as a nifty example of "a song starting out Jewish and turning black."

So deeply had he turned black by plunging into Charleston's ghetto that the handful of white characters in *Porgy and Bess* (such as cops and lawyers) utter only a clipped speech that does not unfold into song. Musicologist Wilfrid Mellers speculated that, in the story of a cripple living on Catfish Row, Gershwin discovered a moving "parable about oppression, alienation, corruption and the inviolability of a radical innocence of spirit." Such music was understandably the product of "an archetypal White Negro and poor-boy Jew, who, making good, knew much that was to be known about spiritual isolation, and had opportunity enough to learn about corruption."[45]

Whatever the composer's psychic wound, *Porgy and Bess* was as difficult to categorize as, say, *Moby-Dick* (which resisted "a distinct classification," the editor of the *New York Literary World* complained upon publication in 1851, "as fact, fiction, or essay"), and as daringly original as Fallingwater (the 1936 house which Frank Lloyd Wright boasted "has no limitations as to form").[46] When the "folk opera" was staged in 1935, the *Times* assigned both its first-string drama critic, Brooks Atkinson, and its chief music critic, Olin Downes, to write reviews in adjacent columns. Though Levant acknowledged the work to be "a folk opera," he slyly added a qualification: "a Jewish folk opera." Harburg had spent the Saturdays of his boyhood in synagogue and later claimed that cantorial music moved him more than any other kind. He was stunned upon first hearing "Summertime"; this lullaby made him feel "as if I had known it all my life." Audiences, however, were nonplussed, and the original production ground to a halt after a mere 124 performances. A revival seven years later ran for 286 performances. *Porgy and Bess* was not a box-office triumph if classified as a musical but, if ranked as an opera, is unrivaled as the most successful such work an American ever composed.[47]

But however it is labeled, an aura of fraudulence has lingered over it. Black critics in particular have hung *Porgy and Bess* out to dry. Historian Harold Cruse denounced it "as the most perfect symbol of the Negro creative artist's cultural denial, degradation, exclusion, exploitation and acceptance of white paternalism." While wishing that blacks had produced their own folk opera, he was confident that such a work "would never have been supported, glorified and acclaimed, as *Porgy* has, by the white cultural elite of America." Ellington was at first very dismissive as well, and the

Pulitzer Prize–winning dramatist August Wilson called Gershwin's opera "a bastardizing of our music and our people."

It ain't necessarily so. Perhaps no composer was a more fertile inspiration for black singers and instrumentalists working in jazz. Consider the impact of *Porgy and Bess*, whether recorded by Miles Davis (with Gil Evans), or as was evident in the collaboration of Louis Armstrong and Ella Fitzgerald on its songs, or in excerpts by Sarah Vaughan and by Nina Simone.[48] Sadly, an album entitled *Ella Sings Gershwin* was not issued until a dozen years after the composer's death. But the lyricist was around to express his gratitude. "I never knew how good our songs were," Ira Gershwin remarked, "until I heard Ella sing them."

Such cross-fertilization and reciprocal relations between Jewish and black artists would so enrich American culture that *Porgy and Bess* could be effectively distorted during the cold war to signify that race relations were better than foreigners presumably believed. The *New York Times* reported that touring companies in Central and Eastern Europe in the 1950s "created a new perspective here for a communist-led people sensitive to reports of American race prejudice and exploitation." It was an odd conclusion to be drawn from so unsparing a portrayal of Catfish Row. But irony marked the interpretive fate of *Porgy and Bess*. What Virgil Thomson had called at its premiere "a piquant but highly unsavory stirring-up together of Israel [and] Africa," flawed by "gefiltefish orchestration," had become an authentic reflection of a multiracial, multiethnic nation.[49]

Second only to Gershwin in writing American music, according to Streisand, was Hyman Arluck, a.k.a. Harold Arlen. He too, according to Harburg (his collaborator on *The Wizard of Oz*), synthesized "Negro rhythms and Hebraic melodies," and achieved a mélange of Africa and Israel. No white Broadway composer, with the possible exception of Gershwin, was more influenced by blues and jazz. Arlen supplied the music for Cotton Club songs for Cab Calloway, Lena Horne and Ethel Waters, and wrote "Stormy Weather" (1932) for Calloway. But after Waters sang it under a lamppost with a blue spotlight shining on her, "Stormy Weather" became her signature song.

Then Arlen joined forces with Johnny Mercer, a white Episcopalian who had grown up in Savannah listening to "race" records aimed at the black market. Mercer trained himself to write lyrics by listening to the songs of Berlin and Kern, after which Mercer linked up with composers like Rube Bloom. Having mastered the appropriate style, Mercer supplied the lyrics for Arlen's "Blues in the Night" (1941), though it was the composer who suggested starting with the lines, "My momma done tol' me / when I was in knee pants." (The sentimental instincts of popular music were unerringly matrifocal.) "Blues in the Night" was intended to be sung by a black man, stuck in a jail cell, in a movie called *Hot Nocturne*. But so haunting was the song that Warner Brothers changed the title of the film to plug the song. The next year came Arlen and Mercer's "That Old Black Magic." In 1946 they collaborated on *St. Louis Woman*, the musical that marked the debut of Pearl Bailey. The black writers Arna Bontemps and Countee Cullen collaborated on the libretto. The blues and jazz were so decisive in influencing Arlen that even his final major work was a black musical, *Jamaica* (1957).[50]

Jazz was composition; it was *created*. But jazz was also interpretation. Playing in the orchestra pit for the Gershwins' *Strike Up the Band* (1930) was a clarinetist whose career would also suggest hybridization: Benny Goodman. When Teddy Wilson joined his trio in 1935, and then when Lionel Hampton joined Goodman's quartet two years later, jazz was publicly and triumphantly desegregated, more than a decade before Jackie Robinson donned a Dodgers uniform. After four other black musicians joined Goodman's band, the manager of a New York hotel told him that they would have to walk through the kitchen to avoid the lobby. He threatened to quit, and the subject was dropped. Among those to hear America swinging was William (Count) Basie. "No matter where we were every Saturday night," he recalled in 1956, "we'd have to hear Benny Goodman's band on the old *Camel Caravan*," a radio program in the 1930s. "That was a wonderful band," a "listening thrill." (But then, according to Lenny Bruce's revisionist dualism, Basie was Jewish anyway.) Goodman had started out in Chicago too poor to have taken music lessons anywhere besides his *shul* and at Hull House; when he got to Carnegie Hall early in 1938, the highlight of that famous jam session was "Bei Mir Bist Du Schön." Under his auspices Secunda's song was rejudaized while somehow remaining fully Americanized—and was sanctified in the nation's citadel of high culture not long after the tumultuous reception the song had received in Harlem's Apollo Theatre. In repudiating racial discrimination, Goodman encouraged others, like the bandleader and clarinetist Artie Shaw (*né* Arthur Arshawsky), to forge important relationships with black musicians like Billie Holiday and Roy Eldridge.[51]

Goodman was hardly alone in helping to desegregate popular culture in the decades before the Supreme Court advised public schools to proceed similarly, with all deliberate speed. In 1937 NBC's *The Jack Benny Show* brought "Rochester" (Eddie Anderson) into the mainstream, and thus tilted the existing imbalances of status toward subtleties of equalization. By the early 1940s Anderson had star billing. The actor was, to be sure, known and addressed offstage as "Rochester," as though he had no surname. But the rest of the Benny ensemble adhered closely enough to the characters whom they played to disappear into their own fictional selves as well. Eugene Patrick McNulty *became* Dennis Day, and Sadie Marks, Benny's wife in private life, was dejudaized into the public figure of Mary Livingstone.

Even when it was not Sunday night, the performers were expected to stay in character. The former Benny Kubelsky made a revolution; he doomed vaudevillian wisecracks and deprived himself of a monopoly of all the good lines. As historian Joseph Boskin has shown in a valuable addition to Jack Benny studies, the effect on the relationship between the "Boss" and his servant and chauffeur was especially important. Because the "Boss" became the butt of the others' humor, Rochester benefited more than anyone else from the redistribution of power (more so on radio than later on television). Nonetheless, his right to inflict ridicule did not prevent Baraka from abusing *The Jack Benny Show* in his play entitled *Jello* (1970), a corrosive parody which makes Rochester into a scalding, let's-get-even militant —and incidentally reduces Dennis Day to a "highvoiced fag."[52]

In elevating Anderson's status, Benny did the right thing, without self-righteousness. As did Cantor in hiring Thelma Carpenter in 1945. She became the first black female vocalist given a regular slot on network radio. Though Cantor's sponsor wanted her to be identified as his maid, the comedian refused to go along: "I didn't cast Dinah Shore or Nora Martin as maids. They were my vocalists, like Thelma. That's how Thelma will be introduced—as my vocalist."[53]

These gestures probably mattered less, however, than Benny Goodman's own deep involvement in the music that blacks invented. Artistic miscegenation punctuated his career and thus suggests the impossibility of confining the history of jazz to a single minority group. Take "Body and Soul," which the Goodman ensemble (including Teddy Wilson) had recorded in 1935, on the tour that ended Jim Crow in jazz. Saxophonist Coleman Hawkins recorded "Body and Soul" four years later, and in 1946 "Lady Day" sang it on a Los Angeles program right after "Strange Fruit." "Body and Soul" was written by a New York Jew named Johnny Green, a bandleader who served as MGM's music director. His jazz standard would give its name to the 1947 film that, through the intertwined careers of a Jewish and a black boxer (John Garfield and Canada Lee), would replicate the minority bonding that "Body and Soul" exhibited. The movie hinted at the ordeal of an oppressed race, and such ardently "progressive" views ensured that director Robert Rossen and scenarist Abraham Polonsky would soon be blacklisted.[54]

Though leftist Jews had the greatest predisposition to accentuate the racial egalitarianism that was the credo of the Communist Party, receptivity to black artistic aspiration was strikingly characteristic even of the apolitical. The Jewish eagerness to showcase and to promote black talent is a noteworthy feature of the history of show business. Dorothy Fields helped ease the ordeal of the Great Depression with the lushly romantic lyrics to "The Way You Look Tonight" (1936). But during the Jazz Age her songs for the all-black revue *Blackbirds of 1928* included "Doin' the New Low Down" and "I Can't Give You Anything But Love, Baby." In the same era, Jack and Bert Goldberg were responsible for producing several black musicals, most famously the *Shuffle Along* series in the 1920s.

Four decades later, even when opportunities for blacks were much enlarged, a Jewish imprint could not be erased. When Ossie Davis's play about the vulnerability of Southern blacks to white supremacy, *Purlie Victorious* (1961), was adapted into a Broadway musical entitled *Purlie* (1970), Gary Geld and Peter Udell were responsible for its gospel-style score. Davis himself cited the inspiration of the tales of Sholom Aleichem. The Brooklyn-born, Catskills-honed Irving Gordon wrote the Nat "King" Cole standard, "Unforgettable" (1951), to which his daughter Natalie added her own voice four decades later, creating a posthumous duet that won a 1992 Grammy for best song. Gordon also wrote for Ellington (providing the lyrics to his "Prelude to a Kiss," for example), and wrote "Me, Myself and I" for Billie Holiday. Burt Bacharach joined lyricist Hal David in catapulting singer Dionne Warwick to stardom. A compact disk was released (on the Tzadik label) in 1997, blatantly entitled *Great Jewish Music: Burt Bacharach*. But that was obviously a mere marketing device; from such Warwick hits as "I Say a Little Prayer" (1967), a turn toward piety could not be inferred.[55]

Bacharach had learned composition from Darius Milhaud, a French Jew who spent much of his career in the United States. His 1923 ballet, *La Création du Monde*, incorporated jazz into a symphonic score a year ahead of *Rhapsody in Blue*, and used black performers as the Adam and Eve who are present at the creation. Leonard Bernstein's senior thesis discovered less of a black musical influence in "a consciously Negroid work like the *Création du Monde*" than in Milhaud's *Chants Populaires Hébraïques* (1925). And because "the only really universal racial influence in America has been the Negro," Bernstein declared,[56] it was not bizarre of Kurt Weill to complete his own Americanization with *Lost in the Stars* (1949). It was the last musical for which Weill finished the score; he died the following year. The lead was Todd Duncan, who had been the first Porgy fifteen years earlier. The musical was set in South Africa.

Born and raised in Vienna, the director and producer Otto Preminger had not exhibited deep involvement in the experiences of blacks. But he was responsible for two instances of "film noir" set to music, cast only with black performers. The first was *Carmen Jones* (1954), adapted from Billy Rose's 1943 Broadway revue; Hammerstein supplied the lyrics. The second was *Porgy and Bess* (1959), for which Previn won an Oscar for adapting Gershwin's score. These two film musicals may have lifted ever so slightly the veil that mainstream movies generally took for granted, even as the power of Jim Crow was about to collapse.

If "coon songs" could be written and sung by both Jews and blacks, if the blues could be Harold Arlen as well as Ethel Waters and other black interpreters of his work, if jazz could be Benny Goodman as well as his admirer Count Basie, then the vernacular musical culture that flourished in roughly the first half of the century confounds the purist seeking some sort of essentialism to define blackness.

Nor did the black-Jewish musical alliance evaporate when the fashion for big jazz bands declined, and when something new came along. Rock and roll was activated not only by kinetic black performers like Chuck Berry and Little Richard, who wrote their own material, but also by rockers (like Presley) who did not. The 1950s differed musically from the 1940s in part because of one songwriting team: Leiber and Stoller. If, on Broadway, successful tunesmiths had to learn to "write Jewish," the explosion of rock and roll made it extremely helpful—if not downright necessary—to "write black." That is what Leiber and Stoller did. By their mid-twenties, their songs had sold more than forty million records (which exceeded Kern's sales over his lifetime).[57]

Jerry Leiber's father had been a *melamed* in Poland but died in Baltimore when the future lyricist was still a boy, leaving his mother to operate a grocery store near a large black neighborhood. Growing up making deliveries, Leiber later described her customers in terms that have come to be clichés, but there is no reason to doubt that the neighbors' vitality and energy and ease were infectious. Mike Stoller was born in Brooklyn; at an interracial summer camp, the future composer was playing boogie-woogie piano even before he was a teenager. The attraction he felt toward black music began early and did not dissipate.

The postwar era marked what Deborah Dash Moore has traced as one of the great migrations of American Jewry, toward the Sunbelt; and both families joined the exodus to Los Angeles, where the lyricist and the composer met.[58] What Leiber and Stoller had in common was an eagerness to cross the color line. "We thought of ourselves as black," Stoller told an interviewer, because "blacks were warmer. They were sharper. Everything about them was somewhat heightened." Leiber concurred: "We were so steeped in black culture, both of us, the inside jokes, the walk, kind of arrogant, kind of a challenge." Their own project was to write "black songs for black people," he remarked; while still teenagers, the duo met that challenge with "Hound Dog" (1953). This defiant woman's repudiation of a unfaithful and worthless lover was written for a black rhythm and blues singer named Willie Mae "Big Mama" Thornton. But Presley made it famous, turning "Hound Dog" into an anthem of young rebels without a cause, but with vague yearnings to resist adults and other authorities, as insouciant and cool Negroes seemed to be doing.[59]

"Hound Dog" marked the success of race-mixing in music a year before the desegregation of public schools was mandated. Leiber and Stoller continued to write for white performers. Peggy Lee's 1969 query ("Is That All There Is") was theirs; and they provided the soundtrack for *Jailhouse Rock* (1957), arguably Presley's best film. (The competition is not keen.) He would later snarl, in a pop paean to "Little Sister" (1961), that "she's mean and she's evil / Like a little ol' boll weevil." That analogy was region-specific. But you didn't have to be Southern to write such a lyric, which was penned by a Brooklyn Jew named Jerome Felder, who called himself Doc Pomus; the music was composed by Mort Shuman. However indebted Presley was to such teams, prudence, not gratitude, undoubtedly led him, in his final years, to wear a Star of David. "I wouldn't want to be kept out of heaven on a technicality," he explained.

Leiber and Stoller were the most important of these teams, however, and wrote most successfully for black groups. The Coasters were given such hits as "Kansas City," "Spanish Harlem," "Charlie Brown," "Searchin'," "There Goes My Baby," "Stand By Me," "Along Came Jones," "Black Denim Trousers and Motorcycle Boots," and "Little Egypt." The sassy "Yakety Yak" made talking black virtually synonymous with talking back. "Love Potion Number 9" was the unofficial anthem of the sixth World Festival of Youth and Students, held in Moscow in the summer of 1957, as disaffected Soviet youth known as *stiliagi* (style-hunters), plus some Eastern European *bitniki*, dug rock and roll enough to alter the life of the Party.

As producers for The Drifters, Leiber and Stoller added strings to make a more "orchestral" sound. They worked so many ingenious variations on the twelve-bar blues and the two-minute limit to the adolescent attention span that by 1995 these writers-producers fulfilled the promise of their 1962 song "On Broadway" (for which they shared credit with the Brill Building's Cynthia Weill and Barry Mann). The staging of *Smokey Joe's Café* confirmed how proficiently Leiber and Stoller had translated "race music" into national fare. Broadway certification also giddily connected the dots back to Porter, Hart, and Berlin, whom Leiber hailed as his songwriting idols—just as a photo of the adolescent Stoller at the piano shows Gershwin's photo on the wall.[60]

How white musicians and audiences absorbed "rhythm and blues" is the story of rock and roll, according to Jerry Wexler, the producer whose Atlantic label was central to that saga. He had grown up in the Great Depression, the son of immigrants from Poland and Germany who lived in the Washington Heights section of Manhattan. His father was a window-washer whose own father was engrossed in the Talmud, and Wexler's mother was an ardent champion of her son's ambitions. "As a Jew, I didn't think I identified with the underclass," he recalled. "I *was* the underclass." Odets had in effect already portrayed how Wexler grew up. Such was the poverty his family experienced that his autobiography draws the following lesson, via Lenny Bruce: "Suffering teaches us only that suffering has absolutely no value." Music was a way out, if not necessarily up; and in that melting-pot to which Wexler was exposed there "simmered . . . a slow-cooking gumbo of New Orleans jazz, small Harlem combos, big bands, Western swing, country, jukebox race music, pop schmaltz." Writing for *Billboard* magazine after the Second World War, he discarded the term "race music" and coined "rhythm and blues" instead to describe the mix of blues, gospel, and boogie that somehow blended into something distinctive and compelling.[61]

He soon left journalism for Atlantic Records, which was cofounded in 1947 by a talent scout for National Records named Herb Abramson. A dentist as well, Abramson was drafted during the Korean War, leaving Wexler to become vice president as well as the chief creative figure of a company that had begun as a "race" label. By the mid-1950s, the audience for Atlantic records could no longer be kept inside the ghetto; and rhythm and blues would become an international phenomenon. When Allen Ginsberg recounted his effort to master pain, to mourn the death of his mother, in "Kaddish" (1959), he wrote not only of reciting aloud the mostly Aramaic doxology that has helped bereaving Jews for a millennium, but also of "listening to Ray Charles," courtesy of Atlantic records.

Wexler himself produced many of the hits sung not only by Charles but also by Aretha Franklin, a former gospel prodigy and the daughter of Detroit's Reverend C. L. Franklin, whose sermons and gospel music Phil and Leonard Chess preserved and released on their Chess Records. Wexler had the savvy to bring Aretha Franklin to Muscle Shoals, Alabama, and in collaboration with other gospel-trained singers and rhythm and blues musicians, she communicated a range of emotions from exhilaration to sorrow that deepened and magnified the range of popular music. "I urged Aretha to be Aretha," he recalled.[62] The stimulus of the Deep South was not enough. One song indelibly associated with her was "(You Make Me Feel Like) A Natural Woman" (1967), credited not to soulful alumni of the black church but to the New Yorkers Carole King and her husband Gerry Goffin (as well as Wexler).

Such music is inescapably the product of what Winston Churchill termed a "magpie society," and belonged to no one in particular. Culture is an import-export business, with trade going in both directions. Take "Eyli, Eyli," which was possibly written in 1896 by Thomashefsky and/or by Jacob Koppel Sandler. During the First World War, Cantor Josef (Yossele)

Rosenblatt, who would be heard on the soundtrack of *The Jazz Singer*, featured "Eyli, Eyli" in his fundraising concerts. He called it the most "popular song in the entire field of Jewish music." No wonder that the crowd-pleasing Jolson did his own Yiddish version. But so did the blues singer Ethel Waters, without creating the impression that this Yiddish song was somehow foreign to her. Though medieval theologians were obliged to think of the universe itself in terms of creatio ex nihilo, historians of the vernacular arts know better than to imagine their subject in such terms. The operative word is eclecticism, not purism. Thus a calypso singer like Harry Belafonte, raised in the Caribbean, could sing "Hava Nagila" in Hebrew and make it so famous that (as he once recalled with astonishment) eight thousand members of the audience once sang it along with him—in Japan.[63]

The history of the Jewish adaptation of black styles thus suggests something reciprocal as well; the exchanges were not one-sided in a culture that has long consisted, as Ralph Waldo Ellison argued, of a mishmash: "interchange, appropriation, and integration." Those terms referred not to elusive ideals but to facts. Thus Louis Armstrong could make records of his scat-singing—an early sensation was "Heebie Jeebies" (1925)—which may have derived from observing Orthodox Jews at prayer. As a philo-Semite who ate *matzoh* most of his life, "Satchmo" never publicly acknowledged davening as a source of scat-singing, however, since he feared any inference that he was ridiculing such worship.[64] The amalgam of culture does not only mean that white Americans are part-black, as Woodward once put it. The historical logic of the claim that any number can play also means that all Americans, including blacks, can be considered part-Jewish. But only part. Such terms are intelligible only if the minorities that have enriched the national culture can continue to renew themselves, can participate in American life without unduly depleting their own resources or consuming at too rapid a rate their own seed-corn. Unless the story that is recounted in this chapter is to have an end, these two minorities must be able to remain culturally distinguishable. I have emphasized how black culture has influenced what Jews have created on native grounds. Now a conclusion might serve to rectify a possible imbalance by underscoring what makes Jewish culture viable.

The Zionist historian Ben Halpern drew a crucial distinction between the two "classic American minorities" in *Jews and Blacks* (1971). Removed from their ancient homelands, both were subjected to discrimination and to bigotry. But blacks, whose lives in the United States have been far more intolerable and circumscribed, did not differ from Jews merely because their rights were far more appallingly violated. They have had, Halpern argued, no ideological claim to separateness, no way to vindicate their own marginality. Jews by contrast aroused opposition not for who they were, and not primarily for what they looked like, but rather for what they believed and did. Their "peculiar practices," Harvard president A. Lawrence Lowell insisted in 1923, would have to be abandoned before Jews could expect to receive equal treatment.[65] Jews have constituted an "ideological minority," which means one destined to resist utter integration, even when that option is available.

Jewry has not held itself together historically because of "tribal" instincts arising from genetic homogeneity. Nor was survival for two millennia in the Diaspora due to the political links forged with other Jews; they are not a homogeneous nation. What enabled them to imagine themselves as a community is the eschatology to which they have subscribed. Their history has a point, which is to accelerate the coming of the Messianic age. They have felt bound to one another not merely because of outside pressure but also, according to the Saadya Gaon, the medieval Babylonian scholar, "because our nation is only a nation by reason of its Torah."

This is a people that is not only persecuted; it is also a people that is chosen. Pawnbroker Sol Nazerman, the man whom Harlem slang identifies as having "the Jew's balls," tells his assistant Jesús Ortiz of the deficiencies of a dispersed minority. The ex-professor and Holocaust survivor tabulates the erasures of Jewish experience: in land, in arms, in security. But what counts, he explains, is a "great bearded legend" to "convince you that there *is* something special about you, even in your poverty." Jews are signatories to a Covenant; and the sense of election, Freud speculated, gave Jews "a particularly high opinion of themselves," a feeling of being "superior to other[s]." Their self-definition as participants in a majestic and eternal destiny "makes them proud and confident."[66] Such a psychology cannot have come from suffering, even if suffering might be made endurable; this attitude can only spring from an ideology.

Such observations have been updated and contextualized, applied to the particularities of "the classic American minorities." The Jewish people have managed to survive even genocide, philosopher Laurence Thomas has conjectured, because of the blessing of a "narrative": a set of beliefs, rituals, myths, and symbols that have ensured "group autonomy." Probably no other phenomenon explains more pointedly why, in the wake of terrible and indeed ineffable historical disasters, Jews somehow "flourished," nowhere more spectacularly than in the United States. By 1969, for example, the per capita income of Jews was nearly twice that of Gentiles, an income gap wider than between whites and blacks. Jews and blacks have shared historical traumas: the shock of displacement, radical vulnerability, mass murder. But Judaism (to which Thomas adheres) has conserved its adherents, has constituted a "positive good" in guaranteeing solidarity despite oppression. Even though suffering is not redemptive, it need not reduce its victims to despair. Even the literary critic and political spokesman Edward W. Said lamented that Palestinians, unlike Jews, have lacked a narrative.

Nor can Thomas discern among his fellow blacks an equivalent ideology, a centripetal syndrome of ideals, a collective memory of having gone up from slavery. "Skin color," he has asserted, "does not make a narrative." Even if the saga of going up from slavery, ascending from plantation to ghetto and beyond, were to be designated the functional equivalent of a narrative, it would not apply to the rest of the African diaspora or to Africa itself. And if the United States were to become a colorblind society, what would be the point of affirming a separate identity? Why would American blacks insist on sustaining their own community? The Jews' duty to continue to live as an intact unit, by contrast, is not supposed to be affected either by oppression or by tolerance or by liberty. The antisemitism of some blacks, Julius Lester has surmised, may stem from "envy of the Jewish narrative, and the painful longing for a healing narrative of their own."[67]

To prevail over adversity, it helps to be an ideological minority, and some blacks have been seeking to devise *sancta* that might be interpreted as counterparts to Jewish ritual. Consider the scheduling of Kwanzaa, for instance. This African-American holiday, invented in Los Angeles after the Watts riots in 1965, occurs not only around Christmas but also around Chanukah, and is celebrated with seven nights of candle-lighting and of exchanging gifts (plus the inevitable objections to "commercialization").[68] Nor could malice alone account for the decision of the Nation of Islam to sponsor an African-American Day of Atonement on 16 October 1997.

Inevitably the seminars in comparative suffering come around to disparities in commemoration as well. In 1993, during the visit of a black delegation to Israel, Gerald Early, a professor of African and Afro-American Studies, claimed to have "learned this about the black American mind: That blacks are in awe and jealous of the enormous achievements of Jews and, as we see it, their privileges." He wrote, "We feel inferior to them." The obligatory itinerary of Yad Vashem raised questions in the ensuing discussion. Why had the horrors of slavery in the South not been evoked so centrally? Why had lesser efforts been expended on preserving the memories and the traumas of blacks?[69]

The Holocaust helped spur an unseemly competition to calibrate and to proclaim how much others besides Jews had suffered. A kind of bidding war broke out among groups with historic grievances. Two years after genealogist Alex Haley's comet soared to the top of the ratings when ABC televised a miniseries based on his historical novel, a black friend of journalist Letty Cottin Pogrebin's told her that NBC's *Holocaust* was criticized by other blacks as "the Jews' way of stealing the spotlight from *Roots*."[70] And two "minority" novelists joined in the effort to "top" the Holocaust. According to the endpapers of Leslie Marmon Silko's novel, *Almanac of the Dead* (1991), in the sixteenth century alone, "sixty million Native Americans died." Never mind that such a figure then served to rationalize the struggle for "nothing less than the return of all tribal lands." Nor did she note the coincidence of a number that was exactly ten times the estimate of Jews killed during the Holocaust. The novelist did no more than imply that white Europeans were solely responsible for so shockingly high a figure. Silko's figure was absurdly inflated. (The common scholarly guess had been an indigenous population of about eight million in the Western Hemisphere.) But in establishing a new historical standard of genocide, Silko matched the dedication of Toni Morrison's *Beloved* to "Sixty Million and more." The Nobel laureate claimed that her number is "the smallest number I got from anybody," with some historians' estimates of slave deaths as high as two hundred million.[71]

No factual warrant for such irresponsible figures exists. The Nigerian historian Joseph Inikori estimated that 15.4 million at least *started* on the Middle Passage; but even that figure stemmed, he admitted, "from my intuition, my *feeling* about the evidence." The numbers game can be played so easily that a contributor to the *Nation* claimed, citing no source, that "slavery brutalized and murdered 600 million black people."[72] Why not 300 million? Or a billion? One figure is about as casual and unsupported as another. The effect may or may not be advertent: to weaken the sense of the distinctive horror of the Holocaust, which American culture was in general unequipped to fathom. The human condition was pushed to its extreme limits in the death camps. How to measure those limits, with humility and with realism, and how to represent the ferocity of history posed a challenge that could neither be evaded nor satisfactorily met. Nothing in human annals seemed as unintelligible as the Holocaust, or so effective in frustrating the aspiration to enlist reason and art in efforts of understanding. Some American Jews nevertheless struggled to get closer to the abyss, to come to grips with an unbearable catastrophe. Yet they could do so only within the groove of their own country's culture.

SHOAH

JEFFERSON'S FIRST INAUGURAL ADDRESS THANKED PROVIDENCE FOR having so "kindly separated" his country from the Old World, by placing an ocean between the new republic and "the exterminating havoc" of Europe.[1] He thus contributed to and shared a dream of innocence: the new nation was supposed to be exempt from the burden of history, from complicity with its inextricable cruelties and injustices. Such a dream ill equipped American culture to absorb the meaning of unfathomable evil, to understand the ease with which good is defeated.

No wonder then that probably the most popular magazine founded in the century was the *Reader's Digest*. The monthly promised to cover a comprehensive range of topics, but *not*, according to founders DeWitt and Lila Wallace of Pleasantville, New York, despair. One analysis of the magazine claimed that its only taboo was "defeatism." Curiously enough, a translator employed for the French edition was Samuel Beckett, whose work grated against America's sunny-side-up spirit. One summer, at a cricket match in London, a companion mentioned to the playwright that the weather was so lovely it made one "glad to be alive," to which he replied: "Oh, I don't think I would go quite so far as to say that."[2]

Have-a-nice-day was much more the first commandment of the New World. Indeed, "evil is not an American concept," Sartre averred in 1949. "Americans are not pessimistic about human nature." From the United States, the principle of negativity itself was believed to have been expelled. A French sociologist added: "Americans have simply decided not to believe in evil." According to Michel Crozier, "What is missing in American culture . . . is . . . the acknowledgment that evil exists."[3] When Dore Schary signed on in 1948 as vice president in charge of production of Hollywood's biggest studio, MGM's press release quoted him as saying: "Under the leadership of L. B. Mayer, I offer my associates a program of work dedicated to the production of good films about a good world." The death camps had been liberated only three years earlier, and yet Schary could not be accused of living in a dream-world. He was atypical among studio executives in actively opposing bigotry, and would later chair the Anti-Defamation League. Two years before his ascension, an apt, red-white-and-blue title was bestowed on a film partly written by Frances Goodrich and Albert Hackett: *It's a Wonderful Life*.[4]

In that epoch there was something grotesque about such a title, for a terrifying chasm had opened up in human experience. Our species had revealed itself to be capable of sadism for which perhaps the only precedent consisted of medieval depictions of Hell, relocated and actualized in places that had names like Treblinka and Mauthausen and Auschwitz. Hell could be specified and enacted on earth. By determining how most efficiently to crush the spirit, and by reducing the body to an object to test how excruciating the pain that might be inflicted upon it, the Nazis left others speechless and inert. The Holocaust left "our metaphysical faculty . . . paralyzed," Theodor Adorno later wrote. Political action was short-circuited as well. In 1943, when a courier from the Polish underground secured an interview with Justice Felix Frankfurter to tell him of the atrocities, the Viennese-born jurist told Jan Karski: "I am unable to believe you." Frankfurter explained that he did not suspect that the messenger was not telling the truth, only that believing him was impossible. And Frankfurter did nothing.[5]

Few bystanders did anything. The scale of the *Shoah* was so appalling that conscience was numbed. The statistics were too staggering for the ordinary moral intelligence to confront, without flinching. On 5 March 1770, British troops in Boston had killed five colonials, an event American historians still refer to as a "massacre." In 1903, when an estimated fifty-nine Jews were killed during a pogrom in Kishinev, the outrage in the part of the world that fancied itself "civilized" was audible. In the spring of 1941, Sir Martin Gilbert wrote, the Germans entered Kishinev and in two weeks murdered about ten thousand people. What happened there was no different in intensity or scale than about five dozen other such slaughters that occurred *that month*. But this time there was silence. Such was the magnitude of the devastation that the *New York Times* minimized the massacre of two million Jews in the East, positioning the 9 December 1942 story on page 20.[6] Why the civilized world failed to decelerate the pace of genocide is a mystery that political, diplomatic, and military historians have tried to solve.

How the Holocaust has sometimes been represented—on stage, on screen, in architecture—is the theme of this chapter, which suggests the difficulty of operating within a culture not known for its appreciation of the tragic. To confront the *Shoah* is both impossible and necessary, and the artistic difficulties may be insurmountable. The suffering the Third Reich inflicted allows for no redeeming qualities. No grief or retribution is sufficient. With such losses no vengeance or restitution is commensurate. That American culture was not quite up to the task is not necessarily due to

IN SEARCH OF AMERICAN JEWISH CULTURE

imaginative limitations. Who could live and breathe with full knowledge of what the Holocaust revealed? Who could stare for long into that abyss of deranged fury, of degradation without limit, of massive killing without remorse, of death without martyrdom?

The Bund (the Polish Jewish Labor Party) was the first organization to provide an account of the full-scale extinction of Polish Jewry; yet, when the *Jewish Frontier* translated the report into English, even its editors did not grasp the implications of the news that had been so desperately smuggled out of the Greater Reich. The report was relegated to the back pages of the September 1942 issue. In the next issue, however, the monthly was more direct, describing the "systematic" design of Nazi Germany to "exterminate" European Jewry. A "holocaust," the *Jewish Frontier* announced, was overtaking European Jewry.[7] This may have been the first use of the term that would, beginning in the 1960s, generally designate the Final Solution. The specter that had haunted Henry Adams—of half a million New Yorkers "eating kosher, and saved from the drowning they deserve"—could no longer be dismissed as a sour wisecrack.[8] Those unable to get to New York and other havens were not only drowned but also tortured, subjected to gruesome medical "experiments," gassed, hanged, shot, and starved to death.

The Holocaust was not entirely unforeseen. Mordecai Kaplan had written in 1934 that "extermination" was the "remedy" that modern anti-semitism had designed, once Jews could no longer be quarantined from Gentile society. Indeed, in the same year Glatstein's visit to his dying mother in Lublin enabled him to forecast the doom of Polish Jewry; and the poems he wrote in the following half-decade or so, well before the Wannsee Conference, so uncannily adumbrated the Final Solution that they could later be published as "Poems of Remembrance" and "Poems of the Holocaust." But his warnings were unheeded, his vision ignored.[9] He wrote in Yiddish, which had shrunk by the spring of 1945 to the language of what another rescued writer, Avrum Golomb, called "*a yortsayt kultur*" (a mourning culture).[10]

The American Jewish intelligentsia that had sustained close ties to Eastern Europe predictably registered the tremors with greater sensitivity than their more acculturated counterparts. That was evident in a symposium published in the *Contemporary Jewish Record* early in 1944. Eleven writers, all "Under Forty," all of rising prominence, were asked about their feelings as Jews. None of the questions alluded to the war then raging, though indirectly that conflagration could have been addressed, as the symposiasts were invited to reflect on "the revival of anti-Semitism as a powerful force in the political history of our time" in affecting their lives or their writings. Several of the writers failed to mention the war even in passing, and none of the respondents claimed any affiliation with American Jewish culture. Some, like Kazin, Lionel Trilling, Clement Greenberg, and drama critic Louis Kronenberger, confessed an inability to fathom even the presence of such a subculture, however admirable a few of the writers claimed its Yiddish literary antecedents to be. Kazin singled out Sholem Aleichem, I. L. Peretz, and I. J. Singer for praise but acknowledged the greater and more direct impact of Blake, Melville, and Emerson. Muriel Rukeyser confessed to the subliminal power of Jewish feelings but denied the influence of any Jewish culture.[11] So deracinated had these writers become that not even the Holocaust could be explicitly recognized.

The eruptions from the depths were slow in getting to the surface in an era American Jewish historians usually described in terms of suburbanization and embourgeoisement. In his major 1957 survey, Nathan Glazer discerned a "remarkably slight" impact that the Holocaust registered on "the inner life" of American Jewry, and little evidence has emerged since then to alter that assessment. Between 1950 and 1965 the Jewish Publication Society of America published only one book on the Holocaust: Leon Poliakov's *Harvest of Hate* (1954), copublished with Syracuse University Press to reduce the risks of marketplace failure. A one-volume reference work like *The New Jewish Encyclopedia* (1962) provided no separate entry on the Holocaust, to which Columbia University's Raul Hilberg devoted his doctoral dissertation. Academic presses ranging from Columbia to Oklahoma rejected it; and Princeton University Press dismissed Hilberg's manuscript as a "not sufficiently important contribution" to an understanding of the Final Solution, a subject that other scholars had already covered adequately. The anonymous evaluator was Hannah Arendt. Nor was Yad Vashem in Israel interested in getting the dissertation published. Only after a subvention was Quadrangle Books in Chicago persuaded to publish Hilberg's *The Destruction of the European Jews* (1961), which has remained an indispensable scholarly treatment of the topic. When Rabbi Irving Greenberg asked to teach a course on the Holocaust in 1962, Yeshiva University needed two years before giving him its approval, and then only under the title "Totalitarianism and Ideology in the Twentieth Century."[12] Until 1960, when Israeli agents captured Adolf Eichmann in Argentina, the Jews of silence are far more evident to the historian than are those who struggled to confront the *Shoah*.

With one blazing exception: an adolescent's diary written in Dutch in a secret annex. An analysis of the vicissitudes of *The Diary of a Young Girl* can illumine the cultural framework within which this most desolate of historical events was represented. What happened to that book validates the remark made to Edith Wharton on the evening the dramatization of *The House of Mirth* opened in New York. The failure of the play caused William

Dean Howells to observe: "What the American public always wants is a tragedy with a happy ending."[13] That is what the public wanted to make of the death of Anne Frank, which could not have been more haunting or terrible. In 1945 the fifteen-year-old inmate of typhus-ridden Bergen-Belsen was last seen shivering in the cold, covered with only a blanket. What was left of her physically had been reduced to bones and tears. Such denials of life were multiplied, under conditions of maximal suffering, by six million. But her fate made the pain immediate, so searing as to be unforgettable.

The last sentence in her diary was written on 1 August 1944, only three days before the murderers came. Her older sister Margot had also kept a diary, but it was lost. Anne's text, spared from oblivion, would have to be mediated, however. It would be read and adapted to accommodate a postwar audience, in terms that would reflect its sentiments and perspectives. The diary was first published in abbreviated form in Holland in 1947. Three years later translations of *Het Achterhuis* appeared in both French and German, but to little effect. Janet Flanner's "Letter from Paris" bestowed faint praise on the *Diary* as the work of "a precocious, talented little Frankfurt Jewess . . . [who] rightly aimed to be a writer when she grew up."[14]

The posthumous power of her words to give concreteness to the Holocaust began only with *The Diary of a Young Girl*, published in the United States in 1952. The catalyst was Meyer Levin, an American novelist who had read the French translation. He was told by Otto Frank, however, the only survivor among the eight Jews who had been hiding at 263 Prinsengracht, that several American and British publishers had already rejected his daughter's diary. "Unfortunately, they all said, the subject was too heartrending." There was no market. Levin persisted: "I sent the diary to a half dozen editors whom I knew. The reactions were uniform: they were personally touched, but professionally they were convinced that the public shied away from such material."

Then, in the annual literary issue of the *American Jewish Congress Weekly*, he urged publication of "the most important human document to have come out of the great catastrophe. . . . The holocaust at long last comes home, and . . . we weep." Serialized in *Commentary*, the diary was hailed as a classic (by Levin) on the front page of the *New York Times Book Review*. Brandished with Eleanor Roosevelt's introduction, *The Diary of a Young Girl* has been translated into fifty-one languages and has sold more than sixty million copies.[15] Even Abbie Hoffman, who read it as an undergraduate and claimed, near the end of his life, that no other book had so affected him, picked her house in Amsterdam as one of the only two sites where the outlaw of the 1970s signed his own name. (The other was the birthplace of the Mexican revolutionary Emiliano Zapata.)[16] In late March 1990, at a UNICEF benefit in New York, Tilson Thomas conducted his own composition entitled "From the Diary of Anne Frank," and later conducted the New World Symphony in a tour that featured the concert piece. Its narrator was Debra Winger, the only U.S.-born movie star ever to undergo Israeli military training. Critics gave the concert piece a mixed reception, with negative notices charging that the music resembled a film score.

Levin also attempted to write a theatrical version, even though producer Herman Shumlin warned him: "It's impossible. You simply can't expect an audience to come to the theater to watch on the stage people they know to have ended up in the crematorium. It would be too painful. They won't come." Producer Cheryl Crawford also passed up the opportunity to support Levin's adaptation of *The Diary of a Young Girl*, and would soon duplicate so erroneous a judgment by declining to produce *West Side Story* as well. A stage adaptation of the *Diary* other than Levin's was nevertheless produced in 1955, which led to its republication in German.

The *Tagebuch* stunned German readers, and then audiences. Attending a stage version in West Berlin in 1956, British critic Kenneth Tynan recorded "the most drastic emotional experience the theatre has ever given me. It had little to do with art, for the play was not a great one; yet its effect, in Berlin, at that moment of history, transcended anything that art has yet learned to achieve." After it was over, "the house-lights went up on an audience that sat drained and ashen, some staring straight ahead, others staring at the ground, for a full half-minute. Then, as if awakening from a nightmare, they rose and filed out in total silence, not looking at each other." Tynan heard "no applause, and there were no curtain-calls." He acknowledged that his report was "not drama criticism. In the shadow of an event so desperate and traumatic, criticism would be an irrelevance. I can only record an emotion that I felt, would not have missed, and pray never to feel again."[17]

Though the Broadway production, in Tynan's opinion, "smacked of exploitation," its emotional force was overwhelming enough to run for 717 performances. An inspired fourteen-year-old in attendance was Barbara (as she then spelled her given name) Streisand; *The Diary of Anne Frank* was the first play she ever saw. Pivotal to the effect on audiences was the staging of director Garson Kanin, whose films had exerted an international impact. Indeed, when visiting the tiny cubicle in Amsterdam, he noticed on the wall above Anne's bed a Dutch movie poster among the photos of Hollywood stars that the young diarist had collected. The poster announced: "*Tom, Dick and Harry*—starring Ginger Rogers, directed by Garson Kanin." (Anne's own photo, she wistfully wrote on 10 October 1942, might someday give her "a chance to come to Hollywood.")[18]

Among the ten actors picked for the New York production was a living link to the shattered Jewish communities of Europe. Joseph Schildkraut had won an Academy Award as Captain Dreyfus in Warner Brothers' *The Life of Emile Zola* (1937). But the 1,068 times Schildkraut played Otto Frank, over the course of three years, "were probably the most important and decisive of my whole life," he wrote. "Because I did not merely act a part, but had to live as Otto Frank through the whole terrible and shattering experience of an era which can never be erased from the memory of my generation."

He could not deny the force of the play: "It was, I believe firmly, not accidental that *The Diary of Anne Frank* became the culmination of my professional life." Himself the son of a leading stage actor who had come from the Balkans to revive for German audiences a love of their own classics, Joseph Schildkraut had "never before . . . felt such an intimate relationship to a play, never such an identification with a part." For the diary "actually wrote the epitaph to a whole period of the history of Europe, the history of Germany, [and] the tragedy of the Jews." At one Zionist rally in Madison Square Garden, a torch was brought from Israel to light a menorah on stage. Schildkraut lit it and said the prayer just as he had done in the final scene in act 1 on Broadway. "Thirty thousand people filled the arena, a sea of humanity," he recalled. "And like powerful waves the murmurs, sighs, prayers of that mass rose up to me, engulfed me, carried me away. I felt sorrow and exultation. My eyes burned, my heart ached in pride and grief."[19]

Schildkraut repeated the role in the movie, which Twentieth Century–Fox released in 1959. But the task of making sense of the senseless was exceedingly difficult; director George Stevens had to make intelligible for wider audiences this microcosm of a historical catastrophe. Some American moviegoers found *The Diary of Anne Frank* baffling, apparently not realizing that it was based on a family's actual experience. They assumed that what they were viewing was fictional. An early cut of the film ended at Bergen-Belsen, which so vexed a preview audience that the conclusion was changed so that, like the play, an optimistic note prevails. "In spite of everything," Anne Frank proclaims earlier in her diary (on 15 July 1944), "I still believe that people are really good at heart." That reverberant testament is heard (twice) in the play and the film, but in her diary is followed by the portent of "the ever-approaching thunder," the doom of "the suffering millions."[20] Such phrases film audiences were spared, as the point was less to disenchant than to inspire.

Otto Frank himself realized that audiences responded as much to the pathos of adolescent yearning as to the horror outside the secret annex,[21] which is undoubtedly why the diary and its dramatizations made such an impact. Even though the Soviet Union officially ignored the Holocaust, lumping Jews anonymously among other victims of fascism, a Russian translation of the diary was allowed to be published in 1960. Deserving credit for such a breakthrough was Ilya Ehrenburg, who provided an introduction to the volume. "Six million were asphyxiated in the gas chambers, shot in ravines or in forests, condemned to a slow death from hunger," the cosmopolitan intellectual wrote in *Dnevnik Anne Frank*. "One voice speaks for these six million. It is not the voice of a wise man or a poet, but of an ordinary girl." Soon thereafter, at a ravine near Kiev, Yevtushenko would imagine himself as her. The poet professed to feel the excitement of love as "they're battering in the door. The roar of the ice." In Norway the effects were felt as well. Debuting as Anne Frank on the stage was the future international film star Liv Ullmann, whose grandfather had been deported to Dachau for the crime of hiding Jews.[22]

In the United States not even the term "Holocaust" was yet widely in use. No name was readily available to specify this evil of the Third Reich, and neither knowledge of nor interest in the Nazi genocide was conspicuous. Thus morally serious artistic impulses were frustrated. The theatrical and cinematic distortions of *The Diary of a Young Girl* must be situated, however, in the context of the 1950s. A vigorous and various pluralism was still subdued for the sake of a consensus that emphasized social stability. Even Alain Resnais's *Night and Fog* (1955), betrays the same evasion of what specifically happened to the Jews. This much-admired documentary film failed to name the primary victims of the Nazis, and their programmatic responsibility for mass murder is subordinated to an abstract meditation on evil. The sensibility of the 1950s tended toward moral generalizations, at the expense of historic specificity. Such an aesthetic blurred the identities of the annihilated and the executioners and torturers, as though wickedness were so universal that nothing need be done about it or even accusations articulated.[23] In pretending that antisemitism was irrelevant to the policies of the Third Reich, *The Diary of Anne Frank* was not unique.

The most bitter controversy that the play generated was its evasion of the distinctively Jewish character of the ordeal in Amsterdam. Levin was quick to blame the playwrights who were given the chance to adapt the diary he had wanted to stage. Oscar-winners for the scenario for *Seven Brides for Seven Brothers* (1954), Albert Hackett and Frances Goodrich were a husband-and-wife team credited with writing thirty-one other films as well. These were mostly light comedies and musicals like *Easter Parade* (1948); their classic *It's a Wonderful Life* had been inspired by a Christmas card. The team had also adapted the Dashiell Hammett series *The Thin Man*, which may account for Lillian Hellman's suggestion that Hackett and Goodrich could transfer *The Diary of a Young Girl* to the stage.

Granted, they were not Jewish. But MGM's head of production later assured Levin that, in researching the Chanukah scene for the adaptation, the team solicited the help of Max Nussbaum, "the most prominent Reform rabbi in Hollywood."[24] Even if Levin was accurate in blaming Hellman and her nominees for minimizing the Jewish dimension of the diary, the erasure was explicable in other terms: it was a cultural mandate. Had anyone else put *The Diary of a Young Girl* on Broadway, similar distortions would have resulted. Audiences in the early 1950s were still uneasy with hearing invocations of particularism and peoplehood, and with facing the lethal implications of Diaspora history. The terminus of the camps, it was widely assumed, had to be understood within the framework of universalism instead. What happened to Anne Frank might have happened to anyone (though it didn't).

For example, the diarist herself wondered:

> Who has made us Jews different from all other people? Who has allowed us to suffer so terribly up till now? It is God who has made us as we are, but it will be God, too, who will raise us up again. If we bear all this suffering and if there are still Jews left, when it is over, then Jews, instead of being doomed, will be held up as an example. Who knows, it might even be our religion from which the world and all peoples learn good, and for that reason and that reason only do we have to suffer now. We can never become just Netherlanders, or just English, or just . . . representatives of any other country for that matter, we will always remain Jews, but we want to, too.

This echo of the Covenant is posthumously twisted into something radically different in both the play and the film. "We're not the only people that've had to suffer," Anne is made to say. "There've always been people that've had to. . . . Sometimes one race. . . . Sometimes another." The alteration was so drastically unfaithful to the diarist's own sentiments that Levin was right to ask: "Why had her Jewish avowal been censored on the stage?" He called her pronouncement "a pure and perfect expression of the search for meaning in the Holocaust, for all humanity, Jewish or not. Nowhere in the substitute drama [of Hackett and Goodrich] is this touched upon. This brazen example of the inversion of a dead author's words epitomizes the programmatic, politicized [*sic*] dilution of the Jewish tragedy. Millions of spectators the world over were unaware they were subjected to idea-censorship."[25] Imagine an equivalent, like a play about Jefferson in which he extols Providence for embroiling America in the exterminating havoc of Europe.

But Anne Frank's belief in the uniqueness of Jewish destiny was precisely what Kanin wanted to stamp out, historian Ralph Melnick charged. The director demanded that the Hacketts comply with what he considered a "serious point": "Anne says 'We're not the only Jews that've had to suffer. Right down through the ages, there have been Jews and they've had to suffer.' This strikes me as an embarrassing piece of special pleading. Right down through the ages, people have suffered because of being English, French, German, Italian, Ethiopian, Mohammedan, Negro, and so on." Kanin could not advise "how this can be indicated, but it seems to me of utmost importance. The fact that in this play the symbols of persecution and oppression are Jews is incidental, and Anne, in stating the argument so, reduces her magnificent stature." The director believed that "it is Peter [Van Daan] who should be the young one, outraged at being persecuted because he is a Jew, and Anne, wiser, pointing out that through the ages, people in minorities have been oppressed. In other words, at this moment the play has an opportunity to spread its theme into the infinite."[26]

Jews were thus grotesquely converted into mere "symbols of persecution and oppression," as though something about Nazi malevolence were capricious, floating outside of any Western patrimony of antisemitism, as though other peoples—like the English or the Germans—had been designated for utter annihilation. To have specified how Jewry itself was to be extinguished was a diarist's error the director corrected.

Nor were the actors in the Chanukah scene to sing in Hebrew because, as the playwrights explained to Otto Frank, to do so "would set the characters in the play apart from the people watching them. . . . The majority of our audience is not Jewish. And the thing that we have striven for . . . is to make the audience understand and identify themselves." Changing "Maoz Tsur" to "Rock of Ages" at least made clear to audiences the persistence of the "raging foes," whose presence outside the annex was directly suggested. But successive drafts of the play had the effect of obscuring the particular anguish of Jewish suffering, leaving the audience to figure out for itself why these Dutch civilians were in hiding. The *Diary* almost appeared to portray a family experiencing a housing shortage. One draft had Mrs. Frank's Sabbath prayer of salvation uttered; later it was eliminated. *Het Achterhuis* recorded the desire of Anne's sister Margot to be a nurse in Palestine, had she survived the war, but neither onstage nor onscreen was her Zionist sentiment mentioned.[27] And though Susan Strasberg had drawn raves for her Broadway portrayal of Anne Frank, Twentieth Century–Fox honored casting custom by substituting a non-Jew, Millie Perkins.

The directors of stage and screen were not alone, however, in misreading Anne Frank's actual text, to say nothing of recent European history. Nor could the innocence of the Jews operating within a culture prone to deny particularist claims be held accountable. Otto Frank was a universalist too. When the Anne Frank Foundation issued a pamphlet in March 1960, soliciting funds for the creation of an International Youth Center in Amsterdam, the Holocaust itself was unmentioned (unless equated with "a period of immorality and injustice"). Neither did words like "Jews" and

"Nazis" appear in print; only a phrase like "enemies of humanity" made reference to the perpetrators of genocide. The extinction of a million Jewish children was transformed into "the suffering of Anne and two million other children." Her father was quoted as calling her diary "a demonstration of the human experience, that in times of distress one learns to know one's true friends and that in the end the powers of evil are not equal to good will and mutual understanding."

No evidence whatsoever was provided for so thoughtless a claim, which the Final Solution itself belied. Anne had indeed become "a symbol for the whole world," but so global a phrasing seemed to negate any effort to concretize her death as a Jew. The denial of the tragic was hardly confined to one side of the Atlantic, or to those who had been spared the relentless terror of Nazi occupation and domination.

The expulsion of nullity from American culture itself was nevertheless impressive, so that the upbeat would be stressed even in a play inspired by a disaster at the heart of Western civilization. The Holocaust had to be put in soft focus. Specialists in light comedy were deemed fit to adapt the diary; indeed, credits like *Naughty Marietta* (1935) strengthened the case for Hackett and Goodrich, who were delighted by their assignment. *The Diary of Anne Frank* "seems to us to lend itself admirably to play form with its tense drama, the possibility of great intimacy in the scenes," they wrote, "and moments of lovely comedy which heighten the desperate, tragic situation of the people." At the outset Broadway producer Kermit Bloomgarden was explicit in his insistence that the script would not be "wringing tears out of people." He added that "the only way this play will go is if it's funny." Get audiences to laugh, Bloomgarden told the pair at their first meeting, to make it "possible for them to sit through the show." No "breast beating," as if the point was not already clear.

Each revision of the script put further daylight between the furies encircling the diarist herself and the gaiety that was the hook supposedly needed to grab an American audience. So far a deviation from the *Diary of a Young Girl* caused Hackett and Goodrich to wonder whether they risked betrayal of the text itself. They were striking so many ludic keys that Otto Frank "may be shocked at the amount of comedy we have in it," they feared. But such a tone "is true to the character of Anne," they concluded, "and consequently in the spirit of the book." The adapters further rationalized why Bloomgarden had chosen them: "He wanted comedy . . . and there is certainly a great deal of comedy already in the book."

How successful those responsible for the Broadway version were in transforming the negative into the positive can be gleaned from the praise of Brooks Atkinson, who admired the omission of any allusion to Bergen-Belsen or to the systematic horror of the Final Solution. Such reticence, he claimed, showed "taste rare in the theater." The *Times* reviewer was pleased that Hackett and Goodrich "do not dwell on the shocking conclusion to Anne's brief career in human society." The play constituted "a record of homely things and human reactions—gratitude for sanctuary in the garret, the disciplines needed to keep their presence a secret, petty irritations, rebellion, treachery, ridicule, callousness, love, forgiveness. It is basically a portrait of Anne keeping alive her interest in life, her faith in the sweetness of the passing moments and her confidence in the future." Atkinson hailed the talents of those who had extended themselves on Broadway, demonstrating themselves to be "dedicated artists with a mission."[28] The play, the *Times* added, was "a lovely, tender drama" about "the shining spirit of a young girl."

The *New York Daily News* called it "not in any important sense a Jewish play"; and the praise of the *New York Post* was even more reassuring that nothing irritating would spoil the enjoyment: "There isn't a Nazi in it."[29] Onstage no one is tortured; no one is killed; no one dies. What better way to draw an audience into an awareness of the *Shoah*?

Nevertheless the benefit ticket sales were initially not so strong as expected, and Kanin suspected that a reputation for gloom hovered over the play. Three days before it opened, he told the *Times* that neither was the tone of the *Diary* melancholy nor was its subject the Second World War. Instead the drama dealt "mainly . . . with human courage, faith, hope, brotherhood, love and self-sacrifice. We discovered as we went deeper and deeper that it was a play about what Shaw called 'the life force.' Anne Frank was certainly killed, but she was never defeated."

A phrase like "life force" might have been applicable to the last seconds of desperation as the Zyklon B was injected in the gas chambers, in the scramble for a final gulp of oxygen. But Shaw's term made little sense otherwise. The interview did not mention to which "race" this gallant girl and her loved ones had belonged, nor that they had been caught in the machinery of mass murder that claimed nearly six million other victims. Kanin called the *Diary* "the honest telling of a breathlessly exciting story . . . a thrilling observation of Anne's necessarily swift, yet magical, journey from childhood through adolescence to passionate young womanhood." He added that it was "a chronicle of the dignity and nobility of common people; a salute to the great spirit of man alive."

What had made that maturation "necessarily swift" was left unexplained; why this particular family and others had needed to summon resources of "dignity and nobility" was not specified. Even more bizarre was Kanin's claim that Anne's words "have bubbled with amusement, love and self-discovery, words so wondrously alive, so near that one feels it might be the people living next door to you." The horror had been so fervently excised, the immediate past so blandly transferred to a fantastic realm of delusion and amnesia that the misrepresentation cannot be ascribed to one director's moral and artistic obtuseness. His interpretation was sanitized of the ineffable terror that Nazism perpetrated. The diarist had assumed as early as 9 October 1942 that most of the Jews transported to the "barbarous" east would be "murdered," and she noted that "the English radio speaks of their being gassed." But such passages were omitted from the play.

The New York Drama Critics' Circle named *The Diary of Anne Frank* the best American play of the year, and Hackett and Goodrich picked up a Pulitzer Prize for drama as well. Howells's remark to Wharton was vindicated when the Pulitzer committee lauded "the miracle" that the playwrights had wrought, which was to guarantee that "the sense of doom is never as important as the will to live." *The Diary of Anne Frank* was, to be sure, a "tragedy"—but one in which the elements of "comedy and a romance" were blended.[30] Eight people had lived hidden in a single room for two years before they were betrayed, and all but one were hideously murdered. But the Pulitzer Prize jury was undeterred from hailing the play as "a statement, courageous and immensely human, of the need of a people in their daily lives to live not merely with death but above it"—an easy way to praise the doomed without having to reconsider so generous a view of our species.

By defining the experience the diarist had recorded into a saga of courage in general, such interpretations denied the wretched vulnerability of one European minority in particular, and evaded a serious exploration of the Holocaust even in the process of seeming to put it on stage. The "race" shared by the *Diary*'s characters was rarely mentioned in the newspaper reports of the Pulitzer Prize for drama. The *New York Times* also alluded to "a young girl's sweetness, courage and confidence in the future."

So sappy a reading—and rereading—of *The Diary of a Young Girl* did not go unchallenged. A critic in Amsterdam's *Het Parool* sharply condemned the deviation of the Broadway play from the diary itself and wondered why the adaptation had been so unfaithful to the adolescent's own words and beliefs: "Even the passages of the *Diary* which are read by an invisible Anne are not citations but fabricated by Miss Goodrich and Mr. Hackett. Their play is a new product which is sailing under a false flag, trash which I hope we shall not see here."[31]

A different issue was raised in a 1957 article entitled "Betrayal of Anne Frank." Rabbi Jacob Weinstein of Chicago sympathized with Levin's outrage that her Jewish voice had been weakened if not suppressed, and asked if there had been "a pattern of omission in the Broadway version that reflects an ideology opposed to strong Jewish identification." Was Levin right in his opinion "that the sentiment attached to the girl's diary has been exploited by persons whose actions do not show them in full sympathy with her ideas?" If that was true, Weinstein argued, "then the control of the *Diary* as it is presently constituted is a bitter travesty on Jewish fate." Otto Frank's response was cosmopolitan: to notice the uniqueness of the Holocaust would somehow contradict his daughter's "message of hope, faith and understanding." So obtuse a denial of the particular fate of the Jews led Weinstein to pose another question: "Does the Jewish people have a right to its own cultural material?"

That issue, however, is either undecidable or is a query that must be answered in the negative.[32] For Jewry has had no single legal and corporate existence through which to invoke rights. In the largest community of the Diaspora, no organization (whether religious or secular) has been recognized (either within or outside the community) as representing that people. Anyone can profess to speak in its name; and anyone, Jew or Gentile, pro-Zionist or anti-Zionist, cosmopolite or particularist, has been free to use (or misuse) its "cultural material." That is a consequence of Emancipation.

Because Hackett and Goodrich barely changed their play in transferring it to the screen, the limitations of the Broadway production were left intact. The *Hollywood Reporter* exulted in the movie's "glowing promise of universal sisterhood and brotherhood." The review was a kind of perfect culmination of the way that the optimistic imperatives of American culture in the 1950s inexorably interpreted the diary. The film was said to amplify "Anne's final philosophy [as] expressed in her diary—that other peoples have also suffered persecution but always there have been some people . . . who have taken a stand for decency. This proved to her that the world is fundamentally and enduringly good." No passages in the diary itself could have been cited as manifest evidence of her "final philosophy," or of her ecumenism on the subject of human suffering. Some of her neighbors did behave more than decently; the courageous Miep Gies helped protect the Jews and also salvaged the diary. But no "righteous Gentiles" are shown on the screen; and no examples are mentioned in the review, which claimed that "every second of [the film] rings with the fresh-minded tone of veracity."

Assuming that the reviewer had accurately represented Anne Frank's belief in the fundamental beneficence of humanity, no explanation was offered for the eruption of wickedness and no interest in its extent or persistence was exhibited. If the world is fundamentally good, how could the Holocaust have happened? Such an obvious question was not even raised, as it seemed out of bounds, ideologically. What one family experienced could not easily conform to Hollywood's approach to representation. Though the situation at 263 Prinsengracht might be regarded as claustrophobic, the film was shot in CinemaScope, and just as oddly won an Academic Award in the category of set decoration. Shelley Winters won an Oscar for Best Supporting Actress and managed, in her acceptance speech, to thank both her agent from the Music Corporation of America *and* Anne Frank. "This isn't a Jewish picture," the president of Twentieth Century–Fox declared. "This is a picture for the world."[33]

Even though *The Diary of Anne Frank*, like *The Diary of a Young Girl*, spares the mass audience the torment of the camps, American culture was not yet prepared to plunge into the depths of torture and turpitude that defined the extremity of the Holocaust. Frequently impervious to the sadness and anguish that serious artists were trying to convey, mass culture has almost compulsively promoted the need for eupeptic resolutions to unsolvable conditions. Early in the nineteenth century, Nahum Tate's revised version of *King Lear* was popular because Edgar and Cornelia fall in love and because she and her father remain alive. Scorned for changing the tragedy so radically, actor Edmund Kean claimed to have tried to be faithful to the original, but "ascertained that a large majority of the public—whom we live to please, and must please to be popular—liked Tate better than Shakespeare."

Hollywood continued such concessions. When *Death of a Salesman* was transposed to the screen, Columbia Pictures initially wanted to add a short documentary, after Willy's funeral, in praise of selling as a career. When *The Crucible* (1953) was staged on Broadway, Ed Sullivan resented its theme; the CBS variety show host wondered why Miller had not written instead a celebration of the nation's colonial heritage. In the Warner Brothers adaptation of Tennessee Williams's *The Glass Menagerie* (1950), loneliness is remedied at the end because Laura Wingfield (Jane Wyman), luckily enough, will soon be welcoming another Gentleman Caller. When Schary adapted *Miss Lonelyhearts* (1933) into *Lonelyhearts* in 1959 (the same year that Stevens's *Diary of Anne Frank* was released), the ending was distorted. MGM's protagonist stops suffering after all, which provoked one acerbic movie critic to note how American was the preference for "an uncrucified Christ."

That is another way of saying that American readers were not yet prepared for Elie Wiesel's lengthy memoir published in Yiddish in Argentina, *Un di velt hot geshvign* (And the world remained silent). For French readers he condensed his account of Auschwitz and Buchenwald; *La Nuit* appeared in 1958. Americans were still not ready; two years later *Night* came out, after twenty publishers had rejected it. No one devoted himself more conscientiously than the author to the problem of how the dead might be remembered and how the living might learn from the Holocaust. Born a year before Anne Frank (in disputed territory between Rumania and Hungary), he was eastern European. He was also poor and pious. Hers was a middle-class German family, so Reform as to be pleased that in 1943 Chanukah occurred so close to Saint Nicholas's Day and Christmas.[35] The little Frankfurt Jewess was therefore a more endearing and accessible icon of violated innocence than was Wiesel. For most Jews as well as non-Jews in the United States, identification with her was thus smoother, reinforcing an interpretation of the Holocaust that generalized it into the signature event of universal suffering.

Though Anne had dreamed of visiting Palestine, her biggest fantasy was to travel all over the world and to become a writer, which is the kind of life that Philip Roth has led. In his novella *The Ghost Writer*, a twenty-three-year-old Zuckerman visits an older and more austere Jewish writer, and imagines that Amy Bellette, a young researcher who is also staying in the house, is an Anne Frank who has somehow survived Bergen-Belsen. Roth's tale is a gesture of imaginative resistance to the Holocaust, as though wondering how something so unbearable might just possibly be less so. *The Ghost Writer* is also a melancholy acceptance of the finality of the Final Solution. Amy Bellette is only herself. "When the sleeve of her coat fell back," Zuckerman "of course saw that there was no scar on her forearm. No scar; [and therefore] no book" after all.

In the very act of dreaming of a universe so benign that Anne Frank might not have perished, in the very realization that such a universe does not exist, Roth confronted the terrible truth to which a mere fiction can point, and did so in part through the subtle indirection of mentioning as well a writer whose own sisters the Nazis had gassed. Anne Frank was, *The Ghost Writer* suggests, "like some impassioned little sister of Kafka's, his lost little daughter—a kinship is even there in the face, I think. Kafka's garrets and closets, the hidden attics where they hand down the indictments, the camouflaged doors. . . . What he invented, she suffered."

Anne Frank could *not* still be alive, and hers are only the words of a ghost-writer. She can "live" only in memory, only in representation. In the United States she could also "live" as a fragile symbol of Jewish identification, as an inspiration. Though Zuckerman's scandalous fiction is supposed to have disgraced New Jersey's embattled Jewry, redemption is still possible, as Judge Leonard Wapter (a distant family friend) writes in a letter to the errant young novelist. "If you have not yet seen the Broadway production of *The Diary of Anne Frank*," the judge tells Zuckerman, "I strongly advise that you do so. Mrs. Wapter and I were in the audience on opening night; we wish that Nathan Zuckerman could have been with us to benefit from that unforgettable experience."

Zuckerman refuses to reply, and tells his father:

> "Nothing I could write Wapter would convince him of anything. Or his wife."

"You could tell him you went to see *The Diary of Anne Frank.* You could at least do that."

"I didn't see it. I read the book. *Everybody* read the book."

"But you liked it, didn't you?"

"That's not the issue. How can you *dis*like it?"[36]

Anne's diary eludes such categories of judgment, even as her brief life has eluded oblivion. "I want to go on living even after my death!" she wrote in the spring of 1944; and in a way she has. In 1991, an expanded edition of the *Diary* appeared, restoring passages that her father had excised to avoid giving offense. (For example, the diary cited the rule in the annex to "speak softly at all times. . . . all civilized languages are permitted, therefore no German!" Otto Frank had altered the rule to "all civilized languages, but softly.")[37] In 1996 *Anne Frank Remembered* won an Oscar for Best Documentary, even as its director, Jon Blair, continued to speak as a universalist. The Holocaust, he insisted, should not be reduced to "a uniquely Jewish experience," nor should the story of Anne Frank "be about the genocide of the Jews specifically."[38]

But Meyer Levin was partly vindicated in 1997, when *The Diary of Anne Frank* returned to Broadway. Wendy Kesselman's new adaptation was based on the restored text. This time "Maoz Tsur" was sung in Hebrew, without apparently provoking demands for refunds at the box office. Anne was exposed as the essentialist she was, telling Peter Van Daan when he considers conversion: "You'll always be Jewish in your soul." Though the further evil that Nazism inflicted is explicitly described in an epilogue, in a soliloquy in which the father recounts the arrests and the deaths of the others, director James Lapine explained: "The diary is a lot about growing up." He added: "Like any good yarn, it makes you think, 'My God, how would I have acted in that situation?' Hopefully, it's first of all a good story. I tried to humanize it and not make it an emblematic story or something moralistic or noble." Lapine, who won Tonys for his libretto and his directing of Sondheim's *Into the Woods,* welcomed children in the audience: "It's not without humor. . . . It's a very entertaining piece of theater. It shouldn't feel like spinach, like you have to come because it's good for you."[39]

True enough, the story put on stage could indicate that, even during the Holocaust, the will to survive, with self-respect intact, was not completely extirpated. That a remnant of European Jewry outlasted the Third Reich is a tribute to fortitude and tenacity, plus miraculous luck. Hitler did not win the war against the Allies. But he did not lose the war against the Jews.

In American thought and expression, the subject of the Holocaust was at first only slowly and rarely broached. In films, for example, even Stanley Kramer's moralistic *Judgment at Nuremberg* (1961) managed to depict Nazism without inserting any major or even minor Jewish characters. Not until Sidney Lumet's *The Pawnbroker* (1965) did Hollywood directly tackle the *Shoah* again; when the protagonist, Sol Nazerman (Rod Steiger), shows the numbers tattooed on his arm to his assistant, the comparison is made to "a secret society." The subject of the Holocaust was still mostly tacit, in important ways still a secret. The Jewish identity of Nazerman is altered as he becomes like Christ, the "Nazarene" showing his stigmata.[40] A trickle of films would nevertheless gather force, helping to shape the sensibility of American Jews—and of many of their neighbors.

The inexplicable somehow had to get explained. Much got lost in translation, but enough seeped through to widen the contours of the culture and to allow serious glimpses of the horror. Awareness of it was heightened in 1978. It was front-page news that year when a faction of American Nazis sought permission to march in Skokie, Illinois, where a remnant of survivors resided. The Office of Special Investigations was created to deport Nazi war criminals. In 1978 Jimmy Carter also formed the President's Commission on the Holocaust as a way of repairing relations with American Jewry, which feared that legitimization of Palestinian nationalist aspirations would become official policy. (The nation's first Holocaust center had been created two years earlier in Brooklyn.) In 1978 NBC also presented a miniseries called *Holocaust*, which earned extremely high ratings even as it stirred criticism for tastelessness. Depictions of the machinery of mass murder were interrupted by commercials, for example. In one instance, just after Adolf Eichmann (Tom Bell) complains how the stench of his victims' corpses made pleasant dining impossible, the virtues of Lysol were hawked. No wonder that Wiesel called the program "offensive" and "cheap."[41]

The trickle had become a flood, and some works distinguished themselves. In 1986 Art Spiegelman put a spin on the claim of Nathanael West, who had called his second book "a novel in the form of a comic strip." Even more than *Miss Lonelyhearts*, *Maus* was a novel in the form of a comic book, a two-volume family history as well as a memoir of how such a history was reconstructed. Born in Stockholm in 1948, Spiegelman cofounded and coedited *Raw* magazine. *Maus* depicts Germans as cats, Jews as mice, and Poles as swine, and is set mostly in New York and in Poland, where Isaac Bashevis Singer recalled in his autobiography a boyhood haunted by the shriek of a mouse a cat was torturing. In comics, Spiegelman asserted, the essentials could be crisply conveyed: "It's a great medium for artists who can't remember much anyway." Though he once noticed "a book whose title summed it all up: *Memoirs of an Amnesiac*," he quipped that he was unable to recall "who wrote it or even if I ever read it."

Spiegelman nevertheless performed a culturally more significant gesture of remembrance than Oscar Levant's book of anecdotes had. *Maus* was a product of the detritus of the graphic arts and other bits of vernacular culture (like *The Cisco Kid, Howdy Doody, Captain Video,* and *Mad*) that shaped a baby-boom childhood in Queens. Ransacking the memory bank formed not only by the comic books he adored but also by the experiences of his family in the late 1930s and 1940s,[42] Spiegelman created a work original enough to dispel comparisons with the iconic influences that formed him and striking enough to win a Pulitzer Prize in 1992 for both "a survivor's tale" and "and here my troubles began." Cartoonist Edward Sorel praised him for having "stretched the boundaries of the comic-strip form and created a work of immense power," "an epic in miniature."[43]

The Holocaust had become so important that a 1989 survey revealed that it ranked first as a marker of identity for American Jews. Second in shaping their sense of themselves happened to be the High Holidays of Rosh Hashonah and Yom Kippur, followed by American antisemitism. In fourth place was God. But however urgent, how to articulate the meaning of the Holocaust continued to be elusive. In 1992 the historian (and Holocaust survivor) Saul Friedländer coined a phrase: "the limits of representation." He raised a question whether something about the Holocaust was so dreadful, so unimaginable, so incongruous in relation to everyday reality that this historical phenomenon was not amenable to the talents and techniques of the artist, regardless of medium.[44] Wiesel himself had indicated something similar, in claiming that, with the exception of his first book, he had not written about the Holocaust, but only "around" it. The effect would have been like staring into the sun.

Claude Lanzmann respected those limits in making a documentary that refused to use a single frame of film taken from the 1940s, as though sedulously honoring the prohibition against graven images. Because *Shoah* (1985) is made up of interviews, audiences are compelled to imagine for themselves the harrowing experiences that survivors recount. "The Holocaust is unique in that it creates a circle of flames around itself, a limit which cannot be crossed because a certain absolute horror cannot be transmitted," Lanzmann insisted. "Pretending to cross that line is a grave transgression." In only approaching that fiery circle, *Shoah* earned the praise of the director Marcel Ophuls (*The Sorrow and the Pity, The Memory of Justice*) as "the greatest documentary on contemporary history ever made."[45]

But Lanzmann was a Parisian. Friedländer was a Czech-born Israeli who had been rescued in France. Though based in New York, Wiesel continued to write primarily in French. Theirs, it is fair to say, was not an American sensibility. The year after "the limits of representation" had been coined, an American Jew would test those limits, would push and risk exceeding them.

As a boy in Cincinnati, Steven Spielberg had first learned to read numbers from the tattooed forearm of an Auschwitz survivor. As a Hollywood director, he would be responsible for the film that, more than any other single artifact in mass culture, would end the secrecy of the society of those who had endured the Holocaust. Universal released *Schindler's List* in Germany on 1 March 1994, and in Israel two days later. When the Motion Picture Academy of Arts and Sciences named it Best Picture that spring, the veil of silence was penetrated as never before, and the fate of European Jewry made more accessible. But *Schindler's Ark* (1982), the book on which the film was based, was written by Thomas Keneally, an Australian and a Gentile, which makes more intricate the puzzle of how to define American Jewish culture.

Nor was that the only problem of classification. Keneally had won the Booker Prize for fiction, which is how his book was categorized by its American publisher, Simon and Schuster, or rather, as a "non-fiction novel," in which he presented "a factual account done with fictional techniques." He himself claimed "to use the texture and devices of a novel to tell a true story," and called *Schindler's Ark* a "documentary novel," "a nonfiction novel," and a "faction."[46] From that ambiguous and unfastidious base, further transmutation occurred, widening the distance from verifiable events.

Take, for example, what the movie reviewer for the *New Yorker* called "the most terrifying sequence ever filmed," as the camera follows a group of naked women directly into the showers of Auschwitz-Birkenau. Little in cinematic history can generate the level of anxiety that scene suggests: is the gas about to be turned on, as it was for an estimated 10,000 a day, *every* day, when the killing facilities were operating at maximal efficiency? Can the camera be that remorseless, that unsparing, that cruel? Is there any episode that cannot, that should not, ever be shown? But what gushes out of the showerhead is water, as fright and terror dissolve into the release of laughter. But though that scene is in the book, the screen raises the ante to a stomach-wrenching degree. Yet both "inmates" and audience are granted a reprieve; the chimneys of the crematoria are totems that remained taboo. There *are* limits of representation,[47] however unbounded the actual devastation the Third Reich inflicted.

But not even Spielberg's own prodigious gifts enabled him to portray the most common actuality of the Holocaust. The way that the noose was tightened around the neck of the Jews was too steady and remorseless, as was the unsparing daily worsening of the ordeal inflicted in the ghettos as well as the camps. A working person generally needs a minimum of three thousand calories. Already by 1941 the average daily caloric intake in the ghettos was five hundred. Such malnutrition constituted a death sentence. But emaciation is difficult to convey visually, and the actors in Plaszów inevitably look more hale and hearty than were the inmates whose flesh hung so precipitously on their bones that the cadavers could be stacked like cordwood. When Buchenwald was liberated, Wiesel looked at himself in the mirror and saw "a corpse" returning his gaze, a skeleton on which skin was hanging. Such walking cadavers were not amenable to reenactment.[48]

"The list is life," the ad campaign for the film announced. Yet consider the opening sentence of the survivor Jakov Lind's "Soul of Wood" (1962): "Those who had no papers entitling them to live lined up to die."[49] For nearly six million Jews, lists were *not* life. They were edicts of death, under conditions of maximal physical and psychic torment. In *Schindler's List* the selection process brings salvation, and the protagonist in the Nazi uniform turns out be a savior.

By 1993 the hero could be an even better German than the "good Germans" who had been distinguished from Nazis under the impact of the cold war, when the moral asymmetry between West and East had to be maintained. Striking the right balance in that era had been difficult to achieve. For example, a 1960 production of *Playhouse 90* dealt with the revolt in the Warsaw Ghetto. "In the Presence of Mine Enemies" starred Charles Laughton. But because the sympathetic characters included a Nazi (played by Robert Redford in his television debut), novelist Leon Uris (*Mila 18*) protested to CBS against "the most disgusting dramatic presentation in the history of American television" (despite the Jewish provenance of the teleplay, written by Rod Serling). The exigencies of the cold war had produced a reverent biopic about Dr. Wernher Von Braun, entitled *I Aim at the Stars* (1960). The director of the rocketry program in Alabama had been pivotal to the V-1 and V-2 programs of the Third Reich, so it was left to a Jewish comedian, Mort Sahl, to suggest a subtitle for *I Aim at the Stars*: "But I Hit London."

The end of the cold war and the firmness with which Germany remained solidly and safely democratic ensured the persistence of the "good German," even if none was quite so amazing as the Sudeten German Oskar Schindler. In *Schindler's List* nearly all the good people—Jew and Gentile—make it to V-E Day, film critic J. Hoberman complained. Most of those for whom the audience is rooting do survive, and the *Schindlerjuden* get through the catastrophe without any obvious psychic scars.[50] Though the Holocaust is the strongest proof of unspeakable inhumanity, the film singles out an exceptional act of goodness, and thus continues the tradition of uplift that allows audiences to turn away from a realistic depiction of recent history.

By 1993, however, the Holocaust had seeped so fully into consciousness that the context in which goodness could be shown had altered; to focus on an exceptional act of courage could not be dismissed or reduced to mere sentimentality. Oskar Schindler *had* saved about eleven hundred Jews.

Even if neither the historical record nor the film itself permitted any psychological penetration into his motives, his behavior stands out precisely because of the magnitude of the evil surrounding him.

In *Schindler's List* certain scenes are likely to be etched in memory: the destruction of the Kraków ghetto, the capricious murders that Amon Goeth commits from his balcony and the immersion of the children hiding in excrement to escape the brutal finality of the roundup and execution. Few cinematic representations of the Holocaust are likely to haunt the imagination more powerfully, or to convey some sense of the encounters with absolute terror and with systematic sadism. "I was highly suspicious of *Schindler's List*," Bellow admitted, "but I was moved by it just the same." Having himself created a Holocaust survivor as the protagonist of *Mr. Sammler's Planet* (1970), the novelist "couldn't deny that at the end I was carried away by some of the terrible things that had never been shown on film before, like the young woman presuming to offer advice, shot and killed right before your eyes. You can't help but be moved by that. Violently moved."[51] By getting closer than anyone else to the circle of fire, Spielberg illumined a rare decision like Schindler's to save lives. Such acts were missing in the abstractions of *The Diary of Anne Frank*.

Nor is it quite fair to blame Spielberg for depicting this exceptional trace of goodness, when Hollywood in general had been so reluctant to tackle the Holocaust directly. He bore no responsibility for ensuring the release only of films in which virtually all the Jews die, or in which no one finds refuge in Palestine. Nor could he be held accountable for the failure of other cinematic versions of the Final Solution to compete in the marketplace. *Schindler's List* should not be judged as though it was required to sum up for a mass audience the extent of the desolation, which is so beyond reckoning that probably only miniaturization can provide some sort of human scale. No story can satisfy the requirements of typicality; there are limits to representativeness too. Alan Pakula's *Sophie's Choice* (1982) was not widely criticized because its protagonist is a Polish Catholic rather than a Polish Jew, nor was Agnieszka Holland's *Europa, Europa* (1991) scoffed at because its protagonist also manages to end up in Israel (which is, incidentally, where *Shoah* ends).

There, at the Ghetto Fighters' Kibbutz, Itzhak Zuckerman, who had been second-in-command of the Jewish Combat Organization in the Warsaw Ghetto, tells Lanzmann: "If you could lick my heart, it would poison you." Though the focus of *Schindler's List* on a good German has a detoxifying effect, though the protagonist is a Gentile, the film was still banned from commercial release in Egypt, which had signed a peace treaty with Israel, and throughout the rest of the Arab world as well.[52] Its inhabitants were thus prevented from honoring the recommendation of President

Clinton, who "implored" the public to see the movie. Oprah Winfrey took his advice and testified on her television show: "I think that I'm a better person as a result of seeing *Schindler's List.*"

Christoph Meili of Zurich saw the film too. In January 1997 it inspired the twenty-eight-year-old night watchman at the Union Bank of Switzerland to blow the whistle on the shredding of banking records from the era of the Second World War, even as Jewish survivors and their descendants were seeking to reclaim their accounts.[53] *Schindler's List* is not classified as a documentary, but has been widely shown in Europe for *educational* purposes.

Even though no Americans were cast for the major roles in Spielberg's only black-and-white film, shot on location with a crew that was markedly European, *Schindler's List* probably suffered from the presumption that a Hollywood movie had to be less artistically mature and sophisticated than one directed and produced by a European. Had the first frame announced, say, Film Polski instead of Amblin Entertainment, film critic Stanley Kauffmann speculated, probably "fewer nerves would have been grated right from the start. I can't remember that any European film, of the dozens that have been made about the Holocaust, has aroused much opposition."

Nor is the genre of the documentary film inherently more authentic, more fair, more representative, freer from the danger of distortion. The historian Omer Bartov pointed out that Lanzmann wanted to locate "witnesses who were both strong enough to testify at some length and coherence, and weak enough to finally break down in front of the camera under the incessant pressure of his questions." Lanzmann's warning against transgression continues to be valid, even as he still insisted upon the inaccessibility of the Holocaust (which the use of actors and actresses violates); the *univers concentrationnaire* resists re-creation or absorption into our own mundane world.[54]

Spielberg's film was released abroad shortly before the Broadway opening of Arthur Miller's *Broken Glass.* Set in 1938 and deriving its title from *Kristallnacht*, the play got mixed reviews, before getting a more favorable reception in London in the summer of 1994. By reexamining the compact with civil society ripped apart in the Holocaust, *Broken Glass* offers further evidence that the degree of Miller's own assimilation can easily be exaggerated.

In Brooklyn, the borough where the playwright himself grew up, Sylvia Gellburg is so disturbed by news accounts and photographs of *Kristallnacht* that she becomes paralyzed, unable to move. Like Glatstein visiting Poland, she sees a catastrophe that too many others prefer to ignore or minimize. Neither her assimilated husband nor her assimilated physician can appreciate her prescience, nor can they share her empathy for the Jewish victims of Nazi terror. Her paralysis is intensified by the disbelief of those who are close to her in the atrocities that she foresees. Her husband Philip is so uncomfortable with his own origins that he resents mistakes like being called "Goldberg." For two decades he has also been sexually impotent as well as emotionally dead; the "broken glass" with which the formal ceremony of the Jewish wedding ends here may refer to the shattered Gellburg marriage as well. Miller's great contemporary had earlier put on the Broadway stage a crippled female protagonist, yearning for a male suitor but emotionally at ease only with her glass menagerie. *Broken Glass* is the Jewish version, with fields of force driven by politics overseas to dispel the illusions of innocence, to puncture the national immunity from history.

Philip Gellburg is guilty of wife-beating too, and is thus so utterly unsympathetic a character that the plot makes a striking point: in dying, he will be punished less for his failures as a husband than his betrayal of his people. Not his cruelty to those close to him but his indifference to the cruelty inflicted on the Jews does him in. Upon learning how much of a bigot his Gentile boss is, Philip suffers a heart attack and must pass from self-hatred to self-recognition. His own shame has obscured how fully Jews are threatened abroad and disliked at home. But what happens to his wife, whose physical immobility seems to have given her emotional strength in her marital struggles? Miller himself was unsure, veering between having Sylvia stand triumphant after her husband has died and having her desperately try to rise on her own and do so just barely.[55] But her visionary acuity lacks political consequences. The ring will close; the political paralysis will not be abated in time.

Broken Glass played in New York a year after the U.S. Holocaust Memorial Museum opened in Washington, D.C. There, on 22 April 1993, President and Mrs. Clinton, Vice President and Mrs. Gore, and the official representatives of thirty-two other nations attended the dedication ceremony, which Cable News Network broadcast to the rest of the planet. The program included a reading by Liv Ullmann, and Wiesel identified the double-sided mission of the museum. "Though the Holocaust was principally a Jewish tragedy," he announced, "its implications are universal."[56] This view was shared by Michael Berenbaum, who then served as deputy director of the President's Commission on the Holocaust. The *Shoah* "is essentially Jewish," he wrote, "yet its interpretation is universal."[57]

How to fulfill and reconcile both of those purposes would dog the formation of the museum itself. *The Diary of Anne Frank* had achieved one purpose: by denying the Jewish dimension of the "tragedy," the play universalized a "girl next door." *Schindler's List* showed the terror-stricken and helpless Jews. But they are often relegated to the background. Spielberg's film presented the Holocaust as a clash of wills between two Gentiles: a good German and an SS Commandant. The formation of the U.S. Holocaust Memorial Museum faced similar choices. Those designing it and giving it direction had to connect the particular to the universal, to respect the uniqueness of what befell the Jews while appealing to other Americans to examine the human proclivity for evil. Such choices were formulated in a setting quite different from Broadway and Hollywood, and the political conflicts and consequences were more overt.

When Wiesel referred to the museum as not "an answer . . . but [as] a question mark," he may have meant even so fundamental a problem as the designation of the victims. President Carter, who created the commission that built the $90 million museum, spoke of eleven million—including six million Jews—killed in the Holocaust. How that figure was derived was left unexplained. Polish-American representatives insisted that the murdered Jews and Gentiles from Poland were numerically comparable. Both groups, it was claimed, were considered subhumans whose extinction was the policy of a national state. The president of the Polish American Congress hoped that the museum would also memorialize Poles whom the NKVD massacred in the Katyn Forest in 1940, and would acknowledge the deaths of other Slavs besides Poles. Ukrainian-Americans also proclaimed that Ukrainians were entitled to the status of Holocaust victims; to put only the fate of the Jews on the agenda therefore smacked of parochialism.

So extensive had the culture of complaint become that Secretary of the Interior James Watt announced his approval of the location of the museum on federal property near the Mall by professing to feel the burden of "persecution." He spoke as an evangelical Christian. The Bible he read condemned certain practices as an "abomination." Homosexuals had also been killed by the Nazis, who persecuted those wearing the pink triangle for who they were. In 1997, when New York City's Museum of Jewish Heritage opened, sixteen Orthodox rabbis announced a public boycott, because a plaque memorializing gay victims of Nazism had been erected at the museum's Living Memorial to the Holocaust.[58]

The contours of the Holocaust were debated in an exchange between its two most prominent American historians. Hilberg insisted that the perpetration of genocide had not begun with the Second World War, or even with the Nazi ascent to power six years earlier, but rather with the Turkish slaughter of the Armenians in 1915. Nor did he confine the circle of the Nazis' victims to the Jews, as so many Gypsies (known, more accurately, as Romani) had also been killed. Indeed, in their terminology, what the Nazis inflicted constituted the Porrajmos, the "great devouring." The Romani representatives in Washington did not want the possibility of retrospective justice to be foreclosed any more than did the Jewish representatives, and their arguments were consistent with Wiesel's description of memory as "not only a victory over time, it is also a triumph over injustice." Remembrance would keep the victims from vanishing (again).

But Lucy S. Dawidowicz rebutted Hilberg by insisting that the war to exterminate Jewry was unique. Holding the first chair in Holocaust history, established by Yeshiva University in 1976, she argued that the Nazis' Judeophobia marked a caesura in history itself: "Never before had one people denied another people the fundamental right to live." The Holocaust did not exhaust the annals of genocide, Dawidowicz acknowledged; but neither should the term refer to all the killings of civilians perpetrated by the Third Reich. The sheer obsessiveness with which one people was rounded up to be slaughtered—from the very young to the very old, from the healthy to the infirm, from inmates locked in mental institutions to practicing Christians descended from "non-Aryan" grandparents—was unprecedented. An apt term that emerged later is Judeocide.[59]

Such arguments did not affect the fundamental character of the museum, which was to be American. But because all Americans are partly Jewish, the polity is too, so the building is closed every year on the tenth of Tishri (the Day of Atonement). The U.S. Congress refuses to transact any public business on Yom Kippur either. Such signals are inevitably mixed. While focusing on the Jewish fate, the museum is closed on Christmas, which is when New York's Jewish Museum as well as the Museum of Jewish Heritage–A Living Memorial to the Holocaust are both open. Even as representatives of each group invoked their claims and argued for inclusion within the circle of fire which was the *Shoah*, the centrality of Jewish annihilation was not seriously challenged. But the museum itself was still a public project: the council was federally sponsored, the land was federally donated, the funds for construction and then for operating costs were partly federally appropriated.

In one other way, this was an American museum. One inscription for the wall at the Hall of Remembrance was considered but rejected because it was too bleak: "Earth do not cover my blood; Let there be no resting place for my outcry!" (Job 16:18).[60] Constructed on a site renamed Raoul Wallenberg Place in 1986, even a building consecrated to the Holocaust was expected to be a place called hope. The director who was hired was a Warsaw-born Israeli named Jeshajahu (Shaike) Weinberg, but the tone he wanted to achieve is associated with American show business. He wanted to "trigger in the visitor's heart feelings of emotional identification with the victims," which, he acknowledged, precluded subtlety and nuance. A "crude method of expression" was needed,[61] though that intent does not do justice to the tact and conscientiousness of the final result, which had attracted ten million visitors in the first five years.

The work of architect James Ingo Freed merited exceptional acclaim. "The building invites interpretation but confounds analysis," wrote the *Times* critic Herbert Muschamp. The "monumental forms appear to be shaped not by architecture but by history." Muschamp's assessment also sought to sidestep the question of representation. He could not ascertain whether the power of the building derived primarily from its design or from its subject, from its artistic sobriety or its historical associations, from the sublime aesthetic skill of the architect or from the moral vacuity of Nazism that texture and space so cunningly conveyed. Such criteria of judgment might be formulated but the next step could not be taken; the building resisted an effort to sort out distinctions of form and theme.

Here it is enough to note how overwhelmed countless visitors have been. The interior of the building, one of them noted, "seems to have been distilled, but not abstracted, from its subject. Its principal materials are brick and steel and brick bolted with steel," Leon Wieseltier of the *New Republic* wrote. "The industrial atmosphere is ominous. This is an atrium without air. . . . The skylight, too, puts you in mind of a train station, until you begin to notice that this gigantic frame of steel is warped, twisted, a derangement of rational design. Above the skylight, from one of the glass bridges that connect the towers, the deformity is truly terrifying. The building seems to be held together by what is tearing it apart." Especially powerful are the photos collected by Holocaust scholar Yaffa Eliach and exhibited in a tower. They show the Jews in one Lithuanian town, Eishishok, where they had lived for nine centuries. In two days of carnage, that history was suddenly and completely terminated. The tastefulness evident in the Hall of Remembrance, at the end of the exhibitions, is also admirable: a chamber seventy feet high, with six unadorned limestone walls. Perhaps each side could represent a million deaths, or a point of the star of the people whose extinction served to gratify a paranoiac frenzy. The floor of cold marble is also blank and empty enough to encourage contemplation and prayer.[62]

The museum managed to obliterate the distinction between why Jews mourned and what others might understand about the Final Solution. The unspeakable had been made accessible without a significant dilution of meaning. Even though the director of communications defined the "ultimate goal" as memorializing "not . . . what the Germans did to the Jews but what people did to people,"[63] the museum was no Babi Yar, the Soviet memorial where the Jews were indistinguishable "victims of fascism."

But whether the *Shoah* deserves to be treated in quite so official a fashion, and made so directly a part of national purpose, is not easy to justify. Even when the duties of bystanders are taken fully into account, even when their failure to decelerate the machinery of annihilation is condemned, even if more could have been done to widen the quotas for immigrants and for refugees, even if military measures might have been taken apart from making V-E Day happen as soon as possible, even if public warnings could have been more explicit that perpetrators of crimes against humanity could expect the full force of Allied justice, the Holocaust Memorial Museum is not located in an appropriate spot. Even if the Holocaust Memorial Museum has a more expansively educational purpose than does Yad Vashem, Israel is a more obvious setting, and a united Germany has a past to reckon with that is quite distinct from the historical tragedies with which the U.S. government is entangled. The devastation of native Americans and the enslavement of African-Americans both constitute historical injustices inviting official redress. Washington's indifference to the trapped and doomed Jews of Europe must be judged quite differently. As "insiders" (and not only as "outsiders"), Jews had the "political influence and economic wherewithal" to get the museum constructed, David Biale has noted. "Almost by definition, the real emblematic minorities are precisely those whose story no one wants to hear." [64]

There is a problem with silence. There can also be a problem with speech, when sentiments of grief and pain are expressed too easily. There is a problem with undue familiarity, when the Holocaust demands full awareness of dislocation. The ineffable barbarism of the Third Reich raised unanswerable questions about the beneficence and even the existence of God, about the unappeasable power of evil, about the frailty of goodness, and about the purpose of a Jewish collective life. Such questions, which Jews themselves had been reluctant to raise for roughly two decades after the war, had become common property. Holocaust memorials were built in places as distant as El Paso and Palm Springs; and by 1997 Clark University created a Center for Holocaust Studies, becoming the first institution of higher learning in the country to offer a doctoral program in Holocaust history. Clark's undergraduates could also enroll in a program in Holocaust and genocide studies.

The ease with which the Holocaust could be slipped into public discourse did not necessarily mean that a genuine grappling with the nihilism it portended had occurred; so smooth a meshing of the gears probably meant that the *Shoah* had been made too much like other forms of hatred and discrimination. The Holocaust had become a less extraordinary example of wickedness. To make it intelligible, the power to disturb has been attenuated. When the Marine Band played "Zog Nit Kaynmal" at the museum in 1995, the power to shock was reduced; to tread near the abyss had become a little too easy. In making the *Shoah* accessible, silence was less pervasive, however necessary in order to meditate upon so disruptive an episode in modern history.

The mystery has been punctured—perhaps fatally. It needed the distance that the logic of American culture (what Emerson called "pitiless publicity") was ordained to close. In contemplating the Final Solution, those who were fortunate enough not to have been there, Wieseltier wrote after visiting the Museum, "must stand away." He continued, "If we are not strangers, if the names of the killers and the places of the killing and the numbers of the killed fall easily from our tongues, then we are not remembering to remember, but remembering to forget."[65] Such oblivion would only ensure the perpetuation of an obliviousness to catastrophe.

FAITH

THROUGHOUT NAZI-OCCUPIED EUROPE, THE AFFILIATION OF A GRAND-parent could suffice to block the escape routes from Jewish identity, and the consequences could be lethal. The Holocaust had therefore raised the question of whether Judaism was worth dying for. Across the Atlantic, however, a different question was posed: was Judaism worth living for? Religion has historically been neither necessary nor sufficient for Jews or their culture to flourish in the United States. But if content were to determine how that culture is defined, religion is irrepressible. That is why the fate of Judaic belief and practice in America merits separate consideration.

Although the Judeo-Christian tradition is often invoked, historic Judaism cannot be fully accommodated to Christendom, even if intolerance were removed from the equation. The closest Hebrew equivalent to "religion" is *dat*, a term borrowed from the Persian and found primarily in the biblical book of Esther (which nevertheless does not mention God). That *dat* also means "law" hints at how the function and meaning of Judaism were transformed after its adherents were emancipated. Even as freedom of worship was formally guaranteed, modern civil society inevitably defined religion in a way that altered a Judaism that had previously been transmitted as practices more than a theology, as codes more than doctrines. Jews were promised freedom of religion, but what most were not quite entitled to enjoy was the freedom to define religion in a way that owed nothing to the prevailing conception in Christendom.[1]

In the United States a society that was Christian coexisted with a state that was not. Because no church was established, religion was encouraged to be voluntaristic. Its exercise was so free under the First Amendment that an American is also virtually free *from* religion. The yearning to flee from an established church could easily become a desire to flee from *any* church. Which meant that, like other faiths in the New World, historic Judaism had to persuade (or even please) its adherents. It could not command fealty. And when rejection of Judaism imposed little if any social or moral penalties, to mend it seemed the only way not to end it.

That happened not only in America. But when its Declaration of Independence defined truth as what is self-evident, there was barely any ideological alternative to personalism, which sociologists Charles Liebman and Steven M. Cohen have defined as "the tendency to transform and evaluate the tradition in terms of its utility or significance to the individual." The standard is modern: no longer submission to the will of God but instead to the dictates of conscience. Rather than emulate Abraham obeying the injunction to sacrifice Isaac (the *akedah*), the modern American Jew wonders, like Woody Allen's Yahweh, why "some men will follow any order . . . as long as it comes from a resonant, well-modulated voice." Tradition is granted a vote, but not a veto, and individual choice is itself given an aura of sanctity. The modern American Jew, Marshall Sklare observed, plucks what is credible from a "vast sacramental heritage," and locates the *mitzvot* that are "subjectively possible" to accept.[2] In encouraging "each person to work out for himself the method whereby he can best express himself religiously," William James might have been speaking in a recognizably American accent. But the source of that quotation is Rabbi Mordecai Menahem Kaplan of the Jewish Theological Seminary, writing in 1928.[3]

And because the Declaration of Independence also includes the pursuit of happiness among the inalienable rights that the Creator bestowed upon humanity, religion also had to acknowledge the pleasure principle, and account for the yearning for comfort in this world. In a beneficent universe, why should duty require the deferment of gratification? Upon seeing republican preachers in action, Tocqueville could parse no distinction between eternal life and felicity on earth. However important Puritanism was to the stern builders of the Massachusetts Bay colony and to the formation of the New England mind, the logic of self-satisfaction was irrevocable. Religion would boost confidence and be cheerful.

Television viewers got a chance to observe the culmination of this sensibility in 1993, when the most consistently admired American of the last half-century chatted with four Jewish comedians. The Reverend Billy Graham assured Milton Berle, George Burns, Red Buttons, and Shecky Green that God loves those who make other people laugh. These favorites of the Friars Club were thus God's favorites too. To support his guarantee of salvation, the eminent evangelist cited no biblical passage (nor did he indicate any other reference). But why risk popularity in a nation of optimists by alluding to the severity of the final judgment? Nine Americans in ten believe in heaven, and regard their own chances of getting there as fair-to-excellent. A paltry 6 percent have revealed to pollsters their expectations of suffering eternal damnation.[4] What an agreeable sensation it must be to live among Christians who are so perky and so virtuous.

In such an atmosphere religion could not be too *inconvenient*: it was expected to accommodate to secular values, not radically challenge them or propose that adherents secede from modern society. In case of conflict with prevailing American norms of secular origin, it is religion that is expected to compromise, or to adapt, or to surrender. The Holy Spirit must conform to the Zeitgeist, not the other way around. In 1978, for example, when racial egalitarianism had to be taken seriously, even so stolid and implacable a sect as the Church of Jesus Christ of Latter-Day Saints wilted; after much prayer, the prophet-president announced a revelation—the first of the modern era—that ended the ban against blacks in the priesthood. Given the national commitment to a colorblind ideal, the deity did not want the Mormons to be marginalized as zealots. (Doctrine continued to bar women from the priesthood, however.)

No segment of Western Christendom had advanced a stronger claim for the centralization and concentration of authority than the Catholic Church, and more than four out of five of its American adherents continue to label themselves "religious." Yet personalism has so disabled the power and the glory of Rome that 82 percent of American Catholics believe that practicing birth control is "entirely up to the individual," and 64 percent insist that "one can be a good Catholic without going to Mass."[5] Thus they resemble the Protestants who founded and have dominated a nation where authority is intended to be diffuse. What Lenny Bruce once called "the only *the* church" has not successfully resisted the primacy of self-satisfaction over self-abnegation.

Judaism too was expected to bend, in order not to break, in a land that was itself "*trayf,*" according to a pronouncement from abroad by Jacob David Willowski. The prominent Orthodox rabbi nevertheless immigrated in 1903, and quickly perceived that the problem bedeviling faith was the loss of credal uniformity. America was "where groups with varying viewpoints and opinions came to be settled," he complained, "and no one recognizes any authority." Another Orthodox rabbi, Israel Meir Ha-Kohen Kagan, even preferred tsarist autocracy to Western freedom, and advised against mass migration: "Whoever wishes to live properly before God must not settle in these countries."[6] The millions who ignored such advice transplanted and transformed their religious culture, with consequences I wish to specify and appraise here. Judaism cannot be equated historically or made logically identical with Jewish culture. But nothing is more evidently an attribute of that culture than *dat*. There has been Jewish culture without Judaism. But the religious life that has been conducted in America has inevitably affected what kinds of Jews would be consolidating even the largely secularized culture this book examines.

The national impact on the Jewish calendar was noted by Sklare, the sociologist who ingeniously listed five criteria that determine which holidays would be celebrated in the United States: (1) Could the festival be re-defined in modern terms? (2) Could it be centered on children? (3) Could it avoid social isolation? (4) Could it be packaged as a Jewish counterpart to a Christian holiday? (5) Could the holiday be honored annually, or at least infrequently? The first two items account, for example, for the elimination of the fast day of Tisha B'av (quite apart from the incongruity of lamenting the destruction of the First and Second Temples while inhaling the upbeat atmosphere of America, where dwelling upon the particular disasters of Exile is not especially congenial).[7]

The fourth item explains the elevation of two holidays that have been pumped up as substitutes for Christmas and Easter. Already right after Reconstruction, the Young Men's Hebrew Association (YMHA) was promoting the "Grand Revival of the Jewish National Holiday of Chanucka" [sic] "to rescue this national festival from . . . oblivion" and to give Jews a respectable Yuletide alternative. They learned—and yearned—to appropriate the lavishness of gift-giving and the relentlessness of shopping that marked the celebration of the birth of the Savior. Informing children of the exploits of the Maccabees had to be supplemented with the distribution of gelt (money) and with thrill of special foods; even Aunt Jemima claimed to provide "the best flour for latkes." Chanukah thus became something much more than an occasion to be grateful for divine providence. A commemoration of the political and military victory over Hellenization could be made to prefigure the struggle against assimilation, and Jews no longer had to envy the exchanges of presents that occurred at Christmas.[8]

But one of the three pilgrim festivals has eclipsed even Chanukah as probably the most widely observed of Jewish holidays. Passover reflects the religious pluralism that Willowski scorned, and is especially susceptible to revisionist readings. The narrative of the Exodus is a hermeneutic playground. Haggadah simply means "a telling," and the scriptural injunction to involve children tends to discourage a rigid adherence to the past. The standard version of the Haggadah that dominated the typical postwar seder did not result from the deliberations of a Sanhedrin but were the canny marketing ploy of a coffee manufacturer. Supermarkets distributed complimentary Haggadot carrying advertisement for Maxwell House, a company that "has probably done more to codify Jewish liturgy than any force in history," claimed Burton I. Visotsky, a JTS professor.

But not even that marketing-induced center could hold; it too had to yield to improvisation. The choices offered by Manhattan stores have included about seventy-five versions of the Haggadah, ranging from the traditional to the feminist, the pacifist, the vaguely radical. One from Santa Cruz depicts a guru in the full lotus position, and another showing the children of Israel surfing on the Red Sea also originated in (where else?)

California. A lesbian variation features Miriam and highlights her leadership. (And why not? Her brother Moses is not even mentioned in the traditional telling.) A rabbinic sage named Thoreau is cited in another, while vegetarians vow to liberate the paschal lamb. Among the four questions posed in *The Egalitarian Haggadah* is one from an "alienated young Jew" who asks: "What can this chauvinistic tribal rite possibly have to say to me?"[9] The American answer seems to be: whatever you want to make of it, bud.

Though Passover is implicit in the First Commandment, only the Fourth Commandment actually mentions a holiday. But to observe the Sabbath requires piety one day a week, rather than joy one day a year (or eight days a year), and therefore criterion 5 entails a reduction in the attractiveness of the Sabbath. In 1892 the ethnographer Jacob Riis had praised "the patriarchal family life of the Jew," especially on the seventh day, "when he gathers his household about his board, scant though the fare be." That quality time, Riis added, "dignifies the darkest slum of Jewtown." Even then, however, the day of rest was in trouble, as the Yiddish theater was already open for business on Friday evenings and on Saturdays—as well as on Rosh Hashonah. The Gentile servants of the wealthier observant Jews, Bessie Thomashefsky recalled, were nevertheless expected to carry cash to purchase tickets for the Saturday matinees.

Half a century later, Sklare asked residents of suburban "Lakeville" how they defined "a good Jew," and learned that only 4 percent considered Sabbath worship to be "essential."[10] No wonder then that, after he published a dissertation on Conservative Judaism that revealed the gap between official commitment to law and practical lapses, one rabbi told Sklare: "Young man, how dare you tell the truth about Conservative Judaism!" That movement could not sustain a binding sense of tradition. But two other sociologists have recorded lapses in New York City even among Orthodox males under thirty-five. One out of five of them did *not* attend services weekly.[11]

An episode in 1934 also revealed the pliable character of American Judaism. That year the Detroit Tigers were heading for an American League pennant, thanks largely to Hank Greenberg, who ended up batting .339 and driving in 139 runs. The first baseman was not observant. Yet a series of newspaper stories had been sparked by his casual remark near the end of the season that he might be spending Rosh Hashonah in a synagogue rather than against the Red Sox. The *halachic* problem was unprecedented. Should Greenberg's contractual promises to his employer and his ethical obligations to his teammates and fans supersede his faith—especially when the Tigers might beat out the New York Yankees for the league championship? One Detroit rabbi could find no clear prohibition in the classic texts against stepping up to the plate, causing the *Detroit News* to exult in a headline: "Talmud Clears Greenberg for Holiday Play." (No rabbi from opposing Boston was apparently consulted.) Greenberg attended *shul* prior to the New Year, but chose to play on Rosh Hashonah, despite some apprehension of divine displeasure: "I'll probably get my brains knocked out by a fly ball." Instead Greenberg hit two home runs, one of which, in the bottom of the ninth inning, enabled his team to win, 2-1. Neither a god of vengeance nor of wrath, the Holy One was evidently rooting for the Tigers. The hometown *Free Press* was ecstatic. It wished the slugger "Happy New Year" in Hebrew and gave its own seal of approval, pronouncing both homers "strictly kosher." Reaching for a metaphor of its own, a Jewish newspaper in Cleveland announced that "Hank Greenberg . . . blew the *shofar* twice[;] and the ears of the Boston Red Sox are still ringing."

But the Jewish calendar was inexorable, and ten days later came Yom Kippur. Instead of facing the Yankees, Greenberg *davened* at Shaarey Zedek in Detroit, whose team already had a clear shot at the World Series. The city's newspapers praised him for his dignity and self-respect, and omitted comment on the dilemma had the pennant race still been close. Jews felt uplifted; the Tigers were not let down; and Edgar Guest's poem was featured in the *Free Press*:

> Come Yom Kippur—holy fast day world wide over to the Jew,
> And Hank Greenberg to his teaching and the old tradition true,
> Spent the day among his people and he didn't come to play.
> Said Murphy to Mulrooney: "We shall lose the game today!
> We shall miss him in the infield and shall miss him at the bat.
> But he's true to his religion—and I honor him for that."

(Greenberg would become less true to his religion; nonetheless, after leading the league four times in home runs and in RBIs, after hitting 58 homers in 1938, and after serving four years in World War II, he became the first Jew to end up in Cooperstown.)[12]

The youngest player to be inducted into the Baseball Hall of Fame (at the age of thirty-seven) was Sandy Koufax, the man with the golden arm. In 1965 the Dodgers' pitcher honored Greenberg's precedent by not playing on Yom Kippur. But the burden imposed on Koufax was heavier: in 5736 the Day of Atonement coincided with the first game of the World Series against the Minnesota Twins. Los Angeles manager Walt Alston therefore had to schedule Don Drysdale instead, while Koufax *davened* in a Minneapolis *shul*. *Which* one has so far eluded historians, with several local rabbis reportedly insisting that it was in theirs where the southpaw had worshiped, even as the Dodgers were getting crushed, 8-2. As Alston shuffled to the mound in the third inning, the embarrassed Drysdale handed him the ball and quipped: "I bet right now you wish I was Jewish too."[13]

This particular diamond business has bewitched enough Jews to stir their resentment against the scheduling of National League playoffs one season during the Days of Awe. The executive director of the Anti-Defamation League felt obliged to go public, disassociating his agency from any effort to switch a game from the tenth of Tishri. Having to attend synagogue at the very end of a pennant race, the ADL's Nathan Perlmutter ruefully announced, was one price that religious dissenters in America could fairly be expected to pay.[14]

The historic distinction between Jacob and Esau (the archetypes of Jew and Gentile) got so blurred, in a nation mad about sports, that the discontinuity deserves to be noted. Consider the testimony of Maurice Samuel, for example, who asserted that the ancient Hebrews as well as the impoverished immigrants of his own Manchester, England, took no notice of athletics. "The language that my parents and my *Rebbi* spoke," he recalled, "was altogether free from the sporting expressions that were so thickly distributed, in strategic ideological areas, throughout English." A reader of the Bible, the Mishnah, and Talmud who skipped their allusions "to Gentile nations and customs . . . would . . . never suspect that the world of antiquity had been as addicted to sports as is the modern world."[15]

One way of gauging the significance of such activities in accelerating Americanization (and in boosting Jewish pride) was the boast of Benny Friedman, who served as the first athletic director at Brandeis University. The ex-Wolverine quarterback told one undergraduate: "You know the two greatest things that ever happened in the history of the Jewish people? Well, I'll tell you. The first was when the Jews got up an army and walloped the British, and the second was when I made All-American twice for Michigan."[16]

Stadiums are among the places where Americans have been known to worship. Synagogues are such buildings too. "Let them make me a sanctuary" is a divine request that the Hebrews and their descendants honored (Exodus 25:8). But however exact some of the specifications, the Lord preferred to leave some decisions about design up to architects, who concocted what historian Rachel Wischnitzer termed the "flexible plan." It was first used consciously on a large scale by the German-born and -trained Eric Mendelsohn, who arrived from Palestine in 1939. The layout that he devised for St. Louis's B'nai Amoona, completed in 1946, doubled the seating capacity for the High Holy Days, with folding walls joining the sanctuary, foyer, and auditorium. To be sure, Albert Kahn's Temple Beth El Synagogue in Detroit had used folding walls four decades earlier; and in the 1920s the *American Hebrew* advised the construction of accordion-

shaped houses of worship to accommodate the contrasting seating requirements for the Sabbath and for the High Holy Days. In the year that B'nai
Amoona was finished, architect Percival Goodman published a paper rec-
ommending the "flexible plan." But Mendelsohn pioneered in perfecting
it: suburbanization had facilitated the exploitation of the horizontal space
that the density of ethnic neighborhoods in the city prohibited.[17]

Architectural history is an ideal demonstration of the difficulty (if not
impossibility) of separating Jewish worship from osmotic influences. In synagogues in Muslim lands, Jews prayed by sitting along the four walls on a
floor covered by mats; that is how Allah is beseeched. In the West, Jews
have seated themselves on chairs or benches, like Christians. Peter Harrison's Touro Synagogue (1763) in Newport, Rhode Island, boasted a facade
like the Congregational meeting-houses of the colonial era; and the basil-
ica and the high steeple of Congregation Beth Elohim made it resemble
the Georgian churches of Charleston, where, after a destructive fire, the
new synagogue (1841) was built in Greek Revival. In the same era the Egyptian Revival that was popular for prisons and monuments led William Strick-
land to design Philadelphia's Mikveh Israel (1825) in that style. A little more
than a generation later, the Gothic Revival could be seen in the first two
synagogues built in San Francisco, although the first Jewish architect in the
United States, Prague-born Leopold Eidlitz, used Romanesque for New
York's Congregation Shaaray Tefila (1847). Having gotten the commission
to design P. T. Barnum's home, an opulent pleasure dome nicknamed
"Iranistan," Eidlitz put Moorish decoration atop a Gothic plan for New
York's Temple Emanu-El (1868). When Kahn revised his Temple Beth El
in 1922, it resembled the Lincoln Memorial, dedicated that year.[18]

Nor did modernism impose a distinctive style of synagogue architecture: to attach a star of David or two tablets of the law on a building might
have been enough to make it obvious that it was not a church. Some of the
most brilliant modernist achievements were by non-Jews. Wright's Beth
Shalom is the most famous of all. Minoru Yamasaki designed North Shore
Congregation Israel in Glencoe, Illinois (1964) as well as Temple Beth El
in Birmingham, Michigan (1974); and Paul Rudolph was responsible for
Congregation Beth El in New London, Connecticut (1973).

Their ecumenical counterpart was Louis Kahn, perhaps the most admired postwar architect of Jewish descent. *His* buildings included a Unitarian church, a priory, a convent, and a mosque in Bangladesh. He also
designed four synagogues, of which only one was actually built, in Chap-
paqua, New York: Temple Beth-El (1972), which critic Paul Goldberger
praised as "a masterpiece of simplicity, where space and light create a serene
environment, a place where the spirit may rest or soar." Reminiscent of
the vanished wooden structures of eighteenth-century Poland and Russia,

this modest *shul* eschews their use of folk art ornamentation (some of which had been borrowed from Polish Catholics anyway). Born into an observant family in Estonia, Kahn had put aside formal religious affiliation after his bar mitzvah, to pursue his self-proclaimed ideals of "light and silence." In seeking no distinctive Jewish aesthetic, he was the opposite of Percival Goodman, whose more than fifty synagogues made him the most popular architect of such houses of worship in American history. But Goodman did not consistently draw on historical references or symbolic preferences, and whether he found an apt and unique aesthetic for Jewish worship is dubious.[19]

No wonder then that, after surveying American synagogue designs in the first three postwar decades, art historian Gary Tinterow tabulated such a multiplicity of styles that he despaired of locating anything "singularly expressive of a Jewish architecture." What revealed "the specifically Jewish activity within" was elusive. No clear answer therefore emerged to the question posed by Lewis Mumford in 1925: "Should a synagog [*sic*] be in harmony with the buildings around it, or should it stand out and proclaim the cultural individuality of the Jewish community?" That meant resolving a larger problem: "the general relation of Jewish culture to Western civilization."[20]

Such categories may be too broad; that dichotomy obscures too many variations. What worked in eastern Europe could not be duplicated in America, though both are part of "Western civilization." The functions of the synagogue resembled the attributes of Protestant churches. The *beth hamedrash*—a house of prayer, study, and much else brimming with communal life—could not be successfully reconstituted where, ironically enough, the "flexible plan" may be the most Jewish feature of synagogue architecture.

The ideological pressures of American democracy would also cause a distinctively Judaic notion to crack: the divine election of Israel. Belief in it could not easily be squared with egalitarian and pluralist ideals, and what happened to chosenness reflects how an ancient faith confronted the rationalism of the post-Enlightenment. The problem is not, as sculptors sometimes require, "site-specific." Election, it can be assumed, has hardly flourished among Australian or British or French Jewry either. But the limited ideological license that the United States has granted to hierarchy and to anything that might smack of "elitism" has exerted an especially heavy strain, and the liturgical center was deeply affected. A prayer like the *kiddush* expresses gratitude to a deity "Who has chosen us from all peoples by giving us His Torah," and the *aleinu* acknowledges that God has granted Jews a unique destiny. When they cleave the Sabbath from the new week, they are enjoined to separate the sacred and the profane, and light from darkness. Jews are made aware of another explicit contrast: between Israel and the nations (*ha-goyim*). No sense of being distinct could be more succinct; no binary opposition could be more stark. Belonging to a people designated as the instrument of revelation, believing Jews proclaim daily: "Blessed art Thou, O Lord, Ruler of the Universe, Who hast not made me a Gentile." (This is not a benediction that Jews relish repeating at interfaith conclaves.)

The salience of election should not be underestimated. Certainly Arnold M. Eisen does not. As the author of a very able book on how American Jewish religious ideologists have wrestled with the idea, he has insisted that "chosenness marks the point at which the three lines of relation which define Jews—those binding them to God, to their fellow-men, and to each other—of necessity intersect." The phrase "*am segulah*" refers to the people that have been plucked out among others as a "peculiar treasure."[21] Yet Scripture leaves the selection process obscure; there is no hard evidence for the virtue nor for the grandeur of a minor nomadic tribe. Nor does the Bible explain God's motives, even though the contract is binding. The provisions are fully enforceable, but one of the two parties has to puzzle its way through interpretations of what is meant. The teleology is plain enough, however. Fidelity to the Torah and to God is expected to unite the generations, until eventually all peoples can recognize the religious truths granted first to only one of them, and thus humanity itself will be redeemed.

The claims of an *am segulah* troubled even medieval Jewish philosophy. Why did an omnipotent deity have to choose anyone, rather than reveal the majesty of the moral law to all? The difficulty of formulating a satisfactory answer may account for the exclusion of election from the thirteen articles of faith that a rationalist like Maimonides propounded. The omission cannot have been an oversight. Whether or not the treasure is peculiar, the *idea* of it certainly is: a preposterously small but inextinguishable people is offered a set of religious ideas that are universally applicable. All are the children of God, Who mysteriously decided to make an irrevocable Covenant with a tiny fraction of them.

But wait: it gets worse. To accept Revelation—a divine intervention that occurred at Sinai—requires belief in a single event that occurred in an expanding universe that is so large that astronomers now realize that it spans thirteen billion light-years. In the midst of this vast, unimaginable emptiness, an eternal and ubiquitous deity suddenly rent the fabric of time to pluck out some ragtag refugees from an ancient empire that happens to be located on a planet spinning in a minor solar system. They are offered an unchanging and absolute moral law by a remote providence responsible for the order of the universe. For Exodus 19:5 to be credible, an intuitive sense of the ways of the world has to be askew. No wonder then that Spinoza, the first deracinated Jewish intellectual in Western history, used his *Tractatus Theologico-Politicus* (1670) to assault the notion of "the vocation of the Hebrews." In the same book the prototype of the "non-Jewish Jew" inaugurated the history of biblical criticism.[22]

Election became so enigmatic, so bizarre, that all sorts of convolutions had to be proposed to keep it intact. The ghastly and prolonged suffering inflicted on medieval Jews provoked one drastic reinterpretation; such misery proved that God had indeed singled them out. This theodicy was less persuasive in the modern era, especially during and after the Holocaust. After millions of speakers of the Yiddish language were murdered, who but the deity was left to be addressed in the *mamaloshen*, as the poet Kadya Molodovsky so savagely demanded: "O God of Mercy / For the time being / Choose another people. / We are tired of death, tired of corpses.... Choose another people." Other Jews reduced election to priority alone; Israel was merely the first to have been chosen. Period. Hayim Greenberg argued that election "must not be taken to signify a *superior race* but a *superior faith*, destined to become the faith of the entire world.... The Jew, through his faith, is merely *advanced*, while the rest of the world is *retarded*." Though Jews can see the divine light better than Christians, they have eyes too, and will come around eventually. This argument is not taut, however. If all human souls are indeed spiritually worthy, then Greenberg's defense makes the *goyim* look morally backward. It is difficult to affirm chosenness without offending against both liberalism and rationalism; a champion of both, Leonard Fein, has conceded that such "a declaration [is one] almost none of us can take literally, and few of us can take seriously."[23]

Historical experience can be factored in as well. Belief in chosenness is not a harmless activity like stamp collecting. On top of all the other accusations against Jews, election has piled up charges of exclusivity, insularity, and even racism. If Gentiles have been irritated by the pride implicit in divine election, sociologist Talcott Parsons once explained, that is due to their perception that American Jews are "guests" who somehow "claim a higher status than the 'host' people."[24] Also resentful were British socialists. H. G. Wells objected to the Jews' presumption (to be seated above the salt by the divine host). George Bernard Shaw ascribed their historic persecution to their "enormous arrogance," dismissed the Nordic supremacism of the Third Reich as a stab at imitating "the posterity of Abraham," and interpreted the Nazi revulsion against *Raschenschande* (racial pollution) as "intensely Jewish."

Hitler concurred—at least as an aged, captured (and captivating) Führer in a fable by George Steiner. From the Jews, the agitated escapee in the South American jungle claims to have "learned . . . everything. To set a race apart. To keep it from defilement." This fictional character tells his Israeli captors how he picked up their "arrogance." His "racism" parodied theirs. "What is a thousand-year *Reich* compared to the eternity of Zion? Perhaps I was the false Messiah sent before. Judge me and you must judge yourselves. *Übermenschen*, chosen ones!"[25]

Not that a counterargument is inconceivable. "No people, race, or tribe is without ethnocentricity," Greenberg rebutted. "A certain degree of narcissism is requisite for the survival of an ethnic group." But election "never constituted a theoretical basis for Jewish domination over other, 'inferior,' races or peoples." The Hebrews' conquest of Canaan, he noted, was not based on the rationale of chosenness. The opposite of narcissism is self-hatred, which became noticeable only after Emancipation and threatened collective survival. Before then, despite persecution, Jews who considered themselves superior to Gentiles had, it so happens, found a recipe for continuity. Still, after Emancipation, election had to be reinterpreted, as mission (as what Eisen termed "ethical cooperation"), or as Israel choosing God instead of the other way around.

The notion nevertheless remained problematic, because it circulated in a society that endorsed other commitments: for example, to principles of pluralism and of egalitarianism. So long as the primary vocation of a rabbi was to adjudicate legal disputes among Jews, then chosenness could be finessed. But if a rabbi must defend Judaism among Gentiles, as in America, then public relations requires that election be explained (or explained away). It "legitimated and even demanded an exclusivity" that most Jews "had repudiated," Eisen surmised. "It presumed a covenant with a personal God in whom they for the most part could not believe." Jews became understandably queasy about a particularism based on holding a monopoly on truth. Though their destiny was prescribed directly from heaven, they wanted to be considered good citizens, which commonly meant repudiating whatever risked accusations of ethnocentrism. This dilemma Eisen phrased crisply: "Jews wanted to be part of America, and yet apart."[26]

In 1937 the imperative to stay apart inspired an unflinching assault. The criticism to which this integral Judaic idea was subjected is intriguing, if only because it was hit by friendly fire from a liberal Protestant journal. The *Christian Century* fiercely opposed the antisemitism that was mounting at home and abroad in the 1930s. In challenging the Judaic imperative of separateness, however, the editors of the magazine did not show exquisite timing. Two years earlier the Nuremberg Laws had reimposed medieval restrictions in arguably the most advanced nation in Europe. Tolerance was not posited as the editors' solution to "the Jewish problem" but was instead presented only as the condition in which a rational remedy could be devised and applied.

That solution had to acknowledge the reciprocity of tolerance; a minority in the United States *also* had to appreciate the sensibility of the majority. If Jewry could ever hope to escape persecution and discrimination, the *Christian Century* argued, its unique situation in a nation of minorities had to be altered. The Jewish people "is a racial minority which conceives its racial integrity as the permanent basis of a distinctive culture. Both race and culture are hallowed by a distinctive religion. The word 'racial' is used broadly, in a non-technical sense." The magazine considered the Jews "a *hereditary* group, and this fact constitutes the basic element in the problem of their relation to gentile society. The Jewish religion cannot be shared with non-Jews except at the sacrifice of Jewish racial and cultural unity. The Jewish community therefore entertains no aspiration to universalize its culture or its cult."

This sort of insularity was puzzling to the editors, whose idea of religion was of a good that ought to be more widely shared. And though they did not realize that converts are praised in the liturgy, the magazine favored bridges, not barriers such as the "ceremony accompanied by a drastic physical symbolism" with which "the occasional gentile proselyte" is admitted to Judaism. How circumcision discouraged female converts was unexplained in the editorial, which objected to the Jewish "determination to maintain racial solidarity," whether by stigmatizing exogamy, or by refusing to imitate the Christian commitment to missionary activity. In urging Jews to relinquish their isolation, the editors were therefore willing to bite the bullet: "Can democracy suffer a hereditary minority to perpetuate itself as a *permanent* minority, with its own distinctive culture sanctioned by its own distinctive cult forms?"

A candid Christian answer would be no. Free to practice their faith and thus fully protected by the First Amendment, "our Jewish brethren . . . have no right *in a democracy* to remove their faith from the normal influences of the democratic process by insulating it behind the walls of a racial and cultural solidarity." Then, in the name of a crude majoritarianism, a not-so-subtle warning was issued to their Jewish brethren. "A crisis" might be provoked, the magazine feared, "in which the prejudice and anger generated by their long resistance to the democratic process will flame up to their great hurt," to say nothing of the "disgrace of our democracy, as well as to the shame of our Christian faith."[27]

Who would be responsible for this outburst of antisemitism? Not those who will have demanded uniformity, it would appear. Better to blame the victims, whose religion "rests upon an impossible basis." They are guilty of "trying to pluck the fruits of democracy without yielding itself to the processes of democracy. . . . Any group which deliberately removes itself from participation in this open process of social change, neither striving to modify the social status quo by openly proclaiming its own ideals, nor exposing itself freely to the normal influences of the social process, is in for a hard time," the *Christian Century* warned. "The situation in which the Jewish problem arises is in large measure Jewry's own creation." The magazine was therefore not ignoring the larger and intensifying climate of hate but was clear on its cause: "We hold that the Jew himself is responsible, in a high degree, and that no solution of his problem is possible until his own degree of responsibility is recognized. The first step toward its recognition is to discern that his determination to maintain a permanent racial status is incompatible with democracy."

Then the magazine got even deeper: "The root cause of the Jewish problem is the Jew's immemorial and pertinacious obsession with an illusion, the illusion that his race, his people, are the object of the special favor of God, who requires the maintenance of their racial integrity and separateness as the medium through which, soon or late, will be performed some mighty act involving human destiny." So much for the messianic age. The Jews' "obsession" with their own chosenness, their own "divinely hallowed racial uniqueness," would produce an "inevitable human reaction."

The weekly did not deny historic Christian guilt for oppression but did lay bare the operations of human psychology in assessing culpability: "If this racial group feels that way about itself, and insists upon living apart in biological and cultural, as well as religious, aloofness, let it take the consequences!" The editorial rejected counsel that the contemporary epidemic of antisemitism made resolution of the Jewish question untimely. The editorial countered: what better time? Such bigotry was still weak enough in the United States for Jews themselves to break "the vicious circle"; and the *Christian Century* hoped "for prophets to arise in Judaism who will begin to proclaim the terrible truth: that Judaism has been feeding its racial pride for millenniums on an illusion; that its martyrdom is in large measure self-invited; that its racial integrity is no more important in God's sight than any other race's integrity." Once the Jews themselves realize that "the doctrine of a covenant race" has served as "the prototype of nazism" from which they themselves were so grievously suffering, once election is abandoned in the heat of the melting-pot, "in loyalty to our common adventure" in the United States, once in effect Jews accept a Christian version of what religion is, only then will there be "a solution of the Jewish problem."[28]

Here was the spirit of majoritarian democracy at its most conformist, as well as a liberal cosmopolitan discomfort with difference that came across as a haughty particularism, as well as a Christian bafflement with chosenness as nothing other than an instigation to bigotry. There were of course Jews (if not necessarily "prophets") who were willing to abandon election if feelings of exclusivity and arrogance seemed so crucially to envelop it.

Mordecai Kaplan added an objection that was pragmatic; so powerful an affront to democratic sensitivities could not be a worthy idea. "From an ethical standpoint, it is deemed inadvisable, to say the least, to keep alive ideas of race or national superiority, inasmuch as they are known to exercise a divisive influence, generating suspicion and hatred," he wrote in 1934. "The harm which results from upholding the doctrine of 'election' is not counterbalanced by the good it is supposed to do in inculcating a sense of self-respect." The founder of the Reconstructionist movement thus wanted to drop chosenness from the liturgy—whether in the *aleinu* or in the blessing for the Torah, or in *The New Haggadah* (1941) which he coauthored.[29]

The editorial inadvertently revealed an ineluctable logical consequence of the repudiation of election. The *Christian Century* upheld freedom of worship but doubted whether that right should be forever invoked by a minority whose stubbornness seemed to give its members so much trouble. If Jews no longer referred to themselves as chosen, then disappearance is not necessarily made more desirable. But it is more feasible. To remove the historic raison d'être of a separate destiny is therefore to assign the Jewish people a suicide mission. It is no accident that Spinoza, in impugning the idea of chosenness, also found no warrant for Jewish continuity. Dissenters from his view of their fate probably have to contest his premise as well—even if only according to the pragmatic principles that led Kaplan to an opposite conclusion in abandoning election. Believers may still squirm under the difficult task of reconciling elitism with egalitarianism. But it is ever harder to see how election can be discarded, without violating the sense of distinctiveness upon which the religious (and therefore the collective) personality of Jewry has rested. Otherwise the balance that modern, committed Jews have struggled to find, in Eisen's phrase, "between exclusivity and participation,"[30] might fatally tilt toward a full, defenses-down integration.

That is why, so that Jews would not disappear, the idea of chosenness did not either; it resisted the pressures of secular skepticism, democratic demands, and universalist aspirations. The marrow of Jewish identity requires *some* justification for perpetuating either trouble or duty. The Orthodox requirement that life be micromanaged entails so many inconveniences, and the catastrophes that faith and peoplehood inflicted on other Jews can still stir such fresh memories that the perpetuation of Judaism requires validation and not merely inertia. That need makes the uniqueness of election, however irrational, also irreplaceable.

If any liturgical moment is more notorious than the daily thankfulness in not being born a Gentile, it is the expression of gratitude every morning in not being born a woman.[31] The force of feminist criticism has made difficult a defense of normative Judaism from the accusation of systematic misogyny. Given the longevity of patriarchy, its repudiation centuries or millennia ago cannot be imagined. That sex roles would be rigidly defined, that women would be excluded from what men in black valued, are only what the historian of Judaism would expect. What is historically salient, however, is how inexorably it would yield by the late twentieth century to the claims of feminism.

The independence of unmarried women had impressed the visiting Tocqueville as emblematic of egalitarianism. As *De la démocratie en Amérique* was being published, Rebecca Gratz invented the Jewish Sunday School movement in Philadelphia and, by making women responsible for educating the next generation, enlarged their role. Upon her death in 1869, "the majority of American Jews who received any formal Jewish education at all learned most of what they knew from female teachers," Jonathan Sarna declared. "These teachers, in turn, had to educate themselves in Judaism, which they did with the aid of new textbooks, some of them written by women as well." A legacy provided by Gratz's brother Hyman enabled women by the end of the century to study Judaism at Gratz College, the first of the coeducational Hebrew teachers' colleges.

The Reform movement also asserted a goal of sexual equality "insofar as this is possible"; and the indomitable Isaac Mayer Wise was interpreting the Torah as requiring the fulfillment of that goal. Admittedly the mixed seating that by the late 1870s had become commonplace in Reform synagogues was not due entirely to incipient feminism. In purchasing a church building, Wise's Congregation Anshe Emeth in Albany had cut too deeply into its budget to make extensive renovations; so the pews used by the church remained in place. Feminism was cost-effective. When Temple Emanu-El moved to a new building in Manhattan soon thereafter, redesign was also considered too expensive; and thus the thrift that had induced mixed seating was reinterpreted to vindicate egalitarian ideals.[32] These were proclaimed in the centennial year of the Declaration of Independence, when Rabbi Wise thundered in the *American Israelite* that "according to Moses, God made man, male and female both in his own image, without any difference in regard to duties, rights, claims and hopes." Resenting the confinement of the Jewish woman to "a garret in the synagogue, isolated like an abomination, shunned like a dangerous demon, and declared unfit in all religious observances," Wise did more to live up to such professions than to introduce the family pew. In substituting confirmation for the bar mitzvah ceremony, he ensured that girls and boys would participate equally.[33]

The bounds of female accomplishment within Judaism were stretched in other ways. Take the androgynously named Ray Frank. Born in San Francisco (possibly in 1861), Rachel Frank became (possibly in 1890) possibly the first woman in history to preach from the *bima* on the High Holy Days. What happened in Spokane launched the singular career of the "girl rabbi." The "female messiah" delivered sermons, primarily in the West, and published essays on Jewish women and on the Jewish family. Her commitment to female emancipation was qualified, however, as she opposed the suffrage and praised domesticity. Invited to deliver the invocation at the Jewish Women's Congress, during the World's Columbian Exposition in 1893, Frank was closer to a revivalist than to a figure of learning.

But within a generation feminism would seem entrenched enough to be parodied in a Thomashefsky musical like *Di sheyne amerikanerin*, or "The Beautiful American Girl" (1910). A campaign slogan like "*Vayber, makht mikh far prezident*" ("Women, Make Me President") does not seek to attract the votes of men, who are dismissed as "*mamzeyrim*" (bastards) and "*khazeyrim*" (swine) who are fit for washing diapers ("*Zoln di mener daypers vashn*"). No wonder Reb Smolinsky, the insufferable patriarch of Anzia Yezierska's *Bread Givers*, laments: "Woe to America where women are let free like men." In such a democracy his ambitious and audacious daughter Sara insists on pursuing happiness, despite the curses this particular *halachic* man inflicts upon her. "He could never understand," she realizes. "He was the Old World. I was the New."[34]

So was Judith Kaplan. She would marry a rabbi whose grandfather, Judah David Eisenstein, produced Hebrew and Yiddish translations of the Declaration of Independence. The milestone in her life occurred on the eighteenth of Adar, 5682 (three years before *Bread Givers* was published), when she became the first bat mitzvah in history. Her father was no Reb Smolinsky. Indeed, though Mordecai Kaplan and Yezierska's fictional patriarch each had four daughters, the JTS professor claimed that Judith, Hadassah, Naomi, and Selma were the four reasons for instituting the ceremony. Judith, the eldest, was prepared for the occasion by Max Kadushin, who had trained Lionel Trilling for his bar mitzvah four years earlier. On 18 March 1922, in a brownstone that had once belonged to showman George M. Cohan (*Yankee Doodle Dandy*), the services represented one small step for a woman. But one big step mankind was not quite ready to take; she stood below the *bima* and recited from her own printed copy of the Pentateuch, following the regular service in which men read from the Torah scrolls on the pulpit.[35]

The first girl in the Reform movement to imitate Judith Kaplan apparently did so in 1931. Another two decades would pass before the ceremony became common. Even then it mattered most to Conservatism, as Reform had depreciated the bar mitzvah ceremony and Orthodoxy discouraged gender equality. "During the 1950s and 1960s many Conservative synagogues limited the celebration to the less problematic Friday night services, when the Torah is not read," sociologist Sylvia B. Fishman noted. "By the late 1980s, however, most Conservative and almost all Reform congregations had made bat and bar mitzvah ceremonies virtually identical." The egalitarian logic of the bat mitzvah ceremony could not be evaded; the claims of the Conservative movement to respect *halacha* proved vulnerable to a democratic faith in the spiritual worthiness of women as well as men. What was the point of asking a thirteen-year-old to read from the Torah but then of denying her the honor of an *aliyah* the rest of her life?

Consistency dictated only one answer. The right to equal treatment, Kaplan believed, was granted to the female in American civilization. "There is no reason why the Jewish civilization should persist in treating her in this day and age as though she were an inferior type of human being." Beginning in 1951, his Society for the Advancement of Judaism gave women *aliyot* as well as the right to be counted in the *minyan*; four years later the Committee on Jewish Law and Standards of the Conservatives' Rabbinical Assembly first confronted the issue of granting women *aliyot*. That gave impetus to the fuller equality of the 1970s and thereafter, as feminism swept through the nation itself. Some Orthodox congregations acknowledged the force of feminism with a special *seudat sh'lisht* (third meal) on Saturday afternoon, or on a Sunday morning, when a thirteen-year-old girl was expected to deliver a *d'var Torah*, a homiletic speech marking her maturation. Already by 1960 roughly 250 nominally Orthodox synagogues had reported instituting some sort of mixed seating, before a backlash was mounted against liberalization (and against the feminization of American Jewish culture).[36] The momentum, however, could not be stopped.

The effect of the rising status of women was formidable, and helped decelerate tendencies toward assimilation. Because girls were widely expected to become bat mitzvah, the gender gap that had long marked Jewish education was largely closed. (Judith Kaplan Eisenstein would earn a doctorate and join the faculty of the Teachers' Institute as a specialist in Jewish music.) "Before the bat mitzvah became popular, one-third of American Jewish women used to receive no formal Jewish education whatsoever," Fishman reported. But by the final decade of the century, "bat mitzvah preparations have brought Jewish girls into supplementary schools and day schools at nearly the same rates as their brothers." She argued that adult lives became enriched too: "'Sisterhood Sabbaths' at suburban temples have housewives spending months preparing Torah readings in Hebrew, with cantillation. Lack of formal Jewish education for women may have been a contributing factor in the earlier decline in domestic Jewish observance, such as maintaining kosher homes. In contrast, the multi-faceted ways in which feminism has brought women to the center of Jewish experience represent one of the few heartening contemporary trends." By the end of the 1970s, the family pew and female participation in worship had become a nearly universal feature of Reform and Conservatism.[37]

The ease with which barriers fell cannot be explained without some reference to the incontestible authority of egalitarian ideals. In 1972 a group named Ezrat Nashim, which had explored how women were treated in Judaic texts, presented a series of demands at the annual meeting of the Rabbinical Assembly of the Conservative movement. The group sought the inclusion of women in the requirement to fulfill all *mitzvot* (ritual obligations), membership in synagogues, incorporation in the *minyan*, participation as equals in religious observances, eligibility to be witnesses in Jewish law, the right of women to initiate divorce proceedings, enrollment in rabbinical and cantorial schools, and encouragement to serve as leaders and professionals in synagogues and in Jewish communal organizations. Most of the these goals were quickly attained; and in September 1973, the declaration that women were eligible for the *minyan* was treated as front-page news in the *New York Times*.

That inclusion was newsworthy because the provocative attempt to be counted in the quorum sometimes resulted in ten angry men. From a conventional *halachic* perspective, the break with tradition was sharper than rabbinical ordination. To teach and interpret the law could hardly be said to be beyond the powers of women, whose study of the Torah Maimonides lauded. (His *Mishneh Torah* conceded, however, that "most women are not equipped to study and will distort the words of the Torah according to the whims of their minds.") But a *minyan* entails an equal responsibility to pray. Exempted from the obligation to do so, women who invoked a right to be counted in the quorum were dramatically shattering the rigidity of sex roles that normative Judaism had prescribed. Because Reform saw no need for a quorum, and because Orthodoxy insisted on gender division, again the Conservative movement registered with greatest sensitivity the struggle to reconcile feminism and tradition, and soon gave an affirmative answer to the fifth question novelist Anne Roiphe posed at a *seder*: "Is it possible for a twentieth-century female, educated to have hopes of equality and justice, to accept the traditions of the past that have left her excluded from the law and prevented her from entering the sacred or the *halacha*—how can a feminist feel about the Jewish religion?"[38]

In retrospect the logic of female ordination therefore seemed inescapable. It became imaginable when Henrietta Szold sought to enroll at the Jewish Theological Seminary. As editor of the Jewish Publication Society and of the *American Jewish Year Book*, as a translator and author, Szold exemplified a life of scholarship even before committing herself to a life of Zionist service. But in 1903 she had to assure President Schechter that she desired only to study, and did not want to make trouble by trying to become what her father had been: a rabbi. With that understanding she was admitted to JTS. In 1921 the specter of female ordination was raised at the Hebrew Union College, which refused (in practice, but not in principle) to countenance so drastic a break with tradition.

Only the renascence of feminism in the 1960s would reignite the demand to enter the professions. The intervening four decades were not barren of a sense of injustice, however. The president of HUC-JIR was the archeologist Nelson Glueck, whose wife graduated from medical school in 1934. A hematologist, Helen Glueck was among six women ranked as full professors at the Medical College of the University of Cincinnati, which may have made her husband's consciousness fairly easy to raise. In any event, shortly before his death in 1971, Glueck had expressed (in vain) the hope of living long enough to ordain a woman.[39]

Officially the first female rabbi in history was Sally Priesand, who had been admitted to HUC-JIR three years earlier. A Reconstructionist, Sandy Eisenberg Sasso, joined her two years later, and Amy Eilberg became the first Conservative rabbi in 1985. By 1992 about 280 women had become rabbis; the figure jumped to about four hundred two years later. Indeed the 1993 graduating class at the Reconstructionist Rabbinical College occupied a no-man's land; only women were ordained that year. The exceptionalism of American Jewish history is compounded when rabbis marry one another, as portrayed in one photo in Frédéric Brenner's idiosyncratic volume, *Jews/ America/A Representation* (1996). That sort of marriage is unknown elsewhere in the Diaspora, or in Israel. July 1995 marked another post-Sinai milestone, when Karen Bender, the assistant rabbi at Temple Beth El, in Great Neck, New York, married a woman. Three hundred guests attended the Reform wedding, during which the yarmulkes that were distributed were inscribed with "The Wedding of Rachel and Karen."[40]

It might be argued that the plasticity of the three non-Orthodox denominations (that is, about 90 percent of Judaism) takes no remarkable acumen or research to present. What suggests the insinuating power of the American environment is that even Orthodoxy has had to figure out how to compromise with its social and cultural surroundings. It too has felt obliged (to quote a feminist slogan) to listen to women for a change. However tightly gender roles are defined and circumscribed in traditional Judaism, its modern representatives have not exhibited "zero tolerance" for feminism. Women have been serving on the lay boards of trustees of many Orthodox synagogues, and even on some ritual committees. A few rabbis even recognized the legitimacy of separate women's *tefilot* (prayer services), according to historian Jeffrey S. Gurock. By 1982 such initiatives had become so conspicuous that the Agudat ha-Rabbanim had to denounce them:

God forbid this should come to pass. A daughter of Israel may not participate in such worthless ceremonies that are totally contrary to *halacha*. We are
shocked to hear that "rabbis" have promoted such an undertaking which results in the desecration of God and his Torah. We forewarn all those who assist such "*Minyonim*" that we will take the strictest measures to prevent such
"prayers," which are a product of pure ignorance and illiteracy. We admon-
ish these "Orthodox rabbis": Do not make a comedy out of Torah.[41]

Such astringency of tone suggests the magnitude of the changes against
which defenders of the status quo were bracing themselves.

One president of the Rabbinical Council of America, the main Orthodox organization, dismissed these prayer groups as a "passing fad" of the
late 1980s. Few prophecies have proven more mistaken than Louis Bernstein's. Increasingly, Orthodox women have recited the *kaddish* in synagogues; and legal authorities found themselves devoting more attention to
issues on which women were especially vocal, such as divorce rulings and
reproductive rights. So many girls were studying the Talmud in Modern
Orthodox day schools, historian Deborah E. Lipstadt commented, that
"the gap between formal Jewish education for men and women has narrowed considerably." When the national propulsion toward greater equality and inclusiveness reinforced a traditional reverence for learning, misogyny could gain little traction. Soloveitchik was not alone in endorsing
female study of the Talmud. So too had Menachem M. Schneerson, the
Lubavitcher Rebbe of Crown Heights, New York, who turned out to be a
pragmatist. He argued that women who enter the vastness of the Talmud
would be much more effective in helping their own children with their
studies, and would be far more able to resist the temptation of secular
studies.[42]

Another harbinger was the first International Conference on Feminism
and Orthodoxy in 1997, after which two faculty members at Yeshiva University's Stern College for Women, Rabbis Avi Weiss and Saul Berman, inaugurated a program aimed at making learned women more conversant
with "the ideologies and traditions of Modern Orthodoxy." Weiss firmly
disavowed one inference that the graduates of Torat Miriam might invite,
however: "They are not rabbis. We are talking about something different."
One foe of female ordination was the president of Yeshiva University,
Rabbi Norman Lamm: "It shakes the boundaries of tradition, and I would
never allow it."[43]

Firm boundaries are of course what the dynamic restlessness of American life has long contested, and it is safe to predict that Lamm's opposition
will not be the final word on the subject. Tradition is more loose (or, from
another angle, resilient) than Orthodox Jews have sometimes pretended,

and whether adherence to it pivots on maintaining patriarchal norms is far from obvious. Rules have been changed and not merely reaffirmed. Capital punishment, for instance, was once on the books as a warning to anyone who broke the Sabbath by gathering sticks (Numbers 15:32–36). Somehow moral sensitivity grew, and such a crime was eventually seen as not quite horrendous enough to merit the death penalty. That rulings were altered circuitously and subtly, without belaboring the evidence of ruptures, does not affect the generalization that change is embedded in tradition. Purim, for example, had to be *introduced* as a national festival, over rabbinical objections.[44]

Within American Orthodoxy the delivery of sermons in English and the appreciation of decorum in worship were innovations, thanks in particular to Rabbi Joseph H. Lookstein of Manhattan's Congregation Kehilath Jeshurun. He admired the tranquillity and tastefulness of Reform and Conservative worship, which he wanted Orthodoxy to emulate. According to his son, Lookstein "strove to combine warmth with dignity, the enthusiasm of Orthodoxy with the aesthetics of Reform, the tradition of four thousand years of Jewish practice with the modern active tempo." In 1937, when he founded the Ramaz School (and thus pioneered the day school movement), no classes were scheduled on Sundays or at Yuletide. That vacation was designated a winter break.

Feminists have invoked the same right to test boundaries, to enhance what tradition permits, and to bring sanctity to what affects them as women in particular. One example is the *shalom bat* or *simchat bat*, a ceremony of recent origin that welcomes the birth of a daughter and that has grown in popularity.[45] But how explicitly, or how quickly, greater female education as well as participation in Orthodox institutional life will pursue the same logic as the other movements is beyond the scope of this inquiry.

What is relevant is how such revisions blur any sharp distinction between Judaism and American culture. To claim that national values have somehow infiltrated a religion whose history can be autonomously traced is misleading. For one of the strongest signs of how Jews have helped shape American culture (and one of the most convincing illustrations of reciprocity) was the rise of feminism beginning in the 1960s. Its best-known activists, ideologues, and theorists have disproportionately been Jews. One of them, literary scholar Carolyn Heilbrun, claimed that "to be a feminist one had to have an experience of being an outsider more extreme than merely being a woman." The explanation she provided is, not to put too fine a point on it, *Galut*: "Having been a Jew, however unobserved that identification was, however fiercely I had denied the adamant antisemitism all around me as I grew up—still having been a Jew had made me an outsider. It had permitted me to be a feminist." One might go further: while it is obvious that women are far more likely to be feminists than men, Jewish-ness (in the form of a sense of marginality or as an expression of liberalism) may constitute something like an independent variable. When the Equal Rights Amendment was making its way (unsuccessfully) through the process of ratification in state legislatures, one public opinion poll revealed that a Jewish man was more likely to favor passage than a Gentile woman.[46] A political position is not inherently Jewish because Jews strongly favor it; sociology should be distinguished from religious ideology. No philosophical tradition that can be teased out of the millennia of Judaic practice and legal interpretation *requires* an endorsement of the manifestoes of the National Organization for Women (NOW). But the eventual triumph of feminism not merely among Americans in general but especially among Jews suggests that Judaism can *become* consistent with it, and can be readily made to honor the claims of all those created in the divine image.

The "modern active tempo" with which the environment altered the religion transplanted from the Old World was registered in the paradigmatic career of Mordecai Kaplan, who also deserves attention for redefining Judaism in the broadest cultural terms. Very few American Jewish religious thinkers have been so influential; almost no other twentieth-century rabbi has elicited so many books devoted to his life and thought. Kaplan's career is beset with ironies. Nearly its entirety—fifty-seven years—was spent on the JTS payroll, yet an unresolved issue associated with his legacy is whether he was a religious thinker at all. He was in any event more admired as a teacher than as a theorist, and better known as a champion of communal creativity than as a scholar of the sacred. The movement he created ex nihilo has remained a very tiny segment of a tiny minority group. By the end of the century, Reconstructionism claimed about fifty thousand members, belonging to ninety congregations—barely one percent of about 5.8 million American Jews.[47] Intellectual historians are excused from playing a numbers game. But they need not ignore the chasm between Kaplan's stature as a thinker and the limited impact of the independent movement he forged.

Though haunted by the sense of having been an underachiever as a writer, Kaplan was a graphomaniac. His unpublished diary spans twenty-seven volumes, and he wrote about ten thousand letters. Despite the torrent of words, however, he is remembered for one book: his first, which neither the *New York Times* nor even the *Menorah Journal* saw fit to review. *Judaism as a Civilization* was published in the same year the Talmud cleared Hank Greenberg to play ball. (Both events demonstrated the flexibility of an ancient faith.) The first edition of Kaplan's volume consisted of fifteen hundred copies, of which Macmillan sent the author six hundred and fifty. A second printing came out the following year; of the thousand copies, he purchased half. That meant that for more than two decades, until *Judaism as a Civilization* was reprinted in 1957, almost no one had a chance to purchase it—except from the author, who offered to speak gratis at congregations were they to buy a minimal number of copies.

If readers' indifference was his initial fate, Kaplan managed something much more exotic in 1945, when his Reconstructionist Foundation published the *Sabbath Prayer Book*. Its liturgical novelties exposed the limits of latitudinarianism and provoked a medieval punishment. The Union of Orthodox Rabbis of the United States and Canada issued a *herem* (ban) that accused Kaplan of "atheism [and] heresy," and—rather superfluously—of "disbelief in the basic tenets of Judaism." He was excommunicated. No Jew was permitted to sit within four feet of him, to speak to him within that range, to eat with him, or to include him among the ten men required for prayer. There may even have been a bonfire of the vanities. The *Times* reported, perhaps inaccurately, that the *Sabbath Prayer Book* was burned during a ceremony at the Hotel McAlpin in New York City.[48]

Kaplan still outlived everyone. Death in 1983, at the age of 102, ended a career that spanned nearly the twentieth century, which began not long before he gave voice to the modernism that encased several generations of his "co-religionists." (To have problematized—and clarified—that category is one of his achievements.) Born in Lithuania, Kaplan arrived in New York in 1890 and, until he was twenty-eight, lived at home—which was a traditional one, marked by love of the learning at which his father, Israel Kaplan, excelled. In 1902, the year Schechter became JTS president, the seminary graduated the twenty-one-year-old Kaplan and ordained him as a rabbi. Yet he was already vexed by religious doubts. He first became skeptical about the existence of miracles, and then about the integrity of the Torah, which biblical criticism had led him to suspect was written by many hands rather than by Moses as the conduit of Yahweh. Kaplan concluded that biblical claims were best understood as projections, and multiple authorship led him to infer that Holy Writ constituted the collective yearning of his ancestors to discover their destiny and to invest it with meaning.[49]

Even while serving on the JTS faculty from 1909 until 1963, Kaplan had an equivocal relationship to the *halacha* that Conservative Judaism officially affirmed. His colleague Louis Ginzberg considered him "a menace," Kaplan noted in his diary, and added that the eminent Talmudist "foams at the mouth and shakes his fist as he cries . . . you are destroying Judaism." But if Kaplan did so, it was in order to save it.

By 1906 Kaplan was wondering what might replace a belief in divine authority that traditional Jews had ascribed to the Torah. He proposed to substitute for revelation a "national conception" of Judaism. In that same year, a lecture that Professor Israel Friedlaender of JTS delivered on Jewish culture stimulated Kaplan to think of culture not only "as product but also as process. . . . It should be the cultivation of all those powers possessed by the Jewish people in a spirit which would tend to reinforce the consciousness of kind which otherwise might die out." Three years later he was ready to propose nationality as the most viable foundation of Jewish identity, practices, and beliefs.[50] Peoplehood and faith would reinforce one another when revelation lacked credence. He refused to let that faith be "described in advance" or to foreclose the options of adaptation to modern conditions. But he insisted that if "the aim of readjustment is to enrich Jewish life, Jews need not fear that departure from certain traditional customs will undermine Judaism."[51] That communal standard became the credo of a lifetime.

Though Kaplan was so stirred by Zionism that he proposed making the anniversary of the Balfour Declaration in 1917 into a holiday of the day of redemption (*Yom Ha-Geulah*), he could not settle in Palestine. He praised Zionism for decelerating the drive toward assimilation and for strengthening the Diaspora itself,[52] even while entertaining the possibility that the United States might itself be a redeemer nation: "After all God wants to choose America as the instrument of his will no less than he wanted Israel of old to act as an instrument of this kind." In any event the process of acculturation had worked its magic so seductively that Kaplan wrote in his journal late in 1918: "To love America is simply to love myself, for it is only in this blessed country that I could have achieved what I value most in myself."[53] This touchstone of self-realization he would apply to the generality of human endeavors. Religion itself would have to accede to the criterion of personal value and purpose. Tradition would have to justify itself, he suggested, in the idiom of individualism.[54]

The magical properties ascribed to Americanization seemed to descend easily on Kaplan and his family. One of his first English teachers in New York City was Abraham Cahan, and the pupil proved apt enough to speak an unaccented English. Classes at the seminary were in English, not in Yiddish; and at the outset of his congregational duties, Rabbi Kaplan was hired precisely because he excelled at delivering sermons in the language that Conservative Jews appreciated as evidence of smooth integration. American life was indeed so effective a solvent, he recognized early in the century, that the power of a distinctive community to prevail would be challenged. Kaplan did not expect Judaism in the New World to exert the same influence upon its adherents as it had in Eastern Europe. But the exhortation to flourish in two civilizations would be pointless were Judaism to become increasingly foreign and inaccessible, and were it to be associated with stagnation and superstition.

In rejecting both the melting-pot and pariahdom, Kaplan wished to situate religion within a cultural setting, to define Judaism not as a set of formal beliefs, but as the collective spiritual expression of his people. Its historic religion needed to be salvaged, altered, and redefined so that the Jews could redeem themselves. To prevail within an open society, he argued in 1916, meant making the agenda of education the inculcation of the humane values of Jewish civilization (defined more broadly than in biblical or rabbinical terms).

Receptivity to revision earned Kaplan the enmity of some advocates of the tradition from which he himself had sprung. At the YMHA on Ninety-second Street in 1915, he organized religious services on Saturday afternoons in the hope of competing with the matinees that were popular among the young (some of whom bought their tickets before the shows to avoid too blatant a violation of the Sabbath). Four years later, Kaplan considered switching the day of rest to Sunday, if that would enable Judaism to sustain itself in the Diaspora (though he feared to make the recommendation public). Indeed, the original manuscript of *Judaism as a Civilization* floated the idea of a switch to Sunday, which he considered for other holidays as well. Noticing how well attended Passover services were on Sundays, and hearing the complaints of some rabbis who despaired of assembling a *minyan* on weekdays, he considered keeping the first day of the festival on the Christian Sabbath.

For a while Kaplan actually eliminated the *Kol Nidre* as more legalistic than spiritual. He himself kept kosher, but mounted no defense of dietary laws except in terms of social utility. If the rules of *kashrut* helped deter assimilation, he endorsed them; if they separated Jews from one another and made adherence to Judaism unduly demanding, pragmatism induced a spirit of nonchalance: "Sooner or later Judaism will have to get along without dietary laws." Each morning he continued to put on his prayer shawl and phylacteries. But sometimes, according to biographer Mel Scult, Kaplan declined to recite the daily prayers and read John Dewey instead.[55]

In naming the movement after the Columbia professor's 1920 *Reconstruction in Philosophy* (and in emulating his repudiation of supernaturalism as well), Kaplan placed communal needs above credal claims. He was more sociologist than metaphysician. Religion no longer gave hope that performing *mitzvot* would ensure salvation in the next world but instead gave meaning through solidarity with other Jews in this world. Within it, however, his orientation was toward the future rather the past. He could be petulant in dismissing esoteric fascination with the "stupid Geniza fragments" on which Schechter had made his reputation, and could reject as quickly as any other red-blooded American the "dry as dust scholarship" of pedants. If he taught *Midrash* annually, that was because of its interpretive thrust, from within the tradition, to breathe fresh life into the Bible. But at JTS Kaplan specialized in homiletics, in communicating interest in Judaism, which he very expansively defined as "something far more comprehensive than Jewish religion. It includes the nexus of a history, literature, language, social organization, folk sanctions, standards of conduct, social and spiritual ideals, aesthetic values, which in their totality form a civilization."[56]

That did not quite mean that whatever Jews do is "Jewish." Though critical of the three denominations that constituted the American version of Jewish civilization, he wanted to make tradition relevant. "It is the duty of the Jew," he wrote, "so to interpret and utilize the elements of that heritage as to fulfill himself through it. . . . If he wants to remain a Jew and have Jewish religion, he must find some way of making his heritage of supreme import to him." Its values are the medium through which the prospect of salvation may be found, and not in isolation.

Such views suggest the unfairness of summing up his thought in terms of innovativeness and individualism: his vocation was to Americanize a Judaism that revered tradition and community too. Kaplan was willing to make the definition of religion open-ended: "Whatever helps to produce creative social interaction among Jews rightly belongs to the category of Jewish religion." Its "essential nature" he therefore refused to specify, and doubted that it was yet possible to do so. But he did depend on "a law of its being" to modify his openness to dynamic interventions from outside, not yet foreseen. He wanted to keep "the way open for the assimilation of forms and values that Judaism may not now possess." He refused to indicate in advance "whether a particular attempt to intensify Jewish experience will produce results that are outlandish or those that enrich Jewish life." What he recommended was that this criterion be "the desire to make Jewish experience spiritually satisfying."[57] If guided by the desire to retain the organic, distinctive, and continuous character of Judaism, then change would make the religious heritage of the modern Jew accessible.

Though Kaplan believed that the option of separatism was precluded, he realized that American conditions defied Jews to conserve their sense of "otherness."[58] The impediments to cultivating such distinctiveness have been formidable (as they are for the historian in search of American Jewish culture). In making religion more than worship and practice and doctrine —while invoking the centrality of Judaism to a distinctive Jewish culture— his book constituted a singular achievement. *Judaism as a Civilization* enhanced understanding and appreciation of that culture, and became an ornament of it. How the religious civilization he outlined will largely determine what is meant by American Jewish culture is the argument of the final chapter.

PROSPECTS

SOME OF AMERICA'S BEST FRIENDS ARE JEWS. BUT WHETHER SUCH loyalty is good for them is a question that has simmered, and in recent years these doubts have gathered force. Freedom has proven to be a wonderful stimulus for Jews, whose socioeconomic ascent has validated the immigrants' fondest hopes at the dawn of the century, and whose deep involvement in the formation of a national culture has been suggested in the previous chapters. American Jewry has had every reason to *kvell*; its experience did not seem like Exile. But freedom may be a nemesis for Judaism, without which a vibrant community is unlikely to prevail. The nation has been good to—and for—Jews, very many of whom could live in the past without Judaism. That possibility has receded, however; a secularist future is foreclosed. Only religion can form the inspirational core of a viable and meaningful Jewish culture. Its fate, I claim here, depends on faith.

Already before the dawn of the twentieth century, the texture of Jewish life was thick enough to create a Jewish culture in America that was secular. The associational patterns, the bonds of intimacy in workplace and neighborhood, the direct links to the Old World—all were strong enough to honor the claims of ethnicity, in the absence of religion. For the first few generations, Jewish identity was secure enough to keep intact a community from which a culture could emerge. By the end of the century, however, that identity has destabilized, so that the boundaries between Jews and others have mostly been obliterated. The historian can make religion ancillary to the evolution of Jewish culture, and can define it as what Jews have imagined and perpetuated. Perhaps soon that definition may no longer be useful to the contemporary observer, because Jews have become so indistinct. As the meaning of being a Jew becomes increasingly uncertain and elusive, the odds are lengthened that an American Jewish culture can be enhanced—and the task of describing it may become insurmountable. That integration would pose a challenge to identity has long been acknowledged. That the challenge would be met has been (at least until very recently) widely accepted. That the challenge would be welcome has also permeated the ethos of American Jews, who have shown little interest in romanticizing very different Diaspora conditions. American Jews have not admired the inbred isolation of, say, Yemenite Jewry, exposed for centuries to a static larger environment. Instead, the beneficence of American citizenship has not only been praised but has also been commonly premised on its compatibility with a Jewish birthright. Whatever tension that Jewish life in America might pose was supposed to be creative. Nationality and peoplehood would be effortlessly synthesized, and therefore the saga of American Jewry is commonly recounted as the reconciliation of these two claims upon allegiance.[1] No matter what the ideology, no matter how it contradicted another, a parallel was proclaimed with the nation's genuine values.

At the dawn of the century, historian Eli Lederhendler observed, the menu of opinions and arguments was enormous, yet "how remarkable it is to find them all deemed compatible with American ideals!"[2] Belief in a common and congruent vision ranged across the sectarian spectrum. An Orthodox rabbi like Bernard Drachman, born in America and trained in Germany, professed to subscribe to a "harmonious combination of Orthodox Judaism and Americanism"; in laying the cornerstone of what became Yeshiva University in 1915, Rabbi Bernard Revel could "see no conflict, no inconsistency between Americanism and Judaism." In so hospitable a society, Revel advocated both Torah and secular knowledge, and could not have foreseen that he belongs to philately as one of the "Great Americans" issue of U.S. postage stamps. In linking the "two civilizations, the Jewish and the American," an eminent Conservative rabbi rejoiced that the "synthesis" has been "so spiritually complementary." Harold M. Schulweis saw parallels in "Passover and the Fourth of July, the festival of Sukkot and Thanksgiving, the prophets and the founding fathers of this country, the Sabbaths of multiple faiths, the Decalogue and the Declaration of Independence."[3] A similar claim can be found on the masthead logo of the Reform synagogue in Los Angeles that twinned the Statue of Liberty and Moses. What the Lawgiver looked like, if indeed he existed, is best known to Michelangelo, or—given the location of Temple Israel in Hollywood—Cecil B. DeMille. Ascher, the attorney for the atomic spies in Doctorow's *The Book of Daniel*, was supposed to be writing a volume designed to show "the contributions of the Old Testament to American law," Daniel Isaacson reports.

Another site in Los Angeles was premised on this synthesis; upon its opening in 1996, the Skirball Cultural Center became the most ambitious expression of the belief in harmonization. Jack Skirball had served for a decade in the Reform rabbinate; he then mastered the skills to produce movies like Hitchcock's *Shadow of a Doubt* (1943) and eventually launched an even more prosperous career speculating in real estate. Jack and Audrey

Skirball and the Skirball Foundation led the drive of mostly California donors (including Spielberg) to create a museum that is part of the Hebrew Union College–Jewish Institute of Religion in Los Angeles. But "we're not theologically driven," according to the founder and president of the Skirball Cultural Center, Uri D. Herscher. "We are not dogmatic." But he was certainly upbeat. American Jewish history, he claimed, "may indeed be the most glorious of stories, but it is untold." To convey it required fifteen years of planning and raising $90 million. The Skirball is a three-story, terraced, 125,000 square-foot complex, designed by the Haifa-born Moshe Safdie and located on a fifteen-acre bluff alongside the San Diego Freeway in the Santa Monica Mountains. A large proportion of visitors have come from greater Los Angeles, where the second-largest Jewish community in the nation (and third-largest in the world) is located, but where only one Jew in five was affiliated with any communal organization or synagogue.[4]

The story that the Skirball communicates emphasizes how fully other Americans share the particular "vision and values" on which Jews have predicated their own culture. In evoking not only the arts but also immigration, religion, family, education, occupational structure, and communal organization, the permanent collection pays special attention to items that exemplify consonance: a *hallah* cover on which Old Glory was woven; marriage contracts featuring flags of both the United States and of the Zionist movement; and a red-white-and-blue " 'V' for Victory" flag stemming from the Second World War, invoking prayers for the nation and for President Roosevelt, written in English, Hebrew, and Yiddish. The central symbol of the museum is a Chanukah lamp designed by Manfred Anson in 1985. Each of its nine branches is topped with a tiny brass Statue of Liberty.

An alternative faith—that return to Zion is the fulfillment of Jewish history—is rather subdued. The first object to be encountered in "Visions and Values" is a Torah scroll opened to Genesis 12:1–3. Next to it is the translation: "Go forth . . . and be a blessing to the world." What is omitted refers to the prospect of a "great nation" to be formed in the Holy Land. The ellipsis was necessary, the coorganizer of the core exhibit explained, to avoid undue stress on "the middle lines, which promise a particular land and future to Abraham's offspring." According to Rabbi Robert Kirschner, "we wanted instead to bring out the universal aspect of the command."[5] Indeed, the adjective "Jewish" is absent from the name of the Skirball Cultural Center.

Under the rubric of the "Pursuit of Liberty," one gallery shows eight objects devoted to the sixteenth president, revered for rescinding General Grant's notoriously antisemitic Order 11. "Father Abraham" was a safer choice than Franklin D. Roosevelt, who commanded much greater loyalty among Jewish voters than Lincoln ever did but who has been retrospectively condemned for failing their trapped coreligionists in Europe. Roosevelt's record is too ambiguous and invites disturbing questions about an era when direct help for European Jewry was held to be inconsistent with American national interests. The celebratory tone pervading the museum was not lost on Herbert Muschamp, who exuded: "Without diminishing the meaning or magnitude of the Holocaust, the place gathers rays of light that have penetrated through a dark century." The architectural critic wrote: "Built on the idea that the power to create is stronger than the will to destroy, the display adds up to the stunning proposition that the twentieth century has been nothing less than a golden age of Jewish achievement."[6]

Though dissent from this triumphalism was rare, a few postwar statements can be plucked to show that not everyone was in sync. Some contested the assumption that ideological consonance should be valued as the condition of such success. Immediately after the Holocaust, the novelist and publicist Ludwig Lewisohn wrote in his diary against "the uncritical acceptance of American civilization—a civilization, despite freedom and prosperity, utterly unsuited to the character of the Jew." To adjust to American life, he told the Rabbinical Assembly in 1946, was "the unspeakable sin"; it would incur "moral suicide, ethnic self-liquidation." Eugene D. Borowitz, a Reform rabbi, also proposed "creative alienation" from America, an ethical distance from the "stinking rot near the core of Western industrial democratic society." In 1957 Nathan Glazer offered a tantalizing, if undeveloped, claim that "there comes a time—and it is just about upon us—when American Jews become aware of a contradiction between the kind of society America wants to become—and indeed the kind of society most Jews want it to be—and the demands of the Jewish religion." (Those requirements, he tabulated, include endogamy, separation, and a return to Zion.) Otherwise, however, it is safe to generalize that, for most of the century, Jews have passed (with distinction) F. Scott Fitzgerald's famous "test of a first-rate intelligence," which is a capacity "to hold two opposed ideas in the mind at the same time, and still retain the ability to function."[7]

A maverick position was nevertheless articulated in a 1996 symposium in *Commentary*. Three decades earlier, when the monthly had published a similar symposium, entitled "The Condition of Jewish Belief," no repudiation of ideological compatibility had been proposed. All the 1966 symposiasts were white. All were male. All were rabbis. Among their forty-seven successors were a computer specialist, a radio talk-show host, seven women, and an African-American. Half a dozen of the participants doubted that the American Jewish mind could function with two opposed ideas any longer, and urged readers to realize that American culture is not quite compatible with Judaism.

For example, "the infantile insistence that religious ritual conform to you rather than the other way around," the Yale polymath David Gelernter wrote, "is the essence of modern American culture, and is strangling Judaism." He claimed that "only orthodox prayer and study" were powerful enough to resist the pursuit of private happiness, to keep Jewishness from meaning "nothing." David Singer, the editor of the *American Jewish Year Book*, saw Judaism as locked in an unresolvable conflict with "modernity," which "means secularism." Torah could not be reconciled with "the world of elite culture," which he saw as "largely . . . a poisonous mix of relativism, subjectivism, and outright nihilism." David A. Teutsch, the president of the Reconstructionist College, defined "the greatest challenge to Jewish continuity" as the influence of "the Western commitment to radical autonomy," which undercuts a religion that is satisfactorily adhered to only when embedded "within a fully lived civilization." The JTS historian Jack Wertheimer described "a sharp dissonance between traditional Jewish perspectives and the prevailing cultural outlook within American society," and dismissed as an "exercise in self-deception" the proclivity to declare that "Jewish and American civilizations are not only compatible, but form a seamless tapestry."[8] None of the dissidents were women, however, perhaps because they objected less keenly to a modernity that elevated their own status and that stimulated worship of the God of Sarah, Rachel, and Rebecca as well. But what was noteworthy was the crack in the consensus, the realization that the "way of the land" (*derekh eretz*) looked to some symposiasts like a dead end for Judaism.

Three sources of friction between its values and American culture can be presented here. One that may call the future of American Jewry into question is the impact of individualism. Defined as an exaltation of personal ambition and assertiveness, and as a belief in the importance of upward striving to achieve one's goals in a fluid social order, this ethos has been unmatched as a vindication of the republic itself. From the first paragraph of the first book in which a distinctly American accent can be detected, Benjamin Franklin's *Autobiography*, the attractiveness of the new nation has been expressed in terms of opportunities for personal success. Poverty and obscurity were not supposed to be permanent impediments to wealth or fame. And the character ideal of the self-made man found its philosopher in Emerson, who wrote essays entitled "Success" and "Self-Reliance," and its best-selling novelist in Horatio Alger Jr., who encouraged fantasies of upward mobility in more than a hundred books. The thinness of social bonds, the hesitancy with which the claims of community and reciprocity are advanced, the difficulty of nourishing collective enterprises without appeals to self-interest, the frequency with which "loners" appear on the landscape as well as in novels and other genres—all stem from the pervasiveness of individualism, which has enabled Americans to justify their society to each other and to foreigners too. Caprices of class and ancestry were not supposed to confine anyone who wishes upon a star, who dreams of evading the "social constructions" that limit identity.

A persecuted and exiled people, submitting to an entrenched nobility, was bound to find appealing the promise of upward mobility. Franklin was quickly translated into Yiddish, and was read (however furtively) in *yeshivot* in the Pale of Settlement. Another key text that exalted autonomy and self-reliance, *The Adventures of Robinson Crusoe*, was translated into Hebrew, and inspired a teenager who later called himself Sholom Aleichem to render his own version. Alger himself was a contributor to *The Israelite*, the journal edited by Isaac Mayer Wise; when the international banker Joseph Seligman hired a tutor for his sons George Washington Seligman, Alfred Lincoln Seligman et al., Alger got the job. The ease with which the national ethos was internalized is recorded in *Bread Givers*, when the narrator defiantly tells her authoritarian father: "I'm going to live my own life. Nobody can stop me. I'm not from the old country. I'm American!"[9] "I don't care for nobody," Jake declares in *Hester Street*, Joan Micklin Silver's 1975 adaptation of Cahan's *Yekl*. With an every-man-for-himself insouciance, Jake proclaims: "I'm an American fella."

Individualism does not fit snugly with *k'lal yisrael*, an ideal that subordinates the promotion of self-interest to communal claims. Radical autonomy does not mesh smoothly with historical Judaism, which works out a covenant between a deity and a people. The goal of self-satisfaction is not consistent with accepting the yoke of the Torah. Take Preminger's *Exodus* (1960), which effaces the collective and nationalist spirit of Zionism in the theme song. In "The Exodus Song," crooner Pat Boone veers dangerously close to committing the Noahide crime of blasphemy in announcing: "This land is mine, God gave this land to me." (Italics in "mine" and "me" need not be added.) God did not even give that land to Moses.

A second source of friction is consciousness of the past. The American attitude is incongruent with an imaginable Jewish future. In the United States the slate could be wiped clean, a tabula rasa on which ancestor-worship would not be inscribed. Truth was not to be distilled from the past but would be ascertained by pragmatic tests. "Is it not the glory of the people of America," James Madison asked, "that whilst they have paid a decent regard to the opinions of former times and other nations, they have not suffered a blind veneration for antiquity, for custom, or for names, to overrule the suggestions of their own good sense, the knowledge of their own situation, and the lessons of their own experience?"

From literary precincts, the replies were affirmative. In this "fortunate land," Hawthorne's Kenyon tells Donatello in *The Marble Faun* (1860), "each generation has only its own sins and sorrows to bear." In Europe, by contrast, "it seems as if all the weary and dreary Past were piled on the back of the Present."[10] Howells preferred "to have too little past, as we have, than too much, as they have" abroad; and the friend and novelist whom he championed invented an archetypal no-account boy who "put no stock in dead people" like Moses—especially those to whom Huck was not kin.[11]

But the imperatives of Judaism require such a sense of affiliation—and of memory—to be integral to the sensibility of worshipers. They are enjoined to remember: *zakhor*. This obligation binds the generations, who are expected to recall the bondage in Egypt from which their deity had emancipated them. Participants at the *seder* are supposed to imagine that they themselves had been slaves. Observant Jews do not live only in time but are expected to act as though eternity were at stake. Presentism is by contrast ever-present in American culture, which promotes the desire to travel light. David Levinsky, for example, has immigrated not only to fulfill the self but also to erase it, to substitute a new identity. "The Wandering Jew in me seeks forgetfulness," Mary Antin wrote. "I long to forget. . . . I want now to be of to-day." Rather than remember the days of yore, the point was to escape the tug of generations: "The past was only my cradle, and now it cannot hold me, because I am grown too big." In the same year that *The Promised Land* was published, Kafka wrote his novel about America, tentatively called *Der Verschollene*, which could be rendered as "the man who was forgotten" or "was lost without a trace."[12] Such dissolution is inconsistent with the communal imperative of continuity.

A society that encourages amnesia is not propitious for Judaism, which does more than make remembrance a duty. Religion is itself a lifelong set of duties: Ten Commandments, 613 *mitzvot*, tractates full of laws, endless inconveniences. To be a Jew no longer brings much trouble, but it takes trouble to practice Judaism, which is a product of both the ancient world and of the Old World. Hedonism is a third problem for Judaism.

When Freud denied that "the intention that man should be 'happy' is . . . included in the plan of 'Creation,'" this "godless Jew" had tradition behind him. Such stoicism might be contrasted with the optimistic title that star quarterback Joe Namath gave his autobiography: *I Can't Wait Until Tomorrow* (1969). The subtitle brandishes a narcissism that is the bloated form of individualism: . . . *'Cause I Get Better-Looking Every Day*. In the New World, where the pursuit of personal happiness was asserted as an inalienable right, most of the state constitutions that were ratified before the twentieth century guaranteed the right to *obtain* felicity as well. Built into the social contract was an entitlement to stroll "On the Sunny Side of the Street" (lyrics by Dorothy Fields, the daughter of the vaudevillian Lew Fields). Americans have widely believed that desires can be satisfied, that life will turn out "all right"—which is the first English phrase that young Levinsky learns in the part of the Diaspora where Jewish history was supposed to be put out of its misery. Defecting to the United States in 1967, the daughter of Joseph Stalin explained that she was tired of her "grim" compatriots; Svetlana Alliluyeva had had enough of "pessimism."[13] A pledge of glorious progress is made in the section called Tomorrowland at both California's Disneyland and Florida's Disney World. But at Disneyland Paris, Tomorrowland does not exist.

With its eye cocked on the international market, Hollywood was an especially fine barometer of divergent national sensibilities. When MGM adapted *Anna Karenina* as *Love* (1927), the European version predictably ends with the suicide of the heroine, who hurls herself in front of a train. Such a finale, however faithful, was considered too somber for Americans, who were given an Anna Karenina who finds such joy at the end that a helpless Tolstoy must have *plotzed* in his grave. At least Thomas Hardy was very much alive when MGM adapted *Tess of the D'Urbervilles* in 1924. But in screening the preview, Louis Mayer disliked the ending, in which the heroine is hanged for murdering Alec d'Urberville. Mayer ordered director Marshall Neilan to substitute a happy ending, in which Tess unpredictably earns a last-minute reprieve. Neilan was incensed, even urging Hardy to intervene, but in vain, since rights to the novel had been sold to MGM, which was free to let Tess live. Europeans who bought tickets for the silent epic *The Gold Rush* (1925) saw Charlie's relationship with Georgia Hale as an illusion, a false promise of sweetness. But Chaplin gave Americans a different ending, in which the pair's love is rewarded with happiness and success. No wonder that in 1936, when *Vigilanti cura* criticized Hollywood, the papal encyclical objected to an "unrealistic" portrayal of life as designed for pleasure rather to be measured by service and self-sacrifice.[14]

This was a *Weltanschauung* that Rome and Jerusalem have historically shared. The pleasure principle is incompatible with any of the main varieties of religious experience. The life of a believer is not supposed to be duty-free. But an ideal of sensation that endorses self-satisfaction wreaks special havoc on those expected to form "a kingdom of priests and a holy nation" (Exodus 19:6). Here Judaism diverged from the Church, which established a separate caste of clerisy whose vocation was seen as too demanding for the masses. But though rabbis are presumably more learned, they are not necessarily more pious. More assured in adjudicating conflicts and in issuing legal interpretations, rabbis are not necessarily more observant.

Judaism in the United States can be recounted as an accommodation to the national entitlement to seek happiness. How else might one interpret the synagogue-center movement that Mordecai Kaplan championed? The architecture of the center inspired a quip—"a pool with a school and a *shul*"—which is why Abba Hillel Silver eliminated such an installation in 1929 at The Temple in Cleveland. "If they come to play," the rabbi warned, "they won't stay to pray." His own Reform denomination differed from earlier revitalizing efforts in a way that revealed how tough a sell religion faced after the Declaration of Independence. Reform Judaism made it easier to claim to be a good Jew (unlike Hasidism, for example, which imposed more stringent demands on its adherents than the rabbinic Judaism it challenged). Intention (*kavanah*) assumed a new importance. "Hasidism did not reform Judaism," Hayim Greenberg noted, "it reformed the Jews."[15]

By the end of the twentieth century, however, secularization had become so extensive (or corrosive) that rates of religious observance were barely higher among affiliated Jews than among unaffiliated Jews. By 1990 Reform Jews (38 percent) had outnumbered Conservative Jews (35 percent); 6 percent identified themselves as Orthodox. Among Jews aged between 25 and 44, the gap between Reform (50 percent) and Conservative Jews (33 percent) widened even further, suggesting weakening religious commitments. Certainly trends in the other direction could be cited, from greater emphasis on ritual to more frequent use of Hebrew to the formation of day schools. The sociological generalization is unaffected, however: The practices of the most popular denomination cannot be distinguished statistically from the piety of those who belong to no synagogue at all.[16] Religion barely served as a psychological barrier against subordination to the allure of American civilization.

This integration had become so complete that Jews found themselves in a quandary. The synthesis they took for granted was no longer a solution to minority status but had instead become the problem. "Once one was an American," Eisen asked, "why did one need to be a Jew, if the values of the two cultures were identical?"[17] If American ideals harmonize so easily with the Jewish heritage, why bother to stay Jewish? If being an American means having it all, why cling to the part that is Jewish? The case for synthesis looked less like a way to make Jews feel at home among other Americans (and vice versa) and more like a recipe for disappearance. If American and Jewish values were virtually synonymous, modernity makes the harsher ethos look superannuated and superfluous.

Because of the suspicion that no creative tension can be sustained when the ideological imbalance is so great, fears for a viable American Jewish culture—indeed, for such a *community*—have heightened. When historians turned prophets, they became pessimists (or exemplars of what Lévi-Strauss in another context called "entropology": the science of analyzing the decline of vitality and energy).[18] A 1960 monograph on immigrant historical societies had noted the special vigor of the American Jewish Historical Society, especially in contrast to the neglect with which other ethnic groups organized study of the uprooted. But when the centenary of the Society was celebrated with the publication of a five-volume scholarly monument, *The Jewish People in America*, the author of the volume on the postwar period, Edward S. Shapiro, was pessimistic. High rates of exogamy, low birth rates, apathy and the enfeeblement of identity, he feared, adumbrated a bleak future.

From a much longer perspective, Rabbi Arthur Hertzberg also fingered his worry beads, and considered "the momentum of Jewish experience in America" to be "essentially spent." No dissent came from sociologist Samuel C. Heilman, who described "Jewish cultural integrity" as "more precarious than ever before," and who feared that even those committed to sustaining tradition might find the pressures "against the actively Jewish way of life in America too powerful" to defeat."[19] Such depletion was portended that only a committed (and observant) core might remain; and that remnant would embody the recruiting poster of the U.S. Marine Corps: "the few and the proud." These entropologists could not summon much confidence in the fate of the most populous, the most successful, the most powerful, and the most prosperous of all Diaspora communities.

Its chances of survival could be lengthened only if its particular cultural resources could be more fully recovered, only if it were less committed to integration and assimilation, only if it were to become more Jewish and less American. To equip itself for a certain measure of cultural resistance, however, required of American Jewry a break with its past. The community was unaccustomed to operating according to the description the pagan seer Balaam applied to the Israelites: "It is a people that shall dwell alone" (Numbers 23:9). Separation is not how Jews have generally lived in the United States, where conditions have been sufficiently benevolent to put at risk a distinct religious system on which Jewish culture and Jewish continuity depend. The virtues the community has celebrated may be handicaps in its yearning to endure, and the conditions that have enabled it to achieve so much now imperil it. A ritualistic invocation of the nation's ideological congeniality is not part of the logic of self-segregation; yet to tip the balance so fervently and unwarily toward integration implies extinction.

Dwelling alone maximized the chances of endogamy. But that was easily discredited in an America where romantic love alone was expected to govern marriage. Anita's advice to Maria in *West Side Story* ("Stick to your own kind") was made to look like narrow prejudice, like an illiberal ethnocentrism. Indeed, the first American Jew to appear in American fiction, Achsa Fielding, marries the eponymous hero of Charles Brockden Brown's *Arthur Mervyn* (1799–1800). Achsa Fielding is a wealthy, assimilated widow whose Jewish origin is no absolute impediment to marriage. A century later the intermarriage rates were very low, especially among the eastern

European immigrants and their children, and the advice columnist of the *Forverts* could afford to be a bit cavalier on the subject. Asked by one correspondent in 1908 about the propriety of plans to marry outside the faith, the "worthy editor" of the *bintel brief* replied: "We can only say that some mixed marriages are happy, others unhappy. But then many marriages between Jew and Jew, Christian and Christian, are not successful either. It is true, however, that in some mixed marriages the differences between man and wife create unhappiness. Therefore we cannot take it upon ourselves to advise the young man regarding this marriage. This he must decide for himself." [20]

Because America is supposed to be about the choices that modern life permits, not about the ascription that ancestry determines, the religious and psychological barriers to exogamy continued to fall; by the last third of the century, the majority of Jews who were marrying were doing so outside the faith. By the 1980s attitudes had discernibly shifted toward acceptance of mixed marriage (or, in the phrase of sociologist Egon Mayer, "from outrage to outreach"). A fundamental means by which communal insularity had been achieved was being widely abandoned. By the last decade of the century, according to National Jewish Population Survey data, the majority of children (ages 6–18) living in Jewish households were not being raised as Jews. [21]

As Gentiles increasingly became spouses and in-laws and grandchildren, Jewish fears faded, as did memories of collective vulnerability. Such concerns did not—and could not—entirely disappear. Even on Passover, the most popular Jewish holiday in America, the *Haggadah* informs its readers that "for more than once they have stood against us to destroy us." The third-person plural is left unspecified, as though persecutors were generic; in any event their writ seemed irrevocable. Among the first words that Ruth Gay, the daughter of eastern European immigrants, learned was *sonim*; the assumption that "enemies" surrounded them was one that subsequent generations would shed only slowly. Rooted in experience, precariousness once seemed so indelible a sign of ethnic consciousness that the playwright and scenarist Paddy Chayefsky even endorsed the definition of a Jew as someone who always lives "with one bag packed." Fleeing Berlin on 30 March 1933, Leo Szilard stashed his savings in his shoes. After reading the following day that Nazi guards had begun searching passengers on trains, the physicist always kept two suitcases packed, even after he moved to Chicago and demonstrated his indispensability by helping create the first nuclear chain reaction. Even in the 1990s irrefutable and ubiquitous evidence of tolerance and inclusion did not stop three out of every four Jews from telling pollsters that antisemitism remained a serious problem in the United States. [22]

The belief that American Jews are subjected to bigotry, that they remain victims, must be designated a delusion. The weight attached to anti-anti-semitism also detracts from the reconstruction of a Jewish culture that is strong enough to withstand not their neighbors' hatred but their love. Packed suitcases are no longer (if they ever were) sufficient manifestations of Jewish identity. No people can survive merely by defining itself as a target of hostility; no minority endures merely by defending itself against suspicion or envy. Even elephantine memories are no substitute for the adaptive and recuperative powers that Jewry had earlier exhibited—and that it would have to tap in the United States too.

But that effort cannot gain traction with the marked decline of tribalism, as the actuarial tables registered the receding distance of the Old World. Ethnicity has thinned out into "symbolic ethnicity" and then into little if any ethnicity at all. To be sure, by the end of the century, that terminus had not yet been reached. The nexus of associations and institutions did not lose all of its cohesiveness. Even among those living in the Sunbelt, even among those who were not on Social Security, ethnicity has not been expunged. But its days are numbered. Immigrant ghettos once constituted "a complete world," sociologist Louis Wirth observed in 1928, when the rest of America seemed virtually cut off, however invisible the gates. As the sheer density and intensity of communal experience inevitably fade, as other forms of identification become more available, the answer that one youngster gave to law professor Alan M. Dershowitz's question—Are you Jewish?—will become commonplace: "Only on my parents' side."[23]

That will cut the lifeline to the sense of a shared fate that once made it possible to be Jewish—and to exist in a Jewish culture—without Judaism. A century earlier secularism was a viable option. Thomashefsky never bothered to attend synagogue; nor did he ever see Palestine—though he frequently visited Europe. Nonetheless, he never ceased to be a culture hero, much less a Jew. Secularism then found its greatest advocates in Zhitlowski, Dubnow, and Ahad Ha-Am, Russian-born theorists who had little use for rabbinic Judaism. They condemned competitive individualism; they invoked the claims of collective memory. But their ideas did not prove durable. At the end of the twentieth century, the task of Americanizing their ideas looks somewhat funereal. To attempt to resurrect an ideology, however admirable, that has already proved its ineffectuality looks like the future of an illusion. The ethnic foundation that once permitted the community's numerous "freethinkers" to operate has simply collapsed. The "non-Jewish Jew" was once familiar. He epitomized universalist yearnings and sought to emancipate humanity, yet he sprang from a recognizable and particular minority; he was not merely a figment of Isaac Deutscher's imagination. Indeed, Deutscher had come from a thickly Jewish world. The

Marxist and atheist had been a child prodigy as a Talmudic scholar in his native Chrzanów before he joined an internationalist movement that would transcend the narrowness of Judaism and all other religions.[24] In 1930, when one of Deutscher's exemplary figures asked himself, in writing the introduction to the Hebrew edition of *Totem and Taboo*: "What is left to you that is Jewish?" Freud answered: "The essence." The purveyor of the talking cure "could not now express that essence clearly in words," however.[25] Later generations of the articulate would be even more frustrated in describing that essence, and it seemed to be the destiny of a godless, postethnic version of Jewishness to expire. The historic options available to a Jewish culture without content have shrunk.

It has become increasingly difficult to imagine how an attachment to the Jewish people can be secured without affirming a personal connection to Judaism. In a poignant 1961 essay, the sociologist Daniel Bell proposed establishing a bond of loyalty to the past primarily through *yizkor*, the tie of memory. But he barely referred to the future and offered no strategy to engage later generations of Jews who might feel less compulsion to say *yizkor*. What happens when a collective memory cannot be transmitted because the community itself is fragmented, dispersed, losing its sense of a common destiny? What happens when particular memories are not enough to sustain the sense of how the generations are linked? What happens when living in America produce very different memories? "A Parable of Alienation" was composed in the shadow of Bell's elders, and did not envision what the father (or grandfather) could transmit, if Judaism itself were forsaken. Though Bell became a perceptive analyst of religion and sought to validate a hospitality to the transcendent, he could not resolve the quandary that Jews faced: that their America would inevitably define the sacred as Christian. In such a scheme the status of Jews, whose version of faith is only partly compatible with majority piety, remained ambiguous.[26]

Is there any other way for the godless to invoke a vibrant Jewish identity in the United States? A literary specialist responded quite differently from Bell. "I am Jewish precisely because I am not a believer," Elaine Marks declared, "because I associate from early childhood the courage not to believe with being Jewish."[27] Such a credo also has its limitations—apart from the curious claim that disbelief requires any sort of courage whatsoever. In academic settings like Madison, Wisconsin, where Marks has taught, her stance is unlikely to incur social penalties; and the consequences of such bravura in the afterlife have not been researched sufficiently to be evaluated.

What is unwarranted is the claim that radical skepticism is somehow "Jewish." No Judaic texts of any historical or theological authority can be cited to justify such a self-definition. Faith may not be rationally defensible, but refusing it does not constitute Jewishness. Disbelief is a style, but it does not add up to a culture—unless a skeptical stance is worked out *within* a culture. That is not what Marks had in mind. However elastic a tradition that embraces rabbis and their revisionists, and that makes room for all sorts of mystics and *magidim* and false messiahs, nothing in their legacy sanctions the denial of God's existence as eligibility for membership in the community. Abraham smashed only idols he believed to be false. Even the Prophets, in denouncing social injustice, remained closely anchored to their own people and its beliefs.

The peculiar ways by which learning and piety interacted in rabbinic Judaism did admittedly encourage a disputatious mentality, stimulating habits of interpretive ingenuity that have anticipated trends in hermeneutics and fascinated scholars in fields like Marks's own. The marginality that the history of the Diaspora has imposed undoubtedly made orthodoxies of time and place look more questionable than to the Gentile majority. But radical skepticism is foreign to the Judaic tradition. Even more crucially, because Jewish identity inevitably springs from a functioning and ongoing community, nonbelief is hardly something that can be viably transmitted to another generation. Having no formal content, no creed into which the young can be inducted, skepticism leaves no footprints. Logically, children in such a situation would be skeptical of skepticism and would turn themselves into believers—but without an institutional context for them, Judaism would not be the obvious destination.

The sterility of a merely antireligious stance was exposed in the childhood of novelist Anne Bernays, who was called a Jew in school and asked her father about the accuracy of the accusation. Public relations counsellor Edward L. Bernays happened to be an atheist; and his reply, she recalled, was "devastating": "You're nothing."[28] His own uncle, Sigmund Freud, might have found that paternal putdown very, very interesting. In any event nothingness is too sterile to be transmissible.

There is simply no longer a serious way of being Jewish—and of living within Jewish culture—without Judaism. As the various secular bases of Jewish life have vanished or have been discredited, religion alone remains standing. Indeed its staying power and its enduring appeal are extraordinary. To convert anyone to it in the Roman Empire had been a capital crime, and in the Middle Ages Jews could also be put to death for proselytizing in defiance of Christian triumphalism. In the nineteenth century western Jews who became emancipated found very few new coreligionists; as the prestige of Christianity was so much higher, conversions tended to go from bottom to top.

But in the United States, Judaism was not despised, and to choose to subscribe to it did not look like slumming. Especially after the Second World War, Judaism was no longer treated as the junior partner in the work of salvation. Instead, Judaism was elevated in the public sphere to a plane of equality with Protestantism and Catholicism. Respected as the ancient sponsor of Christianity, Judaism has also come to be accepted as a legitimate alternative to it. Attacks launched by liberal Protestant editors upon the notion of chosenness ceased, as did disdain for the "peculiar practices" of Jewish undergraduates at Harvard. In 1953, the Day of Atonement coincided with "football Friday" in a Mississippi hamlet named Rolling Fork. On the high school varsity, four of the starting players were Jews, as was drum major Bettye Sue Kline, who recalled: "When we reported that we wouldn't be at the game because of Yom Kippur, the people in town simply changed the game to Thursday night. No arguments. No controversy. . . . They respected us more for it." Sometimes appreciation exceeded knowledge, as when Secretary of State John Foster Dulles was given a Torah by David Ben-Gurion and, in thanking the Israeli prime minister, asked him whether it contained the New Testament.[29] Or when Ronald Reagan expressed his enjoyment in looking out from the White House at Lafayette Park, seeing "the huge menorah, celebrating the Passover season."[30] But the value of the sentiment should not be discounted.

The ecumenism and latitudinarianism that are the conditions to which religion in America aspires have installed expressions of Judaism in places that would have astonished its adherents a century ago. Attached to the office doorpost of Father Theodore Hesburgh, who served as president of Notre Dame from 1952 until 1987, was a mezzuzah; and at the All Souls Unitarian Church on the Upper East Side of Manhattan, the *shofar* is blown. "High Holiday" services (including an abbreviated rendition of *Kol Nidre*) are held in other Unitarian churches, which have also built *sukkot*, lit *chanukiot* and conducted the *seder*.[31] Christmas has become less sectarian, and its public manifestations more inclusive—thanks in part to Eddie Cantor, the singer who popularized "Santa Claus is Comin' to Town" (1934), and to Johnny Marks, who wrote the words and music to "Rudolph the Red-Nosed Reindeer" (1949). Under the lines that once separated the two faiths, the ground is crumbling; in postwar America the prestige of Judaism has been at least as high as it ever was in Puritan New England.

A glum assessment of Judaism as the core of a cogent culture can also be presented, however. When writing "The Religion of American Jews," the final chapter of *American Judaism*, Glazer had to admit that so little serious research had been done on the topic that his readers were obliged to trust him. The chapter was mostly "based on personal observation." What did he observe? Jews believed, he wrote, that "religion should keep in step with science, psychotherapy, and liberal politics, and that as long as it does so it is doing its job." Religion also mattered for the sake of "Jewish self-respect—a kind of adjunct to the defense agencies engaged in fighting anti-semitism." Finally Judaism functioned to preserve Jews as an intact unit, "a kind of adjunct to the work of the Zionist groups."

But Glazer could locate little "spiritual experience." Worldliness dwarfed encounters with the supernatural, and the desire to repair this world vastly exceeded interest in the next one. An ideology (made up mostly of rationalist and liberal elements) proved easier to describe than the Jews' cosmology, and their politics was more evident than their piety. Though post-1960s revitalization could be discerned in the greater appreciation for ritualism and mysticism, and even in a spurt of volumes devoted to theology, to classify Jews as a "religious group" is a bit of a misnomer. One in five (or about 1.1 million) answered "none" to a question, posed in 1990, about religious identification.[32] Such Jews define themselves merely as non-Christians.

Here the discontinuity is interesting. Even an antisemite like Arnold J. Toynbee had praised the ancient Hebrews for their "mighty feat of spiritual intuition." The nineteenth-century German Reformer Abraham Geiger had argued that the Jewish people was historically characterized by a "religious genius." Wittgenstein wrote cryptically—and self-deprecatingly—that "amongst Jews 'genius' is found only in the holy man. Even the greatest of Jewish thinkers is no more than talented. (Myself for instance.)"[33] Whatever the aptness of such claims, the American cousins have not exactly been awash in a sea of faith.

Not until 1840 did an ordained rabbi, the Bavarian Abraham Rice, reach these shores, which means that American Jewry got along for nearly two centuries without such clergy, and in the succeeding century and a half, millions of Jews felt that they could still manage without rabbis. Opinion surveys have revealed that Jews do not keep pace with other Americans in congregation membership or in frequency of worship. When Americans were asked about the place of religion in their lives, 55 percent tell pollsters that it is "very important." Only 30 percent of Jews say so. Though only 14 percent of all Americans are willing to admit that religion plays no role in their lives, the Jewish percentage is thirty-five. In a national survey conducted in 1988, the pursuit of equality and of social justice ranked much higher than religion itself as the Jewish value that mattered most. When Jews were asked which of three qualities most effectively shaped their own identity, more than half answered "equality," a fifth said "Israel," and another fifth said "religion." According to a 1990 survey, the label of an "ethnic" group was considered more accurate than a "religious" group,[34] even as ethnicity itself was receding.

As an ancient people as well as a "model minority," Jews have thus exhibited a curious duality. Their ethical monotheism can be traced to the most distant origins, and yet the high levels of education that catapulted them to social success also gave them an antidote to what can be impugned as superstition. The result is that the people responsible for imagining the deity their neighbors worship have generally shown little faith in faith. In the admittedly arcane field of theology, American Jewry has always suffered from manpower shortages. The pool of candidates that might be drawn from the intelligentsia has been so thin, Zhitlowski commented, that "one would have to be a failure in all other scientific and liberal professions in order to make Jewish theology a profession."

That is unfair to the most admired students of the sacred: Abraham J. Heschel, Soloveitchik, Emil Fackenheim, and (in his own way) Wiesel. But all were foreign-born and -educated. For Americans the formal study of the ways of God is very much of an acquired taste. That is why the best-known American-born theologian was very much of an outsider. Will Herberg typified the proclivity to make up Jewish culture as he went along. Neither ordained as a rabbi nor formally trained as a theologian, he was so open to Christian influences that he contemplated conversion. The Reverend Reinhold Niebuhr dissuaded him, offering the rationale that only a good Jew could become a good Christian, and Herberg decided to settle for being the former. His own institutional affiliations were ecumenical: he taught at Drew University, a Methodist institution, and served as religion editor of the *National Review*, the brainchild of the Roman Catholic William F. Buckley. In *Judaism and Modern Man* (1951), Herberg gave his faith an idiosyncratic, existentialist twist, and even adopted the doctrine of original sin. That indebtedness to Christianity helps explain why, though he had many readers, he had no significant Jewish disciples.[35]

Yet without Judaism, and without the religious injunction of some measure of separation from Gentiles, Jews are reduced to another American minority group. As an ethnic group, Jewry can erect little if any defense against assimilationist pressures. As an ethnic group, its customs will seem increasingly quaint and replaceable. Nor will its cuisine (however delicious) or its patchwork of phrases (however colorful) be enough to constitute a rich and distinctive identity (and often adopted by the majority anyway, making the case for differentiation even harder to formulate). As an ethnic group, Jews cannot make an incontestible moral case for survival. The authoritative *Harvard Encyclopedia of American Ethnic Groups* has 106 listings from Acadians to Zoroastrians; were that figure to drop to 105, or fewer, no principle could be formulated that would make that decline or disappearance heartbreaking.

A *religious* case, however, can be advanced from within the tradition, and therefore American Jewry can be saved—if at all—on faith alone. "This is obviously true for the relatively small minority who are personally devout," sociologists Seymour Martin Lipset and Earl Raab write, "but it is also probably true for the much larger body of Jews who are primarily affiliated for communal reasons. If they yield their sense of the religious tradition and history attached to the Jewish community, they will eventually lose any sense of its particularity [so that] other communal and familial involvements will not sustain commitment." What makes Jews different is, finally and fundamentally, only Judaism. As discrimination disappears and love of America is fully reciprocated, what is there to live for but an *am olam*, an eternal Israel? Christians no longer make it something to die for, and merely to dissent from their belief in the Resurrection hardly makes for an impregnable rationale for Jewish identity. The Jew in the pew is pivotal. "Take religion out," Mordecai Kaplan warned in 1934, and Jewish civilization "becomes an empty shell." It is therefore possible to envision a simplified future, when a precise definition will be possible: a Jew is someone who subscribes to Judaism. Period.[36]

A simplified future may not of course be a viable one. To situate Judaism at the irreducible core of American Jewish culture is to rely upon its most vulnerable feature, the part for which this minority has shown the least aptitude. That is why those who are committed to continuity can sometimes give the impression of fighting for a lost cause. To these entropologists, four rebuttals can nevertheless be offered.

One is the consolation that concern for the caliber of Judaism is nothing new. Fears for a community going into remission were expressed even when William McKinley was living in the White House. The callow and vulgar repudiation of Judaic norms weighed heavily in the indictment. At the dawn of the century, rabbis and other cultural custodians were denouncing the bar mitzvah ceremony for its profane ostentatiousness, the Sabbath for being more honored in the breach and so poorly observed, and the elevation of Chanukah to a demeaning facsimile of Christmas. Even intermarriage, in an era when its rates were in low single digits, when its occurrence was rare enough to be newsworthy, provoked warnings that the primacy of romantic love was defeating a sense of collective destiny.[37] Anthropologist Maurice Fishberg feared that American Jews were "paying a high price for their liberty and equality—self-effacement."

That warning was issued in 1907. Four years later Arthur Ruppin did not confine his anxieties to the United States in lamenting that "the structure of Judaism, once so solid, is crumbling away before our very eyes." The sociologist prophesied a "thinning [of] the ranks of Jews."[38] Abba Hillel Silver noted how effectively Jews had resisted "hostility." But he worried that they had "not yet learned how to resist prosperity . . . [and] keep our soul intact . . . under freedom and opulence." That warning flare was sent up in 1924.

The following year, to celebrate the fiftieth anniversary of Chicago's Anshe Sholom Congregation, Rabbi Saul Silber turned killjoy: "What will become of our children? Do we want them to grow up pinochle players and poker sharks, or do we want them to grow up men and women who have an understanding of the problems of life, who know the history of their ancestors, who are proud Jews, and who will be a credit to us?" he wondered. "Our children are running away from us. . . . Let us build houses of worship, social centers and Hebrew schools, and let us provide the means for the coming generation to learn and to know."[39]

Of course the standards of holiness that this culture was expected to satisfy were different (probably higher). Perhaps the most learned of Talmudic scholars to immigrate in that era, Chicago's "chief rabbi," published a biblical commentary in 1904. In its introduction Willowski remarked that Jews had prospered and been honored in the United States. "But the ways and customs of this land militate against the observance of the laws of the Torah and the Jewish way of life," he warned, and those who strayed from observance would "mostly . . . descend to the Gehenna [Hell]." He speculated (in 1904!) that "if we do not bestir ourselves now, I am sore afraid that there will be no Jew left in the next generation."

Willowski's indignation and anxiety could not be readily countered by offering proof of a thriving high culture, despite the reputation for literacy that the community enjoyed. In the era of the First World War, only one Jew out of 250 belonged to the Jewish Publication Society of America. Even after commercial firms as well as other Jewish houses competed for readers of books of Jewish interest, it was puzzling that only 3,182 Jews living in New York State belonged to the JPS. "A terrifying percentage of our young people are absolutely without the slightest religious training," attorney and activist Louis Marshall complained to the president of Hebrew Union College. "They are growing up in total ignorance of the noble traditions of our faith . . . and the Bible itself is to them a sealed book."[40] That lament was recorded in 1920, when the Jewish core of an American Jewish culture was at its most dazzling and most susceptible to the tendency of posterity to romanticize a more glorious past.

The long view suggests that it may be too soon to tell whether fears are warranted, that the installation of a field like entropology is premature. That is a second rebuttal, and was the position of Salo W. Baron, who made brevity the soul of his historical defense of American Jewry. Centuries were needed, he argued, before any of the previous centers of Jewish creativity and learning could be established. By contrast the evolution of an American Jewish culture has so far barely spanned a century, "yet it already has great achievements to its credit." He did not explicitly address one unprecedented challenge, however: the sheer velocity, the quickened tempo of history itself, which a joke can illustrate. A physician telephones a patient, and gives him the mixed blessing of good news and bad news. The good news is that the patient has twenty-four hours to live. "That's the *good* news? What could be worse? So what's the *bad* news?" the patient frantically demands. The doctor replies: "I've been trying to reach you since yesterday." When demographic depletion was so apparent, when no hope could be nurtured of replenishment from abroad, when even the definition of a Jew was fracturing the community, would it have enough time to invest in its cultural resources? Did American Jewry still enjoy the luxury to revitalize as well as conserve its investment in learning? Or was the pace of change already too revved up to matter? Nor did Baron, famous for his repudiation of a merely "lachrymose" Jewish past, measure in any careful way the difficulty of strengthening the marrow of Jewish culture.[41]

Fears may be premature; entropology is not, after all, an exact science. The singularity of the Jewish experience has defeated historical generalization, and defying the odds is a habit that has now lasted millennia. There is something "mysterious, miraculous, unique" about the survival of his fellow Jews, Sir Isaiah Berlin asserted, "not only as a religion, but as a community, a scattered nation, a race, held together by ties of kinship, language, common memories, habits, and a sense of belonging." Historical laws do not seem quite applicable to a people that believes that it has a covenant to honor and promises to keep. Deuteronomy 7:7 blithely ignores the determinism of demography: "The Lord did not . . . choose you because you were more numerous than any people—for you were the fewest of all peoples." But even were the study of the past prescribed as an antidote to an irrational surrender to the inexplicable, the lessons of Jewish history might well offer not only enlightenment but also reassurance. The Jewish experience exhibits agency as well as weakness, initiative as well as victimization. Jews have made their own history and not merely submitted to it. Already during the Babylonian exile, the powers of this people seemed spent and its national struggles already old. Yet even as the lament was uttered, "Our bones are dried, and our hope is lost" (Ezekiel 37:11), the Bible itself was being written or arranged. Such renewal has also been a consoling, recurrent feature of the Diaspora.[42]

The committed core that is observant attests to the tenacity of Orthodoxy, which was supposed to be an anachronism confined to immigrants. A 1937 survey disclosed that four out of every five Orthodox rabbis had been born abroad, and their strict version of Judaism was expected to be a "sunset industry." The Rabbi Isaac Elchanan Theological Seminary, the acorn from which the oak of Yeshiva University grew, did not get around to hiring an English instructor until well after the seminary had been founded, and his way of acclimating the future rabbis to their new country was to translate *David Copperfield*, line by line, into Yiddish. Introduced to an East Side public school administrator who is in love with Sara Smolinsky, her learned father is astonished at his expression of interest in the holy tongue. "Hebrew?" Reb Smolinsky asks incredulously. "An American young man, a principal, and wants to learn Hebrew?" Attending a *seder* at the Kaplans' home, David Levinsky is amazed to discover that their youngest son is enrolled in an East Side yeshiva: "That an American schoolboy should read Talmud seemed a joke to me." Yet watching him interpret a passage, the wealthy cloak manufacturer admits: "I was deeply affected."

In an era when Levinsky's own atheism was widely shared, who could have divined the persistence—indeed the Americanization—of Judaic tradition? Falling in love with a very observant young woman in 1906, a freethinker asked the advice of the *Forverts*, which believed that such a marriage might be viable. Lest more die of heartbreak, however, patriarchy had to be operable: "The fact that the girl is religious and the man is not can be overcome if he has enough influence on her." It was piety itself that was assumed to be outmoded. Yet, other than feminism, no ferment has been more striking or decisive to American Judaism than Orthodoxy, which has come to exercise an influence far out of proportion to its numbers.[43]

A third reason to challenge entropology is the official repudiation, especially in recent decades, of cultural uniformity. Space has thus been opened up for minority groups, who are encouraged to take pride in their own "cultures" and who are no longer obligated to imitate the aspirations of the once-dominant group. Proponents of "Anglo-conformity" no longer enjoy a chokehold on the definition of the good life. Even though narrower versions of multiculturalism have barely noticed the most ancient minority of all, Jews are not in principle discouraged from making their religion integral to a distinctive culture. What it might resemble has been suggested by novelist Nessa Rapoport, whose "people . . . gave the world monotheism, the Sabbath, psychoanalysis, the theory of relativity, [and] American feminism, among many other contributions."

But demanding the right to be taken seriously was not the point the author of *Preparing for Sabbath* (1981) wished to make. Such bragging rights were not exercised merely to suggest how American (or how liberal) Jews are. Her intention was to validate "an authentic, engaged Jewish culture," because "people need culture not in order to live, but in order to have something to live for." Rapoport generalized that "if they do not know how to find their own culture, they will claim somebody else's. And if they cannot be proud of their Jewish culture, they are going to find some other culture to be proud of," to explore and to perpetuate.[44] And though Jewish culture has been available to anyone who seeks to know it, as is Ashanti or Inuit or any other culture, no one but a Jew would want—or would be expected—to sustain and transmit Jewish culture in a milieu in which minority identities are legitimated and even expected to flourish.

That is why Diaspora history may provide no precedent. In Wilhelmine and Weimar Germany, intermarriage rates also soared, and a famously acculturated, modernized, and prosperous community seemed to have earned a secure status. But an appreciation for cultural variety was very limited. Even a liberal like Max Weber was antipluralist, believing that the radical assimilation of this "pariah people" was not only possible but necessary (either through conversion or through intermarriage). Weber could not imagine German Jews belonging to the *Volk* without identifying fully with its common consciousness and historical memory; the particularity and "self-segregation" of those who wished to remain affirming Jews unnerved him.[45] Such denial of Jewish difference is neither demanded nor expected in the United States, where a recognizable Jewish culture can be seen as a source of national enrichment rather than a stimulus to resentment.

A fourth and final rebuttal to the pessimists closes this book on the question raised in the first chapter: essentialism. Scholars who have been most apprehensive about the prospects for survival have tended to believe in a normative Judaism. According to Charles Liebman, such an essence can be located historically, and under modern conditions Orthodoxy has come closest to it. The practices of very observant Jews, he has insisted, have been more likely to ensure communal continuity. By measuring the American Jewish experience against a normative standard, he has posited "a point where Judaism or Jewishness might so transform itself that it can no longer be called Judaism." According to an ironic David Singer, American Jewry could not vanish, thanks to "the simple device of redefining Jewishness in such a way as to include all kinds of people whose *bona fides* would not previously have been acceptable." According to historian Jerold S. Auerbach, "normative Judaism" entails at a minimum a historical attachment to the law and the land—and a century of American Jewish history can be recounted as largely a betrayal of that bedrock pair of beliefs, so that a community only nominally Jewish remains.[46] Such scholars insist that Judaism is a set of claims and practices that can in principle be defined (though perhaps not agreed upon in practice), and that such a religion can be demarcated so that inauthenticity can also be recognized. Only by specifying those boundaries and upholding what is legitimate can resistance be mounted to assimilation. A viable American Jewish culture is thus imperiled when too little remains of a Judaism that meets normative standards, when the allure of American culture constantly subjects what is truly Jewish to downward redefinition. The history of Jewish life is therefore a story of declension, predicated on essentialism. Its champions are among the most reflective and serious observers of American Jewry.

Nevertheless their position is unconvincing. The strongest objection is historical: Judaism has been so manifestly affected by varying conditions over millennia that no effort to describe its essence, to fix it in place, can succeed. In 1936 a German rabbi published *The Essence of Judaism*. In its time it was regarded as a classic. But its author was not Orthodox, as might have been guessed from Liebman's argument, but Leo Baeck, a Reform leader whose views could not be reconciled with other versions of what is "normative." His views and emphases are not the same as *Basic Judaism*, published eleven years later. Its author, Milton Steinberg, was a leading Conservative rabbi, with strongly Reconstructionist sympathies. "The essence of Judaism is the affirmation that the Jews are the chosen people," Arthur Hertzberg announced in 1966. "All else is commentary." He too is a Conservative rabbi. Yet Steinberg would have sharply disagreed, having argued that election was a claim that could only be invoked (he winced) "half-allegorically."[47] When Maimonides compressed Judaism into thirteen principles, other Judaic thinkers were shocked, though they were presumably essentialists too.

The only way to adjudicate such conflicts is to stipulate that the disputants are no longer describing an essence but instead a changing though not infinitely malleable phenomenon. All essentialists are vulnerable to the same difficulty of trying to freeze in place the dynamic receptivity of the Jews to varying stimuli that marks the evolution of this religion. Values, symbols, and ideas have circulated so freely that Judaism was never static for long. The festivals that punctuate the presumably unique Jewish calendar were mostly picked up from the Canaanites, or at least adapted from them. Moses and Aaron were once Egyptian names, and it is a commonplace that even the idea of God has changed. The deity of Maimonides (or of Mordecai Kaplan) bears little resemblance to the volatile and passive-aggressive Yahweh. Among the most famous *midrashim* is one that has Moses himself at a loss in following the discourse of the rabbis, who, it can be safely assumed, would have been mystified by the rites of American Jews who nevertheless profess to trace their lineage all the way back to his era.

No system of belief based on interpretations of texts that invite further interpretations can be stabilized. "Whatever was or was not Jewish," Jacob Neusner has claimed, "a great many things have *become* so," which may be why Gershom Scholem pointedly denied that an "essence" can be ascribed to Judaism. Its boldest twentieth-century historian could not regard it "as a closed historical phenomenon," nor consider it "defined by or with any authority." To equate Judaism with *halacha*, he snorted, was "utter nonsense."[48] Thus at least indirectly he validated Martin Buber's antinomianism. Because Franz Rosenzweig downplayed Zion, Jerold Auerbach's concise formulation—Law and Land are the sine qua non—would collide rather awkwardly with the two most creative and influential Jewish thinkers of twentieth-century Germany. This kind of essentialism does not nullify the Jewishness of Buber and Rosenzweig, but has the odd effect of disparaging their claim to have believed in Judaism.

Like religion, culture should not be regarded as the stable expression of a people with an immutable set of attributes. The features that are more evident are borrowing, adaptation, and inventiveness as well as continuity. Culture is the fluid expression of a historically contingent people (even if that people fancies itself to be eternal). The effort to formulate an unalterable and peculiar essence of American Jewish culture is no more likely to succeed than was, say, the struggle of Slavophiles to locate an irreducible spiritual core, a "national ego" that could be contrasted with the corrupt soul of Western rationalism. However the historical and future importance of Judaism is assessed, there is no essential American Jewish culture, just as there is no fixed Jewish identity in the United States.

But what has not changed is the challenge posed to American Jews. They remain obliged to reconcile the right to be equal with the option to be different. Suspended between those two alluring ideals, Jews can look back upon the grand cultural legacy they have fashioned over the past century, aware that the task ahead is not unfamiliar. It will require resourcefulness as well as stamina. American Jews must be of two minds. They must learn to adjust to differing historical circumstances while somehow remaining continuous with their past. To live creatively and durably with that ambivalence has been more than the hope of American Jews. That double vision has also been their predicament—and their fate.

Notes

PREFACE (PP. XI–XVI)

1. Delmore Schwartz, in "Under Forty: A Symposium," *Contemporary Jewish Record* 7 (February 1944), 14.
2. Arthur A. Goren, *The American Jews* (Cambridge, Mass.: Harvard University Press, 1982), 2.
3. "Marlon Brando's Heart of Darkness?" *Forward*, 12 April 1996, 7.
4. Matthew Arnold, "Civilisation in the United States" (1888), in *The Complete Prose Works of Matthew Arnold*, ed. R. H. Super (Ann Arbor: University of Michigan Press, 1977), 11:357, 358, 363, and 368; Lionel Trilling, *Matthew Arnold* (New York: Columbia University Press, 1949), 404.
5. Quoted in David H. Weinberg, *Between Tradition and Modernity: Haim Zhitlowski, Simon Dubnow, Ahad Ha-Am, and the Shaping of Modern Jewish Identity* (New York: Holmes and Meier, 1996), 246; Ruth Gay, *Unfinished People: Eastern European Jews Encounter America* (New York: Norton, 1996), 286; Jonathan D. Sarna, "Jewish Scholarship and American Jewish Continuity," in *Toward an American Jewish Culture: New Perspectives on Jewish Continuity*, ed. Richard A. Siegel (New York: National Foundation for Jewish Culture, 1994), 5.
6. Quoted in Louis Harap, *The Image of the Jew in American Literature: From Early Republic to Mass Immigration* (Philadelphia: Jewish Publication Society of America, 1974), 446–47.
7. Ibid., x–xi, 11, 23; Harley Erdman, *Staging the Jew: The Performance of an American Ethnicity, 1860–1920* (New Brunswick: Rutgers University Press, 1997), 107–13; Joel Rosenberg, "Jewish Experience on Film—An American Overview," *American Jewish Year Book* 96 (Philadelphia: Jewish Publication Society of America, 1996), 5; Neal Gabler, *An Empire of Their Own: How the Jews Invented Hollywood* (New York: Crown, 1988), 105.
8. Noel Stock, *The Life of Ezra Pound* (New York: Pantheon, 1970), 306.
9. Philip Roth, *Portnoy's Complaint* (New York: Random House, 1969), 274.

DEFINITIONS (PP. 1–31)

1. Kenneth Aaron Kanter, *The Jews on Tin Pan Alley: The Jewish Contribution to American Popular Music, 1830–1940* (New York: KTAV, 1982), 70–71; "'Bei Mir' Now Leads Best-Selling Songs," *Life* 4 (31 January 1938), 39; Victoria Secunda, *Bei Mir Bist Du Schön: The Life of Sholom Secunda* (Weston, Conn.: Magic Circle, 1982), 73–75, 129–33, 144–51, 153–57; Sammy Cahn, *I Should Care:*

The Sammy Cahn Story (New York: Arbor House, 1974), 63–71; Marvin Caplan, "The Curious History of 'Bei Mir Bist Du Schön,'" American Jewish *Congress Monthly* 62 (January–February 1995), 13–16.

2. Saul Bellow, "I Took Myself as I Was . . . ," *ADL Bulletin* 33 (December 1976), 3; Donald Altschiller to author, 24 November 1998.

3. Jay Mechling, Robert Merideth, and David Wilson, "American Cultural Studies: The Discipline and the Curriculum," *American Quarterly* 25 (October 1973), 369.

4. Stephen Greenblatt, "Culture," in *Critical Terms for Literary Study*, ed. Frank Lentricchia and Thomas McLaughlin (Chicago: University of Chicago Press, 1990), 225; Raymond Williams, *Keywords: A Vocabulary of Culture and Society*, rev. ed. (New York: Oxford University Press, 1983), 87–92.

5. Stefan Collini, "Escape from DWEMsville," *Times Literary Supplement*, 27 May 1994, 3; Clifford Geertz, *The Interpretation of Cultures: Selected Essays* (New York: Basic Books, 1973), 5, 12, 30, 89, and 312.

6. Didier Eribon, *Conversations with Claude Lévi-Strauss*, trans. Paula Wissing (Chicago: University of Chicago Press, 1991), 152; Alexis de Tocqueville, *Selected Letters on Politics and Society*, ed. Roger Boesche, trans. James Toupin and Roger Boesche (Berkeley and Los Angeles: University of California Press, 1985), 38.

7. Shelly Fisher Fishkin, *From Fact to Fiction: Journalism and Imaginative Writing in America* (New York: Oxford University Press, 1988), 31; Henry James, "Americans Abroad," in *The American*, ed. James W. Tuttleton (New York: Norton, 1978), 359; Boris Emmet and John E. Jeuck, *Catalogues and Counters: A History of Sears, Roebuck and Company* (Chicago: University of Chicago Press, 1950), 13–14.

8. Quoted in Richard Gilman, "The City and the Theater," in *New York: Cultural Capital of the World, 1940–1965*, ed. Leonard Wallock (New York: Rizzoli, 1988), 202.

9. Quoted in Stephen Spender, *Love-Hate Relations: A Study of Anglo-American Sensibilities* (London: Hamish Hamilton, 1974), 27; Frederick Jackson Turner, "The Significance of the Frontier in American History" (1894), in *American Historians: A Selection*, ed. Harvey Wish (New York: Oxford University Press, 1962), 318, 329–30; Ralph Waldo Emerson, *Essays and Lectures*, ed. Joel Porte (New York: Library of America, 1983), 261.

10. Quoted in Ann Douglas, *Terrible Honesty: Mongrel Manhattan in the 1920s* (New York: Farrar, Straus and Giroux, 1995), 185, and in Neil Jumonville, *Critical Crossings: The New York Intellectuals in Postwar America* (Berkeley and Los Angeles: University of California Press, 1991), 74; J. Hoberman, *Vulgar Modernism: Writing on Movies and Other Media* (Philadelphia: Temple University Press, 1991), 232; Max Lerner, "Six Revolutions in American Life," in *The Revolutionary Theme in Contemporary America*, ed. Thomas R. Ford (Lexington: University of Kentucky Press, 1965), 1.

11. Werner Sollors, "A Critique of Pure Tolerance," in *Reconstructing American Literary History*, ed. Sacvan Bercovitch (Cambridge, Mass.: Harvard University Press, 1986), 255; Saul Bellow, "Starting Out in Chicago," *American Scholar*

44 (Winter 1974–75), 72; Lawrence Grobel, "Playboy Interview: Saul Bellow," *Playboy* 44 (May 1997), 60.

12. Hayim Greenberg, *The Inner Eye: Selected Essays* (New York: Jewish Frontier Association, 1953), 39; Charles S. Liebman and Steven M. Cohen, *Two Worlds of Judaism: The Israeli and American Experiences* (New Haven: Yale University Press, 1990), 23; William Scott Green, "Old Habits Die Hard: Judaism in *The Encyclopedia of Religion*" (1989), in *The Challenge of America: Can Judaism Survive in Freedom?*, ed. Jacob Neusner (New York: Garland, 1993), 154.

13. Theodor Reik, *Jewish Wit* (New York: Gamut, 1962), 102.

14. Laurence J. Silberstein, "Others Within and Others Without: Rethinking Jewish Identity and Culture," in *The Other in Jewish Thought and History: Constructions of Jewish Culture and Identity*, ed. Laurence J. Silberstein and Robert L. Cohn (New York: New York University Press, 1994), 2; Ahad Ha-Am, "Slavery in Freedom" (1891), in *Selected Essays*, trans. and ed. Leon Simon (Cleveland, Ohio: Meridian, 1962), 194; Enrique Krauze, "An Interview with Isaiah Berlin," *Partisan Review* 50 (Winter 1983), 22–23; Jeremy Tarsh and Jonny Wolfson, "A Conversation with Isaiah Berlin," *The Windmill* 1 (1986), 16.

15. Lev Kopelev, *The Education of a True Believer*, trans. Gary Kern (New York: Harper and Row, 1980), 102 and 112–13.

16. Laura Z. Hobson, *Gentleman's Agreement* (New York: Simon and Schuster, 1947), 195; Charles E. Silberman, *A Certain People: American Jews and Their Lives Today* (New York: Summit, 1985), 68–69.

17. Max Lerner, Leslie Fiedler, and Philip Roth in "The Jewish Intellectual and American Jewish Identity," in *Great Jewish Speeches Throughout History*, ed. Steve Israel and Seth Forman (Northvale, N.J.: Jason Aronson, 1994), 169, 171–72, and 177–78.

18. Kim Chernin, "In the House of the Flame Bearers," *Tikkun* 2 (July–August, 1987), 57; Joyce Antler, *The Journey Home: Jewish Women and the American Century* (New York: Free Press, 1997), 315.

19. Stuart Hall, "Cultural Identity and Diaspora," in *Identity: Community, Culture, Difference*, ed. Jonathan Rutherford (London: Lawrence and Wishart, 1990), 225.

20. Kenneth Stow to author, 3 March 1997; Lionel Kochan, *The Jew and His History* (New York: Schocken, 1977), 89; David H. Weinberg, *Between Tradition and Modernity: Haim Zhitlowski, Simon Dubnow, Ahad Ha-Am, and the Shaping of Modern Jewish Identity* (New York: Holmes and Meier, 1996), 152.

21. Quoted in S. S. Prawer, *Heine's Jewish Comedy* (New York: Oxford University Press, 1983), 16; Hannah Arendt, "The Jew as Pariah: A Hidden Tradition" (1944), in *The Jew as Pariah: Jewish Identity and Politics in the Modern Age*, ed. Ron H. Feldman (New York: Grove, 1978), 69 and 79–81.

22. Deborah Dash Moore, "Jewish Women on My Mind," *culturefront* 5–6 (Winter 1997), 162.

23. Walter Benn Michaels, *Our America: Nativism, Modernism, and Pluralism* (Durham: Duke University Press, 1995), 138.

24. David Biale, "Confessions of an Historian of Jewish Culture," *Jewish Social Studies*, n.s. 1 (Fall 1994), 43; Susanne Klingenstein, *Jews in the American*

Academy, 1900–1940: The Dynamics of Intellectual Assimilation (New Haven: Yale University Press, 1991), xiii.

25. George Santayana, *Character and Opinion in the United States* (Garden City, N.Y.: Doubleday Anchor, 1956), 29; Marjorie Garber, *Vested Interests: Cross-Dressing and Cultural Anxiety* (New York: Routledge, 1992), 16; Biale, "Confessions," 44–45; David A. Hollinger, "Jewish Identity, Assimilation and Multiculturalism," in *Creating American Jews: Historical Conversations About Identity*, ed. Karen S. Mittelman (Philadelphia: National Museum of American Jewish History, 1998), 52–59.

26. Quoted in Albert Goldman, "Laughtermakers," in *Next Year in Jerusalem: Portraits of the Jew in the Twentieth Century*, ed. Douglas Villiers (New York: Viking, 1976), 230, and in Robert Brustein, *Cultural Calisthenics: Writings on Race, Politics, and Theatre* (Chicago: Ivan R. Dee, 1998), 85.

27. Quoted in *The Big Book of Jewish Humor*, ed. William Novak and Moshe Waldoks (New York: Harper and Row, 1981), 60; John Cohen, ed., *The Essential Lenny Bruce* (London: Panther, 1975), 56.

28. Leslie Fiedler, *Fiedler on the Roof: Essays on Literature and Jewish Identity* (Boston: David R. Godine, 1991), 179.

29. Jean-Paul Sartre, *Anti-Semite and Jew*, trans. George J. Becker (New York: Grove, 1960), 85; Susan Rubin Suleiman, "The Jew in Jean-Paul Sartre's *Réflexions sur la question juive*: An Exercise in Historical Reading," in *The Jew in the Text: Modernity and the Construction of Identity*, ed. Linda Nochlin and Tamar Garb (London: Thames and Hudson, 1995), 212 and 216; Anthony Heilbut, *Exiled in Paradise: German Refugee Artists and Intellectuals in America from the 1930's to the Present* (New York: Viking, 1983), 348–49.

30. Quoted in Joshua Rubenstein, *Tangled Loyalties: The Life and Times of Ilya Ehrenburg* (New York: BasicBooks, 1996), 13, 79, and 331.

31. Quoted in Avishai Margalit, "Isaiah Berlin at Eighty," in *On the Thought of Isaiah Berlin*, new ed. (Jerusalem: Israel Academy of Sciences and Humanities, 1990), 7, and in "The Philosopher of Sympathy," *New Republic* 212 (20 February 1995), 35–36; Tarsh and Wolfson, "Conversation with Isaiah Berlin," 15.

32. Quoted in Sylvia Rothchild, "Rav Soloveitchik: Talmudic Scholar and Philosopher," *Present Tense* 4 (Summer 1977), 43.

33. Chaim Weizmann, *Trial and Error* (New York: Schocken, 1966), 152; Thomas L. Friedman, *From Beirut to Jerusalem* (New York: Doubleday Anchor, 1990), 429; Randolph S. Bourne, "The Jew and Trans-National America" (1916), in *War and the Intellectuals: Essays, 1915–1919*, ed. Carl Resek (New York: Harper and Row, 1964), 128.

34. Philip Gleason, *Speaking of Diversity: Language and Ethnicity in Twentieth-Century America* (Baltimore: Johns Hopkins University Press, 1992), 18–19; Werner Sollors, *Beyond Ethnicity: Consent and Descent in American Culture* (New York: Oxford University Press, 1986), 150–52, 182–86, and 224; John Higham, *Send These to Me: Jews and Other Immigrants in Urban America* (New York: Atheneum, 1975), 203–8.

35. Sarah Schmidt, *Horace M. Kallen: Prophet of American Zionism* (Brooklyn, N.Y.: Carlson, 1995), 19–20, 26–27, and 165; Lewis S. Feuer, "Horace M. Kallen

on War and Peace," in *The Legacy of Horace M. Kallen*, ed. Milton R. Konvitz (Rutherford, N.J.: Fairleigh Dickinson University Press, 1987), 45–46; Milton R. Konvitz, "H. M. Kallen and the Hebraic Idea," in *The Legacy of Horace M. Kallen*, 66–74.

36. Seth Korelitz, "The Menorah Idea: From Religion to Culture, from Race to Ethnicity," *American Jewish History* 85 (March 1997), 75–100; Robert Alter, "Epitaph for a Jewish Magazine: Notes on the *Menorah Journal*," *Commentary* 39 (May 1965), 51–55; Ira Eisenstein, "Henry Hurwitz: Editor, Gadfly, Dreamer," in *The "Other" New York Jewish Intellectuals*, ed. Carole S. Kessner (New York: New York University Press, 1994), 193–98, 201, and 203.

37. Walter Lippmann to Henry Hurwitz, 24 December 1916, in folder 21, box 18 of Horace M. Kallen Papers, American Jewish Archives (Cincinnati).

38. Leslie A. Fiedler, *To the Gentiles* (New York: Stein and Day, 1972), 69–75; Louis Harap, *The Image of the Jew in American Literature: From Early Republic to Mass Immigration* (Philadelphia: Jewish Publication Society, 1974), 455–71; Susan [Sontag] Rieff, "Henry Harland: The Philo-Semite as Anti-Semite," *Chicago Jewish Forum* 10 (Spring 1952), 199–205; Malcolm Bradbury, *Dangerous Pilgrimages: Trans-Atlantic Mythologies and the Novel* (New York: Penguin, 1996), 224–26.

39. Richard I. Cohen, *Jewish Icons: Art and Society in Modern Europe* (Berkeley and Los Angeles: University of California Press, 1998), 21.

40. Bette Roth Young, *Emma Lazarus in Her World: Life and Letters* (Philadelphia: Jewish Publication Society, 1995), 55–56 and 61–62.

41. Quoted in Ira B. Nadel, *Joyce and the Jews: Culture and Texts* (Iowa City: University of Iowa Press, 1989), 139; James Joyce, *Ulysses* (New York: Modern Library, 1961), 487; Neil R. Davison, *James Joyce, Ulysses, and the Construction of Jewish Identity: Culture, Biography and "The Jew" in Modernist Europe* (Cambridge: Cambridge University Press, 1996), 9, 10, 204, 218, 243 n. 2, and 276 n. 26.

42. Meyer Schapiro, "The Nature of Abstract Art" (1937), in *Modern Art: 19th and 20th Centuries* (New York: George Braziller, 1978), 196.

43. Arnold Jacob Wolf, "The Joy of Genesis," *Hadassah* 79 (October 1997), 44.

44. Robert P. Crease and Charles C. Mann, "How the Universe Works," *Atlantic Monthly* 254 (August 1984), 71–72; "Analyzing Jewish Comics," *Time* 112 (2 October 1978), 76.

45. Jane Perlez, "Hungary Sadly Reflects on the Continuing Drain of Its Big Brains," *International Herald Tribune*, 21–22 March 1998, 1 and 5; M. F. Perutz, "An Intellectual Bumblebee," *New York Review of Books* 40 (7 October 1993), 19; Eugene P. Wigner, as told to Andrew Szanton, *The Recollections of Eugene P. Wigner* (New York: Plenum, 1992), 45–46, 49–51, and 120–22; Clifford Krauss, "So, Argentina, Start at the Beginning . . . ," *International Herald Tribune*, 30–31 May 1998, 1 and 4.

46. Quoted in Thomas Schatz, *The Genius of the System: Hollywood Filmmaking in the Studio Era* (New York: Pantheon, 1988), 286, in "Aaron Copland," in *American Jewish Biographies*, ed. Murray Polner (New York: Lakeville, 1982), 73.

47. Quoted in Robert Sklar, "Lies and Secrets at New York Film Festival," *Forward*, 11 October 1996, 10.

48. Quoted in Glenn Kaye, "A Certain Simon Schama," *Harvard Magazine* 93 (November–December, 1991), 51; "The Art of Fiction" (1984), in *Conversations with Philip Roth*, ed. George J. Searles (Jackson: University Press of Mississippi, 1992), 181.

49. James Conant, "An Interview with Stanley Cavell," in *The Senses of Stanley Cavell*, ed. Richard Fleming and Michael Payne (Lewisburg: Bucknell University Press, 1989), 49–50; Raphael Patai, *The Jewish Mind* (Detroit: Wayne State University Press, 1996), 359.

50. Erich Auerbach, *Mimesis: The Representation of Reality in Western Literature* (Princeton: Princeton University Press, 1953), 13.

51. Quoted in James R. Oestreich, "Finding the Human Drama in a Monument by Bach," *New York Times*, 16 March 1997, and in Israel Shenker, *Coat of Many Colors: Pages from Jewish Life* (Garden City, N.Y.: Doubleday, 1985), 278–79, 280, and 281; Oscar Wilde, *Salomé* (New York: Hartsdale House, 1947), 31 and 32.

52. Vladimir Nabokov, *Strong Opinions* (New York: McGraw-Hill, 1973), 90–91; "The Art of Fiction" (1974), in *Conversations with Joseph Heller*, ed. Adam J. Sorkin (Jackson: University Press of Mississippi, 1993), 108; Ruth Gay, *Unfinished People: Eastern European Jews Encounter America* (New York: Norton, 1996), 67.

53. Norman Podhoretz, *Making It* (New York: Random House, 1967), 123; Margaret Brenman-Gibson, *Clifford Odets: American Playwright: The Years from 1906 to 1940* (New York: Atheneum, 1981), 22 n; Nathan Glazer, "The National Influence of Jewish New York," in *Capital of the American Century: The National and International Influence of New York City*, ed. Martin Shefter (New York: Russell Sage Foundation, 1993), 167 and 172.

54. Quoted in Varian Fry, *Surrender on Demand* (New York: Random House, 1945), 130.

55. Quoted in Martin Gottfried, *Broadway Musicals* (New York: Abrams, 1979), 241.

56. Daniel Royot, *L'humour et la culture américaine* (Paris: Presses Universitaires de France, 1996), 245; John Rockwell, "Woody Allen: France's Monsieur Right," *New York Times*, 5 April 1992; John Lahr, "The Imperfectionist," *New Yorker* 71 (9 December 1996), 79.

57. Wendy Wasserstein, *The Heidi Chronicles and Other Plays* (New York: Vintage, 1991), 195.

58. Quoted in Joseph Boskin, "The Urban Comic Spirit," *culturefront* 5–6 (Winter 1997), 138.

59. Rael Meyerowitz, *Transferring to America: Jewish Interpretations of American Dreams* (Albany: State University of New York Press, 1995), 27.

60. Quoted in Mark Hodin, "Class, Consumption, and Ethnic Performance in Vaudeville," in *Prospects* (New York: Cambridge University Press, 1997), 22:202; James Gleick, *Genius: The Life and Science of Richard Feynman* (New York: Pantheon, 1992), 97, 410, and 411; Abbie Hoffman, *Soon To Be a Major*

Motion Picture (New York: Putnam, 1980), 166 and 281; John Murray Cuddihy, *The Ordeal of Civility: Freud, Marx, Lévi-Strauss, and the Jewish Struggle with Modernity* (New York: Basic Books, 1974), 189–97.

61. "Letter to *The Day*," 11 November 1915, in Irving Howe and Kenneth Libo, *How We Lived: A Documentary History of Immigrant Jews in America* (New York: Richard Marek, 1979), 246; Bruce Cook, *The Beat Generation* (New York: Scribner, 1971), 103; "Isaac Bashevis Singer" (1968), in *Writers at Work*, ed. George Plimpton (New York: Viking, 1981), 5th ser., 77.

62. Wilfrid Sheed, *The Good Word and Other Words* (New York: Penguin, 1978), 156; Sergio Della Pergola, "Changing Cores and Peripheries: Fifty Years in Socio-Demographic Perspective," in *Terms of Survival: The Jewish World since 1945*, ed. Robert S. Wistrich (New York: Routledge, 1995), 15.

63. Michael A. Meyer, "German-Jewish Identity in Nineteenth-Century America," in *Toward Modernity: The European Jewish Model*, ed. Jacob Katz (New Brunswick, N.J.: Transaction, 1987), 258–59; Jonathan D. Sarna, *JPS: The Americanization of Jewish Culture, 1888–1988* (Philadelphia: Jewish Publication Society, 1989), 29–30 and 37.

64. Efraim Shmueli, *Seven Jewish Cultures: A Reinterpretation of Jewish History and Thought*, trans. Gila Shmueli (Cambridge: Cambridge University Press, 1990), xiii, 12–15, and 178.

65. Ludwig Wittgenstein, *Culture and Value*, ed. G. H. von Wright and Heikki Nyman, trans. Peter Winch (Chicago: University of Chicago Press, 1980), 19e; Sander L. Gilman, *Smart Jews: The Construction of the Image of Jewish Superior Intelligence* (Lincoln: University of Nebraska Press, 1996), 140; Ahad Ha-Am, "Imitation and Assimilation" (1894), in *Selected Essays*, 117; George Steiner, *After Babel: Aspects of Language and Translation* (New York: Oxford University Press, 1975), 115.

66. Quoted in Irving Howe, with Kenneth Libo, *World of Our Fathers* (New York: Harcourt Brace Jovanovich, 1976), 452, and in Thomas Meehan, "Public Writer No. 1?" *New York Times Magazine*, 12 December 1965, 44–45 and 136.

CONDITIONS (PP. 32–58)

1. Quoted in F. O. Matthiessen, *American Renaissance: Art and Expression in the Age of Emerson and Whitman* (New York: Oxford University Press, 1941), 29.

2. Quoted in Alfred Kazin, "Introduction: The Jew as Modern American Writer," in *The Commentary Reader*, ed. Norman Podhoretz (New York: Atheneum, 1967), xv; Louis Harap, *The Image of the Jew in American Literature: From Early Republic to Mass Immigration* (Philadelphia: Jewish Publication Society, 1974), 288–89; Bette Roth Young, *Emma Lazarus in Her World: Life and Letters* (Philadelphia: Jewish Publication Society, 1995), 6–7, 24, and 44.

3. Hans Wysling, ed., *Letters of Heinrich and Thomas Mann, 1900–1949*, trans. Don Reneau (Berkeley and Los Angeles: University of California Press, 1998), 66; Michael Brenner, *The Renaissance of Jewish Culture in Weimar Germany* (New Haven: Yale University Press, 1996), 4.

4. Quoted in Emma Felsenthal, *Bernhard Felsenthal: Teacher in Israel* (New York: Oxford University Press, 1924), 19; Michael A. Meyer, "German-Jewish Identity in Nineteenth-Century America," in *Toward Modernity: The European Jewish Model*, ed. Jacob Katz (New Brunswick, N.J.: Transaction, 1987), 261–62; Joseph A. Levine, "Music, Cantorial," in *Jewish-American History and Culture: An Encyclopedia*, ed. Jack Fischel and Sanford Pinsker (New York: Garland, 1992), 414.

5. Rudolf Glanz, *Studies in Judaica Americana* (New York: KTAV, 1970), 230 and 232.

6. Quoted in Peter Grose, *Israel in the Mind of America* (New York: Knopf, 1983), 82; Ann Douglas, *Terrible Honesty: Mongrel Manhattan in the 1920s* (New York: Farrar, Straus and Giroux, 1995), 120.

7. Jonathan D. Sarna, *JPS: The Americanization of Jewish Culture, 1888–1988* (Philadelphia: Jewish Publication Society, 1989), 39–42; David G. Dalin, "Mayer Sulzberger and American Jewish Public Life," in *An Inventory of Promises: Essays on American Jewish History in Honor of Moses Rischin*, ed. Jeffrey S. Gurock and Marc Lee Raphael (Brooklyn, N.Y.: Carlson, 1995), 40–41.

8. Quoted in Bryan Cheyette, "Englishness and Extraterritoriality: British-Jewish Writing and Diaspora Culture," in *Studies in Contemporary Jewry*, ed. Ezra Mendelsohn (New York: Oxford University Press, 1996), 12:23.

9. Cynthia Ozick, *Metaphor and Memory: Essays* (New York: Knopf, 1989), 174; Hasia R. Diner, "Before the Promised City: Eastern European Jews in America before 1880," in *Inventory of Promises*, 45, 57, and 61; Meyer, "German-Jewish Identity," 249; David H. Weinberg, *Between Tradition and Modernity: Haim Zhitlowski, Simon Dubnow, Ahad Ha-Am, and the Shaping of Modern Jewish Identity* (New York: Holmes and Meier, 1996), 85; Morris Hillquit, *Loose Leaves from a Busy Life* (New York: Rand School Press, 1934), 8, 17, and 37.

10. Moses Rischin, *The Promised City: New York's Jews, 1870–1914* (Cambridge, Mass.: Harvard University Press, 1962), 117; Abraham Cahan, *Yekl and The Imported Bridegroom and Other Stories of the New York Ghetto* (New York: Dover, 1970), 41 and 49–50; Fred Somkin, "Zion's Harp by the East River: Jewish-American Popular Songs in Columbus's Golden Land, 1890–1914," *Perspectives in American History*, n.s., 2 (1985), 207.

11. Ruth Gay, *Unfinished People: Eastern European Jews Encounter America* (New York: Norton, 1996), 64–65; J. Hoberman, *Bridge of Light: Yiddish Film Between Two Worlds* (New York: Schocken, 1991), 65; Esther Romeyn and Jack Kugelmass, *Let There Be Laughter! Jewish Humor in America* (Chicago: Spertus, 1997), 28.

12. Henry James, *The Question of Our Speech and The Lesson of Balzac* (Boston: Houghton Mifflin, 1905), 42 and 43; Ozick, *Metaphor and Memory*, 152–53; Robert McCrum, William Cran, and Robert MacNeil, *The Story of English* (New York: Viking, 1986), 267.

13. Rischin, *Promised City*, 116; Nathan Glazer, "Social Characteristics of American Jews, 1654–1954" (1955), in *The Challenge of America: Can Judaism Survive in Freedom?* ed. Jacob Neusner (New York: Garland, 1993), 115; Gerald Sorin,

Tradition Transformed: The Jewish Experience in America (Baltimore: Johns Hopkins University Press, 1997), 85.

14. Somkin, "Zion's Harp," 219, 220; Barbara W. Grossman, *Funny Woman: The Life and Times of Fanny Brice* (Bloomington: Indiana University Press, 1991), 27–28; Donald Weber, "Memory and Repression in Early Ethnic Television: The Example of Gertrude Berg and *The Goldbergs*," in *The Other Fifties: Interrogating Midcentury American Icons*, ed. Joel Foreman (Champaign: University of Illinois Press, 1997), 152.

15. Abraham Cahan, "The Russian Jew in America" (1898), in *The Jew in the Modern World: A Documentary History*, ed. Paul Mendes-Flohr and Jehuda Reinharz (New York: Oxford University Press, 1980), 377; Steven Cassedy, *To the Other Shore: The Russian Jewish Intellectuals Who Came to America* (Princeton: Princeton University Press, 1997), 78, 148, and 150; Henry L. Feingold, *Lest Memory Cease: Finding Meaning in the American Jewish Past* (Syracuse: Syracuse University Press, 1996), 175–76.

16. Quoted in Gay, *Unfinished People*, 294; Anita Norich, "Isaac Bashevis Singer in America: The Translation Problem," *Judaism* 44 (Spring 1995), 209–10; Janet Hadda, "Isaac Bashevis Singer in New York," *Judaism* 46 (Summer 1997), 350, 354, and 360; Cassedy, *To the Other Shore*, 101 and 150; Laura Z. Hobson, *Laura Z.: A Life* (New York: Arbor House, 1983), 23.

17. Yankev Glatshteyn, *Selected Poems of Yankev Glatshteyn*, trans. and ed. Richard J. Fein (Philadelphia: Jewish Publication Society, 1987), 101 and 103; Ruth R. Wisse, "Found in America," *New Republic* 213 (18 and 25 September 1995), 55 and 56, and "Language as Fate: Reflections on Jewish Literature in America," in *Studies in Contemporary Jewry*, ed. Ezra Mendelsohn (New York: Oxford University Press, 1996), 12:132.

18. Hoberman, *Bridge of Light*, 235, 247–53, and 265; Lauren N. Antler, "The Search for Paradise: Yiddish Film and Jewish Radicalism in 1930s America," Barnard College senior thesis (1998), 27–35; Paul Buhle, "The Hollywood Blacklist and the Jew: An Exploration of Popular Culture," *Tikkun* 10 (September–October, 1995), 37–38.

19. Haim Zhitlowsky, "Our Future in America" (1915), in *Jew in the Modern World*, 388–89; Weinberg, *Between Tradition and Modernity*, 110, 120, 138, 139, and 140.

20. Solomon Schechter, "English and Hebrew Must Be the Languages of American Jewry" (1904), in *Jew in the Modern World*, 390; William Chomsky, *Hebrew: The Eternal Language* (Philadelphia: Jewish Publication Society, 1957), 272 and 277.

21. Gerson D. Cohen, "The Blessings of Assimilation in Jewish History" (1966), in *Challenge of America*, 48–49; Raphael Patai, *The Jewish Mind* (Detroit: Wayne State University Press, 1977), 81–83 and 94–95.

22. Susanne Klingenstein, *Enlarging America: The Cultural Work of Jewish Literary Scholars, 1930–1990* (Syracuse: Syracuse University Press, 1998), 277–84 and 302; Gerson Cohen, "The Scholar as Chancellor," in *Creators and Disturbers: Reminiscences by Jewish Intellectuals of New York*, ed. Bernard Rosenberg and Ernest Goldstein (New York: Columbia University Press, 1982), 210–11.

23. Eli Lederhendler, *Jewish Responses to Modernity: New Voices in America and*

Eastern Europe (New York: New York University Press, 1994), 21; McCrum, Cran, and MacNeil, *Story of English*, 19.

24. Lawrence W. Levine, *The Opening of the American Mind: Canons, Culture, and History* (Boston: Beacon, 1996), 133–35; Robert Warshow, "An Old Man Gone" (1951), in *The Immediate Experience: Movies, Comics, Theatre, and Other Aspects of Popular Culture* (Garden City, N.Y.: Doubleday Anchor, 1964), 67–79.

25. Noam Chomsky, "Interview," in *The Chomsky Reader*, ed. James Peck (New York: Pantheon, 1987), 11, 13.

26. Quoted in Cassedy, *To the Other Shore*, 113, and in Bernard G. Richards, introduction to Cahan, *Yekl and The Imported Bridegroom*, vii.

27. John Higham, *Send These to Me: Jews and Other Immigrants in Urban America* (New York: Atheneum, 1975), 88–100; Hasia R. Diner, *In the Almost Promised Land: American Jews and Blacks, 1915–1935* (Westport, Conn.: Greenwood, 1977), 32 and 33; Rischin, *Promised City*, 126; Cassedy, *Other Shore*, 117–19 and 140; Harap, *Image of the Jew*, 491–92; Sorin, *Tradition Transformed*, 168.

28. Quoted in Rischin, *Promised City*, 160.

29. Ibid., 127; Kenneth Aaron Kanter, *The Jews on Tin Pan Alley: The Jewish Contribution to American Popular Music, 1830–1940* (New York: KTAV, 1982), 34–35, 117, and 196.

30. Quoted in Nicholas Dawidoff, *The Catcher Was a Spy: The Mysterious Life of Moe Berg* (New York: Pantheon, 1994), 60; Roger Angell, "Congratulations! It's a Baby!" *New Yorker* 73 (15 December 1997), 139; Cheryl Greenberg, "Pluralism and Its Discontents: The Case of Blacks and Jews," in *Insider/Outsider: American Jews and Multiculturalism*, ed. David Biale, Michael Galchinsky, and Susannah Heschel (Berkeley and Los Angeles: University of California Press, 1998), 66.

31. Hoberman, *Bridge of Light*, 270–72.

32. Paul Berman, *A Tale of Two Utopias: The Political Journey of the Generation of 1968* (New York: Norton, 1996), 236.

33. Nahma Sandrow, *Vagabond Stars: A World History of Yiddish Theater* (New York: Harper and Row, 1977), 97; Robert Brustein, *Cultural Calisthenics: Writings on Race, Politics, and Theatre* (Chicago: Ivan R. Dee, 1998), 223–28; Judith Laikin Elkin, "Adler, Stella," in *Jewish Women in America: An Historical Encyclopedia*, ed. Paula E. Hyman and Deborah Dash Moore (New York: Routledge, 1997), 1:19–21; Margaret Brenman-Gibson, *Clifford Odets, American Playwright: The Years from 1906 to 1940* (New York: Atheneum, 1981), 254.

34. Selma G. Lanes, *The Art of Maurice Sendak* (New York: Abrams, 1984), 40, 43, 45, 138, and 140–42; Joan Acocella, "The Big Bad Wolf is Back," *New Yorker* 74 (30 November 1998), 112.

35. Quoted in Moses Rischin, "The Jews and Pluralism: Toward an American Freedom Symphony," in *Jewish Life in America: Historical Perspectives*, ed. Gladys Rosen (New York: KTAV, 1978), 77; Barrett Wendell to Horace M. Kallen, 5 June 1912, in *Barrett Wendell and His Letters*, ed. M. A. De Wolfe Howe (Boston: Atlantic Monthly Press, 1924), 249.

36. Budd Schulberg, *What Makes Sammy Run?* (New York: Modern Library, 1941), 249.

37. Quoted in Daniel Itzkovitz, "Secret Temples," in *Jews and Other Differences: The New Jewish Cultural Studies,* ed. Jonathan Boyarin and Daniel Boyarin (Minneapolis: University of Minnesota Press, 1997), 196; Harold E. Stearns, ed., preface to *Civilization in the United States: An Inquiry by Thirty Americans* (New York: Harcourt Brace, 1922), vii.

38. Henry James, *The American Scene,* ed. Leon Edel (Bloomington: Indiana University Press, 1969), 85 and 131; Donald Weber, "Outsiders and Greenhorns: Christopher Newman in the Old World, David Levinsky in the New," *American Literature* 67 (December 1995), 732 and 740.

39. Somkin, "Zion's Harp," 191 n; Gershom Scholem, *On Jews and Judaism in Crisis: Selected Essays,* ed. Werner J. Dannhauser (New York: Schocken, 1976), 61–90.

40. Quoted in *Truman Capote: Conversations,* ed. M. Thomas Inge (Jackson: University Press of Mississippi, 1987), 287–88; Virgil Thomson, *A Virgil Thomson Reader* (Boston: Houghton Mifflin, 1981), 549 and 551; Ezra Mendelsohn, ed., "On the Jewish Presence in Nineteenth-Century European Musical Life," in *Studies in Contemporary Jewry,* 10:10.

41. Seymour Martin Lipset, *American Exceptionalism: A Double-Edged Sword* (New York: Norton, 1996), 151; Alan M. Dershowitz, *The Vanishing American Jew: In Search of Jewish Identity for the Next Century* (Boston: Little, Brown, 1997), 343.

42. Quoted in Neal Gabler, *An Empire of Their Own: How the Jews Invented Hollywood* (New York: Crown, 1988), 325; Tom Dardis, *Some Time in the Sun* (New York: Scribner, 1976), 8, 80, 113, 114, 118, 140, 144, and 149.

43. Quoted in Larry Swindell, *Spencer Tracy* (New York: World, 1969), 139; Alfred Appel Jr., *Nabokov's Dark Cinema* (New York: Oxford University Press, 1974), 21 and 307.

44. Quoted in Ivan Kalmar, *The Trotskys, Freuds and Woody Allens: Portrait of a Culture* (New York: Viking, 1993), 245 and 353; Mark Winokur, *American Laughter: Immigrants, Ethnicity, and 1930s Hollywood Film Comedy* (New York: St. Martin's, 1996), 180; Barry Rubin, *Assimilation and Its Discontents* (New York: Times Books, 1995), 81; Woody Allen, *Four Films of Woody Allen* (New York: Random House, 1982), 4.

45. Lederhendler, *Jewish Responses to Modernity,* 107–10; Leslie Fiedler, in "The Jewish Intellectual and American Jewish Identity," in *Great Jewish Speeches Throughout History,* ed. Steve Israel and Seth Forman (Northvale, N.J.: Jason Aronson, 1994), 177–78; Weber, "Outsiders and Greenhorns," 740; Hélène Cixous, "Sorties: Out and Out: Attacks/Ways Out/Forays," in Hélène Cixous and Catherine Clement, *The Newly Born Woman,* trans. Betsy Wing (Minneapolis: University of Minnesota Press, 1986), 71.

46. Quoted in Michael R. Marrus, "Are the French Antisemitic? Evidence in the 1980s," in *The Jews in Modern France,* ed. Frances Malino and Bernard Wasserstein (Hanover: University Press of New England, 1985), 225; Joanna McGeary, "Echoes of the Holocaust," *Time* 149 (24 February 1997), 40.

47. Lawrence Wechsler, "Oy, Spock," *New Yorker* 71 (4 September 1995), 34; Leonard Nimoy, "What Being Jewish Means to Me," *New York Times*, 22 December 1996, and *I Am Spock* (New York: Hyperion, 1995), 67–69.

48. Quoted in Harap, *Image of the Jew*, 220 and 237–38; "Marlon Brando's Heart of Darkness?" *Forward*, 12 April 1996, 7.

49. Kazin, introduction, xvi; H. L. Mencken, *The American Language*, rev. ed., ed. Raven I. McDavid Jr. and David W. Maurer (New York: Knopf, 1963), 234 and 235; Robert Muccigrosso, *Celebrating the New World: Chicago's Columbian Exposition of 1893* (Chicago: Ivan R. Dee, 1993), 155–56 and 165–68.

50. Quoted in "Heaven's Window," *New Yorker* 74 (27 April and 4 May 1998), 116.

51. Leslie A. Fiedler, "What Shining Phantom: Writers and the Movies" (1967), in *The Collected Essays of Leslie Fiedler* (New York: Stein and Day, 1971), 2:447; Kazin, introduction, xvii; Eugene Goodheart, *Culture and the Radical Conscience* (Cambridge, Mass.: Harvard University Press, 1973), 57; Pauline Kael, *Deeper into Movies* (Boston: Little, Brown, 1973), 327.

52. Quoted in Harap, *Image of the Jew*, 389, and in Douglas, *Terrible Honesty*, 430.

53. Douglas, *Terrible Honesty*, 449.

54. John Russell Taylor, *Strangers in Paradise: The Hollywood Emigrés, 1933–1950* (New York: Holt, Rinehart and Winston, 1983), 80–81 and 210; Anthony Heilbut, *Exiled in Paradise: German Refugee Artists and Intellectuals in America from the 1930's to the Present* (New York: Viking, 1983), 48 and 280–81; Gabler, *Empire of Their Own*, 165 and 180.

55. Quoted in Hannah Arendt, *Men in Dark Times* (New York: Harcourt, Brace and World, 1968), 170; T. W. Adorno, "Scientific Experiences of a European Scholar in America," trans. Donald Fleming, in *The Intellectual Migration: Europe and America, 1930–1960*, ed. Donald Fleming and Bernard Bailyn (Cambridge, Mass.: Harvard University Press, 1969), 369.

56. Van Wyck Brooks, "America's Coming-of-Age" (1915), in *Three Essays on America* (New York: Dutton, 1970), 17–18 and 20.

57. Michael Kammen, *The Lively Arts: Gilbert Seldes and the Transformation of Cultural Criticism in the United States* (New York: Oxford University Press, 1996), 9, 10–11, 69–70, 80, 88, and 94.

58. Norman Podhoretz, ed., preface to *Commentary Reader*, ix; Lionel Trilling, *The Last Decade: Essays and Reviews, 1965–75*, ed. Diana Trilling (New York: Harcourt Brace Jovanovich, 1979), 9–10; Alan M. Wald, *The New York Intellectuals: The Rise and Decline of the Anti-Stalinist Left from the 1930s to the 1980s* (Chapel Hill: University of North Carolina Press, 1987), 31–33; Norman Cantor, *The American Century: Varieties of Culture in Modern Times* (New York: HarperCollins, 1997), 62.

59. Abraham Cahan, *The Rise of David Levinsky* (New York: Harper and Bros., 1917), 167.

60. Higham, *Send These to Me*, 100; H. L. Mencken, *Prejudices: A Selection*, ed. James T. Farrell (New York: Vintage, 1958), 97; Nicolas Slonimsky, *Perfect Pitch: A Life Story* (New York: Oxford University Press, 1988), 96; Mendelsohn, "Jewish Presence in Musical Life," 11.

61. Quoted in Rubin, *Assimilation*, 159.
62. Burton Bernstein, *Family Matters: Sam, Jennie and the Kids* (New York: Summit Books, 1982), 137–38 and 183; Lukas Foss and Paul Myers in *Conversations about Bernstein*, ed. William Westbrook Burton (New York: Oxford University Press, 1995), 7–8 and 62; John Rockwell, "Bernstein Triumphant," *New York Times Magazine*, 31 August 1986, 19; "Leonard Bernstein, February 10, 1980," in Don Hewitt, *Minute by Minute . . .* (New York: Random House, 1985), 145.
63. Quoted in Theodor Reik, *Jewish Wit* (New York: Gamut, 1962), 51; David Diamond and Justin Brown in *Conversations about Bernstein*, 28, 29, and 99.

MUSICAL THEATER (PP. 59–87)

1. John Dizikes, *Opera in America: A Cultural History* (New Haven: Yale University Press, 1993), 502; Geoffrey Block, *Enchanted Evenings: The Broadway Musical from* Show Boat *to* Sondheim (New York: Oxford University Press, 1997), 210.
2. Quoted in John Lahr, "The Lemon-Drop Kid," *New Yorker* 72 (30 September 1996), 74.
3. Quoted in Block, *Enchanted Evenings*, 147.
4. David Gelernter, *1939: The Lost World of the Fair* (New York: Free Press, 1995), 25 and 65.
5. Quoted in Israel Shenker, *Coat of Many Colors: Pages from Jewish Life* (Garden City, N.Y.: Doubleday, 1985), 284; Kenneth Aaron Kanter, *The Jews on Tin Pan Alley: The Jewish Contribution to American Popular Music, 1830–1940* (New York: KTAV, 1982), 42–43.
6. Quoted in Martin Gottfried, *Broadway Musicals* (New York: Abrams, 1979), 143.
7. William Goldman, *The Season: A Candid Look at Broadway* (New York: Harcourt, Brace and World, 1968), 149; Abraham Cahan, *The Rise of David Levinsky* (New York: Harper and Row, 1960), 157, 505–6; Nahma Sandrow, "Yiddish Theater and American Theater," in *From Hester Street to Hollywood: The Jewish-American Stage and Screen*, ed. Sarah Blacher Cohen (Bloomington: Indiana University Press, 1983), 23.
8. Quoted in Hugh Fordin, *Getting to Know Him: A Biography of Oscar Hammerstein* (New York: Random House, 1977), 125–26.
9. Gottfried, *Broadway Musicals*, 221, 257–59, 317, and 343; Craig Zadan, *Sondheim & Co.*, 2d ed. (New York: Harper and Row, 1986), 3; "He Sent Them Away Humming: Richard Rodgers, 1902–1979," *Time* 115 (14 January 1980), 83; Philip Furia, *The Poets of Tin Pan Alley: A History of America's Great Lyricists* (New York: Oxford University Press, 1992), 95; Kanter, *Jews on Tin Pan Alley*, 162.
10. Richard Rodgers, *Musical Stages: An Autobiography* (New York: Random House, 1975), 88; Furia, *Poets*, 155; Jesse Green, "The Song is Ended," *New York Times Magazine*, 2 June 1996, 51; Charles Schwartz, *Cole Porter* (New York: Dial, 1977), 117–18; Alec Wilder, *American Popular Song: The Great In-*

novators, 1900–1950 (New York: Oxford University Press, 1972), 244, 246, and 251; Gottfried, *Broadway Musicals*, 202 and 203–4; Laurence Bergreen, *As Thousands Cheer: The Life of Irving Berlin* (New York: Viking, 1990), 417.

11. Quoted in Schwartz, *Cole Porter*, 155.

12. Block, *Enchanted Evenings*, 360; Lahr, "Lemon-Drop Kid," 70 and 71; Yip Harburg, "From the Lower East Side to 'Over the Rainbow,'" in *Creators and Disturbers: Reminiscences by Jewish Intellectuals of New York*, ed. Bernard Rosenberg and Ernest Goldstein (New York: Columbia University Press, 1982), 139.

13. Quoted in Dizikes, *Opera in America*, 71–72 and 79.

14. Green, "Song is Ended," 30.

15. Robert W. Creamer, *Babe: The Legend Comes to Life* (New York: Simon and Schuster, 1974), 133 and 207–9; Block, *Enchanted Evenings*, 159; Rodgers, *Musical Stages*, 238; Ethan Mordden, *Better Foot Forward: The History of the American Musical Theatre* (New York: Grossman, 1976), 190; Fred Goodman, *The Mansion on the Hill: Dylan, Young, Geffen, Springsteen, and the Head-On Collision of Rock and Commerce* (New York: Times Books, 1997), xi.

16. Theodore H. White, *In Search of History: A Personal Adventure* (New York: Harper and Row, 1978), 518–24; Gene Lees, *Inventing Champagne: The Worlds of Lerner and Loewe* (New York: St. Martin's, 1990), 33; Richard Corliss, "The Trip Ends," *Time* 146 (21 August 1995), 60; Green, "Song is Ended," 30.

17. Ronald Sanders, "The American Popular Song," in *Next Year in Jerusalem: Portraits of the Jew in the Twentieth Century*, ed. Douglas Villiers (New York: Viking, 1976), 209; John Lahr, *Light Fantastic: Adventures in Theatre* (New York: Dial, 1996), 256; Gottfried, *Broadway Musical*, 175 and 176; Wilfrid Mellers, "An American in New York," *New Republic* 208 (14 June 1993), 44, 45, and 46; "He Sent Them Away Humming," *Time*, 83.

18. Quoted in Lahr, *Light Fantastic*, 245, and in "Lemon-Drop Kid," 72; Harburg, "From the Lower East Side," 150; Furia, *Poets of Tin Pan Alley*, 209.

19. Walter Benjamin to Gershom Scholem, 17 April 1931, in *The Correspondence of Walter Benjamin, 1910–1940*, ed. Gershom Scholem and Theodor W. Adorno, trans. Manfred R. Jacobson and Evelyn M. Jacobson (Chicago: University of Chicago Press, 1994), 378.

20. Ira Gershwin, *Lyrics on Several Occasions* (New York: Knopf, 1959), 241.

21. Quoted in Block, *Enchanted Evenings*, 120.

22. Quoted in John Lahr, "Song of the Suits," *New Yorker* 71 (24 April 1995), 117.

23. Quoted in Kanter, *Jews on Tin Pan Alley*, 174; Block, *Enchanted Evenings*, 104.

24. Quoted in William A. Henry III, "Master of the Musical," *Time* 130 (7 December 1987), 80.

25. Quoted in Lees, *Inventing Champagne*, 135.

26. Ibid., 188–98 and 311–12.

27. Zadan, *Sondheim & Co.*, 14; Gottfried, *Broadway Musicals*, 54 and 64.

28. Quoted in Isaiah Berlin, *Russian Thinkers*, ed. Henry Hardy and Aileen Kelly (New York: Viking, 1978), 92.

29. Green, "Song is Ended," 33; "He Sent Them Away Humming," *Time*, 83.

30. Quoted in Brad Leithauser, "Here To Stay," *New York Review of Books* 43 (17 October 1996), 36.

31. Quoted in Richard Corliss, "The Most Snappy Fella," *Time* 138 (16 September 1991), 67; Gottfried, *Broadway Musicals*, 60 and 61; Michael Feinstein, "His Words Add Music to the Music," *New York Times*, 1 December 1996.

32. Quoted in Block, *Enchanted Evenings*, 70, and in Deena Rosenberg, *Fascinating Rhythm: The Collaboration of George and Ira Gershwin* (Ann Arbor: University of Michigan Press, 1997), 321.

33. Quoted in Leithauser, "Here To Stay," 38; Mellers, "American in Paris," 48; Gottfried, *Broadway Musicals*, 221, 222, 225, 230, and 231.

34. Ibid., 225 and 229.

35. Quoted in Fordin, *Getting to Know Him*, 270.

36. Dizikes, *Opera in America*, 502; Barry Singer, *Black and Blue: The Life and Lyrics of Andy Razaf* (New York: Schirmer, 1992), 216–19; Gottfried, *Broadway Musicals*, 257–59.

37. Quoted in Lahr, "Lemon-Drop," 72.

38. Ibid., 70; Mordden, *Better Foot Forward*, 213 and 214.

39. Margo Jefferson, "Culture Clashes Still Intrigue in *King and I*," *New York Times*, 28 April 1996; Judith Miller, "Making Money Abroad, and Also a Few Enemies," *New York Times*, 26 January 1997.

40. Israel Zangwill, *The Melting-Pot: Drama in Four Acts* (New York: Macmillan, 1922), 86–87, 160, 185, and 204; Neil Larry Shumsky, "Zangwill's *The Melting Pot*: Ethnic Tensions on Stage," *American Quarterly* 27 (March 1975), 29–41; Arthur Mann, *The One and the Many: Reflections on the American Identity* (Chicago: University of Chicago Press, 1979), 98–106, 109–16, and "The Melting Pot," in *Uprooted Americans: Essays to Honor Oscar Handlin*, ed. Richard L. Bushman, Neil Harris, et al. (Boston: Little, Brown, 1979), 292–314; Judah L. Magnes, "The Melting Pot" (1909), in *Dissenter in Zion: From the Writings of Judah L. Magnes*, ed. Arthur A. Goren (Cambridge, Mass.: Harvard University Press, 1982), 101 and 102.

41. Nathan Glazer and Daniel Patrick Moynihan, *Beyond the Melting Pot: The Negroes, Puerto Ricans, Jews, Italians and Irish of New York City* (Cambridge, Mass.: MIT Press, 1963), 174.

42. Rodgers, *Musical Stages*, 4.

43. Henry L. Feingold, *Lest Memory Cease: Finding Meaning in the American Jewish Past* (Syracuse: Syracuse University Press, 1996), 175–76; Lahr, *Light Fantastic*, 307; Mordden, *Better Foot Forward*, 99 and 100.

44. Quoted in Lahr, *Light Fantastic*, 306.

45. Vincent Canby, "Confronting a Classic, Head On," *New York Times*, 9 October 1994; Mordden, *Best Foot Forward*, 105; Gottfried, *Broadway Musicals*, 12, 19, 164, and 167.

46. Howard Teichmann, *George S. Kaufman: An Intimate Portrait* (New York: Atheneum, 1972), 91–93; Bergreen, *As Thousands Cheer*, 247–51.

47. Quoted in Stephen Holden, "*Show Boat* Makes New Waves," *New York Times*, 25 September 1988; Mordden, *Better Foot Forward*, 101 and 109.

48. Dizikes, *Opera in America*, 488; Leonard Bernstein, *The Joy of Music* (New York: Simon and Schuster, 1959), 172; Lahr, *Light Fantastic*, 306–7 and 308–10.

49. Canby, "Confronting a Classic," 5; interview with Yael Margalit Levine, Elkins Park, Pennsylvania, 25 February 1997; Lahr, *Light Fantastic*, 308–10.

50. Sanders, "American Popular Song," 203; Gottfried, *American Musicals*, 161, 162, 164, and 167; Block, *Enchanted Evenings*, 14 and 19; Edna Ferber, *A Peculiar Treasure* (New York: Doubleday, Doran, 1939), 304–6.

51. Quoted in Lahr, *Light Fantastic*, 308; Martin Bauml Duberman, *Paul Robeson* (New York: Knopf, 1988), 113–15; Furia, *Poets of Tin Pan Alley*, 185–86.

52. Holden, "*Show Boat* Makes New Waves," 27; Lahr, *Light Fantastic*, 308–9; John S. Simmons, "School Censorship: No Respite in Sight," *Forum* 19 (Winter 1996–1997), 15; Miles Kreuger, Show Boat: *The Story of a Classic American Musical* (New York: Oxford University Press, 1977), 211–12; Block, *Enchanted Evenings*, 72.

53. Clyde H. Farnsworth, "Blacks Accuse Jews in *Show Boat* Revival," *New York Times*, 1 May 1993.

54. Furia, *Poets of Tin Pan Alley*, 18, 186–87, and 189; Lahr, *Light Fantastic*, 251; Mordden, *Better Foot Forward*, 187–88; Gottfried, *Broadway Musicals*, 13 and 19.

55. Quoted in Amy Henderson and Dwight Blocker Bowers, *Red, Hot and Blue: A Smithsonian Salute to the American Musical* (Washington, D.C.: Smithsonian Institution Press, 1996), 144.

56. Dizikes, *Opera in America*, 504; Stephen Holden, "Their Songs Were America's Happy Talk," *New York Times*, 24 January 1993: Gottfried, *Broadway Musicals*, 186 and 189.

57. Quoted in Mordden, *Better Foot Forward*, 188; Block, *Enchanted Evenings*, 117; Henderson and Bowers, *Red, Hot and Blue*, 146; Dizikes, *Opera in America*, 504; James Agee, "Pseudo-Folk," *Partisan Review* 11 (Spring 1944), 219–23.

58. Ethan Mordden, *Rodgers and Hammerstein* (New York: Abrams, 1992), 27–28; Holden, "America's Happy Talk," 6; Andrea Most, "'We Know We Belong to the Land': The Theatricality of Assimilation in Rodgers and Hammerstein's *Oklahoma!*," *PMLA* 113 (January 1998), 79–87; Bruce Pomahac, letter to the editor, *New York Times*, 14 February 1993; John Steinbeck, *The Grapes of Wrath* (New York: Viking, 1939), 45.

59. Quoted in Philip Taylor, *The Distant Magnet: European Emigration to the U.S.A.* (New York: Harper Torchbooks, 1972), 249; Gottfried, *Broadway Musicals*, 175, 186, and 189; Holden, "America's Happy Talk," 1 and 6.

60. Quoted by Carol Lawrence in *Conversations about Bernstein*, ed. William Westbrook Burton (New York: Oxford University Press, 1995), 180.

61. Quoted in Zadan, *Sondheim & Co.*, 17.

62. Avery Corman, "Sharks and Jets Are Ready to Rumble Again," *New York Times*, 14 May 1995; Martha Duffy, "West Side Glory," *Time* 145 (29 May 1995), 64–65; Gottfried, *Broadway Musicals*, 103.

63. Moira Hodgson, "Robbins Leaps From Ballet to Broadway," *New York Times*, 10 February 1980; Jefferson, "Culture Clashes Still Intrigue," 4; Gottfried, *Broadway Musicals*, 47; Mordden, *Better Foot Forward*, 263.

64. Quoted in Duffy, "West Side Glory," 64–65; Leonard Bernstein, "Excerpts from a *West Side Story* Log" (6 January 1949), in *Findings* (New York: Simon and Schuster, 1982), 144.

65. Hodgson, "Robbins Leaps," 4; Michael Walsh, "Here Comes the Show Boat!"

Time 132 (7 November 1988), 114; Mordden, *Better Foot Forward*, 263–64; Lawrence in *Conversations about Bernstein*, 171; Gottfried, *Musicals*, 54 and 64; Duffy, "West Side Glory," 64–65.

66. Stanley Kramer, with Thomas M. Coffey, *A Mad, Mad, Mad, Mad World: A Life in Hollywood* (New York: Harcourt Brace, 1997), 34–35; Memo from Adrian Scott, appendix 5, in Larry Ceplair and Steven Englund, *The Inquisition in Hollywood: Politics in the Film Community, 1930–1960* (Garden City, N.Y.: Doubleday, 1980), 443; Robert J. Corber, *Homosexuality in Cold War America* (Durham: Duke University Press, 1997), 86.

67. Lawrence in *Conversations about Bernstein*, 169, 170, 171, 172, and 177; Jonathan Miller in *Conversations about Bernstein*, 108; Block, *Enchanted Evenings*, 259.

68. Lawrence in *Conversations about Bernstein*, 170; Bernstein, *Joys of Music*, 56–57; Burton, ed., introduction to *Conversations about Bernstein*, xxxi.

69. George Steiner, "Some 'Meta-Rabbis,'" in *Next Year in Jerusalem*, 75.

70. Quoted in Henry, "Master of the Musical," 80 and 82; Gottfried, *Broadway Musicals*, 175 and 176; "He Sent Them Away Humming," *Time*, 83; Holden, "America's Happy Talk," 6.

71. Gottfried, *Broadway Musicals*, 29, 32, 127, 319, 320–21, and 322; Frank Rich, "Sondheim Says Goodbye To Broadway—For Now," *New York Times*, 24 July 1983; Sylviane Gold, "The Ups and Downs are Part of the Ride," *New York Times*, 23 March 1997; Henry, "Master of the Musical," 80; John Lahr, "The Wizard of Loss," *New Yorker* 71 (23 October 1995), 103–4, 105.

72. Quoted in Zadan, *Sondheim & Co.*, 124 and 125–26; Henderson and Bowers, *Red, Hot and Blue*, 227 and 230.

73. Quoted in Stefan Kanfer, "A Landmark and a Missed Mark," *New Leader* 78 (4 December 1995), 30, and in Zadan, *Sondheim & Co.*, 124.

74. Quoted in Scott Baldinger, "*Company* Enters a New, Scary Stage of Life," *New York Times*, 17 September 1995.

75. Kanfer, "Landmark," 30 and 31; Margo Jefferson, "Listen to *Company*, Tune Out the Book," *New York Times*, 15 October 1995.

76. Brad Leithauser, "Time Shift," *Time* 146 (16 October 1995), 95–96; Zadan, *Sondheim & Co.*, viii; James Spada, *Streisand: Her Life* (New York: Crown, 1995), 425.

77. Green, "Song is Ended," 48; Anthony Tommasini, "For Sondheim, The New Has Always Been Old," *New York Times*, 21 July 1996.

78. Quoted in Henry, "Master of the Musical," 82; Zadan, *Sondheim & Co.*, 6; Dizikes, *Opera in America*, 508–9; Gottfried, *Broadway Musicals*, 327.

79. A. R. Gurney, "Coming Home To a Musical That Sounds Like America," *New York Times*, 8 September 1996; Joseph Berger, "His Tunes Make Disney's World Go Round," *New York Times*, 13 July 1997.

80. Green, "Song Is Ended," 51.

MUSIC (PP. 88–114)

1. Quoted in Yohanan Boehm, "Music," in *Encyclopedia Judaica* (Jerusalem: Macmillan, 1971), 12:555.

2. Lucy Dawidowicz, *The Jewish Presence: Essays on Identity and History* (New York: Harcourt Brace Jovanovich, 1977), 32–45; Alexander L. Ringer, *Arnold Schoenberg: The Composer as Jew* (Oxford: Clarendon Press, 1990), 194–205.

3. Michael Walsh, "A Song to Remember: Arthur Rubinstein, 1887–1982," *Time* 121 (3 January 1983), 81; Harvey Sachs, *Rubinstein: A Life* (New York: Grove, 1995), 13–14, 15, 20, 21, 36–37, 119–20, 297–300, 338–39, 393–94, and 401.

4. Ruth Ellen Gruber, "Filling the Jewish Space in Europe," *American Jewish Committee, International Perspectives* 35 (September 1996), 1, 2, 15–17, and 35–36.

5. Michael Alpert, "As If It Were Yesterday," in *Klezmer Music: A Marriage of Heaven and Earth*, ed. Candace Ward (Roslyn, N.Y.: Ellipsis Arts, 1996), 15.

6. Raphael Patai, *The Jewish Mind* (Detroit: Wayne State University Press, 1996), 363 and 364–66; Debra Nussbaum Cohen, " 'Jewish Sax' Sounded as Clinton Joins New Year's Services," Jewish Telegraphic Agency clipping (in possession of author); Alan M. Dershowitz, *The Vanishing American Jew: In Search of Jewish Identity for the Next Century* (Boston: Little, Brown, 1997), 91–92.

7. Ezra Mendelsohn, "On the Jewish Presence in Nineteenth-Century European Musical Life," in *Studies in Contemporary Jewry*, ed. Ezra Mendelsohn (New York: Oxford University Press, 1993), 9:4, 7, and 10–12; Christopher Fifield, *Max Bruch: His Life and Works* (New York: George Braziller, 1988), 16 and 169; Peter Gay, *Freud, Jews and Other Germans: Masters and Victims in Modernist Culture* (New York: Oxford University Press, 1978), 189.

8. Laurel E. Fay, "The Composer Was Courageous, But Not as Much as in Myth," *New York Times*, 14 April 1996; Peter Stadlen, "The Composer," in *Next Year in Jerusalem: Portraits of the Jew in the Twentieth Century*, ed. Douglas Villiers (New York: Viking, 1976), 310 and 312.

9. Quoted in Louis Harap, *The Image of the Jew in American Literature: From Early Republic to Mass Immigration* (Philadelphia: Jewish Publication Society, 1974), 456–57; Werner Sollors, *Beyond Ethnicity: Consent and Descent in American Culture* (New York: Oxford University Press, 1986), 66; Mark Slobin, "Some Intersections of Jews, Music and Theater," in *From Hester Street to Hollywood: The Jewish-American Stage and Screen*, ed. Sarah Blacher Cohen (Bloomington: Indiana University Press, 1983), 33–34.

10. Quoted in Harap, *Image of the Jew*, 390; Aaron Copland and Vivian Perlis, *Copland since 1943* (New York: St. Martin's, 1989), 34, 36, and 53; Peter M. Rutkoff and William B. Scott, "Appalachian Spring: A Collaboration and a Transition," in *Prospects* (New York: Cambridge University Press, 1995), 20:215–16.

11. Leonard Bernstein, "The Absorption of Race Elements into American Music" (1939), in *Findings* (New York: Simon and Schuster, 1982), 98–99; Bernard Lewis, *Semites and Anti-Semites: An Inquiry into Conflict and Prejudice* (New York: Norton, 1987), 224.

12. Kenneth Aaron Kanter, *The Jews on Tin Pan Alley: The Jewish Contribution to American Popular Music, 1830–1940* (New York: KTAV, 1982), 15–19.

13. Quoted in Amy Henderson and Dwight Blocker Bowers, *Red, Hot and Blue: A Smithsonian Salute to the American Musical* (Washington, D.C.: Smithsonian Institution Press, 1996), 48.

14. Quoted in Nick Marinello, "Songs of the South," *Tulanian* 67 (Spring 1996), 22; David Ewen, *The Life and Death of Tin Pan Alley: The Golden Age of American Popular Music* (New York: Funk and Wagnalls, 1964), 18; Kanter, *Jews on Tin Pan Alley*, 93–94; Victor Greene, *A Passion for Polka: Old-Time Ethnic Music in America* (Berkeley and Los Angeles: University of California Press, 1992), 62.

15. Laurence Bergreen, *As Thousands Cheer: The Life of Irving Berlin* (New York: Viking, 1990), 42–43; Ann Douglas, *Terrible Honesty: Mongrel Manhattan in the 1920s* (New York: Farrar, Straus and Giroux, 1995), 15.

16. Philip Furia, *The Poets of Tin Pan Alley: A History of America's Great Lyricists* (New York: Oxford University Press, 1990), 76–77; F. Scott Fitzgerald, *The Great Gatsby* (New York: Scribner's, 1925), 96–97.

17. Alex Berlyne, "After the Bawl," *Jerusalem Post Magazine*, 14 October 1983, 12 and 13; Martin Gottfried, *Broadway Musicals* (New York: Abrams, 1979), 249.

18. Furia, *Poets of Tin Pan Alley*, 72–75 and 80–81; Neal Gabler, *Winchell: Gossip, Power, and the Culture of Celebrity* (New York: Knopf, 1995), xii; Leo P. Ribuffo, *Right Center Left: Essays in American History* (New Brunswick, N.J.: Rutgers University Press, 1992), 80 and 83–84.

19. Fred Somkin, "Zion's Harp by the East River: Jewish-American Popular Songs in Columbus's Golden Land, 1890–1914," *Perspectives in American History* (Cambridge, Mass.: Harvard University Press, 1985), n.s., 2:185–87, 190, 191, and 193; Greene, *Passion for Polka*, 59–63.

20. Bergreen, *As Thousands Cheer*, 66–67; Abraham Cahan, *The Rise of David Levinsky* (New York: Harper and Row, 1960), 529.

21. Quoted in Lee Davis, *Bolton and Wodehouse and Kern: The Men Who Made Musical Comedy* (New York: Heineman, 1993), 232; also in Alexander Woollcott, *The Story of Irving Berlin* (New York: Putnam, 1925), 215–16.

22. Quoted in Josh Rubins, "Genius Without Tears," *New York Review of Books* 35 (16 June 1988), 30; Alec Wilder, *American Popular Song: The Great Innovators, 1900–1950* (New York: Oxford University Press, 1972), 120.

23. John Lahr, "The Lemon-Drop Kid," *New Yorker* 72 (30 September 1996), 71; Bergreen, *As Thousands Cheer*, 40, 131, 277–78, 285, and 286; Gottfried, *Broadway Musicals*, 236; Furia, *Poets of Tin Pan Alley*, 47 and 60.

24. Quoted in Gerald Bordman, *American Musical Theatre: A Chronicle*, 2d ed. (New York: Oxford University Press, 1992), 476; Wilder, *American Popular Song*, 93 and 108–10; Bergreen, *As Thousands Cheer*, 344–45.

25. Quoted in Bergreen, *As Thousands Cheer*, 362.

26. Bergreen, *As Thousands Cheer*, 314, 321, 380, 386–87, 409, 454–55, 466, 570, 576, and 581; Walter L. Hixson, *Parting the Curtain: Propaganda, Culture, and the Cold War, 1945–1961* (New York: St. Martin's, 1997), 6; Kanter, *Jews on Tin Pan Alley*, 144; Jesse Green, "The Song is Ended," *New York Times Magazine*, 2 June 1996, 48.

27. Quoted in Michael Freedland, *Irving Berlin* (New York: Stein and Day, 1974), 17; Kanter, *Jews on Tin Pan Alley*, 136; Marc Slobin, *Tenement Songs: The Popular Music of Jewish Immigrants* (Champaign: University of Illinois Press, 1982), 176; Bergreen, *As Thousands Cheer*, 51, 128, and 529.

28. Bergreen, *As Thousands Cheer*, 27, 30, 46, and 199; Ann Douglas, "Siblings and Mongrels," *Common Quest* 2 (Summer 1997), 11.

29. Quoted in Bergreen, *As Thousands Cheer*, 121.

30. Philip Roth, *Operation Shylock: A Confession* (New York: Simon and Schuster, 1993), 157; Stephen Holden, "Their Songs Were America's Happy Talk," *New York Times*, 24 January 1993; Ethan Morddan, *Rodgers and Hammerstein* (New York: Abrams, 1992), 211 and 213.

31. Quoted in Kanter, *Jews on Tin Pan Alley*, 153.

32. Henderson and Bowers, *Red, Hot and Blue*, 28; Kanter, *Jews on Tin Pan Alley*, 34–35; Sigmund Spaeth, *A History of Popular Music in America* (New York: Random House, 1948), 512–13; Shawn Levy, *King of Comedy: The Life and Art of Jerry Lewis* (New York: St. Martin's, 1996), 215–16.

33. Quoted in Michael Rogin, *Blackface, White Noise: Jewish Immigrants in the Hollywood Melting Pot* (Berkeley and Los Angeles: University of California Press, 1996), 145.

34. Berlyne, "After the Bawl," 12 and 13; Gottfried, *Broadway Musicals*, 235, 236, and 249; Rubins, "Genius," 30; Bergreen, *As Thousands Cheer*, 27, 90–91, 135–36, 258, and 365–66.

35. Bergreen, *As Thousands Cheer*, 581; Herbert Kupferberg, "Bernstein's Gift," *Reform Judaism* 23 (Summer 1995), 62 and 63; Ralph Blumenthal, "FBI's Endless Bid to Peg Bernstein as 'Red,'" *International Herald Tribune*, 30–31 July 1994, 18.

36. Quoted in Michael Walsh, "The Best and the Brightest: Leonard Bernstein, 1918–1990," *Time* 136 (29 October 1990), 113; Burton Bernstein, *Family Matters: Sam, Jennie, and the Kids* (New York: Summit Books, 1982), 140 and 142–45.

37. Quoted in Kupferberg, "Bernstein's Gift," 62; Bernstein, *Family Matters*, 145–49.

38. Quoted in John Ardoin, "Israel Gives Bernstein a 30-Year Retrospective," *New York Times*, 17 April 1977; Yaacov Mishori in *Conversations about Bernstein*, ed. William Westbrook Burton (New York: Oxford University Press, 1995), 162; Kupferberg, "Bernstein's Gift," 62 and 67.

39. Quoted in Ralph Tyler, "Signs of a New Spirituality in the Arts," *New York Times*, 11 November 1979; Bernstein, *Family Matters*, 14–15 and 116–17; Lukas Foss and David Diamond in *Conversations about Bernstein*, 7 and 17.

40. Burton, ed., and Joan Peyser in *Conversations about Bernstein*, xi, xvii, and 44–45.

41. Quoted in Harold Livesay, *Samuel Gompers and Organized Labor in America* (Boston: Little, Brown, 1978), 85.

42. Lukas Foss, Jonathan Miller, and Paul Myers in *Conversations about Bernstein*, 6, 13, 63, 109, and 111; Aaron Copland, "1949: The New 'School' of American Composers," in *Copland on Music* (Garden City, N.Y.: Doubleday, 1960), 172–73; John Rockwell, "Bernstein Triumphant," *New York Times Magazine*, 31 August 1986, 19.

43. Quoted in Ardoin, "30-Year Retrospective," 16.

44. Quoted in Shuly Rubin Schwartz, *The Emergence of Jewish Scholarship in*

America: The Publication of the Jewish Encyclopedia (Cincinnati, Ohio: Hebrew Union College Press, 1991), 86.

45. Quoted in Burton, ed., and Harold Schonberg, *Conversations about Bernstein*, xix, xvi, xxvi, and 33–34.

46. Schonberg in *Conversations about Bernstein*, 36; Burton, ed., introduction to ibid., xxxiii; Miller in ibid., 113.

47. Joseph Horowitz, "Professor Lenny," *New York Review of Books* 40 (10 June 1993), 42; Rockwell, "Bernstein Triumphant," 24.

48. Robert L. Carringer, *The Making of Citizen Kane* (Berkeley and Los Angeles: University of California Press, 1985), 106–9; Alex Ross, "The Music That Casts The Spells Of *Vertigo*," *New York Times*, 6 October 1996; Mstislav Rostropovich in *Conversations about Bernstein*, 137.

49. Allan Kozinn, "A Weary Maestro Marches to a Relentless Drummer," *New York Times*, 5, May 1996.

50. Quoted in David Schiff, "An Older, Wiser, Humbler Wunderkind," *New York Times Magazine*, 20 August 1995, 30 and 31; Michael Walsh, "Hitting the High Notes," *Time* 147 (1 April 1996), 74.

51. Schiff, "Older, Wiser," 30–31.

52. Quoted in ibid., 31.

53. Beverly Sills, *Bubbles: A Self-Portrait* (Indianapolis: Bobbs-Merrill, 1976), 12–13, 16–18, 26, 27–32, 45, 210–12, 215, and 227–29; Beverly Sills and Lawrence Linderman, *Beverly: An Autobiography* (New York: Bantam, 1987), 339–40; Craig Zadan, *Sondheim & Co.*, 2d ed. (New York: Harper and Row, 1986), 260.

54. Douglas, "Siblings and Mongrels," 10; Charles Hamm, *Irving Berlin: Songs from the Melting Pot: The Formative Years, 1907–1914* (New York: Oxford University Press, 1997), 213–14; Bergreen, *As Thousands Cheer*, 75; Aaron Fuchs, "Boppin' the Blues," in *The Fifties Book*, ed. Jay Berman (New York: Berkley Medallion, 1974), 79.

55. E. Anthony Rotundo, "Jews and Rock and Roll: A Study in Cultural Contrast," *American Jewish History* 72 (September 1982), 82, 84, 85–87, and 88–89.

56. Michael Rothschild to author, 3 August 1996; Rotundo, "Jews and Rock and Roll," 92–93 and 103; Greg Shaw, "Brill Building Pop," in *The Rolling Stone Illustrated History of Rock and Roll*, ed. Jim Miller (New York: Random House, 1976), 122–27.

57. Ellen Willis, "Dylan" (1967–68), in *Beginning to See the Light: Pieces of a Decade* (New York: Knopf, 1981), 6; Rotundo, "Jews and Rock and Roll," 101, 105, and 106.

58. Quoted in Linda Kuehl, "Talk with Mr. Knopf," *New York Times Book Review*, 24 February 1974, 21.

59. Quoted in Lahr, "Lemon-Drop Kid," 74; Green, "Song is Ended," 52.

60. Quoted in Thomas Meehan, "Public Writer No. 1?" *New York Times Magazine*, 12 December 1965, 44–45 and 136; Joel Lewis, "At 90, Kunitz Remembers a Lifetime of Poetry," *Forward*, 15 December 1995, 13–14.

61. Rotundo, "Jews and Rock and Roll," 100; Jimmy Carter, *Why Not the Best?* (Nashville: Broadman, 1975), 9–10.

62. Quoted in Anthony Scaduto, *Dylan* (New York: Signet, 1973), 150.

63. Quoted in Mikal Gilmore, "Bob Dylan at Fifty," *Rolling Stone*, 30 May 1991, 60; Fred Goodman, *The Mansion on the Hill: Dylan, Young, Geffen, Springsteen, and the Head-On Collision of Rock and Commerce* (New York: Times Books, 1997), 90–91; *Lennon Remembers: The Rolling Stone Interviews*, ed. Jann Wenner (New York: Popular Library, 1971), 44.

64. Quoted in Bergreen, *As Thousands Cheer*, 423.

65. Wenner, ed., *Lennon Remembers*, 32.

66. Jon Pareles, "A Wiser Voice Blowin' in the Autumn Wind," *New York Times*, 28 September 1997.

67. Quoted in Kurt Loder, "Bob Dylan" (1984), in *The Rolling Stone Interviews: The 1980s*, ed. Sid Holt (New York: St. Martin's / Rolling Stone Press, 1989), 95 and 96.

THEATER (PP. 115–138)

1. Alexis de Tocqueville, *Democracy in America*, ed. Phillips Bradley (New York: Knopf, 1945), 2:154–57; Paul R. Mendes-Flohr, "Werner Sombart's *The Jews and Modern Capitalism*: An Analysis of its Ideological Premises," *Year Book of the Leo Baeck Institute* (London: Secker and Warburg, 1976), 21:87–107.

2. Gerald Weales, *Odets the Playwright* (New York: Metheun, 1985), 183–84.

3. Robert Warshow, *The Immediate Experience: Movies, Comics, Theatre and Other Aspects of Popular Culture* (Garden City, N.Y.: Doubleday Anchor, 1962), 30–31.

4. Clifford Odets, *Six Plays* (New York: Modern Library, 1939), 48, 65, 66, 89, and 95; John Lahr, *Light Fantastic: Adventures in Theatre* (New York: Dial, 1996), 214; Warshow, *Immediate Experience*, 23; R. Baird Shuman, *Clifford Odets* (New Haven: Twayne, 1962), 55–65.

5. Quoted in Lahr, *Light Fantastic*, 213; Odets, *Six Plays*, 57 and 94; Margaret Brenman-Gibson, *Clifford Odets, American Playwright: The Years from 1906 to 1940* (New York: Atheneum, 1981), 250 and 326.

6. Lillian Hellman, *An Unfinished Woman: A Memoir* (Boston: Little, Brown, 1969), 4, and *Collected Plays* (Boston: Little, Brown, 1971), 183, 188, and 206; Bonnie Lyons, "Lillian Hellman: 'The First Jewish Nun on Prytania Street,'" in *Hester Street to Hollywood*, 106–22; William Wright, *Lillian Hellman: The Image, the Woman* (New York: Simon and Schuster, 1986), 17–18, 20–21, 146, 150, and 154.

7. Quoted in Rachel Shteir, "Championing Odets, Unfashionable as That Is," *New York Times*, 27 April 1997.

8. Quoted in Arthur Holmberg, "It's Never Easy to Go Back," *American Repertory Theatre News* 18 (March 1997), 12; Abbie Hoffman, *Soon to be a Major Motion Picture* (New York: Putnam, 1980), 5; David Mamet, *Make-Believe Town: Essays and Remembrances* (Boston: Little, Brown, 1996), 139; Ed Siegel, "More Jewish Than Thou?" Boston *Globe*, 9 November 1997, K6.

9. Arthur Miller, "Introduction to *Collected Plays*" (1957), in *Death of a Salesman: Text and Criticism*, ed. Gerald Weales (New York: Viking, 1967), 161; Elia Kazan, *A Life* (New York: Knopf, 1988), 355–59.

10. Mary McCarthy, *Sights and Spectacles, 1937–1956* (New York: Farrar, Straus and Cudahy, 1956), xv and xvi; Leslie Fiedler, *Waiting for the End* (New York: Stein and Day, 1964), 91; Diana Trilling in "The Jewish Writer and the English Literary Tradition," *Commentary*, 8 (September 1949), 216; Edgar Rosenberg, *From Shylock to Svengali: Jewish Stereotypes in English Fiction* (Stanford: Stanford University Press, 1960), 303.

11. Sidra DeKoven Ezrahi, rev. of Ellen Schiff, *From Stereotype to Metaphor: The Jew in Contemporary Drama* (Albany: State University of New York Press, 1982), in *Studies in Contemporary Jewry*, ed. Peter Y. Medding (Bloomington: Indiana University Press, 1986), 2:388.

12. Mamet, *Make-Believe Town*, 139–40; Arthur Miller, "Responses to an Audience Question and Answer Session," *Michigan Quarterly Review* 37 (Fall 1998), 821–22; Siegel, "More Jewish Than Thou?" K6.

13. Jonathan D. Sarna, *Jacksonian Jew: The Two Worlds of Mordecai Noah* (New York: Holmes and Meier, 1981), 6–7, 12, and 47–50; Donald Margulies, *The Loman Family Picnic* (Garden City, N.Y: Fireside Theatre, 1994), 95.

14. Quoted in Leslie Fiedler, *Fiedler on the Roof: Essays on Literature and Jewish Identity* (Boston: David R. Godine, 1991), 132; Enoch Brater, "Ethnics and Ethnicity in the Plays of Arthur Miller," in *Hester Street to Hollywood*, 124; Norman Mailer, *Marilyn: A Biography* (New York: Grosset and Dunlap, 1973), 159; Stanley Kauffmann, "Marcellino," *New Republic* 216 (3 February 1997), 30.

15. George Ross, "*Death of a Salesman* in the Original" (1951), in Miller, *Death of a Salesman*, ed. Weales, 259, 261, 262, and 263.

16. Miller, "Introduction to *Collected Plays*," in *Death of a Salesman: Text and Criticism*, 170.

17. Gordon F. Sander, *Serling: The Rise and Twilight of Television's Last Angry Man* (New York: Dutton, 1992), xviii, 3, 6, 20, 100–102, 103, 184, 207, 209, and 221.

18. Carolyn Clay, "Mamet and Supermamet," *Boston Phoenix*, 18 February 1986.

19. David Mamet, *American Buffalo* (New York: Grove, 1976), 72–73.

20. Quoted in James Kaplan, "Miller's Crossing," *Vanity Fair*, no. 375 (November 1991), 246.

21. Larry Swindell, *Body and Soul: The Story of John Garfield* (New York: Morrow, 1975), 110–11; Patricia R. Erens, *The Jew in American Cinema* (Bloomington: Indiana University Press, 1985), 182.

22. Arthur Holmberg, "The Old Neighborhood," *American Repertory Theatre News* 18 (March 1997), 7.

23. Quoted in ibid., 8; Peter Brunette, "Mamet Views Cops Through a New Lens," *New York Times*, 10 February 1991; Jonathan Lieberson, "The Prophet of Broadway," *New York Review of Books* 35 (21 July 1988), 3; David Mamet, *Some Freaks* (New York: Viking, 1989), 9, 16–18, and 19.

24. David Mamet, *Speed-the-Plow* (New York: Grove Weidenfeld, 1987), 56 and 81–82.

25. Schiff, *From Stereotype to Metaphor*, 70–72; Miller, "Introduction to *Collected Plays*," 161; Jerry Sterner, "Playwright, or Businessman?" *New York Times Magazine*, 9 June 1991, 34.

Notes

26. Quoted in Strobe Talbott, "Why They Backed Bush," *Time* 140 (23 November 1992), 51.
27. Quoted in Felicity Barringer, "U.S. Communists' Meeting Has Its Own Fractionalism," *New York Times*, 9 December 1991, 14.
28. Robert B. Reich, *The Resurgent Liberal (And Other Unfashionable Prophecies)* (New York: Random House, 1989), 15–16 and 235; Phoebe Hoban, "The Family Wasserstein," *New York* 26 (4 January 1993), 32–37; Wendy Wasserstein, *Bachelor Girls* (New York: Knopf, 1990), 83–84.
29. Arthur Miller, *Timebends: A Life* (New York: Grove, 1987), 314; Wendy Wasserstein, *The Heidi Chronicles and Other Plays* (New York: Vintage, 1991), 232.
30. Quoted in Clay, "Mamet and Supermamet," 10.
31. Reich, *Resurgent Liberal*, 18.
32. William A. Henry III, "Reborn with Relevance," *Time* 140 (2 November 1992), 69, and "The Gay White Way," *Time* 141 (17 May 1993), 62–63; Carolyn Clay, "Heavenly Power," *Boston Phoenix*, 10 March 1995; Tony Kushner, *Angels in America: Millennium Approaches* (New York: Theatre Communications Group, 1993), 45.
33. Robert Leiter, "If You Ask Paul Rudnick . . . ," *Forward*, 28 July 1995, 1 and 10; Marilyn Cantor Baker, letter to the editor, *New York Times*, 27 October 1996.
34. Odets, *Six Plays*, 55.
35. Quoted in Leslie Bennetts, "An Uncommon Dramatist Prepares Her New Work," *New York Times*, 24 May 1981; Wendy Wasserstein, *The Sisters Rosensweig* (San Diego: Harcourt Brace, 1993), 27.
36. Wasserstein, *Heidi Chronicles and Other Plays*, 149–50.
37. Wasserstein, *Sisters Rosensweig*, 53 and 74.
38. Wasserstein, *Heidi Chronicles and Other Plays*, 61–63 and 71; William Novak, "Are Good Jewish Men a Vanishing Breed?" in *Jewish Possibilities: The Best of Moment Magazine*, ed. Leonard Fein (Northvale, N.J.: Jason Aronson, 1987), 60–66; Edward S. Shapiro, *A Time for Healing: American Jewry since World War II* (Baltimore: Johns Hopkins University Press, 1992), 139–43.
39. Quoted in "Wendy Wasserstein," in *Interviews with Contemporary Women Playwrights*, ed. Kathleen Betsko and Rachel Koenig (New York: Morrow, 1987), 426.
40. Wasserstein, *Heidi Chronicles and Other Plays*, 82, 85, 97, 103–4, 110, 120, 124, 138–39, 143, 148, and 152.
41. Quoted in *Interviews with Contemporary Women Playwrights*, 420 and 425; Benedict Nightingale, *Fifth Row Center: A Critic's Year On and Off Broadway* (New York: Times Books, 1986), 132–33.
42. Robert Wright, "The Evolution of Despair," *Time* 146 (28 August 1995), 53.
43. Quoted in "But Can He Cook?" *New York Times*, 15 June 1986; Alfred Kazin, *A Walker in the City* (New York: Grove, 1958), 44 and 60.
44. Wasserstein, *Sisters Rosensweig*, 88.
45. Quoted in "Wasserstein's World," *Reform Judaism* 21 (Summer 1993), 45; Randall Jarrell, "A Girl in a Library" (1951), in *The Complete Poems* (New York: Farrar, Straus, and Giroux, 1969), 18; Wasserstein, *Sisters Rosensweig*, 30, 103, and 106.

46. Wasserstein, *Sisters Rosensweig*, 12, 36–38, and 81; Calvin Trillin, "Drawing the Line," *New Yorker* 70 (12 December 1994), 56.

47. Wasserstein, *Sisters Rosensweig*, 79–80; Howard Kissel, "The Banker, the Writer, and the Yenta," *Reform Judaism* 21 (Summer 1993), 44–45; Hoban, "The Family Wasserstein," 35; Judith Miller, "The Secret Wendy Wasserstein," *New York Times*, 18 October 1992.

48. Nancy Backes, "Wasserstein, Wendy," in *Notable Women in the American Theatre: A Biographical Dictionary*, ed. Alice M. Robinson et al. (Westport, Conn.: Greenwood, 1994), 901; Wasserstein, *Sisters Rosensweig*, 30, 31, 65, 68, 77, 94, and 96.

49. Hiram Wesley Evans, "The Klan's Fight for Americanism" (1926), in *The Culture of the Twenties*, ed. Loren Baritz (Indianapolis: Bobbs-Merrill, 1970), 93; Ari Roth, "Cross-Cultural Collaboration: Remaking a Melting Pot" (copy in possession of author).

50. Martha Minow, "Too Much Justice," *Common Quest* 1 (Fall 1996), 55–56; David Biale, "The Melting Pot and Beyond: Jews and the Politics of American Identity," in *Insider/Outsider: American Jews and Multiculturalism*, ed. David Biale, Michael Galchinsky, and Susannah Heschel (Berkeley and Los Angeles: University of California Press, 1998), 27.

RACE (PP. 139–167)

1. Jean Genet, *The Blacks: A Clown Show*, trans. Bernard Frechtman (New York: Grove, 1960), 3.

2. Quoted in Ann Douglas, *Terrible Honesty: Mongrel Manhattan in the 1920s* (New York: Farrar, Straus, and Giroux, 1995), 166 and 521; also in Earl R. Beck, *Germany Rediscovers America* (Tallahassee: Florida State University Press, 1968), 83–84; James Hoberman, "The Show Biz Messiah, or Today I Am An Entertainer," in *No Rose* 1, no. 3 (Spring 1977), 6; C. Vann Woodward, "Clio with Soul" (1969), in *The Future of the Past* (New York: Oxford University Press, 1989), 45.

3. Quoted in David Levering Lewis, "Parallels and Divergences: Assimilationist Strategies of Afro-American and Jewish Elites from 1910 to the Early 1930s," in *Bridges and Boundaries: African Americans and American Jews*, ed. Jack Salzman, Adina Back, and Gretchen Sullivan Sorin (New York: Braziller, 1992), 18; James Weldon Johnson, *Along This Way* (New York: Viking, 1933), 326–28; Alain Locke, ed., "The Negro Spirituals," in *The New Negro* (New York: Boni, 1925), 199.

4. Quoted in James R. Oestreich, "When the Big Break Came for Bernstein, He Was Not a Bit Shy," *New York Times*, 14 November 1993; Leonard Bernstein, "The Absorption of Race Elements into American Music" (1939), in *Findings* (New York: Simon and Schuster, 1982), 40 and 49.

5. Quoted in Eileen Southern, *The Music of Black Americans: A History*, 2d ed. (New York: Norton, 1983), 265; Bernstein, *Findings*, 50; Israel Zangwill, afterword to *The Melting-Pot: Drama in Four Acts* (New York: Macmillan, 1922),

207; Werner Sollors, *Beyond Ethnicity: Consent and Descent in American Culture* (New York: Oxford University Press, 1986), 71; Charles Hamm, *Irving Berlin: Songs from the Melting Pot: The Formative Years, 1907–1914* (New York: Oxford University Press, 1997), 41.

6. Johnson, *Along This Way*, 326–28.

7. Quoted in Malcolm Bradbury, *Dangerous Pilgrimages: Trans-Atlantic Mythologies and the Novel* (London: Penguin, 1995), 303; Raphael Patai, *The Jewish Mind* (Detroit: Wayne State University Press, 1996), 114, 121–22, 157, and 378.

8. Nahma Sandrow, "Yiddish Theater and American Theater," in *From Hester Street to Hollywood: The Jewish-American Stage and Screen*, ed. Sarah Blacher Cohen (Bloomington: Indiana University Press, 1983), 19.

9. Jack Kerouac, *On the Road* (New York: Penguin, 1991), 180.

10. Langston Hughes, "Dream Variations," in *The Collected Poems of Langston Hughes* (New York: Knopf, 1994), 40.

11. John Cohen, ed., *The Essential Lenny Bruce* (New York: Bell, 1970), 31; Jonathan Mahler, "Searching for Clues in Mystery of PEN," *Forward*, 18 April 1997, 1 and 2; Murray Friedman, with Peter Binzen, *What Went Wrong?: The Creation and Collapse of the Black-Jewish Alliance* (New York: Free Press, 1995), 121; Joyce Johnson, *Minor Characters* (Boston: Houghton Mifflin, 1983), 214–15.

12. Milton Mezzrow and Bernard Wolfe, *Really the Blues* (Garden City, N.Y.: Doubleday Anchor, 1972), 11–12, 14–15, 42, 79–80, 96, 176, 177, 181, 186, 198, 257–58, 261, 271, 282, 285, and 290.

13. Quoted in Hilary Mills, *Mailer: A Biography* (New York: Empire Books, 1982), 55; Norman Mailer, "The White Negro: Superficial Reflections on the Hipster" (1957), in *Advertisements for Myself* (New York: Putnam's, 1959), 341 and 347; Irving Howe, *A Margin of Hope: An Intellectual Autobiography* (New York: Harcourt Brace Jovanovich, 1982), 240; Eldridge Cleaver, *Soul on Ice* (New York: Dell, 1968), 98.

14. Alan Trachtenberg, ed., *Memoirs of Waldo Frank* (Amherst: University of Massachusetts Press, 1973), 102–3 and 105; Douglas, *Terrible Honesty*, 79 and 81; Daniel S. Terris, "Waldo Frank and the Re-discovery of America, 1889–1929" (Ph.D. diss., Harvard University, 1992), 296, 313, 336, 341–42, 343, and 346.

15. Quoted in Eugene Levy, *James Weldon Johnson: Black Leader, Black Voice* (Chicago: University of Chicago Press, 1973), 313, and in *Selected Writings of Gertrude Stein*, ed. Carl W. Van Vechten (New York: Vintage, 1972), 338.

16. Stein, *Selected Writings*, ed. Van Vechten, 5 and 224; Douglas, *Terrible Honesty*, 117; Martin Luther King Jr., "Letter from Birmingham City Jail" (1963), in *The Negro in Twentieth-Century America*, ed. John Hope Franklin and Isidore Starr (New York: Vintage, 1967), 158.

17. George Washington Cable, *The Grandissimes: A Story of Creole Life* (New York: Scribner, 1880), 200; Franz Kafka, *Amerika*, trans. Edwin Muir (New York: New Directions, 1962), 286; J. Hoberman, *Vulgar Modernism: Writing on Movies and Other Media* (Philadelphia: Temple University Press, 1991), 143 and 147; Lawrence Grobel, "Playboy Interview: Saul Bellow," *Playboy* 44 (May 1997), 66; Bradbury, *Dangerous Pilgrimages*, 282–83.

18. Quoted in Joyce Antler, *The Journey Home: Jewish Women and the American Century* (New York: Free Press, 1997), 69–70; Linda K. Kerber, "Annie Nathan Meyer," in *Notable American Women: The Modern Period*, ed. Barbara Sicherman and Carol Hurd Green (Cambridge, Mass.: Harvard University Press, 1980), 473.

19. Quoted in Michael Kammen, *The Lively Arts: Gilbert Seldes and the Transformation of Cultural Criticism in the United States* (New York: Oxford University Press, 1996), 203.

20. Quoted in Hasia R. Diner, *In the Almost Promised Land: American Jews and Blacks, 1915–1935* (Westport, Conn.: Greenwood, 1977), 59.

21. Barrington Moore, *Social Origins of Dictatorship and Democracy* (Boston: Beacon, 1966), 445; Martin Bauml Duberman, *Paul Robeson* (New York: Knopf, 1988), 353.

22. Joyce Milton, "The Old Left," *New Republic* 215 (4 November 1996), 13; Billie Holiday, with William Duffy, *Lady Sings the Blues* (New York: Lancer, 1965), 82–84; Michael Meeropol and Robert Meeropol, letter to the editor, *New York Times Book Review*, 26 November 1995, 4.

23. Theodor Herzl, *Old-New Land*, trans. Lotta Levensohn (New York: Bloch, 1941), 170; Alan Wald, "The Subaltern Speaks," *Monthly Review* 43 (April 1992), 17–19, 20.

24. Paul Buhle, "The Hollywood Blacklist and the Jew," *Tikkun* 10 (September–October, 1995), 40; Sarah Blacher Cohen, "Yiddish Origins and Jewish-American Transformations," in *Hester Street to Hollywood*, 11.

25. Quoted in J. Harvie Wilkinson III, *One Nation Indivisible: How Ethnic Separatism Threatens America* (Reading, Mass.: Addison-Wesley, 1997), 86; also in Sheila Rule, "Black Film Portrait Back on Screen," *New York Times*, 16 March 1993, C13; Jim Davidson, "Telling a Story: The Making of *Nothing But a Man*," *Common Quest* 3 (Summer 1998), 8–23; Alex Haley, *The Autobiography of Malcolm X* (New York: Ballantine, 1992), 196.

26. W. E. B. Du Bois, *The Autobiography of W. E. B. Du Bois* (New York: International Publishers, 1968), 174–75; Paul Gilroy, *The Black Atlantic: Modernity and Double Consciousness* (Cambridge, Mass.: Harvard University Press, 1993), 135 and 211–12.

27. Quoted in Lawrence W. Levine, *Black Culture and Black Consciousness: Afro-American Folk Thought from Slavery to Freedom* (New York: Oxford University Press, 1977), xiii.

28. Michael Rogin, *Blackface, White Noise: Jewish Immigrants in the Hollywood Melting Pot* (Berkeley and Los Angeles: University of California Press, 1996), 41–42 and 167–68; J. C. Furnas, *Goodbye to Uncle Tom* (New York: Sloane, 1956), 260–84.

29. Quoted in Diner, *Almost Promised Land*, 68–69.

30. Quoted in Gilroy, *Black Atlantic*, 177; Mark Slobin, "Some Intersections of Jews, Music, and Theater," in *Hester Street to Hollywood*, 36; Irving Howe, with Kenneth Libo, *World of Our Fathers* (New York: Harcourt Brace Jovanovich, 1976), 562–63; Ronald Sanders, "The American Popular Song," in *Next Year in Jerusalem: Portraits of the Jew in the Twentieth Century*, ed. Douglas

Villiers (New York: Viking, 1976), 199; Gilbert Seldes, "The Daemonic in the American Theatre," in *The Seven Lively Arts*, rev. ed. (New York: Sagamore, 1957), 178–79.

31. Rogin, *Blackface, White Noise*, 5 and 41.
32. Barrett Wendell to Sir Robert White-Thomson, 31 March 1917, in *Barrett Wendell and His Letters*, ed. M. A. De Wolfe Howe (Boston: Atlantic Monthly Press, 1924), 281–82; Sollors, *Beyond Ethnicity*, 88–89; Seldes, *Seven Lively Arts*, 178–79; Rogin, *Blackface, White Noise*, 43–44.
33. J. Stanley Lemons, "Black Stereotypes as Reflected in Popular Culture," *American Quarterly* 29 (Spring 1977), 107 and 108; Kenneth Aaron Kanter, *The Jews on Tin Pan Alley: The Jewish Contribution to American Popular Music, 1830–1940* (New York: KTAV, 1982), 30, 32–33, 89 and 139; James Lincoln Collier, *Duke Ellington* (New York: Oxford University Press, 1987), 66.
34. Eddie Cantor, with Jane Kesner Ardmore, *Take My Life* (Garden City, N.Y.: Doubleday, 1957), 124–25; Douglas, *Terrible Honesty*, 328, 371; June Sochen, "Fanny Brice and Sophie Tucker," in *Hester Street to Hollywood*, 44; Barbara W. Grossman, *Funny Woman: The Life and Times of Fanny Brice* (Bloomington: Indiana University Press, 1991), 11, 24–28, 31–32, and 39–47.
35. Sochen, "Fanny Brice and Sophie Tucker," 47 and 48–49; Douglas, *Terrible Honesty*, 359; Rogin, *Blackface, White Noise*, 109; Jean-Paul Sartre, *Nausea*, trans. Lloyd Alexander (Norfolk, Conn.: New Directions, n.d.), 234–37; Raymond Sokolov, *Wayward Reporter: The Life of A. J. Liebling* (New York: Harper and Row, 1980), 191–94.
36. Quoted in Philip Furia, *The Poets of Tin Pan Alley: A History of America's Great Lyricists* (New York: Oxford University Press, 1992), 32–33; Sochen, "Fanny Brice and Sophie Tucker," 45; Rogin, *Blackface, White Noise*, 111.
37. Quoted in Diner, *Almost Promised Land*, 68–69, and in Martin Gottfried, *Broadway Musicals* (New York: Abrams, 1979), 341; Michael Freedland, *Jolson* (New York: Stein and Day, 1972), 69–70 and 88–89.
38. Rogin, *Blackface, White Noise*, 177 and 181; Furia, *Poets of Tin Pan Alley*, 33; Hoberman, "Show Biz Messiah," 2; Ann Douglas, "Siblings and Mongrels," *Common Quest* 2 (Summer 1997), 8, and *Terrible Honesty*, 159 and 376.
39. Quoted in Rogin, *Blackface, White Noise*, 190.
40. Quoted in Kammen, *Lively Arts*, 97–98.
41. Seldes, *Seven Lively Arts*, 178–80 and 181–82; Sochen, "Fanny Brice and Sophie Tucker," 50.
42. Charles A. Beard and Mary R. Beard, *The Rise of American Civilization* (New York: Macmillan, 1927), 2:814–17; LeRoi Jones, *Blues People: Negro Music in White America* (New York: Morrow, 1963), 100; Rogin, *Blackface, White Noise*, 97 and 112–13.
43. Samson Raphaelson, preface to *The Jazz Singer* (New York: Brentano, 1925), 9–10; Slobin, "Some Intersections," 35.
44. Quoted in Albert Lee, *Henry Ford and the Jews* (New York: Stein and Day, 1980), 29, and in Kanter, *Jews on Tin Pan Alley*, 23; Douglas, *Terrible Honesty*, 74, 112, and 352.
45. David Schiff, "Ado Over Plenty o' Nuttin'," *New York Times*, 29 June 1997;

Wilfrid Mellers, "An American in New York," *New Republic* 208 (14 June 1993), 44, 45, 46, 48, and 49; Yip Harburg, "From the Lower East Side to 'Over the Rainbow,'" in *Creators and Disturbers: Reminiscences by Jewish Intellectuals of New York*, ed. Bernard Rosenberg and Ernest Goldstein (New York: Columbia University Press, 1982), 146, and 147.

46. Quoted in Michael T. Gilmore, ed., introduction to *Twentieth-Century Interpretations of* Moby-Dick (Englewood Cliffs, N.J.: Prentice-Hall, 1977), 7, and in Robert C. Twombly, *Frank Lloyd Wright: An Interpretive Biography* (New York: Harper and Row, 1973), 205.

47. Oscar Levant, *The Memoirs of an Amnesiac* (New York: Putnam, 1965), 126; Geoffrey Block, *Enchanted Evenings: The Broadway Musical from* Show Boat *to* Sondheim (New York: Oxford University Press, 1997), 13 and 64; Harburg, "From the Lower East Side," 147.

48. Quoted in Robert Brustein, *Cultural Calisthenics: Writings on Race, Politics, and Theatre* (Chicago: Ivan R. Dee, 1998), 36; Harold Cruse, *The Crisis of the Negro Intellectual* (New York: Morrow, 1967), 101–4; Era Bell, "Why Negroes Don't Like *Porgy and Bess*," *Ebony* 14 (October 1959), 50–51 and 54; Hollis Alpert, *The Life and Times of* Porgy and Bess: *The Story of an American Classic* (New York: Knopf, 1990), 121–22, 183, and 281–82; Douglas, *Terrible Honesty,* 102; Gene Lees, *Cats of Any Color: Jazz Black and White* (New York: Oxford University Press, 1994), 223–24.

49. Quoted in Jay Cocks, "The Voice of America: Ella Fitzgerald, 1918–1996," *Time* 147 (24 June 1996), 83; "Yugoslavs Sing Praise of Porgy," *New York Times,* 22 December 1954; Walter L. Hixson, *Parting the Curtain: Propaganda, Culture, and the Cold War, 1945–1961* (New York: St. Martin's, 1997), 137; Alpert, *Life and Times of* Porgy and Bess, 118 and 226–42; Virgil Thomson, *A Virgil Thomson Reader* (Boston: Houghton Mifflin, 1981), 24 and 27.

50. Quoted in Stephen Holden, "How a Star Is Born, and Grows Up," *New York Times,* 22 September 1991; Furia, *Poets of Tin Pan Alley,* 210–11, 245, 247, 264, and 270–71; Harburg, "From the Lower East Side," 146 and 147; Gottfried, *Broadway Musicals,* 253, 255, 332, and 333; Sanders, "American Popular Song," 197.

51. Quoted in Lees, *Cats of Any Color,* 195 and 240; James Lincoln Collier, *Benny Goodman and the Swing Era* (New York: Oxford University Press, 1989), 89 and 172–75; Victoria Secunda, *Bei Mir Bist Du Schön: The Life of Sholom Secunda* (Weston, Conn.: Magic Circle, 1982), 150; Holiday, *Lady Sings the Blues,* 69–81.

52. Amy Henderson, *On the Air: Pioneers of American Broadcasting* (Washington, D.C.: Smithsonian Institution Press, 1988), 72 and 74; Joseph Boskin, *Sambo: The Rise and Demise of an American Jester* (New York: Oxford University Press, 1986), 175–97; Werner Sollors, *Amiri Baraka/LeRoi Jones: The Quest for a "Populist Modernism"* (New York: Columbia University Press, 1978), 208–10.

53. Quoted in Herbert G. Goldman, *Banjo Eyes: Eddie Cantor and the Birth of Modern Stardom* (New York: Oxford University Press, 1997), 248.

54. Rogin, *Blackface, White Noise,* 219–20.

55. Collier, *Duke Ellington,* 66; Gottfried, *Broadway Musicals,* 311; Allen Woll,

Black Musical Theatre: From Coontown *to* Dreamgirls (Baton Rouge: Louisiana State University Press, 1989), 256–57; "Irving Gordon, 81, Songwriter of 1940s," *New York Times*, 8 December 1996; Ben Ratliff, "Jazz Taps a Maverick of Pop Song," *New York Times*, 13 July 1997.

56. Bernstein, *Findings*, 56, 99.

57. John Lahr, *Automatic Vaudeville: Essays on Star Turns* (London: Methuen, 1984), 49.

58. Robert Palmer, *Baby, That Was Rock & Roll: The Legendary Leiber & Stoller* (New York: Harcourt Brace Jovanovich, 1978), 10–23; E. Anthony Rotundo, "Jews and Rock and Roll," *American Jewish History* 72 (September 1982), 91; Deborah Dash Moore, *To the Golden Cities: Pursuing the American Jewish Dream in Miami and L.A.* (New York: Free Press, 1994), 22–24, 27, and 35–38.

59. Quoted in Mark Lisheron, "Rhythm-and-Jews," *Common Quest* 2 (Summer 1997), 30–31; Jon Pareles, "Catchy Tunes Laced with Danger," *New York Times*, 26 February 1995; Nelson George, *The Death of Rhythm and Blues* (New York: Pantheon, 1988), 64–69; Karen De Witt, "Ebonics, Language of Richard Nixon," *New York Times*, 29 December 1996.

60. Quoted in Albert Goldman, *Elvis* (New York: McGraw-Hill, 1981), 578; Rotundo, "Jews and Rock and Roll," 91–92 and 106; Hixson, *Parting the Curtain*, 159; Richard Corliss, "Baby, That's Rock 'n' Roll," *Time* 145 (13 March 1995), 105; Palmer, *Baby*, 10–11.

61. Rotundo, "Jews and Rock and Roll," 94–95; Jerry Wexler and David Ritz, *Rhythm and the Blues: A Life in American Music* (New York: Knopf, 1993), 20–21, 62–63, 127, and 143; Lisheron, "Rhythm-and-Jews," 23.

62. Allen Ginsberg, *Kaddish and Other Poems, 1958–1960* (San Francisco: City Lights Books, 1961), 7; Wexler, *Rhythm and the Blues*, 205–15; Fred Goodman, *The Mansion on the Hill: Dylan, Young, Geffen, Springsteen, and the Head-On Collision of Rock and Commerce* (New York: Times Books, 1997), 137; Lisheron, "Rhythm-and-Jews," 28.

63. Marvin Caplan, "'Eyli, Eyli': From Show Tune to Anthem," *American Jewish Congress Monthly* 63 (November–December, 1996), 13–15; Nadine Brozan, "Chronicle," *New York Times*, 20 January 1994.

64. Quoted in David Remnick, *The Devil Problem and Other True Stories* (New York: Random House, 1996), 243; Laurence Bergreen, *Louis Armstrong: An Extravagant Life* (New York: Broadway, 1997), 58–59 and 267–68.

65. Quoted in Seymour Martin Lipset, "Political Controversies at Harvard, 1636 to 1974," in Seymour Martin Lipset and David Riesman, *Education and Politics at Harvard* (New York: McGraw-Hill, 1975), 146.

66. Quoted in David B. Starr, "This is Only the Fact, but We Have the Idea . . . ," *Jewish Political Studies Review* 9, nos. 1–2 (Spring 1997), 17; Edward Lewis Wallant, *The Pawnbroker* (New York: Manor Books, 1962), 43; Sigmund Freud, *Moses and Monotheism*, trans. Katherine Jones (New York: Vintage, 1955), 134–35.

67. Laurence Mordekhai Thomas, "The Soul of Identity: Jews and Blacks," in *People of the Book: Thirty Scholars Reflect on Their Jewish Identity*, ed. Jeffrey Rubin-Dorsky and Shelley Fisher Fishkin (Madison: University of Wisconsin

Press, 1996), 172–82, and *Vessels of Evil: American Slavery and the Holocaust* (Philadelphia: Temple University Press, 1993), 137, 140, 169, 176–89, and 197–204; Stephan Thernstrom and Abigail Thernstrom, *America in Black and White: One Nation, Indivisible* (New York: Simon and Schuster, 1997), 541; Thomas Sowell, *Migrations and Cultures: A World View* (New York: Basic-Books, 1996), 299; Edward W. Said, *After the Last Sky: Palestinian Lives* (New York: Pantheon, 1986), 5–6, 7, 102–3, and 106; Julius Lester, "Blacks, Jews, and Farrakhan," *Dissent* 41 (Summer 1994), 368.

68. Anna Day Wilde, "Mainstreaming Kwanzaa," *Public Interest*, no. 119 (Spring 1995), 69–73; Gerald Early, "Dreaming of a Black Christmas," *Harper's* 294 (January 1997), 55–56, 59, and 60.

69. Quoted in Lester, "Blacks, Jews, and Farrakhan," 368; Gerald Early, "Who is the Jew? A Question of African-American Identity," *Common Quest* 1 (Spring 1996), 43.

70. Letty Cottin Pogrebin, *Deborah, Golda and Me: Being Jewish and Female in America* (New York: Crown, 1991), 225.

71. Lawrence Osborne, "The Numbers Game," *Lingua Franca* 8 (September 1998), 53–54 and 56–58; Toni Morrison, *Beloved* (New York: Knopf, 1987), n.p.; Bonnie Angelo, "The Pain of Being Black" (1989), in *Conversations with Toni Morrison*, ed. Danille Taylor-Guthrie (Jackson: University Press of Mississippi, 1994), 257; Emily Miller Budick, *Blacks and Jews in Literary Conversation* (Cambridge: Cambridge University Press, 1998), 161–66; Geoffrey H. Hartman, *The Longest Shadow: In the Aftermath of the Holocaust* (Bloomington: Indiana University Press, 1996), 4–5 and 137–38.

72. Quoted in Osborne, "Numbers Game," 53; Laurie Stone, "The Interpretation of Jews," *Nation* 266 (26 January 1998), 35.

SHOAH (PP. 168–196)

1. "First Inaugural Address" (1801), in *The Portable Thomas Jefferson*, ed. Merrill D. Peterson (New York: Viking, 1975), 292.

2. John Heidenry, *Theirs Was the Kingdom: Lila and DeWitt Wallace and the Story of the* Reader's Digest (New York: Norton, 1993), 90 and 263; Anthony Cronin, *Samuel Beckett: The Last Modernist* (New York: HarperCollins, 1997), 469.

3. Michel Contat and Michel Rybalka, eds., *The Writings of Jean-Paul Sartre*, trans. Richard C. McCleary (Evanston: Northwestern University Press, 1974), 1:227; Michel Crozier, *The Trouble with America*, trans. Peter Heinegg (Berkeley and Los Angeles: University of California Press, 1984), 120 and 136; Jean-Philippe Mathy, *Extrême-Occident: French Intellectuals and America* (Chicago: University of Chicago Press, 1993), 122 and 123.

4. Quoted in Thomas Schatz, *The Genius of the System: Hollywood Filmmaking in the Studio Era* (New York: Pantheon, 1988), 446.

5. Quoted in E. Thomas Wood and Stanislaw M. Jankowski, *Karski: How One Man Tried to Stop the Holocaust* (New York: John Wiley, 1994), 188; Theodor

W. Adorno, *Negative Dialectics,* trans. E. B. Ashton (New York: Continuum, 1995), 362.

6. Quoted in Robert Leiter, "Taking History Personally," *Forward,* 2 January 1998, 10; Martin Gilbert, *The Holocaust: A History of the Jews of Europe during the Second World War* (New York: Holt, Rinehart and Winston, 1985), 171–72 and 175; Deborah E. Lipstadt, *Beyond Belief: The American Press and the Coming of the Holocaust, 1933–1945* (New York: Free Press, 1986), 169, 174–75, and 186.

7. Mark A. Raider, *The Emergence of American Zionism* (New York: New York University Press, 1998), 208.

8. Quoted in Alfred Kazin, "The Jew as Modern American Writer," in *The Commentary Reader,* ed. Norman Podhoretz (New York: Atheneum, 1967), xvi.

9. Mordecai M. Kaplan, *Judaism as a Civilization: Toward a Reconstruction of American-Jewish Life* (New York: Macmillan, 1934), 72; Ruth R. Wisse, "Found in America," *New Republic* 213 (18 and 25 September 1995), 55; Alvin H. Rosenfeld, *A Double Dying: Reflections on Holocaust Literature* (Bloomington: Indiana University Press, 1980), 121–26.

10. Quoted in Anita Norich, "'*Harbe sugyes'*/Puzzling Questions: Yiddish and English Culture in America During the Holocaust," *Jewish Social Studies* 5 (Fall 1998/Winter 1999), 97.

11. Ibid., 95 and 102–5; Muriel Rukeyser, Alfred Kazin, et al., in "Under Forty," *Contemporary Jewish Record* 7 (February 1944), 3–4, 5, 6, 9–11, 15–17, 20–22, 23, 26, and 32–33.

12. Nathan Glazer, *American Judaism* (Chicago: University of Chicago Press, 1957), 114; Jonathan D. Sarna, *JPS: The Americanization of Jewish Culture, 1888–1988* (Philadelphia: Jewish Publication Society, 1989), 272–73; Raul Hilberg, *The Politics of Memory: The Journey of a Holocaust Historian* (Chicago: Ivan R. Dee, 1996), 105, 110–19, and 156; Edward T. Linenthal, *Preserving Memory: The Struggle to Create America's Holocaust Museum* (New York: Viking, 1995), 8.

13. Quoted in Edith Wharton, *A Backward Glance* (New York: D. Appleton-Century, 1934), 147.

14. "Genêt" [Janet Flanner], "Letter from Paris," *New Yorker* 26 (11 November 1950), 126.

15. Meyer Levin, "A Classic Human Document," *American Jewish Congress Weekly* 19 (16 June 1952), 12–13, and *The Obsession* (New York: Simon and Schuster, 1973), 35; Lawrence Graver, *An Obsession with Anne Frank: Meyer Levin and the Diary* (Berkeley and Los Angeles: University of California Press, 1995), 14–20 and 24–25; Ralph Melnick, *The Stolen Legacy of Anne Frank: Meyer Levin, Lillian Hellman, and the Staging of the Diary* (New Haven: Yale University Press, 1997), 2–3, 7, 9, and 19.

16. Jonah Raskin, *For the Hell of It: The Life and Times of Abbie Hoffman* (Berkeley and Los Angeles: University of California Press, 1996), 81; Mark Hertsgaard, "Steal This Decade," *Mother Jones* 15 (June 1990), 36; Howard Goodman, "The Last Yippie," *Inside Magazine/Philadelphia Jewish Exponent* 2 (Summer 1989), 66.

17. Quoted in Levin, *Obsession*, 36; William Westbrook Burton, ed., and Carol Lawrence in *Conversations about Bernstein* (New York: Oxford University Press, 1995), xxii–xxiii and 171; Sander L. Gilman, *Jewish Self-Hatred: Anti-Semitism and the Hidden Language of the Jews* (Baltimore: Johns Hopkins University Press, 1986), 345; Kenneth Tynan, "Berlin Postscript" (1956), in *Curtains* (New York: Atheneum, 1961), 450–51.

18. James Spada, *Streisand: Her Life* (New York: Crown, 1995), 32–33; Joseph Schildkraut (as told to Leo Lania), *My Father and I* (New York: Viking, 1959), 233.

19. Ibid., 2–3, 236, and 237–38.

20. Anne Frank, *The Diary of a Young Girl*, trans. B. M. Mooyaart-Doubleday (Garden City, N.Y.: Doubleday, 1953), 237.

21. Judith E. Doneson, *The Holocaust in American Film* (Philadelphia: Jewish Publication Society, 1987), 69 and 73.

22. Joshua Rubenstein, *Tangled Loyalties: The Life and Times of Ilya Ehrenburg* (Boston: Beacon, 1996), 323–24; Yevgeny Yevtushenko, "Babiy Yar" (1961), in *Selected Poems*, trans. Robin Milner-Gulland and Peter Levi (Baltimore: Penguin, 1962), 82–83; Linenthal, *Preserving Memory*, 2.

23. Omer Bartov, "Spielberg's Oskar: Hollywood Tries Evil," in *Spielberg's Holocaust: Critical Perspectives on* Schindler's List, ed. Yosefa Loshitzky (Bloomington: Indiana University Press, 1997), 52–53.

24. Quoted in Levin, *Obsession*, 152; Doneson, *Holocaust in American Film*, 74; Graver, *Obsession with Anne Frank*, 77, 86–87, and 125.

25. Frank, *Diary*, 186–87; Frances Goodrich and Albert Hackett, *The Diary of Anne Frank* (New York: Random House, 1956), 168; Levin, *Obsession*, 29–30; Doneson, *Holocaust in American Film*, 69–70 and 82; Graver, *Obsession with Anne Frank*, 59–60 and 89; Melnick, *Stolen Legacy*, 108–9.

26. Quoted in Melnick, *Stolen Legacy*, 115–18.

27. Quoted in Doneson, *Holocaust in American Film*, 70; Melnick, *Stolen Legacy*, 9, 100–101, 115, 137, 139, 159, and 205–6; Levin, *Obsession*, 126.

28. Quoted in Melnick, *Stolen Legacy*, 92–94, 96, 128, and 187; Graver, *Obsession with Anne Frank*, 61; Cynthia Ozick, "Who Owns Anne Frank?" *New Yorker* 73 (6 October 1997), 80–81, 86, and 87.

29. Quoted in Graver, *Obsession with Anne Frank*, 94; Alvin H. Rosenfeld, "The Americanization of the Holocaust" (Ann Arbor: Jean and Samuel Frankel Center for Judaic Studies of the University of Michigan, 1995), 10–12.

30. Quoted in Alvin H. Rosenfeld, "Popularization and Memory: The Case of Anne Frank," in *Lessons and Legacies: The Meaning of the Holocaust in a Changing World*, ed. Peter Hayes (Evanston: Northwestern University Press, 1991), 252–53 and 256, and in Melnick, *Stolen Legacy*, 126–28, 144, and 147; Frank, *Diary*, 34–35.

31. Quoted in Melnick, *Stolen Legacy*, 144–45.

32. Jacob Weinstein, "Betrayal of Anne Frank," *American Jewish Congress Weekly* 24 (13 May 1957), 5–7; Melnick, *Stolen Legacy*, 164.

33. Quoted in Melnick, *Stolen Legacy*, 178; Ezra Goodman, *The Fifty-Year Decline and Fall of Hollywood* (New York: Simon and Schuster, 1961), 166, 397–98, and 435.

34. Quoted in Lawrence W. Levine, *The Unpredictable Past: Explorations in American Cultural History* (New York: Oxford University Press, 1993), 161; Arthur Miller, *Timebends: A Life* (New York: Grove, 1987), 314–16; William Wiegand, "Arthur Miller and the Man Who Knows" (1957), in Arthur Miller, *Death of a Salesman*, ed. Gerald Weales (New York: Viking, 1967), 294; Maurice Yacowar, *Tennessee Williams and Film* (New York: Frederick Ungar, 1977), 10; Dwight Macdonald, *Discriminations: Essays and Afterthoughts, 1938–1974* (New York: Viking, 1974), 256–61.

35. Frank, *Diary*, 108–13; Gilman, *Jewish Self-Hatred*, 349.

36. Philip Roth, *The Ghost Writer* (New York: Fawcett Crest, 1980), 128, 135, 207, and 209–10.

37. Frank, *Diary*, 46; Rosenfeld, "Popularization and Memory," 267; Edward Rothstein, "Anne Frank: The Girl and the Icon," *New York Times*, 25 February 1996.

38. Quoted in Rothstein, "Anne Frank."

39. Quoted in Carolyn Clay, "*Diary* Reopened," *Boston Phoenix*, 7 November 1997; also in Gary Susman, "Frank Talk," *Boston Phoenix*, 24 October 1997.

40. Annette Insdorf, *Indelible Shadows: Film and the Holocaust* (New York: Vintage, 1983), 6–10 and 23–28; Leonard J. Leff, "Hollywood and the Holocaust: Remembering *The Pawnbroker*," *American Jewish History* 84 (December 1996), 355, 358–60, 365, 372–73, 374–75, and 376.

41. Quoted in Doneson, *Holocaust in American Film*, 189; Linenthal, *Preserving Memory*, 11–12 and 18.

42. Quoted in Alfred Appel Jr., *Nabokov's Dark Cinema* (New York: Oxford University Press, 1974), 78; Isaac Bashevis Singer, *Love and Exile* (Garden City, N.Y.: Doubleday, 1984), 19; Janet Hadda, *Isaac Bashevis Singer: A Life* (New York: Oxford University Press, 1997), 142; Art Spiegelman, "Mein Kampf (my struggle)," *New York Times Magazine*, 12 May 1996, 36–37.

43. Quoted in Judith O'Sullivan, *The Great American Comic Strip: One Hundred Years of Cartoon Art* (Boston: Little, Brown, 1990), 188; Thomas Doherty, "Art Spiegelman's *Maus*: Graphic Art and the Holocaust," *American Literature* 68 (March 1966), 69–84.

44. Steven M. Cohen, "Jewish Continuity over Judaic Content: The Moderately Affiliated American Jew," in *The Americanization of the Jews*, ed. Robert M. Seltzer and Norman J. Cohen (New York: New York University Press, 1995), 397 and 408; Saul Friedlander, ed., introduction to *Probing the Limits of Representation: Nazism and the "Final Solution"* (Cambridge, Mass.: Harvard University Press, 1992), 1–6 and 20.

45. Quoted in Morton A. Reichek, "Out of the Night," *Present Tense* 3 (Spring 1976), 42, and in J. Hoberman, *Vulgar Modernism: Writing on Movies and Other Media* (Philadelphia: Temple University Press, 1991), 218 and 225.

46. Joseph McBride, *Steven Spielberg: A Biography* (New York: Simon and Schuster, 1997), 43–44 and 45; Yosepha Loshitzky, ed., introduction to *Spielberg's Holocaust*, 8; Sarah Lyall, "Book Notes," *New York Times*, 9 March 1994; Pedro E. Ponce, "Making Novels of Life's Ethical Dilemmas," in *Oskar Schindler and His List*, ed. Thomas Fensch (Forest Dale, Vt.: Paul S. Eriksson,

1995), 38; Fritz Lanham, "Keneally's Luck," in ibid., 43 and 46; Sara R. Horowitz, "But Is It Good for the Jews?" in *Spielberg's Holocaust*, 138 n. 1; Thomas Keneally, *Schindler's List* (London: Sceptre, 1982), 13.

47. Terrence Rafferty, "A Man of Transactions," in *Oskar Schindler and His List*, 88; Gilbert, *Holocaust*, 754–55; Bryan Cheyette, "The Uncertain Certainty of *Schindler's List*," in *Spielberg's Holocaust*, 228 and 232.

48. Geoffrey H. Hartman, "The Cinema Animal," in *Spielberg's Holocaust*, 62; Horowitz, "But Is It Good for the Jews?" 122; Bartov, "Spielberg's Oskar," 50; Elie Wiesel, *Night* (New York: Hill and Wang, 1960), 116.

49. Jakov Lind, *Soul of Wood and Other Stories*, trans. Ralph Mannheim (New York: Fawcett Crest, 1966), 9.

50. Hartman, "Cinema Animal," 74 n. 1; Gordon F. Sander, *Serling: The Rise and Twilight of Television's Last Angry Man* (New York: Dutton, 1992), 156; J. Hoberman, "How Steven Spielberg (Re)Invented Hollywood," *Forward*, 30 May 1997, 12.

51. Quoted in Lawrence Grobel, "Playboy Interview: Saul Bellow," *Playboy* 44 (May 1997), 62; Bartov, "Spielberg's Oskar," 44.

52. Claude Lanzmann, *Shoah: An Oral History of the Holocaust* (New York: Pantheon, 1985), 196; Bartov, "Spielberg's Oskar," 46; Haim Bresheeth, "The Great Taboo Broken: Reflections on the Israeli Reception of *Schindler's List*," in *Spielberg's Holocaust*, 206.

53. Quoted in Philip Gourevitch, "A Dissent on *Schindler's List*," *Commentary* 97 (February 1994), 49, and in Loshitzky, ed., introduction to *Spielberg's Holocaust*, 15 n. 22; Margot Hornblower, "Of Mercy, Fame—and Hate Mail," *Time* 151 (1 June 1998), 57.

54. Loshitzky, ed., introduction to *Spielberg's Holocaust*, 5; Stanley Kauffmann, "A Predicament," *New Republic* 213 (11 December 1995), 24; Bartov, "Spielberg's Oskar," 55; Hartman, "Cinema Animal," 63; Miriam Bratu Hansen, "*Schindler's List* is not *Shoah*," in *Spielberg's Holocaust*, 83–84.

55. Joyce Antler, "The Americanization of the Holocaust," *American Theatre* 12 (February 1995), 17–19.

56. Elie Wiesel, "For the Dead and the Living," *New Leader* 76 (17–31 May 1993), 14; Linenthal, *Preserving Memory*, 25.

57. Quoted in Linenthal, *Preserving Memory*, 36.

58. Wiesel, "Dead and the Living," 14; Linenthal, *Preserving Memory*, 27, 39–40, 66, and 187–89; Julie Salamon, "Walls That Echo of the Unspeakable," *New York Times*, 7 September 1997; Jonathan Mahler, "Rabbis Reject Shoah Museum," *Forward*, 12 September 1997, 1.

59. Wiesel, "Dead and the Living," 14; Linenthal, *Preserving Memory*, 113, 116, and 240; William H. Honan, "First U.S. Doctoral Program on Holocaust is Being Created," *New York Times*, 12 October 1997; Yehuda Bauer, "Some Introductory Comments," *Studies in Contemporary Jewry*, ed. Jonathan Frankel (New York: Oxford University Press, 1997), 13:5–6.

60. Linenthal, *Preserving Memory*, 98, 249, 257, and 318–19.

61. Quoted in ibid., 142.

62. Herbert Muschamp, "Shaping a Monument to Memory," *New York Times*, 11

April 1993; Leon Wieseltier, "After Memory," *New Republic* 208 (3 May 1993), 20; Linenthal, *Preserving Memory*, 180–86.

63. Quoted in Rosenfeld, "Americanization of the Holocaust," 17.

64. David Biale, "The Melting Pot and Beyond: Jews and the Politics of American Identity," in *Insider/Outsider: American Jews and Multiculturalism*, ed. David Biale, Michael Galchinsky, and Susannah Heschel (Berkeley and Los Angeles: University of California Press, 1998), 28.

65. Honan, "First U.S. Doctoral Program," 27; Ralph Waldo Emerson, "The Conduct of Life" (1860), in *Essays and Lectures*, ed. Joel Porte (New York: Library of America, 1983), 1067; Wieseltier, "After Memory," 20.

FAITH (PP. 197–223)

1. Jon D. Levenson, *Esther: A Commentary* (Louisville, Ky.: Westminster John Knox, 1997), 17, 18, and 46; Mordecai M. Kaplan, *Judaism as a Civilization: Toward a Reconstruction of American-Jewish Life* (New York: Macmillan, 1934), 125 and 218.

2. Joseph L. Blau, *Judaism in America: From Curiosity to Third Faith* (Chicago: University of Chicago Press, 1976), 10–11 and 19–20; Charles S. Liebman and Steven M. Cohen, *Two Worlds of Judaism: The Israeli and American Experiences* (New Haven: Yale University Press, 1990), 128 and 156; Woody Allen, *Without Feathers* (New York: Warner Books, 1976), 27; Marshall Sklare, *America's Jews* (New York: Random House, 1971), 112–13.

3. Quoted in Mel Scult, *Judaism Faces the Twentieth Century: A Biography of Mordecai M. Kaplan* (Detroit: Wayne State University Press, 1993), 147.

4. Alexis de Tocqueville, *Democracy in America*, ed. Phillips Bradley (New York: Knopf, 1945), 2:135; Neil Postman, *Amusing Ourselves to Death: Public Discourse in the Age of Show Business* (New York: Penguin, 1985), 5; Martin Gottfried, *George Burns and the Hundred-Year Dash* (New York: Simon and Schuster, 1996), 293–94; Russell Shorto, "Belief by the Numbers," *New York Times Magazine*, 7 December 1997, 61.

5. Charles S. Liebman, "Religious Trends among American and Israeli Jews," in *Terms of Survival: The Jewish World since 1945*, ed. Robert S. Wistrich (New York: Routledge, 1995), 299–300; Robert Gottlieb and Peter Wiley, *America's Saints: The Rise of Mormon Power* (New York: Putnam, 1984), 177–86; Shorto, "Belief by the Numbers," 61.

6. Quoted in Jeffrey S. Gurock, *American Jewish Orthodoxy in Historical Perspective* (Hoboken, N.J.: KTAV, 1996), 16 and 51.

7. Sklare, *America's Jews*, 114–17; Liebman and Cohen, *Two Worlds of Judaism*, 134.

8. Quoted in Jonathan D. Sarna, *JPS: The Americanization of Jewish Culture, 1888–1988* (Philadelphia: Jewish Publication Society, 1989), 15; Gerald Sorin, *Tradition Transformed: The Jewish Experience in America* (Baltimore: Johns Hopkins University Press, 1997), 153; Jenna Weissman Joselit, *The Wonders of America: Reinventing Jewish Culture, 1880–1950* (New York: Hill and Wang, 1994), 229–43; Liebman and Cohen, *Two Worlds of Judaism*, 15–16.

9. Quoted in Allen R. Myerson, "Editions of the Passover Tale: This Year in Profusion," *New York Times*, 4 April 1993; Joselit, *Wonders of America*, 198 and 220–28; Joel Lewis, "Choosing a Haggadah," *Forward*, 22 March 1996, 9.

10. Jacob A. Riis, *The Children of the Poor* (New York: Scribner, 1892), 43; Moses Rischin, *The Promised City: New York's Jews, 1870–1914* (Cambridge, Mass.: Harvard University Press, 1962), 144–47; Fred Somkin, "Zion's Harp by the East River: Jewish-American Popular Songs in Columbus's Golden Land, 1890–1914," *Perspectives in American History*, n.s., 2 (1985), 195 n; Marshall Sklare, *Observing America's Jews*, ed. Jonathan D. Sarna (Hanover: University Press of New England, 1993), 206–7.

11. Quoted in Sklare, *Observing America's Jews*, 9; Liebman, "Religious Trends," 304.

12. Peter Levine, *Ellis Island to Ebbets Field: Sport and the American Jewish Experience* (New York: Oxford University Press, 1992), 132, 134–35, 136, and 138.

13. Ibid., 246.

14. David Evanier, "It's Aesthetic When You Win," *American Spectator* 20 (September 1987), 24.

15. Maurice Samuel, *The Gentleman and the Jew* (New York: Knopf, 1950), 103–5.

16. Quoted in Abbie Hoffman, *Square Dancing in the Ice Age* (Boston: South End, 1982), 190.

17. Rachel Wischnitzer, *Synagogue Architecture in the United States: History and Interpretation* (Philadelphia: Jewish Publication Society, 1955), 136–39, 148–52, and 159; Gary Tinterow, "Post–World War II Synagogue Architecture," in *Two Hundred Years of American Synagogue Architecture* (Waltham, Mass.: Rose Art Museum of Brandeis University and American Jewish Historical Society, 1976), 30; Lance J. Sussman, "The Suburbanization of American Judaism as Reflected in Synagogue Building and Architecture, 1945–1975," *American Jewish History* 75 (September 1985), 34–35 and 40–43; Henry L. Feingold, *Lest Memory Cease: Finding Meaning in the American Jewish Past* (Syracuse: Syracuse University Press, 1996), 184.

18. Raphael Patai, *The Jewish Mind* (Detroit: Wayne State University Press, 1996), 362; Gerald Bernstein, "Two Centuries of American Synagogue Architecture," in *Two Hundred Years of American Synagogue Architecture*, 9–10, 11, 12–13, 14, and 16.

19. Paul Goldberger, "A Spiritual Quest Realized But Not in Stone," *New York Times*, 13 October 1996; Rabbi Chaim Stern, letter to the editor, *New York Times*, 27 October 1996; Michael Wise, "A Quest to Build a Tabernacle for Our Age," *Forward*, 27 September 1996, 9; Percival Goodman, "The Character of the Modern Synagogue," in *An American Synagogue for Today and Tomorrow*, ed. Peter Blake (New York: Union of American Hebrew Congregations, 1954), 92 and 94; Tinterow, "Post–World War II Synagogue," 33.

20. Lewis Mumford, "Towards a Modern Synagog Architecture," *Menorah Journal* 11 (June 1925), 225; Lauren B. Strauss, "Staying Afloat in the Melting Pot: Constructing an American Jewish Identity in the *Menorah Journal* of the 1920s," *American Jewish History* 84 (December 1996), 324; Tinterow, "Post–World War II Synagogue," 34.

Notes

21. Arnold M. Eisen, *The Chosen People in America: A Study in Jewish Religious Ideology* (Bloomington: Indiana University Press, 1983), 5 and 169.

22. Hayim Greenberg, *The Inner Eye: Selected Essays*, n. ed. (New York, 1953), 1:55, and *The Inner Eye: Selected Essays*, ed. Shlomo Katz (New York, 1964), 2:66; Eisen, *Chosen People*, 152; *The Philosophy of Spinoza*, ed. Joseph Ratner (New York: Modern Library, 1927), 11–35 and 64–70.

23. Kadya Molodovsky, "God of Mercy," trans. Irving Howe, in *The Penguin Book of Modern Yiddish Verse*, ed. Irving Howe, Ruth R. Wisse, and Khone Shmeruk (New York: Viking, 1987), 330 and 332; Greenberg, *Inner Eye*, 1:17, and *Inner Eye*, 2:56; Leonard Fein, "A Matter of Distinction," *Forward*, 10 October 1997, 7.

24. Talcott Parsons, "The Sociology of Modern Anti-Semitism," in *Jews in a Gentile World*, ed. Isacque Graeber and Stuart Henderson Britt (New York: Macmillan, 1942), 107 and 114–16; Eisen, *Chosen People*, 12 and 33.

25. Quoted in Greenberg, *Inner Eye*, 1:3; Eisen, *Chosen People*, 57 and 198 n. 15; George Steiner, *The Portage to San Cristóbal of A. H.* (New York: Simon and Schuster, 1981), 163–64.

26. Greenberg, *Inner Eye*, 1:5 and 7; Patai, *Jewish Mind*, 462; Eisen, *Chosen People*, 9, 13, 21, 62, 66, and 97.

27. "Jewry and Democracy," *Christian Century* 54 (9 June 1937), 734; Kaplan, *Judaism as a Civilization*, 379.

28. "Jewry and Democracy," *Christian Century*, 735–36; Greenberg, *Inner Eye*, 1:4; Eisen, *Chosen People*, 33–36; Leonard Dinnerstein, *Antisemitism in America* (New York: Oxford University Press, 1994), 109–10.

29. Kaplan, *Judaism as a Civilization*, 43; Eisen, *Chosen People*, 73–98; Scult, *Judaism Faces the Twentieth Century*, 285 and 360–61.

30. Eisen, *Chosen People*, 3–4, 7, 26, 174, and 178.

31. Susan Weidman Schneider, *Jewish and Female: Choices and Changes in Our Lives Today* (New York: Simon and Schuster, 1985), 34, 80, and 82.

32. Tocqueville, *Democracy in America*, 2:209–10; Jonathan D. Sarna, *A Great Awakening: The Transformation that Shaped Twentieth Century Judaism and Its Implications for Today* (New York: Council for Initiatives in Jewish Education, 1995), 19, and "The Debate over Mixed Seating in the American Synagogue," in *The American Synagogue: A Sanctuary Transformed*, ed. Jack Wertheimer (New York: Cambridge University Press, 1987), 366–68; Deborah E. Lipstadt, "The Impact of the Women's Movement on American Jewish Life: An Overview after Twenty Years," in *Studies in Contemporary Jewry*, ed. Peter Y. Medding (New York: Oxford University Press, 1995), 11:90–91.

33. Quoted in Pamela S. Nadell, "'Top Down' or 'Bottom Up': Two Movements for Women's Rabbinic Ordination," in *An Inventory of Promises: Essays on American Jewish History in Honor of Moses Rischin*, ed. Jeffrey S. Gurock and Marc Lee Raphael (Brooklyn: Carlson, 1995), 198–202.

34. Sarna, *Great Awakening*, 22–24; Marc Slobin, *Tenement Songs: The Popular Music of the Jewish Immigrants* (Champaign: University of Illinois Press, 1982), 129 and 131–32; Anzia Yezierska, *Bread Givers* (New York: Persea Books, 1975), 205 and 207.

35. Scult, *Judaism Faces the Twentieth Century*, 235 and 301–2; Carole S. Kessner, "Kaplan and the Role of Women in Judaism," in *The American Judaism of Mordecai M. Kaplan*, ed. Emanuel S. Goldsmith, Mel Scult, and Robert M. Seltzer (New York: New York University Press, 1990), 350–52.

36. Paula E. Hyman, "The Introduction of Bat Mitzvah in Conservative Judaism in Postwar America," *YIVO Annual* 19 (1990), 133–46, and "Bat Mitzvah," in *Jewish Women in America: An Historical Encyclopedia*, ed. Paula E. Hyman and Deborah Dash Moore (New York: Routledge, 1997), 1:126–27; Mordecai M. Kaplan, *The Future of the American Jew* (New York: Macmillan, 1948), 402; Suzanne F. Singer and Judy Oppenheimer, "Reconstructionism: From 'Heresy' to 'It's What Most Jews Are,'" *Moment* 22 (June 1997), 58; Sylvia Barack Fishman, *A Breath of Life: Feminism in the American Jewish Community* (New York: Free Press, 1993), 130, 131, and 155.

37. Scult, *Judaism Faces the Twentieth Century*, 355; Sylvia Barack Fishman, "A Dark Portrait of Jewish Assimilation," *Forward*, 7 June 1996, 9, and *Breath of Life*, 153.

38. Quoted in Fishman, *Breath of Life*, 184; Lipstadt, "Impact of the Women's Movement," 89 and 90; Jonathan D. Sarna, "Response," *Judaism* 44 (Summer 1995), 306; Anne Roiphe, *Generation without Memory: A Jewish Journey in Christian America* (New York: Simon and Schuster, 1981), 18; Jay L. Halio, "Anne Roiphe: Finding Her America," in *Daughters of Valor: Contemporary Jewish American Women Writers*, ed. Jay L. Halio and Ben Siegel (Newark: University of Delaware Press, 1997), 97–110.

39. Michael A. Meyer, *Response to Modernity: A History of the Reform Movement in Judaism* (New York: Oxford University Press, 1988), 379–80; Nadell, "'Top Down' or 'Bottom Up,'" 198–202.

40. Fishman, *Breath of Life*, 201 and 208; Lipstadt, "Impact of the Women's Movement," 86 and 87; Yigal Schleiffer, "Coming Out of the Gay and Lesbian *Shtetl*," *Forward*, 30 May 1997, 15.

41. Quoted in Gurock, *American Jewish Orthodoxy*, 60–61.

42. Lipstadt, "Impact of the Women's Movement," 86, 87, and 93–95; Schneider, *Jewish and Female*, 149–65.

43. Quoted in Jeff Helmreich, "Orthodox Seminary Launches Degree Program for Women," *JUF News* (Chicago), July 1997, 36.

44. Kaplan, *Judaism as a Civilization*, 155; Hershel Shanks, "Tolerance vs. Halachah," *Moment* 22 (June 1997), 8; Elias Bickerman, *Four Strange Books of the Bible: Jonah, Daniel, Koheleth, Esther* (New York: Schocken, 1967), 210.

45. Haskel Lookstein, "Joseph: The Master of His Dreams," in *Rabbi Joseph H. Lookstein Memorial Volume*, ed. Leo Landman (New York: KTAV, 1980), 16–17; Gurock, *American Jewish Orthodoxy*, 37–40 and 336; Fishman, *Breath of Life*, 123 and 124–26.

46. Quoted in Susannah Heschel, ed., introduction to *On Being a Jewish Feminist* (New York: Schocken, 1995), 117–18.

47. Singer and Oppenheimer, "Reconstructionism," 53.

48. Scult, *Judaism Faces the Twentieth Century*, 341, 344, and 360–61; Marc Lee Raphael, *Profiles in American Judaism: The Reform, Conservative, Orthodox,*

and Reconstructionist Traditions in Historical Perspective (San Francisco: Harper and Row, 1984), 183–84; Jeffrey S. Gurock and Jacob J. Schacter, *A Modern Heretic and a Traditional Community: Mordecai M. Kaplan, Orthodoxy, and American Judaism* (New York: Columbia University Press, 1997), 3 and 140–42.

49. Scult, *Judaism Faces the Twentieth Century*, 19, 244, and 247.
50. Quoted in ibid., 90–91 and 211–12; Baila Round Shargel, "Kaplan and Israel Friedlaender: Expectation and Failure," in *American Judaism of Mordecai M. Kaplan*, 102–3.
51. Scult, *Judaism Faces the Twentieth Century*, 64; Kaplan, *Judaism as a Civilization*, 385 and 447.
52. Scult, *Judaism Faces the Twentieth Century*, 334.
53. Quoted in ibid., 169–70, 281, and 317.
54. Kaplan, *Judaism as a Civilization*, 282; Scult, *Judaism Faces the Twentieth Century*, 263; S. Daniel Breslauer, "Kaplan, Abraham Joshua Heschel, and Martin Buber: Three Approaches to Jewish Revival," in *American Judaism of Mordecai M. Kaplan*, 235 and 241.
55. Scult, *Judaism Faces the Twentieth Century*, 32, 48, 125–26, 132, 151–52, 143, 190, 280, 286–90, 294, 296–97, 341, and 343; Kaplan, *Judaism as a Civilization*, x, 216–17, 439–42, and 521–22; Ira Eisenstein, "Kaplan as Liturgist," in *American Judaism of Mordecai M. Kaplan*, 319–322.
56. Allan Lazaroff, "Kaplan and John Dewey," in *American Judaism of Mordecai M. Kaplan*, 186; Scult, *Judaism Faces the Twentieth Century*, 224 and 226; Kaplan, *Judaism as a Civilization*, 178.
57. Kaplan, *Judaism as a Civilization*, 184–85, 327, 328, 335, 413–14, and 513.
58. Ibid., 514–15.

PROSPECTS (PP. 224–247)

1. Charles S. Liebman, *The Ambivalent American Jew: Politics, Religion, and Family in American Jewish Life* (Philadelphia: Jewish Publication Society, 1973), vii and 26–27; Jonathan S. Woocher, *Sacred Survival: The Civil Religion of American Jews* (Bloomington: Indiana University Press, 1986), 87–89; Jonathan D. Sarna, "The Cult of Synthesis in American Jewish Culture," *Jewish Social Studies*, V (Fall 1998–Spring, 1999), 52–79.
2. Eli Lederhendler, *Jewish Responses to Modernity: New Voices in America and Eastern Europe* (New York: New York University Press, 1994), 113 and 137.
3. Quoted in Benny Kraut, "Jewish Survival in Protestant America," in *Minority Faiths and the Protestant Mainstream*, ed. Jonathan D. Sarna (Champaign: University of Illinois Press, 1998), 31; Jeffrey S. Gurock, *American Jewish Orthodoxy in Historical Perspective* (Hoboken, N.J.: KTAV, 1996), 30 and 42; Harold M. Schulweis, "The Embrace of a Community," *Oasis* 1 (Summer 1997), 4; E. L. Doctorow, *The Book of Daniel* (New York: Signet, 1972), 133; Neal Gabler, *An Empire of Their Own: How the Jews Invented Hollywood* (New York: Crown, 1988), 307.

4. Quoted in Robin Cembalest, "Editing Out Abraham in Los Angeles," *Forward*, 19 April 1996, 10, and in Bernard Weinraub, "Jewish History Museum Opening in Los Angeles," *New York Times*, 21 April 1996; "Grand Opening: The Skirball Cultural Center," *Reform Judaism* 24 (Summer 1996), 58; Stanley F. Chyet to author, 2 October 1998; Uri D. Herscher, "In Thrall to Hope," *Oasis* 1 (Fall 1996), 6.

5. Quoted in Cembalest, "Editing Out Abraham," 1; Grace Cohen Grossman and Robert Kirschner, *Visions and Values: Jewish Life from Antiquity to America* (Los Angeles: Skirball Cultural Center, 1996), 5 and 32; Grace Cohen Grossman, ed., "Project Americana," in *New Beginnings: The Skirball Museum Collections and Inaugural Exhibition* (Los Angeles: Skirball Cultural Center, 1996), 92 and 93.

6. Joellyn Wallen Zollman, "At What Cost Liberty?: A Review of the America Galleries in the Skirball Cultural Center's Core Exhibition" (1997), 3 (MS in my possession); Herbert Muschamp, "Architecture of Light and Remembrance," *New York Times*, 15 December 1996.

7. Quoted in Ralph Melnick, *The Life and Work of Ludwig Lewisohn* (Detroit: Wayne State University Press, 1998), 2:378–79, also in Arnold M. Eisen, *The Chosen People in America: A Study in Jewish Religious Ideology* (Bloomington: Indiana University Press, 1983), 121, 122, 141, and 142; Nathan Glazer, *American Judaism* (Chicago: University of Chicago Press, 1957), 9–10; F. Scott Fitzgerald, *The Crack-Up*, ed. Edmund Wilson (New York: New Directions, 1945), 69.

8. David Gelernter, David Singer, David A. Teutsch, and Jack Wertheimer, in "What Do American Jews Believe?: A Symposium," in *Commentary* 102 (August 1996), 36–37, 83, 84, 89, 91, and 92.

9. Seymour Martin Lipset and Earl Raab, *Jews and the New American Scene* (Cambridge, Mass.: Harvard University Press, 1995), 14; Marie Waife-Goldberg, *My Father, Sholom Aleichem* (New York: Simon and Schuster, 1968), 41; Louis Harap, *The Image of the Jew in American Literature: From Early Republic to Mass Immigration* (Philadelphia: Jewish Publication Society, 1974), 272; Gary Scharnhorst, with Jack Bales, *The Lost Life of Horatio Alger, Jr.* (Bloomington: Indiana University Press, 1985), 98–99 and 100; Anzia Yezierska, *Bread Givers* (New York: Persea Books, 1975), 138.

10. *Federalist* 14, in James Madison, Alexander Hamilton, and John Jay, *The Federalist*, ed. Edward Mead Earle (New York: Modern Library, n.d.), 85; Nathaniel Hawthorne, *Novels*, ed. Millicent Bell (New York: Library of America, 1983), 1103.

11. Quoted in Malcolm Bradbury, *Dangerous Pilgrimages: Trans-Atlantic Mythologies and the Novel* (London: Penguin, 1995), 179; Mark Twain, *Adventures of Huckleberry Finn*, ed. Walter Blair and Victor Fischer (Berkeley and Los Angeles: University of California Press, 1985), 2.

12. Mary Antin, *The Promised Land* (Boston: Houghton Mifflin, 1969), xxii and 364; Joyce Antler, *The Journey Home: Jewish Women and the American Century* (New York: Free Press, 1997), 22–23; J. Hoberman, *Vulgar Modernism: Writing on Movies and Other Media* (Philadelphia: Temple University Press, 1991), 143.

13. Sigmund Freud, *Civilization and Its Discontents*, trans. and ed. James Strachey (New York: Norton, 1962), 23; Henry Steele Commager, *Jefferson, Nationalism, and the Enlightenment* (New York: Braziller, 1975), 110; Svetlana Allilu-yeva, *Only One Year*, trans. Paul Chavchavadze (New York: Harper and Row, 1969), 354; Abraham Cahan, *The Rise of David Levinsky* (New York: Harper and Row, 1960), 91.

14. Thomas Schatz, *The Genius of the System: Hollywood Filmmaking in the Studio Era* (New York: Pantheon, 1988), 32 and 34; Joseph Garncarz, "Hollywood in Germany, 1925–1990," in *Hollywood in Europe: Experiences of a Cultural Hegemony*, ed. David W. Ellwood and Rob Kroes (Amsterdam: VU University Press, 1994), 107; Bruno P. F. Wanrooij, "Dollars and Decency: Italian Catholics and Hollywood, 1945–1960," in ibid., 248, 249, and 256.

15. Quoted in Deborah Dash Moore, *At Home in America: Second-Generation New York Jews* (New York: Columbia University Press, 1981), 125, and in Lloyd P. Gartner, "Metropolis and Periphery in American Jewry," in *Studies in Contemporary Jewry*, ed. Jonathan Frankel (Bloomington: Indiana University Press, 1984), 1:343; Marc Lee Raphael, *Abba Hillel Silver: A Profile in American Judaism* (New York: Holmes and Meier, 1989), 52–53; Hayim Greenberg, *The Inner Eye: Selected Essays*, ed. Shlomo Katz (New York: Jewish Frontier Association, 1964), 2:74–75.

16. Sidney Goldstein, "Profile of American Jewry: Insights from the 1990 National Jewish Population Survey," in *American Jewish Year Book*, ed. David Singer (Philadelphia: Jewish Publication Society, 1992), 92:129–30; Charles S. Liebman and Steven M. Cohen, *Two Worlds of Judaism: The Israeli and American Experiences* (New Haven: Yale University Press, 1990), 55 and 181 n.

17. Eisen, *Chosen People*, 41.

18. Claude Lévi-Strauss, *A World on the Wane*, trans. John Russell (New York: Criterion, 1961), 397.

19. John J. Appel, *Immigrant Historical Societies in the United States, 1880–1950* (New York: Arno, 1980), 264–68; Edward S. Shapiro, *A Time for Healing: American Jewry since World War II* (Baltimore: Johns Hopkins University Press, 1992), 229–57; Arthur Hertzberg, *The Jews in America: Four Centuries of an Uneasy Encounter* (New York: Simon and Schuster, 1989), 386; Samuel C. Heilman, *Portrait of American Jews: The Last Half of the Twentieth Century* (Seattle: University of Washington Press, 1995), 6 and 100.

20. Harap, *Image of the Jew*, 40–41, 44, and 72; Leslie A. Fiedler, *To the Gentiles* (New York: Stein and Day, 1972), 67; Michael Warner, *The Letters of the Republic: Publication and the Public Sphere in Eighteenth-Century America* (Cambridge, Mass.: Harvard University Press, 1990), 169–70; Isaac Metzker, ed., *A Bintel Brief: Sixty Years of Letters from the Lower East Side to the Jewish Daily Forward* (Garden City, N.Y.: Doubleday, 1971), 83.

21. Egon Mayer, "From an External to an Internal Agenda," in *The Americanization of the Jews*, ed. Robert M. Seltzer and Norman J. Cohen (New York: New York University Press, 1995), 420; David Van Biema, "Sparse at Seder?" *Time* 149 (28 April 1997), 67; Lipset and Raab, *Jews and the New American Scene*, 72.

22. Ruth Gay, *Unfinished People: Eastern European Jews Encounter America* (New

York: Norton, 1996), 56; Shaun Considine, *Mad as Hell: The Life and Work of Paddy Chayefsky* (New York: Random House, 1994), 299; William Lanouette, with Bela Silard, *Genius in the Shadows: A Biography of Leo Szilard* (New York: Scribner, 1992), 115–16; Elliott Abrams, *Faith or Fear: How Jews Can Survive in a Christian America* (New York: Free Press, 1997), 156; Liebman and Cohen, *Two Worlds of Judaism*, 32 and 42.

23. Louis Wirth, *The Ghetto* (Chicago: University of Chicago Press, 1928), 222; Alan M. Dershowitz, *The Vanishing American Jew: In Search of Jewish Identity for the Next Century* (Boston: Little, Brown, 1997), 45.

24. Fred Somkin, "Zion's Harp by the East River: Jewish-American Popular Songs in Columbus's Golden Land, 1890–1914," *Perspectives in American History*, n.s., 2 (1985), 195 n and 211 n; David H. Weinberg, *Between Tradition and Modernity: Haim Zhitlowski, Simon Dubnow, Ahad Ha-Am, and the Shaping of Modern Jewish Identity* (New York: Holmes and Meier, 1996), 17, 26, 88, and 106; Isaac Deutscher, *The Non-Jewish Jew and Other Essays*, ed. Tamara Deutscher (New York: Hill and Wang, 1968), 5–15, 22–23, and 25–41.

25. Sigmund Freud, *Standard Edition of the Complete Psychological Works*, trans. and ed. James Strachey (London: Hogarth, 1955), 13:xv.

26. Daniel Bell, *The Winding Passage: Essays and Sociological Journeys, 1960–1980* (Cambridge, Mass.: Abt Books, 1980), 317–18 and 347–54.

27. Elaine Marks, "Juifemme," in *People of the Book: Thirty Scholars Reflect on Their Jewish Identity*, ed. Jeffrey Rubin-Dorsky and Shelley Fisher Fishkin (Madison: University of Wisconsin Press, 1996), 346.

28. *The Jews of Boston* (videocassette), written and produced by Lorie Conway for WGBH Boston (1996).

29. Quoted in Lewis Lord, "Matzos and Magnolias: An Exhibit Explores a Lost World of Southern Judaism," *U.S. News & World Report* 124 (25 May 1998), 55; William Lee Miller, *Piety along the Potomac: Notes on Politics and Morals in the Fifties* (Boston: Houghton Mifflin, 1964), 173.

30. Quoted in Paul Slansky, *The Clothes Have No Emperor: A Chronicle of the American '80s* (New York: Simon and Schuster, 1989), 125.

31. Leonard Fein, ed., "A *Moment* Interview with Father Theodore Hesburgh," in *Jewish Possibilities: The Best of Moment Magazine* (Northvale, N.J.: Jason Aronson, 1987), 300; E. J. Kessler, "The Latest Rage for Unitarians—Sukkot, Seders," *Forward*, 6 June 1997, 1 and 2.

32. Glazer, *American Judaism*, 3–7, 129, 133, and 172; Leonard Dinnerstein and Gene Koppel, *Nathan Glazer: A Different Kind of Liberal* (Tucson: University of Arizona, 1973), 22; Goldstein, "Profile of American Jewry," 89–90.

33. Eisen, *Chosen People*, 20; Arnold J. Toynbee, *A Study of History* (London: Oxford University Press, 1939), 4:262; Ludwig Wittgenstein, *Culture and Value*, ed. G. H. von Wright and Heikki Nyman, trans. Peter Winch (Chicago: University of Chicago Press, 1980), 18e.

34. Liebman and Cohen, *Two Worlds of Judaism*, 123; Harold Schulweis, "Are We Losing the Faith?" *Reform Judaism* 20 (Spring 1992), 5; Jeffrey K. Salkin, "The Jews We Don't See," *Reform Judaism* 20 (Winter 1991), 5; George Gallup Jr., and Jim Castelli, *The People's Religion: American Faith in the '90s* (New York:

Macmillan, 1989), 116; Abrams, *Faith or Fear*, 9–10 and 127–28; Lipset and Raab, *Jews and the New American Scene*, 49, 54, and 134.

35. Quoted in Weinberg, *Between Tradition and Modernity*, 123; David G. Dalin, ed., introduction to *From Marxism to Judaism: The Collected Essays of Will Herberg* (New York: Markus Wiener, 1989), xv–xviii and xix.

36. Lipset and Raab, *Jews and the New American Scene*, 71; Mordecai M. Kaplan, *Judaism as a Civilization: Toward a Reconstruction of American-Jewish Life* (New York: Macmillan, 1934), 201, 305–6, and 520; Leonard Fein, "Our Trouble With Boundaries," *Forward*, 26 December 1997, 7.

37. Jenna Weissman Joselit, *The Wonders of America: Reinventing Jewish Culture, 1880–1950* (New York: Hill and Wang, 1994), 44–54, 109–113, 116, 229, 230–33, 239–42, and 251–55.

38. Quoted in Naomi W. Cohen, *Encounter with Emancipation: The German Jews in the United States, 1830–1914* (Philadelphia: Jewish Publication Society, 1984), 172, and in Sara Bershtel and Allen Graubard, *Saving Remnants: Feeling Jewish in America* (New York: Free Press, 1992), 14; Dershowitz, *Vanishing American Jew*, 71.

39. Quoted in Arthur A. Goren, "Between Ideal and Reality: Abba Hillel Silver's Zionist Vision," in *Abba Hillel Silver and American Zionism*, ed. Mark A. Raider, Jonathan D. Sarna, and Ronald W. Zweig (Portland, Ore.: Cass, 1997), 73; also in Lizabeth Cohen, *Making a New Deal: Industrial Workers in Chicago, 1919–1939* (New York: Cambridge University Press, 1990), 54.

40. Quoted in Abraham J. Karp, *Jewish Perceptions of America: From Melting Pot to Mosaic* (B. G. Rudolph Lecture in Judaic Studies, Syracuse University, 1976), 6–7; Louis Marshall to Kaufmann Kohler, 4 June 1920, in *Louis Marshall, Champion of Liberty: Selected Papers and Addresses*, ed. Charles Reznikoff (Philadelphia: Jewish Publication Society, 1957), 2:908.

41. Salo Wittmayer Baron, *Steeled by Adversity: Essays and Addresses on American Jewish Life* (Philadelphia: Jewish Publication Society, 1971), 10 and 542–49; Robert Liberles, *Salo Wittmayer Baron: Architect of Jewish History* (New York: New York University Press, 1995), 317–19.

42. Jeremy Tarsh and Jonny Wolfson, "A Conversation with Isaiah Berlin," *Windmill*, no. 1 (1986), 15; Ahad Ha-am, *Selected Essays*, trans. and ed. Leon Simon (Cleveland, Ohio: World, 1962), 84–85.

43. Eisen, *Chosen People*, 10; Yezierska, *Bread Givers*, 293–94; Cahan, *Rise of David Levinsky*, 397–98; Jeffrey S. Gurock, *The Men and Women of Yeshiva: Higher Education, Orthodoxy, and American Judaism* (New York: Columbia University Press, 1988), 39; Metzker, ed., *Bintel Brief*, 55–56.

44. Nessa Rapoport, "Culture: Nourishment for the Jewish Soul," in *Toward an American Jewish Culture: New Perspectives on Jewish Continuity*, ed. Richard A. Siegel (New York: National Foundation for Jewish Culture, 1994), 15–16.

45. Quoted in Gary A. Abraham, *Max Weber and the Jewish Question: A Study of the Social Outlook of His Sociology* (Champaign: University of Illinois Press, 1992), x–xi and 7; David Ellenson, "Max Weber on Judaism and the Jews: A Reflection on the Position of Jews in the Modern World," in *What is Modern*

about the Modern Jewish Experience? ed. Marc Lee Raphael (Williamsburg, Va.: College of William and Mary, 1997), 85–86.

46. Charles S. Liebman, *Deceptive Images: Toward a Redefinition of American Judaism* (New Brunswick, N.J.: Transaction Books, 1988), 58–59, 68, 70, 79, and 91; Stephen Sharot, "Judaism and Jewishness," in *Studies in Contemporary Jewry*, ed. Ezra Mendelsohn (New York: Oxford University Press, 1993), 9:197; David Singer, "Living with Intermarriage" (1979), in *American Jews: A Reader*, ed. Marshall Sklare (New York: Behrman House, 1983), 408; Jerold S. Auerbach, *Rabbis and Lawyers: The Journey from Torah to Constitution* (Bloomington: Indiana University Press, 1990), x, xi, and 205–6.

47. Arthur Hertzberg in *The Condition of Jewish Belief* (New York: Macmillan, 1966), 90; Milton Steinberg, *The Making of the Modern Jew: From the Second Temple to the State of Israel* (New York: Behrman House, 1948), 179; Eisen, *Chosen People*, 117–18 and 137.

48. Jacob Neusner, ed., "Assimilation and Self-Hatred in Modern Jewish Life" (1971), in *The Challenge of America: Can Judaism Survive in Freedom?* (New York: Garland, 1993), 211; Gershom Scholem, "Judaism," in *Contemporary Jewish Religious Thought: Original Essays on Critical Concepts, Movements, and Beliefs*, ed. Arthur A. Cohen and Paul Mendes-Flohr (New York: Scribner, 1987), 505 and 506; David Biale, *Gershom Scholem: Kabbalah and Counter-History* (Cambridge, Mass.: Harvard University Press, 1979), 111–13.

Acknowledgments

In writing this book, I have incurred many debts. Here is the place to begin to discharge them.

I am deeply indebted to scholars willing to read complete drafts of this book: Joyce Antler, Hasia R. Diner, Lawrence H. Fuchs, Nathan Glazer, Richard H. King, Jerry Z. Muller, Jonathan D. Sarna, and Edward S. Shapiro. In manuscript form huge swaths were read by Donald Altschiller, David Biale, Sylvia Barack Fishman, and Geoffrey B. Levey. In addition Andrea Most read the chapter on musical theater, Robert Brustein the chapter on theater, and Michael T. Gilmore the chapter on race. My gratitude is profound to them all for their conscientious critical reading and for the knowledge they transferred when I needed it. Conversations with Steven Aschheim, Jacob Cohen, Thomas Doherty, Michael Gilmore, Linda Raphael, Marc Lee Raphael, Frank Schwarz, Ray Schwarz, Joyce Seltzer, David B. Starr, and Phillip M. Weitzman also proved very beneficial. Others answered particular queries, saved me from errors, and suggested leads worth pursuing: Marc Brettler, Emily M. Budick, William Flesch, Sylvia Fuks Fried, Hayim Goldgraber, John Bush Jones, Edward K. Kaplan, Gerd D. Korman, Alan Mintz, Antony Polonsky, Moses Rischin, Sharon P. Rivo, Robert Rockaway, Charles P. Schiller, Mel Scult, Richard S. Tedlow, S. Ilan Troen, and David Wolfman. I am most appreciative. For irrepressible blunders of interpretation and fact, however, I am alone accountable.

A conversation with Leonard Fein sparked the necessary orientation of this book when it was stalled; a conversation with Benny Kraut ensured that the act of writing would be unblocked. Others also deserve to be singled out. Donald Altschiller has been an invaluable friend, an indefatigable source of often esoteric knowledge, and a bastion of support in this and other enterprises. Everyone who works in American Jewish historiography has learned from Jonathan Sarna; I am lucky to have him nearby as friend, as colleague, and as general editor of the series in which this volume appears. For well over two decades, I have found it difficult to write a book without wondering—and worrying—about what my friend Richard King would think of it. "Yeah, but what've you done *lately*?" is the question that has kept me cuffed to the word processor. He has served as a model of seriousness and of scholarly rectitude.

To present earlier drafts of this book as lectures has also been opportune. These venues have included the Center for Judaic Studies at the University of Michigan, where Todd M. Endelman invited me to deliver the David W. Belin Lecture in American Jewish Affairs; the Center for Jewish Studies at the University of Wisconsin, where David Sorkin bestowed the honor of Kutler Visiting Lecturer; and the Center for Judaic Studies at the University of Pennsylvania, where David Ruderman welcomed me as well. A conference at Berkeley under the leadership of David Biale was enormously stimulating in helping me to see how America might be situated within the *longue durée* of Jewish history. A preliminary view of American Jewish culture was also presented at an American Studies colloquium at Brandeis; I thank the department's chairperson, Joyce Antler, for her initiative as well as for many other gestures of support and friendship. For graciously guiding me through the Skirball Cultural Center and Museum in Los Angeles, I salute Stanley F. Chyet; for subsidizing part of my visit there, I am indebted to the Mazer Fund of Brandeis University, an institution that has itself been an ideal setting for experiencing and thinking about the themes of this book. Angelina Simeone, the academic administrator of the Department of American Studies, deserves my gratitude in this respect as well.

I also acknowledge the cooperation of editors and publishers for granting me permission to pluck from their pages material that has been altered for this volume. Large chunks of the chapter on theater appeared earlier in different form in the Robert Cohen Memorial Volume of the journal *Jewish History* (1994), published jointly by Haifa University Press and the University Press of New England and edited by Kenneth R. Stow, and in *Daughters of Valor: Contemporary Jewish American Women Writers*, edited by Jay L. Hallo and Ben Siegel and published by the University of Delaware Press in 1997. A portion of the chapter on the *Shoah* appeared in volume 8 of the annual *Studies in Contemporary Jewry*, published by Oxford University Press and edited by Peter Y. Medding in 1992.

In three graduate readings courses at Brandeis, I seized the opportunity to exchange views on the topic of American Jewish culture with students in the Department of Near Eastern and Judaic Studies. Especially fruitful were the contributions of Felicia Herman, Seth Korelitz, Jonathan D. Krasner, Andrea Most, Mark A. Raider, and Rona Sheramy.

My literary agent, Gerard McCauley, has exhibited loyalty, forbearance and generosity. I am grateful to him.

The staff of the University Press of New England deserve my special gratitude for their terrific editorial help—Phyllis Deutsch and Philip M. Pochoda in particular. But even their patience and encouragement are dwarfed by the help of Lee C. Whitfield, who has lived long enough with this book and who even supplied its title. She has left the most appreciable mark of all; to her are hereby recorded my most heartfelt thanks and my love.

Index of Names

Index of Names

Blitzstein, Marc, 66, 106
Bloch, Ernst, 93
Bloch, Rolf, 50
Block, Geoffrey, 67
Bloom, Harold, 118
Bloom, Rube, 157
Bloom, Solomon, 52
Bloomfield, Mike, 110
Bloomgarden, Kermit, 178
Boas, Franz, 34
Bontemps, Arna, 158
Boone, Pat, 229
Borowitz, Eugene D., 227
Boskin, Joseph, 159
Bourne, Randolph, 15, 16–17, 49
Brandeis, Louis D., xii, 34
Brando, Marlon, xi–xii, xiii, 44, 51
Brecht, Bertolt, 66
Brenner, Frédéric, 216
Breslawsky, Solomon, 103
Brice, Fanny, 37, 59, 98, 150, 152, 154
Britton, Joe, 153
Broch, Hermann, 54
Bronfman, Edgar, 50
Brooks, Richard, 82
Brooks, Shelton, 152
Brooks, Van Wyck, 34, 54–55
Brown, Charles Brockden, 233
Brown, Lew, 97
Bruce, Lenny, 12, 13, 20, 22, 26, 112, 143, 145, 158, 163, 199
Bruch, Max, 91
Buber, Martin, 20, 246, 247
Buckley, William F., Jr., 240
Burnett, Carol, 108
Burns, George, 150, 198
Burrows, Abe, 62, 63
Burton, Richard, 60
Butterfield, Paul, 110
Buttons, Red, 198

Cable, George Washington, 146
Caesar, Irving, 94–95, 100, 101
Cahan, Abraham, 6, 35, 36, 37, 39, 41–42, 46, 49, 56, 95–96, 117, 221, 229
Cahn, Sammy, 2, 52
Calloway, Cab, 157
Cantor, Eddie, 2, 13, 59, 149, 150, 151–52, 153, 154, 159, 238

Capone, Al, 153
Capote, Truman, 46–47
Capra, Frank, 54
Carpenter, Thelma, 159
Carson, Johnny, 108
Carter, Jimmy, 111, 185, 192
Cavell, Stanley, 23
Cerf, Bennett, 47
Chagall, Marc, 25, 88
Chaplin, Charlie, 10, 18, 231
Charles, Ray, 13, 163
Chayefsky, Paddy, 234
Chekhov, Anton, 23, 134, 137
Chernin, Kim, 9
Chess, Leonard and Phil, 163
Chomsky, Noam, 41
Chomsky, William, 39, 41
Churchill, Winston, 163
Chwolson, Daniel, 57
Cimino, Michael, 98
Cixous, Hélène, 49
Cleaver, Eldridge, 144
Clinton, Bill, 64, 90, 126, 127, 189–90, 191
Clurman, Harold, 44
Cobb, Lee J., 118
Cohan, George M., 35, 149, 213
Cohen, Elliot E., 55–56
Cohen, Gerson D., 40
Cohen, Hettie, 143
Cohen, Steven M., 198
Cohn, Harry, 54
Cohn, Roy, 128
Cole, Nat "King" and Natalie, 160
Coltrane, John, 64
Copland, Aaron, 22, 68, 78, 92–93, 104, 106
Correll, Charles, 142
Crane, Hart, 92
Crawford, Cheryl, 173
Crosby, Bing, 96, 97, 149
Crozier, Michel, 168
Cruse, Harold, 156
Cullen, Countee, 158
cummings, e. e., 55

Da Ponte, Lorenzo, 64
David, Hal, 160
Davies, Marion, 96
Davis, Miles, 64, 157

298

Index of Names

Manchester, Melissa, 109
Manilow, Barry, 109, 110
Mann, Barry, 110, 162
Mann, Thomas, 28, 33
March, Fredric, 118
Margulies, Donald, 120, 124
Marks, Edward, 93
Marks, Elaine, 236–37
Marks, Gerald, 101
Marks, Johnny, 238
Marshall, Louis, 242
Marx Brothers, 43, 53, 74, 96, 151
Marx, Groucho, 48
Marx, Karl, 3, 41, 129, 144
Mason, Jackie, 12–13
Mastroianni, Marcello, 121
Mayer, Egon, 234
Mayer, Louis B., 52, 168, 231
McCarthy, Mary, 119
Medem, Vladimir, 10
Meier, Richard, 52
Meili, Christoph, 190
Mellers, Wilfrid, 156
Melnick, Ralph, 176
Melville, Herman, 40, 171
Mencken, H. L., 56
Mendelsohn, Eric, 203, 204
Mendelssohn, Felix, 91, 103
Menken, Alan, 86
Mercer, Johnny, 157–58
Merman, Ethel, 65
Merrick, David, 61
Meyer, Annie Nathan, 146
Meyerbeer, Giacomo, 91
Mezzrow, Milton, 143–44
Michelson, Albert, 33
Midler, Bette, 109
Mikhoels, Solomon, 147
Milhaud, Darius, 160
Miller, Arthur, 118–21, 123, 126, 127, 129, 182, 190–91
Miller, Jonathan, 24, 60, 82, 104
Minghella, Anthony, 97
Molnár, Ferenc, 64
Molodovsky, Kadya, 207
Monroe, Marilyn, 10–11, 120
Moore, Deborah Dash, 10–11, 60, 161
Moore, Marianne, 55

Morrison, Toni, 167
Mumford, Lewis, 205
Munch, Charles, 104
Muni, Paul, 118
Muschamp, Herbert, 194, 227
Myers, James, 109

Nabokov, Vladimir, 25, 28
Namath, Joe, 230
Nathan, George Jean, 34
Neilan, Marshall, 231
Nelson, Willie, 98
Neusner, Jacob, 246
Newman, Barnett, 19
Newman, Randy, 110
Nichols, Anne, 17
Nichols, Lewis, 78
Niebuhr, Reinhold, 240
Nimoy, Leonard, 50–51
Noah, Mordecai Manuel, 120, 134
Nosseck, Max, 43
Nussbaum, Max, 175–76
Nyro, Laura, 110

Odets, Clifford, 25, 44, 115–17, 118, 121, 123, 125, 126, 129, 163
Offenbach, Jacques, 91
O'Neill, Eugene, 129, 142
Ophuls, Marcel, 186
Oppenheim, James, 34
Oppenheimer, J. Robert, 33

Pachter, Henry, 14
Pakula, Alan, 189
Paley, William S., 47
Panofsky, Erwin, 24
Parsons, Talcott, 207
Patai, Raphael, 141
Patinkin, Mandy, 97
Peerce, Jan, 43
Penniman, "Little" Richard, 161
Peretz, I. L., 171
Perkins, Carl, 108–9
Perkins, Millie, 177
Perl, Arnold, 148
Perlmutter, Nathan, 203
Picasso, Pablo, 55
Picon, Molly, 36

Index of Names

Wilder, Billy, 54
Williams, Bert, 151, 152
Williams, Raymond, 3, 20
Williams, Tennessee, 129, 182
Willowski, Jacob David, 199, 200, 242
Wilson, August, 157
Wilson, Teddy, 158, 159
Wilson, Woodrow, 153
Winchell, Walter, 95, 151
Winfrey, Oprah, 190
Winger, Debra, 173
Winters, Shelley, 181–82
Wirth, Louis, 235
Wischnitzer, Rachel, 203
Wise, Isaac Mayer, 35, 212, 229
Witmark Brothers, 93
Wittgenstein, Ludwig, 29, 111, 239
Wolf, Lucien, 34
Wolfe, Bernard, 143
Wolfson, Harry, xiv
Woodward, C. Vann, 140, 164
Woollcott, Alexander, 96, 99
Wouk, Herman, 3

Wright, Frank Lloyd, 17, 156, 204
Wright, Richard, 143, 145, 149
Wyman, Jane, 182

X, Malcolm, 148

Yamasaki, Minoru, 204
Yeltsin, Boris, 126
Yerushalmi, Yosef Hayim, 40
Yevtushenko, Yevgeny, 91, 175
Yezierska, Anzia, 213
Young, Joe, 100

Zamenhof, Ludwig Lazar, 23
Zametkin, Adella Kean and Michael, 38
Zangwill, Israel, 34–35, 72–73, 125, 137, 138,
 140–41, 153
Zhitlowski, Haim, 35, 38–39, 235, 240
Ziegfeld, Florenz, Jr., 74, 76–77, 95, 98,
 100, 151
Zippel, David, 86
Zuckerman, Itzhak, 189
Zukor, Adolph, 5

UNIVERSITY PRESS OF NEW ENGLAND publishes books under its own imprint and is the publisher for Brandeis University Press, Dartmouth College, Middlebury College Press, University of New Hampshire, Tufts University, and Wesleyan University Press.

LIBRARY OF CONGRESS CATALOGING-IN-PUBLICATION DATA
Whitfield, Stephen J., 1942–
In search of American Jewish culture / by Stephen J. Whitfield.
    p.   cm. — (Brandeis series in American Jewish history,
culture, and life)
Includes bibliographical references and index.
ISBN 0–87451–754–0 (cl. : alk. paper)
1. Jews—United States—Intellectual life. 2. American
literature—Jewish authors—History and criticism. 3. Jewish
entertainers—United States. 4. Popular culture—United States.
5. United States—Ethnic relations. I. Title. II. Series.
E184.35.W45 1999
305.8924073—dc21   99–30390